Sustaining Early Childho

C000120943

How gains from early childhood experiences are initiated, increased, and sustained, and how they affect life-course development, is fundamental to science and society. These matters also have increasing policy relevance, given public investments in early learning programs and the need to measure their effectiveness in promoting well-being. With contributions from leading researchers across many disciplines, this book emphasizes key interventions and practices over the first decade of life and the elements and strategies through which gains can be enhanced by schools, families, communities, and public institutions. Three critical themes are addressed: firstly, the importance of documenting and understanding the impact of investments in early childhood and school-age years. Secondly, increased priority on elements and principles for scaling effective programs and practices to benefit all children. Thirdly, a focus on multiple levels of strategies for sustaining gains and promoting long-term effects, ranging from early care and family engagement to school reform, and state and federal policy.

Arthur J. Reynolds is a professor in the Institute of Child Development at the University of Minnesota. A leading expert in the early intervention field, he directs the Chicago Longitudinal Study, one of the largest studies of the effects of early education.

Judy A. Temple is a professor in the Humphrey School of Public Affairs at the University of Minnesota. Her research focuses on the evaluation of long-term effects of early educational interventions and policy evaluation.

"This book has it all. Sustaining early learning gains is a top education policy priority. The content is first rate and the authors offer a plethora of effective recommendations that will strengthen programs and practices. The authors themselves are a who's who list of educational and developmental scientists with vast experience in knowing what works. The book clearly shows that good early childhood education policy and effective school reform go hand in hand."

Arne Duncan, *Former Secretary, United States Department of Education*

"This research reinforces why we're taking significant strides to expand early education, which is fundamentally about giving every child in every neighborhood their best chance to succeed. Reynolds and Temple show us that these significant investments in our children will help level the playing field, further close the achievement gap, and build stronger communities for generations to come."

Rahm Emanuel, *Mayor, City of Chicago*

"This volume focuses on one of the most crucial issues facing us today: how to build upon and sustain the gains from early intervention. The editors and authors are clear that we need a multi-year commitment to continuity and quality. The work presented here provides powerful justification for this comprehensive investment."

Samuel J. Meisels, *Founding Executive Director, Buffett Early Childhood Institute, University of Nebraska*

"The research is ripe with insights and directives gleaned from years of investments, programming, and evaluations. This is well-timed and well-aimed as public and private investments in early childhood seek to spur an increasingly greater impact. It is an invaluable volume for practitioners, policymakers, and all those who care about providing young children accessible pathways of opportunity."

Rip Rapson, *President and CEO, The Kresge Foundation*

"Investing in children's early learning is an investment in our shared future. Much has been written about the importance of early learning for brain development, but this book provides important research and insights into how to sustain those early gains through the K-3 years and beyond. This is a valuable resource for practitioners, researchers, policymakers, and philanthropists."

Kate Wolford, *President, McKnight Foundation*

Sustaining Early Childhood Learning Gains

Program, School, and Family Influences

Edited by

Arthur J. Reynolds
University of Minnesota

Judy A. Temple
University of Minnesota

CAMBRIDGE
UNIVERSITY PRESS

University Printing House, Cambridge CB2 8BS, United Kingdom

One Liberty Plaza, 20th Floor, New York, NY 10006, USA

477 Williamstown Road, Port Melbourne, VIC 3207, Australia

314-321, 3rd Floor, Plot 3, Splendor Forum, Jasola District Centre, New Delhi - 110025, India

79 Anson Road, #06-04/06, Singapore 079906

Cambridge University Press is part of the University of Cambridge.

It furthers the University's mission by disseminating knowledge in the pursuit of
education, learning and research at the highest international levels of excellence.

www.cambridge.org
Information on this title: www.cambridge.org/9781108441896
DOI: 10.1017/9781108349352

© Cambridge University Press 2019

First published 2019
First paperback edition 2020

A catalogue record for this publication is available from the British Library

Library of Congress Cataloging in Publication data
Names: Reynolds, Arthur J., editor. | Temple, Judy A., editor.
Title: Sustaining early childhood learning gains : program, school, and family
influences / edited by Arthur J. Reynolds and Judy A. Temple.
Description: Cambridge ; New York, NY : Cambridge University Press, 2019. |
"The book is based on a national invitational conference that was held at the
Federal Reserve Bank of Minneapolis in October 2015. The chapters are updated
versions of those presented at the conference" – Chapter 1. | Includes
bibliographic references and index.
Identifiers: LCCN 2018039866 | ISBN 9781108425926 (hbk.)
Subjects: LCSH: Early childhood education – Evaluation. | Early childhood
education – Planning.
Classification: LCC LB1139.25 .S87 2019 | DDC 372.21–dc23
LC record available at https://lccn.loc.gov/2018039866

ISBN 978-1-108-42592-6 Hardback
ISBN 978-1-108-44189-6 Paperback

Contents

Figures

Tables

Contributors

LAURA BORNFREUND New America Foundation
BARBARA A. BOWMAN Erikson Institute
MARGARET BURCHINAL University of North Carolina at Chapel Hill
GREGORY CAMILLI Rutgers University
FRANCES A. CAMPBELL University of North Carolina at Chapel Hill
JUAN C. CHAPARRO Universidad EAFIT, Colombia
GREG J. DUNCAN University of California at Irvine
MADELYN GARDNER Learning Policy Research Institute
KAREN HANSON University of Minnesota
MOMOKO HAYAKAWA University of Minnesota
NATHAN HUEY University of Minnesota
JADE M. JENKINS University of California at Irvine
DAVID KIRP University of California at Berkeley
ABBIE LIEBERMAN New America Foundation
ANDREW J. MASHBURN Portland State University
BETH MELOY Learning Policy Research Institute
CHRISTINA F. MONDI University of Minnesota
TUTRANG NGUYEN University of California at Irvine
SUH-RUU OU University of Minnesota
YI PAN University of North Carolina at Chapel Hill
CRAIG T. RAMEY Virginia Tech Carilion Research Institute, Virginia Tech
SHARON LANDESMAN RAMEY Virginia Tech Carilion Research Institute,
  Virginia Tech
ARTHUR J. REYNOLDS University of Minnesota
LAWRENCE J. SCHWEINHART HighScope Educational Research Foundation
  (Emeritus)
EMILY K. SNELL Temple University
AARON J. SOJOURNER University of Minnesota
DEBORAH J. STIPEK Stanford University
JUDY A. TEMPLE University of Minnesota
BARBARA A. WASIK Temple University
MARJORIE WECHSLER Learning Policy Research Institute
RITA YELVERTON Portland State University

Foreword

This volume presents the proceedings of a research conference convened by the Human Capital Research Collaborative (HCRC), hosted by the Federal Reserve Bank of Minneapolis, on the critically important topic of increasing and sustaining early childhood development gains. I welcome the opportunity to provide a brief foreword for the proceedings, as I am grateful for the work of these scholars on this crucial topic.

By way of background, let me note that, as Provost and Executive Vice President of the University of Minnesota, I had the privilege of working with the members of our Twin Cities campus community to create and implement a campus strategic plan that reinvigorates our commitment to the land-grant mission of the University. The HCRC exemplifies two of the campus plan's four main strategic pillars, so the work presented at this conference clearly aligned with our institution's central aspirations.

One pillar of our campus plan is a commitment to capitalize on the extraordinary breadth, as well as the quality, of our research capacity, in order to address the world's grand challenges. We understand "grand challenges" to be not only deep and difficult problems, but also multi-faceted challenges, requiring expertise and ideas drawn from many spheres and disciplines in order to be effectively addressed. These grand challenges are among the most important and complex problems facing local communities, states, nations, and the world.

Enhancing individual and community capacity for a changing world, ensuring that everyone has the opportunity to realize his or her potential, is one of the aims of the HCRC, and it is also among the five grand challenges explicitly identified as a priority research focus for our university. This is a meaningful alignment of goals, one that promises constructive synergies.

Another central pillar of our campus strategic plan is a commitment to reciprocal engagement with our various communities, a commitment to draw on and respond to our specific location in a vibrant but complicated metropolitan area. The University of Minnesota wants to work *with* community, government, nonprofit, and corporate partners on *shared* priorities, with mutually inflected identification of issues and of pathways forward.

For more than ten years, the HCRC has exemplified reciprocal engagement. The HCRC is focused on the links between human capital and economic development, public health, and K–12 education. In another iteration of this reciprocity, it must be noted that the future of the University of Minnesota – which exists to develop human potential – also depends upon our community's commitment to develop the potential of its children.

Thus, I'm delighted that this center brought together researchers, policymakers, and funding organizations to focus on the challenge of sustaining early childhood developmental gains. I want to thank Arthur Reynolds, Judy Temple, and Art Rolnick for leading this effort, and all of the participants of the conference and contributors to the volume for this signally important work.

KAREN HANSON
Executive Vice President and Provost
University of Minnesota

Acknowledgments

This volume is a product of the Human Capital Research Collaborative (HCRC), an interdisciplinary research center at the University of Minnesota. Since 2006, HCRC has been dedicated to promoting public policies and programs for young people through research and practice from birth to early adulthood. In support of this mission, HCRC conducts research on the determinants of well-being; investigates the efficacy and cost-effectiveness of social programs; synthesizes, integrates, and disseminates knowledge on socially significant topics; and designs and implements interventions to promote healthy development (http://hcrc.umn.edu).

This is the third volume designed to highlight leading research and practice on critical topics in human capital, education, and child development. The first two books by HCRC, published by Cambridge University Press, were *Childhood Programs and Practices in the First Decade of Life: A Human Capital Integration* (2010) and *Health and Education in Early Childhood: Predictors, Interventions, and Policies*. The current volume's focus on early learning gains and well-being is timely and of great social significance. Increasing and sustaining gains from many kinds of positive early childhood experiences is one of the major goals of our time in all human services. This volume provides many perspectives and strategies for effectively addressing both the challenges and opportunities.

Preparation of this volume was supported, in part, by grants from the National Institute of Child Health and Human Development, the Bill & Melinda Gates Foundation, and the US Department of Education. We thank the Federal Reserve Bank of Minneapolis for hosting the conference upon which this volume is based, and for help in organizing the initial drafts of the chapters presented at the conference. We also thank Linda Rees-Christianson for assisting in the editing and administrative process in completing the final chapter preparations. We are grateful for the support of the College of Education, the Institute of Child Development, and the Humphrey School of Public Affairs at the University of Minnesota for sharing and advancing common interests with HCRC in promoting the well-being of children and youth.

1 Introduction
Increasing and Sustaining Gains in Early Learning

Arthur J. Reynolds and Judy A. Temple

How gains from early childhood experiences are initiated, increased, and sustained is fundamental to developmental and educational science, and has increasing policy relevance given new public investments over the past decade. The effectiveness of these investments in producing gains is also critical for accountability and identifying future investment priorities. The challenge of maintaining gains has received increased attention as early childhood programs expand. Evidence from recent evaluations of state prekindergarten (Lipsey, Farren & Hofer, 2015) and federal Head Start programs (Puma, Bell, Cook et al., 2012) shows positive benefits but reduced gains as children matriculate into elementary school. Directly supporting the theme of this volume, more recent evidence reported by Johnson & Jackson (2018) demonstrates that the longer-term benefits of the early intervention of Head Start are bolstered by subsequent greater investments in public schools. Another example is Ansari & Pianta's (2018) study that shows linkages between elementary school quality and the persistence of preschool effects. This is further supported by Reynolds, Ou, & Temple's (2018) study of the long-term benefits of programs that continue into elementary school.

This volume emphasizes not only key interventions and practices over the first decade of life that promote healthy development, but also elements and strategies through which learning gains can be enhanced by schools, families, communities, and public institutions. Scaling and expansion of effective programs also are considered. The approaches and principles covered in the volume that show evidence of enhancing learning gains include: (a) program dosage and quality; (b) teacher background, curriculum, and instruction; (c) preschool to third grade (P–3) continuity and alignment; and (d) school quality and family support. Lessons from long-term studies since the 1960s and from current practices will be described to help move the field forward.

The chapter authors are leading researchers and thought leaders in the multidisciplinary fields of human development, education, and behavioral science. Coverage of topics has a strong emphasis on policy and program improvement as well as translational research. Many implications for policy and practice are discussed. The book is based on a national invitational conference that was held at the Federal Reserve Bank of Minneapolis in October 2015. The chapters are updated versions of the papers presented at the conference. Sponsored by the Human Capital Research Collaborative (http://hcrc.umn.edu), an interdisciplinary research center at the University of Minnesota, this book is the third in the series on education and child development.

Themes for Promoting Effectiveness

The book addresses three key themes for research, policy, and practice. They have been a focus of multidisciplinary scholarship for decades, but have increased in priority as access to early education has expanded and evidence of effectiveness is more valued.

Theme 1: Assessing the Impacts of Increased Investment in Early Childhood. The first is the importance of documenting the impact of increased federal and state investments in early childhood development. In recent years, public funding of early childhood programs has continued to grow. The US Department of Education's Race to the Top and Preschool Development Grants to states, enhancements in federal Head Start programs and Child Care and Development Block Grants, and state expansion of prekindergarten programs total more than $5 billion in new funding over the past five years. Total public funding at all levels exceeds $30 billion annually (Council of Economic Advisors, 2015, 2016), which is a doubling of investment over the past two decades (US General Accounting Office, 1999). Public–private sector initiatives, such as Pay for Success, have also been implemented to expand access (Government Accountability Office, 2015; Temple & Reynolds, 2015). Documenting and understanding the extent to which these investments lead to sustained gains in the elementary grades is of great importance not only for accountability but for identifying the elements of programs and contexts that promote longer-term effects on achievement, socio-emotional learning, and educational attainment.

As a consequence of new investments, program participation has increased. Figure 1.1 shows that enrollment of 4-year-olds in public preschool (state pre-K, Head Start, special education) has increased from a decade ago to 43% (NIEER, 2017). For 3-year-olds, 16% are enrolled. Because these rates do not include federal Title I and local funding, they are likely to have been underestimated by at least 5 percentage points. Full-day preschool enrollment also has increased to 54% (includes 3- and

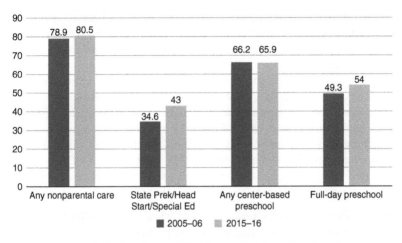

Figure 1.1 Percentage of US 4-year-olds in early education

4-year-olds). Although 80% of 4-year-olds are in nonparental care for at least part of the day (about 3.2 million out of 4 million children), this is relatively unchanged from a decade ago (US Department of Education, 2017). This indicates that it is the type of early education that has changed the most rather than enrollment itself. Consequently, understanding and addressing ways to improve quality and the size of impacts over time has the potential to improve the well-being of millions of young children each year. It also increases the importance of regular accountability to ensure programs are providing sufficient benefits that can be sustained.

Differences in enrollment by socio-economic status, race, and ethnicity continue to be large. Parental education is a good predictor of enrollment in center-based programs, as 18% of children whose parents were high school dropouts were enrolled in such programs compared to 41% for those with advanced degrees (US Department of Education, 2016). A similar pattern occurs for family income, with enrollment in center-based programs nearly three times higher for nonpoor children than poor children (US Department of Education, 2016). Hispanic and American Indian children are less likely to participate in center- and school-based preschools (42% and 46%, respectively) compared to White and Black children (49% and 53%, respectively). Dual-language learners of all ethnicities are underrepresented in programs (42%) relative to English-language-only children (48%; Park et al., 2017). Participation across P–3 should be fully inclusive and strive to tailor instruction to promote learning optimally.

Many chapters discuss the lessons from landmark and current projects to inform policy and program improvement. Extensive research has consistently shown that participation in effective preschool and early education programs can improve school readiness skills and subject matter achievement, and can reduce the need for later remedial education services (Camilli et al., 2010; Cannon et al., 2017). Ensuring that these benefits continue for contemporary programs and for children from diverse backgrounds and experiences is a major goal. Access to high quality programs that support the transition to school and can also lead to long-term benefits is highlighted. The measurement of sustained effects and methodological issues about successfully tracking cohorts and monitoring implementation quality is salient as well.

Theme 2: Focus on Key Elements and Principles of Effectiveness. The second theme of the volume is a comprehensive focus on the elements and principles for sustaining gains in well-being. These elements are also the presumed causes of why continued gains are not observed for many programs and interventions. A major limitation in the field is a focus on one or two of the elements or principles, such as insufficient program quality or poor elementary school quality, without addressing the full scope of possibilities. This may involve, for example, teacher educational and preservice background, class size and support staff, high mobility from preschool to the school grades, differences in class sizes or curriculum, or inconsistent family involvement over time. These explanations have not been fully explored for state pre-K programs, Head Start, and similar programs.

Historically, early childhood programs were designed to promote the development of children with elevated risks of poor cognitive, socio-emotional, and parenting outcomes. Center-based and family-focused programs provided intensive and enriching educational experiences from birth to age 5 to improve foundational skills for school success and social competence (Consortium for Longitudinal Studies, 1983). Influenced by the environmentalism of the 1960s, intellectual effects of programs were emphasized, especially gains in IQ scores (Zigler & Trickett, 1978). Over time, the scope of outcomes expanded to school and social competence, school readiness, and to the current conception of well-being.

Whether improvements in learning and well-being are sustained throughout childhood and into adulthood depends to a large extent on the quality of the program. For example, the landmark prospective cohort studies of the Cornell Consortium, Perry Preschool, Abecedarian Project, and Child–Parent Centers all showed large preschool gains that were sustained to adulthood. For three of the program evaluations, economic returns exceeded costs by at least a factor of 3. The key common elements of the programs were (a) small classes and child-to-staff ratios no higher than 17:2; (b) an intensive focus on language and literacy within a whole-child, developmental philosophy; (c) comprehensive family services; (d) staff compensation that was competitive with public schools; and (e) frequent monitoring and feedback for improvement.

Most current programs financed by states and school districts have few of the key elements of the landmark studies. Child-to-staff ratios are usually 20:2. Family services and expectations for parent involvement are minimal. Curriculum and instruction often lack a strong evidence base, and emphasize teacher-directed activities. Program monitoring is cursory, and is designed for accountability rather than improvement. Costs per child are also lower. As one illustration, the Tennessee Voluntary Prekindergarten program may be classified as a routine state pre-K program based on these criteria. Child-to-staff ratios are 20:2, and although full-day services are provided, none of the comprehensive family services found in the landmark studies are evident. A recent experimental study of the program found positive effects at the end of preschool but no detectable effects on learning from kindergarten to third grade (Lipsey, Farren & Hofer, 2015). This is not surprising given the accumulated evidence that only high-quality programs that follow the established principles of effectiveness from the field yield long-term effects.

Table 1.1 shows three common sets of program elements that promote effectiveness in early childhood programs. Programs for preschool children and beyond that meet more of these elements are likely to have larger and more enduring effects than those meeting fewer of the elements (Cannon et al., 2017; Reynolds et al., 2010). Zigler et al.'s (2006) and the National Institute of Early Education Research's (NIEER, 2017) effectiveness elements are similar in most respects, with the Zigler framework including parent involvement as a key element. The Child–Parent Center (CPC) elements described in Reynolds et al. (2017) also emphasize parent involvement as well as curriculum alignment and continuity across ages and grades. The organizational component of collaborative leadership helps create a positive learning environment that is further enhanced by professional development for staff.

How these common elements align with key principles of effective intervention described by Ramey and Ramey (1998) is noted in the last column. Among the six principles are: developmental timing, program intensity, and ecological and environmental maintenance of development. They are reasonably represented by the three frameworks, though not perfectly. Environmental maintenance of development, which is

Table 1.1 Core elements of early childhood programs and services and linkage to key principles of effectiveness

CPC-P-3 Program Elements Reynolds et al. 2017	Essential Elements of High-Quality Pre-K Gates Foundation 2015	Zigler et al. 2006	NIEER 2016	Key Principles Ramey & Ramey 1998
Collaborative leadership A team led by head teacher to create a strong learning climate Delegated responsibilities for curriculum, family support	Strong leadership Integrated system of learning goals, curriculum, professional development, formative assessments, and data	Monitoring system with on-site observation	Monitoring with site visits at least once every five years	Environmental maintenance of development
Effective learning experiences Small classes (<18 in pre-K; <26 in K–3) Balance of teacher-and child-directed instruction Extended learning time, including full-day, multi-year programs Teacher has BA degree; Assistant has CDA, AA degree, or equivalent Engaged in learning and instruction	Maximum class size of 22, adult:child ratio between 2:15 and 2:22 Two adults in the classroom Learning time: 6–6.5 hours per day, 180–205 days per year Support for dual-language learners Support for students with special needs Teacher–child interactions focused on learning	Maximum of 10 children per teacher or assistant teacher Teacher with BA and EC specialization; Assistant with CDA or equivalent Full-day and two-year option	Maximum ratio of 10 children per staff member Maximum class size of 20 Teacher has BA degree Teacher has specialized training Assistant has CDA or equivalent	Developmental timing Program intensity Direct provision of learning experiences Individual differences in program benefits
Aligned curriculum & practices Evidence-based curriculum Annual curriculum alignment plan Across-grade collaboration	Age-appropriate learning standards Proven (research-based) curriculum Formative assessments Data-driven decision-making	Curriculum is evidence-based Parent involvement plan	Comprehensive learning standards Health screening for vision plus at least one support service 1 meal per day or more	Implement new curricula for increased effectiveness Program breadth and flexibility

Parent involvement & engagement Menu-based system of home and school support Annual parent involvement plan Parent resource teacher and outreach worker Physically located parent room Needs assessment			Individual differences in program benefits Program intensity
Professional development In-person and online coaching support Site mentors Review of online modules	Ongoing professional development focused on teacher–child interactions Education and compensation: Teachers have a BA and early learning credential, and are compensated at the same level as K–3 teachers	System of in-service training for all staff Teachers are compensated at rates competitive with schools	Teacher in-service training of at least 15 hours per year
Continuity and stability Participation from preschool to third grade Colocation or close proximity Outreach efforts to reduce mobility	Public support from elected officials, courts and the policy environment	Funding levels support high quality of programs	Environmental maintenance of development

Note. Some elements may span multiple categories, but have been assigned to the one that fits most closely related to duration, is central to CPC-P–3 but not directly addressed in the others. Relatively few programs include all of the elements at high levels of quality, especially over P–3. Fewer than 10% of students have been shown to experience features similar to CPC-P–3 (Reynolds et al., 2010). Some elements have shown improvement, however, such as full-day kindergarten, in which 83% of 5-year-olds are enrolled compared to 69% a decade ago (US Department of Education, 2017). With these elements and principles as a framework, the volume addresses how changes in quality and alignment of programs and practices can improve long-term outcomes. The elements and principles in Table 1.1 provide a checklist for identifying core features influencing learning and gains over time.

The volume is organized according to the main sources of sustained and long-term effects identified in the literature. These include: (a) dosage and length of participation; (b) program quality in the dimensions of learning experiences, curriculum and instruction, and teacher background and qualifications; (c) continuity and alignment over P–3; and (d) school quality and family support. Federal, state, and local-level institutional funding is also covered. Authors delve into these issues by summarizing what is known, effectiveness, and next steps to better improve program performance and consistency in learning. Examples from programs showing long-term effects include the Child–Parent Centers, Perry Preschool, Abecedarian Project, and Infant Health and Development Program.

The reasons for a drop-off in effects, for example, may vary by outcome. Achievement effects tend to show larger drop-offs over time compared to socio-emotional learning, special education placement, and crime prevention (Reynolds & Temple, 2008). Even if gains in one domain drop off, they may carry over to other domains. A common finding is that benefits on school readiness, for example, carry over to reduced special education even if achievement gains are not sustained (Consortium, 1983; Schweinhart et al., 2005). To illustrate and organize the alternative possibilities for sustaining gains from early childhood experiences, the Five-Hypothesis Model of Effectiveness (5HM; Reynolds, 2000) was developed (described in further detail in the next major section of this chapter). In this model, long-term and sustained effects are evaluated according to the extent to which programs impact (1) cognitive-scholastic skills (cognitive advantage), (2) socio-emotional adjustment, (3) motivation, (4) family support behavior, and (5) school quality and support. Program components such as dosage and intensity can also be assessed according to these hypotheses. Programs showing long-term effects tend to demonstrate impacts on two or more of the five hypotheses. Attention to all five can help enhance impacts and address gaps in program implementation.

Theme 3: Multiple Levels of Programs, Policies, and Practices Need to Be Integrated. The third theme is the focus on multiple levels of strategies for initiating and sustaining learning gains as well as promoting well-being. Approaches for enhancing early childhood learning vary dramatically in scale, breadth, and specificity. With regard to scale, the new Every Student Succeeds Act of 2015 provides, at the federal level, several avenues for enhancing early childhood programs and outcomes. The required school improvement plans prepared by states and districts provide opportunities to include early learning as a key goal, and organize resources and practices to sustain gains in achievement, performance, and socio-emotional learning. How schools will enhance parent involvement and school climate, which are also requirements under the Act, can also spur systemic strategies to bolster P–3 programs and practices.

At the state and district levels, alignment of standards, assessments, and professional development for principals and staff are key to promoting continuity and integration of services across the continuum of early education. Many states, including Minnesota, Washington, New Jersey, and North Carolina, have accelerated P–3 and broader alignment across grades to promote consistency in learning (Takanishi, 2016). Resources for professional development and capacity building also are central to further improvement. States such Wisconsin and California have implemented class-size reduction policies that can further support the continuum of learning in the early grades. Due to discontinuities in instructional support and philosophy between early childhood and school settings, improvements in the integration and alignment of services can improve children's levels of readiness for kindergarten and the early grades that are sustained over time (Takanishi, 2016; Zigler & Styfco, 1993). Increased teacher preparation and ongoing resource support reinforces instructional improvements (Manning et al., 2017).

At the school and classroom levels, many structural and process elements have been shown to increase learning, including teacher background and education, positive teacher–child relationships, engaged instruction, school climate, and small classes (Manning et al., 2017). Professional development and support for teachers and staff also make positive contributions to learning. With regard to specificity within and across levels of scale, enhancements in all of the above elements across the age continuum, from child care through school-age programs, increase the dosage and duration of services. Family and community engagement are also salient to building capacity and support through the schooling process. Given the historic focus on specific elements of reform, including curriculum enhancement and small classes (Reynolds, Magnuson & Ou, 2010), comprehensive approaches may not only have larger effects on child development but may also provide a greater likelihood that gains will be sustained. Principles of effective school improvement developed in the 1970s have not been successfully utilized in early childhood programs and their follow-on efforts (Reynolds et al., 2017; Zigler & Styfco, 1993). Among these are principal leadership, school climate and high expectations of performance, and engaged learning communities (Takanishi & Kauerz, 2008). These principles have been incorporated in school reform, most notably the Five Essentials framework of effective leaders, ambitious instruction, involved families, supportive environment, and collaborative teachers (Bryk, 2010).

Each of these levels is part of the ecological perspective that is necessary to ensure developmental continuity over time and maintain learning gains. State and local efforts and major research projects that have documented effective programs that could be expanded are discussed in many chapters. Consistent with the ecological perspective, this book includes a range of strategies and research findings that have important policy implications.

These themes provide a comprehensive approach to better understanding how to create immediate learning gains and sustain these gains as children transition to elementary schools and beyond. Findings and principles of effectiveness covered in the chapters can be translated to programs and policies at multiple levels of scale. They also support the principle of developmental continuity in which supportive and tailored learning experiences can yield enduring impacts if they occur on a regular basis over extended time periods. Key outcomes addressed in the chapters include school readiness, reading and math achievement, socio-emotional learning, parent involvement, remedial education, delinquency, educational attainment, and socio-economic status, and well-being in young and middle adulthood.

Mechanisms of Long-Term Effects

No volume on promoting long-term and sustained effects would be complete without discussing the long history of research on the processes and mechanisms through which experiences in intervention lead to improved well-being. Because early interventions were largely designed to enhance cognitive development (Consortium for Longitudinal Studies, 1983; Zigler & Trickett, 1978), the mechanism of change was believed to be from IQ to achievement, leading to long-term benefits on social competence and well-being. This conceptualization proved to be too narrow given the broader goals of intervention and the programs being situated within family, education, and community contexts (Bronfenbrenner, 1974; Zigler & Trickett, 1978). As reviewed by Reynolds and Ou (2011), three phases of research have occurred since the 1970s. In the first phase, the cognitive advantage hypothesis was found to be the initiator of long-term effects on school achievement, educational attainment, and economic well-being (Berrueta-Clement et al., 1984; Cornell Consortium for Longitudinal Studies, 1983). Other mediators were not directly assessed. The second phase added family and motivational factors to better document the complexity of influences (Reynolds, Ou & Topitzes, 2004; Schweinhart et al., 1993). Seitz et al. (1983), for example, found that cognitive advantage was a function of increased motivation in accounting for the impact of a Head Start program on school achievement.

In recognition of the complex processes at play over time, the third phase of research has emphasized a comprehensive set of child, family, and school-related mechanisms within a framework of alternative models (Reynolds et al., 2011). These phases are summarized in Figure 1.2 with regard to educational attainment, a key long-term outcome. The Cornell Consortium for Longitudinal Studies (1983), which included 12 model programs of varying types, found support for cognitive advantage as the initiator of long-term effects. Early cognitive advantage leads to reduced special education and retention grades, and better attitudes toward schooling, ultimately leading to higher rates of high school graduation. This was extended upon in the Perry Preschool study – one of the Cornell Consortium projects – as shown in the middle section of Figure 1.2. Teachers and motivational variables contributed to the process of change to higher educational attainment.

In the third phase, the comprehensive approach of 5HM is a further expansion that includes family as well as school support, along with individual cognitive, motivational, and socio-emotional mechanisms. As shown in the bottom portion of Figure 1.2, these hypotheses contribute to the explanation of long-term effects on educational attainment in the CPC program. Early cognitive advantages, as measured by school readiness skills, initiate impacts that culminate through later competencies in higher attainments. Prior studies through young adulthood showed that cognitive advantage pathways accounted for up to 40 percent of intervention main effects on depressive symptoms, school completion, job skills, and criminal behavior (Reynolds & Ou, 2011; Reynolds et al., 2004). Family support and school support pathways accounted for up to 50 percent of impacts on these outcomes.

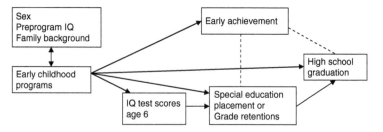

Figure 1.2a Sources of long-term effects from the Consortium for Longitudinal Studies (1983). Arrows for family background are not shown.

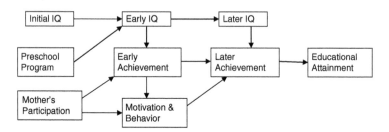

Figure 1.2b Sources of long-term effects from Perry Preschool (Barnett et al., 1998)

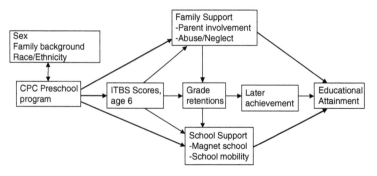

Figure 1.2c Sources of long-term effects from the CPC program (Reynolds, 2000; Reynolds & Ou, 2011). Arrows for family background are not shown.

Figure 1.3 shows the complete specification of 5HM for enhancing children's well-being. Sustained gains in multiple outcome domains are expected as a function of the timing, duration, and quality of intervention, and as the key mechanisms of change are established and reinforced throughout early childhood and into adolescence. The school support and family support hypotheses are particularly relevant to these processes of change.

Documenting mechanisms serves three key purposes. First, it improves program design and modification. Empirically supported paths that are identified can contribute to a variety of improvement efforts. Second, identifying and understanding generative mechanisms can increase generalizability and external validity of findings. To the extent that findings across studies share a common mechanism, program replication and expansion in different contexts would be more likely to be successful. Common mechanisms would also promote sustained effects. Finally, causal inferences are strengthened. Since the length of time between the end of the program and outcome assessment is extensive, documenting the process is essential. These processes are reflected in many chapters and enhance understanding of how impacts are sustained.

Terminology

Given the size and multidisciplinary nature of the early childhood field, a few key concepts are defined. First, we adopt a broad definition of early childhood as the entire first decade of life, from prenatal development up to age 10. This would include through the third grade year as a general endpoint. The historical convention of the preschool period from ages 3 to 5 as defining early childhood has encouraged an unfortunate separate classification of programs and experiences that limit integration. The focus on the continuum of experiences supports a more complete spectrum of services and research approaches. As an operationalization of this continuum, P–3 reinforces the need to optimize learning environments as children grow.

Second, the concept of sustaining gains is synonymous with long-term effects, and other terms such as lasting and enduring effects. These terms are used interchangeably throughout the volume. To conclude that sustained effects occur does not mean that an initial effect on school readiness skills has to be followed by observed effects in the same domain or in the same metric of school achievement for many years. It could be any relevant outcome connected to program goals, such as grade retention, special education, social skills, or crime prevention. We know of no credible evidence that long-term effects occur without the presence of

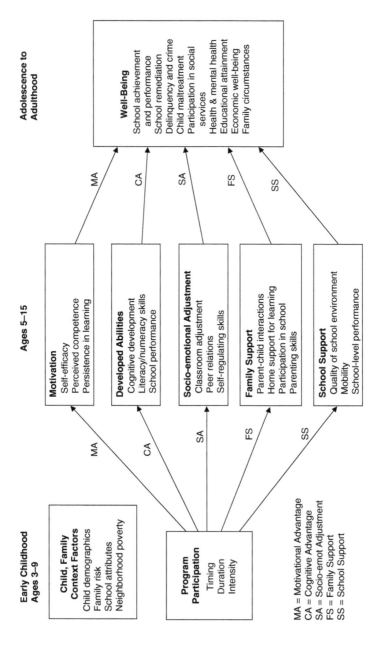

Figure 1.3 Five-hypothesis model of early childhood program effectiveness to youth and adult well-being

immediate or short-term benefits. Certainly, it may take time for the goals of a particular intervention to be achieved, but initial effects or short-term gains are routinely documented. The term "sleeper effect" is often used to refer to the possibility that undetectable early effects are manifested many years later. This view is mistaken. Effects that occur later, such as pre-school preventing crime – which was not fully anticipated in the course of evaluating programs – are traceable to observable earlier benefits in school success and socio-emotional learning (Reynolds & Ou, 2011; Schweinhart et al., 2005). This is true of all other benefits that have been documented in the literature (Cannon et al., 2017).

For how long does a "gain" or program "effect" have to be observed to be regarded as evidence of sustained or long-term benefits? Although this will depend to a large extent on the program theory, our working definition is a minimum of two years, and preferably four to five years, for evidence of sustained effects. This would mean, for example, that a pre-K program would have sustained or long-term effects if it impacted second and third grade outcomes as well as kindergarten performance. A home visiting or parenting program should affect family behaviors and school readiness for preschool children. Some programs, especially if they are high in quality and intensive, demonstrate long-term effects into adult-hood and to midlife. They also have high economic returns. This is ideal, but not necessary for programs to be effective or to show sustained effects. Given the contemporary context in which almost all children receive some degree of center-based early education, the benefits documented in studies from the 1960s and 1970s would not be expected to be fully realized in today's programs.

Although this issue is addressed in several chapters, and more broadly in Chapter 15, many effective programs show sustained effects with no fade-out. The belief that fade-out is inevitable is clearly false. By definition, fade-out means that initial benefits relative to a control condition drop to zero, or no statistically reliable difference for any outcome measured later. It is also the case that the existence of fade-out is a function of program quality. High-quality programs are much less likely to show substantial reduction in effects over time. Of course, there are complex issues to consider. A drop-off in relative effects is likely to occur for some outcomes as a function of maturation and development. The natural variation in performance and in achievement increases with age ("fan-spread" pattern), which substantially increases standard deviations in effect size metrics.

Methodological features such as control group equivalence, measurement validity, and sample retention are also relevant, and can substantially influence whether effects are sustained. If control groups are more advantaged than program groups, a pattern of fade-out or drop-off would be an artifact of this initial non-equivalence, and not evidence of fade-out. Indeed, this was the major methodological problem in the original evaluation of Head Start in the Westinghouse report (Cicarelli, Cooper & Granger, 1969). Given that many early childhood programs seek to enroll the most disadvantaged, impacts may be underestimated. High rates of attrition in follow-up periods are also problematic and may also lead to downward bias, since those lost to follow-up tend to be more disadvantaged.

The scope and focus of this book are unique in the early childhood field. Recent volumes have addressed broad educational (Lee, 2016) and social class themes (Maholmes, 2014; Siraj & Mayo, 2014), or a traditional early childhood focus (Goffin, 2016; Hyson & Tomlinson, 2016). Although contexts of development are covered in depth, they do not specifically address the issues and challenges associated with sustaining or optimizing early learning gains. This is a larger problem in the field. Many disciplines, practitioners, and policymakers want to better understand and address ways to strengthen continuity in learning over childhood. The contents of the volume provide relevant knowledge and approaches for a variety of readers and audiences. Thus, to our knowledge, this is the first book that covers the scientific and programmatic research on the nature, challenges, evidence, and prescriptions for sustaining gains over time for a variety of child and youth outcomes.

Volume Focus

The book includes four parts corresponding to the areas in need of improvement to better sustain gains. The first three parts cover program, school, and family influences at varying levels, while Part IV addresses integrative themes and next steps for ensuring continuing progress. Part I examines program characteristics, teacher background and experience, and curriculum as sources of sustained and long-term gains. As described above, the accumulated research over many decades shows that long-term effects in many domains of well-being are more likely as dosage and quality increases. Although enrollment in public preschool programs has increased in recent years, very few children receive the maximum or optimal duration of services in preschool and over P–3. For example, only half of 4-year-olds are in full-day programs and fewer than a fifth of 3-year-olds enroll in public programs.

In Chapter 2, Barbara A. Wasik and Emily K. Snell synthesize research on preschool dosage and duration. As discussed, understanding the amount of preschool needed to achieve and sustain positive gains is critical as policymakers and educators balance available funding with increasing access to quality programs. The authors make clear that the issue of dosage cannot be addressed independently of the content and quality of programs. An additional year of preschool will not improve learning or strengthen gains if quality is subpar! In a review of the accumulated research up to present-day state and local preschool programs, they find good evidence that some aspects of dosage have positive effects on learning, including session duration (full-day versus half-day), duration (number of years), and threshold dosage (two years versus one year). Studies are limited in other aspects of dosage frequency (days per week), intensity, and cumulative dosage – and need further investigation. The findings of their review of curriculum content are mixed, but indicate that better operationalization and measurement of what elements are delivered, how much, and with what level of quality, are needed. As the authors note, progress in strengthening gains can accelerate if the "content of the preschool experience was more aligned with research-based content, specifically addressing children's language and literacy skills, and early mathematical foundations." Increasing the dosage, duration, and intensity of services is an important avenue for sustaining gains but that quality improvements are fundamental.

In Chapter 3, Gregory Camilli covers four influences on achievement outcomes in early education: the effects of teaching quality, the effects of teacher qualifications, teacher effects, and program interventions intended to improve child outcomes. As noted, they are best considered together. Positive evidence is reviewed for each, but the difficulty of establishing causality is a limitation of most findings, as are measurements of teacher effects. Both comparative evaluations and experiments of many samples corroborate that program benefits – whether teacher qualifications or learning gains – are mediated through teachers. Camilli concludes that "it is both ironic and remarkable that effective programs have been and continue to be designed that have substantial impact on child outcomes." Although teacher and program benefits have been well documented, better understanding of the impact of teachers, and increasing their effects, is a challenge to progress, but positive steps are occurring in many contemporary programs and practices, to the benefit of children.

Preschool curricula are a primary avenue for enhancing children's outcomes. Decades of research have sought to identify the most effective models and key principles of implementation, with mixed success. In Chapter 4, Greg Duncan and colleagues review the findings from many evaluations, including the 2008 Preschool Curriculum Evaluation Research Initiative Study and more recent syntheses. Four types of curricula are considered: literacy- and math-focused, whole-child, and locally-developed models. Math curricula were found to improve classroom activities and achievement relative to HighScope and Creative Curriculum, two widely used whole-child approaches. Literacy curricula showed larger effects on achievement compared to the whole-child approaches but showed no consistent effects on classroom processes. Creative curriculum as evaluated showed some impacts on classroom activities and teacher interactions but no differences in achievement relative to local curricula. Recent syntheses show the benefits of skill-specific curricula focused on reading (e.g., Literacy Express) or math (e.g., Building Blocks). Certainly, it is important to consider implementation fidelity, use of other curricula, and teacher professional development opportunities as influential for both teachers and students. These factors would be expected to vary by context. The authors emphasize that the accumulated evidence favors specific skilled-based curricula over whole-child approaches as currently implemented. They note the importance of building on current knowledge by assessing the impacts of different curricula and to continue to evaluate the effects of existing, new, and revised curricular models to achieve sustained gains of interventions that are known to be possible.

Beth Meloy, Madelyn Gardner, Marjorie Wechsler, and David Kirp in Chapter 5 identify and describe key lessons from well-known state-of-the-art early childhood programs as well as their implications for policy. They draw on evidence from landmark and contemporary studies of the Child–Parent Centers, Michigan's Great State Readiness Program, New Jersey's Abbott Preschool, North Carolina's Smart Start and Pre-K, Oklahoma's universal preschool, and Washington State's Early Childhood programs. Six tenets for enhancing programs and their sustained effects are detained: (1) a strong program structure with relatively small classes and low ratios; (2) engaging and meaningful learning experiences in the classroom; (3) a highly skilled and supported workforce; (4) comprehensive services for children and families; (5) continuous quality improvement; and (6) an early learning continuum up to third grade. The latter one is perhaps the most important and unrealized element in practice and policy, which is reinforced in many chapters (e.g., Chapters 6–8, 14, and 15). As noted by the authors: "while there is variation in the extent to which these six programs invest in the early elementary years or begin interventions prior to preschool, in every case decision-makers have acknowledged that pre-K alone is not enough … each of these programs makes it clear that, while the quality of early learning instruction is important for immediate child outcomes, sustained benefits require far more comprehensive investments in children and their families."

Part II covers P–3 continuity and includes four chapters. The major tenet of P–3 is that gains can be sustained and increased to the extent that kindergarten to third grade experiences build on and are aligned with earlier experiences. This can establish an integrated system of support over many years. Moreover, increased duration of participation is expected to promote sustained gains. Few children experience a strong system of early childhood programs that would satisfy the key elements described in Table 1.1. In Chapter 6, Andrew Mashburn and Rita Yelverton examine the role of instructional practices between preschool and kindergarten in contributing to learning gains. Using data from the national Head Start Impact Study (HSIS), which found no overall effects of the program at the end of kindergarten, the authors examined whether the consistency of instructional practices (i.e., amount of time spent doing literacy/language, math, whole-group, and child-chosen activities) across Head Start and kindergarten classrooms predicted gains in kinder-garten. Results indicated that children's math skills and social-emotional skills during kindergarten were positively associated with the consistency of instructional practices they experienced across Head Start and kinder-garten classrooms. The authors discuss how these findings can strengthen early childhood learning gains in Head Start and other programs.

In Chapter 7, "Quality and Continuity in Young Children's Educational Experiences," Deborah Stipek summarizes research on what constitutes quality at both the preschool level and in the early elementary grades, and discusses dimensions of continuity across grades that might affect how well gains in preschool are sustained over time. Evidence on the nature of high-quality instructional programs, preschool through third grade, is reviewed, along with the potential value of creating continuity in children's educational experience as they move from pre-school through the early elementary grades. Although there is evidence that teaching practices tailored to children's needs and specific interven-tions in both preschool and the early grades promote learning gains, the high prevalence of inconsistent and misaligned instructional practices is a major challenge to the field. Better assessment of instruction, learning environments, and teaching practices is warranted as is enhanced profes-sional development opportunities for teachers across P–3. The goal of achieving greater continuity over P–3 must follow key principles of instructional quality identified in the field.

In Chapter 8, Arthur J. Reynolds describes the revision and scale-up of the Child–Parent Center (CPC) program, which has been the focus of one of largest longitudinal studies of early childhood programs. Beginning in 2012 and based on funding from the US Department of Education, the first expansion of the program outside Chicago was implemented in four districts (Saint Paul, MN; Normal, IL; and Evanston, IL in addition to Chicago expansion). The Midwest CPC expansion was revised as a P–3 school reform model and implemented six key elements: (a) effective learning experiences, including small classes; (b) collaborative leadership; (c) aligned curriculum; (d) parent involvement and engagement; (e) professional development; and (f) continuity and stability. Results of the expansion showed good evidence of fidelity and positive effects on school readiness skills and parent involvement. Duration of participation was linked to learning gains over time, which suggested that the CPC program can be scaled effectively to a broad context of schools and districts. On the basis of the accumulated research in the program, the system of services provided can be implemented in other districts, and resources of support are available for further expansion.

In Chapter 9, Laura Bornfreund and Abbie Lieberman examine trends in states' practices for supporting P–3 efforts to improve reading skills in the third grade benchmark year. As noted, "effective early education policy approaches must combine targeted early literacy initiatives with policies that support, scaffold, and sequence children's learning and development through third grade." Given the influence of state policies on education practice, the potential for impacting child outcomes is large. The authors synthesize data on state P–3 policies that may impact goals for third grade literacy at the agency, school, and classroom level. Among the areas reviewed are educators; standards, assessment, and data; equitable funding; state pre-K; kindergarten; dual-language learners; and third grade reading laws. As noted by the authors, progress is evident in several areas, especially in state-funded pre-K, kindergarten programs, and standards, but aligning and integrating services over P–3 is at the beginning stages. State implementation of the new federal Every Student Succeeds Act may help accelerate future progress.

Part III covers family and school processes that promote learning gains and long-term effects. The environmental contexts that support learning are key influences on child development outcomes. The more comprehensive programs are, and the more they tailor services to children's needs over extended periods of time, the more of a difference they have been found to make in terms of whether long-term effects occur. In Chapter 10, Arthur J. Reynolds and colleagues summarize evidence on three hypothesized mechanisms of long-term effects that have been shown to account for gains in well-being. These are the cognitive-scholastic advantage, family support, and school support hypotheses (see Figures 10.2 and 10.3). In studies of the Child–Parent Centers, Abecedarian, Perry, and other programs that followed participants into adulthood, both the provision of comprehensive family services and school context and quality were important explanations of effects. In the Child–Parent Center program, for example, parent involvement in school and the quality of elementary schools each accounted for 25 to 30 percent of the long-term effects on achievement, educational attainment, and crime prevention. Implications for sustaining gains at population levels are described.

In Chapter 11, Lawrence J. Schweinhart recounts the long history of early childhood education from the eighteenth century to present-day prekindergarten programs. Reflecting on the contributions of HighScope Perry Preschool, one of the landmark studies begun in the early 1960s, Dr. Schweinhart argues that "highly effective" preschool should be the focus of public policy rather than the lower-cost routine programs that are usually implemented. The Perry program had low child-to-teacher ratios, a child-centered curriculum, and weekly home visits. He also notes that the issue of sustained effects is complex, given that, while short-term gains in IQ do not persistent, they mediate the effects on long-term outcomes and positive economic returns. Consistent with the accumulated knowledge, the meaning of IQ gains is not strictly cognitive advantage but broader school readiness or being a "better student academically and behaviorally." Schweinhart makes clear the main lesson from Perry: "we must substantially maintain the quality of early childhood programs if we expect [them] to be highly effective" and "continue to evaluate their results. As a society, we need to invest in these programs and improve the less effective programs that now exist."

Chapter 12, on the Carolina Abecedarian Project, by Frances A. Campbell, Yi Pan, and Margaret Burchinal, and Chapter 13, on the Infant Health and Development Program – a designed replication and extension of Abecedarian – by Juan C. Chaparro, Aaron J. Sojourner, and Nathan Huey, describe the complex benefits of these landmark studies on child development and parenting. Each program provided comprehensive family services as well as intensive educational enrichment that contributed to long-term effects. In the case of Abecedarian, Campbell and colleagues show that positive teacher interactions in kindergarten and the early grades helped account for long-term effects of Abecedarian on achievement, educational attainment, and adult well-being. For the Infant Health and Development Program, Chaparro and colleagues detail the often overlooked benefits of educational enrichment for parents' well-being, as the freed time provided by early education for the child has psychological benefits for parents that may help in increasing quality parenting time, not to mention employment opportunities. Both programs also substantially reduced achievement gaps for participants during childhood. In total, the four chapters in Part III reinforce the need for greater attention to parental involvement and family support in early childhood programs, as well as the role of school quality and context factors in sustaining and possibly increasing gains for early education.

Part IV covers more integrative themes and lessons over the past five decades that can be applied to present and future programs. As such, we expand further on the contributions and implications for the field. In Chapter 14, Barbara Bowman reflects on progress in the field since *Eager to Learn* (Bowman, Donovan & Burns, 2001), a landmark book published by the National Research Council for which Professor Bowman was co-editor. This book was way ahead of its time, and provided succinct summaries of the state of knowledge on effectiveness in early childhood programs and practices that have only increased in importance – curriculum and instructional strategies, balance of academic and socio-emotional learning, the role of play in early development, teacher background and experience, and continuity in leaning gains. The increasing need to close the achievement gap by race/ethnicity and family income was also emphasized, with the main conclusion being that encouraging and reinforcing an enthusiasm for learning throughout childhood is most critical. Indeed, the title of the book reflects this core focus. In reviewing the progress in the field since 2001, Professor Bowman finds success. One is the increase in the number of early childhood teachers with BAs in public schools, and more recently in Head Start. The book recommended that all young children should have teachers with the same level of education as the teachers of children in kindergarten through college. Progress, though slow, is also noted in balancing teacher-directed and child-initiated learning, blending socio-emotional learning with traditional academic content areas, and aligning preschool with kindergarten and the early grades.

On this latter point, Professor Bowman noted that while the concept of preschool to third grade systems is becoming more accepted, progress in service integration to support children's learning has been weak. Part of the reason, as noted, is that increasing preschool funding by itself was easier given available evidence on return on investment. Another reason, though, is the challenge of aligning and integrating different systems of education across ages. Such systems change is more difficult, especially at a large scale. The present book provides avenues for making more progress in P–3 in the future. As noted, "there is a good deal of support for the notion that children learn best when there is an alignment between what they know and what we want them to know. This means that interventions that are sustained over time, building from one level to the next, are likely to result in better long-term achievement."

In the concluding chapter, Craig Ramey and Sharon Landesman Ramey review much of the history of experiments and multifaceted research to promote early childhood development. They have a unique perspective, since between them they have designed and/or directed the Abecedarian Project, Infant Health and Development Project, and the National Head Start/Public School Transition Demonstration Project. They show the high levels of support for the benefit of a variety of well-implemented intervention on cognition, school achievement, reductions in special education and grade retention, and long-term health benefits. Their discussion of the myth of "fade-out" effects is timely given the current attention to expanding early learning programs at the state and national levels. They conclude that high-quality programs of sufficient dosage and duration do sustain their effects and that we can do better as a field to ensure this occurs in all programs.

Building on the accumulated work, they describe 12 hallmarks of programs that show large long-term effects. Among the most notable are that (a) program leaders have a strong interest in the program, equivalent to a shared ownership; (b) intensity and dosage was relatively high, and thus spanned multiple years; and (c) multiple features and components were implemented in the program, and consist with ecological and environmental maintenance models. These can help ensure that program scaling leads to greater effectiveness. As the authors state, these hallmarks can hopefully help "reduce the large and burdensome educational inequalities and health disparities that continue to plague our nation's lowest-income and most marginalized children and families."

Conclusion

As the chapters make clear, the scope and depth of knowledge on the sources of long-term and sustained effects of early childhood programs have grown substantially over the past decade. To fully support the continuum of learning during all of early childhood, high priority should be given to increases in program dosage, duration, and quality; teacher development; school and instructional quality; family support and parenting; and P-3 continuity. These foci are consistent with key principles of effectiveness and are supported by the evidence from the most successful programs. Historically, the concept of the P-3 continuity has been explicit, as expressed at the time of the Head Start planning committee in 1965:

It is clear that successful programs of this type must be comprehensive, involving activities generally associated with the fields of health, social services and education. Similarly, it is clear that the program must focus on the problems of child and parent and that these activities need to be carefully integrated with programs for the school years. (See Richmond, 1997, p. 122.)

Although the importance of P–3 and the continuum of early learning is well documented, systems of support at the local, state, and national levels are only now being built. More integrative programs, policies, and practices are being implemented in many communities. The goal now is to ensure that all children have the opportunity to benefit from these advances and that supportive services for children, families, and schools can be sustained for future generations.

References

Ansari, A. & Pianta, R. C. (2018). The role of elementary school quality in the persistence of preschool effects. *Child and Youth Services Review*, 86, 120–127.

Barnett, W. S., Young, J. W. & Schweinhart, L. J. (1998). How preschool education influences long-term cognitive development and school success: A causal model. In W. S. Barnett & S. S. Boocock (Eds.), *Early Care and Education for Children in Poverty: Promises, Programs, and Long-Term Results*. Albany, NY: State University of New York Press, pp. 167–184.

Berrueta-Clement, J., Schweinhart, L., Barnett, W., Epstein, A. & Weikart, D. (1984). *Changed Lives*. Monograph 8, Ypsilanti, MI: High/Scope Press.

Bill and Melinda Gates Foundation. (2015). *Early Learning: High-Quality Pre-Kindergarten*. Seattle.

Bowman, B. T., Donovan, M. S. & Burns, M. S. (Eds.). (2001). *Eager to Learn: Educating Our Preschoolers*. National Research Council. Washington, DC: National Academy Press.

Bronfenbrenner, U. (1974). Is early intervention effective? *Teachers College Record*, 76, 279–303.

Bryk, A. S. (2010). Organizing schools. *Phi Delta Kappan*, 91(7) 23–30.

Consortium for Longitudinal Studies. (1983). *As the Twig Is Bent . . . Lasting Effects of Preschool Programs*. Hillsdale, NJ: Lawrence Erlbaum Associates.

Council of Economic Advisors. (2015). *Economics of Early Childhood Investment*. Washington, DC: Executive Office of the President.

Council of Economic Advisors. (2016). Inequality in early childhood and effective public policy interventions. *Economic Report of the President*. Washington, DC: Executive Office of the President.

Camilli, G., Vargas, S., Ryan, S. & Barnett, W. S. (2010). Meta-analysis of the effects of early education interventions on cognitive and social development. *Teachers College Record*, 112(3), 579–620.

Cannon, J. S., Kilburn, M. R., Karoly, L. A. et al. (2017). *Investing Early: Taking Stock of Outcomes and Economic Returns from Early Childhood Programs.* Santa Monica, CA: RAND. DOI: 10.7249/RR1993.

Cicarelli, V. G., Cooper, W. H. & Granger, R. L. (1969). *The Impact of Head Start: An Evaluation of the Effects of Head Start on Children's Cognitive and Affective Development.* (Vol. 2, Prepared for the Office of Economic Opportunity.) Athens: Westinghouse Learning Corporation and Ohio University.

Government Accountability Office. (2015). *Pay for Success: Collaboration among Federal Agencies Would Be Helpful as Governments Explore New Financing Mechanisms* (GAO-15-646). Washington, DC: Government Accountability Office.

Goffin, S. (2016). *Early Childhood Education for a New Era.* New York, NY: Teachers College Press.

Hyson, M. & Tomlinson, H. B. (Eds.). (2016). *The Early Years Matter.* New York, NY: Teachers College Press.

Johnson, R. C. & Jackson, C. P. (2018). *Reducing Inequality through Dynamic Complementarity: Evidence from Head Start and Public School Spending.* Working paper 23489. Cambridge, MA: National Bureau of Economic Research.

Lee, J. (2016). *The Anatomy of Achievement Gaps.* New York, NY: Oxford University Press.

Lipsey, M. W., Farren, D. C. & Hofer, K. G. (2015). *A Randomized Controlled Trial of a Voluntary Prekindergarten Program on Children's Skills and Behaviors through Third Grade.* (Peabody Research Institute, Vanderbilt University.)

Maholmes, V. (2014). *Fostering Resilience and Well-Being in Children and Families in Poverty.* New York, NY: Oxford University Press.

Manning, M., Garvis, S., Fleming, C. & Wong, G. T. W. (2017, January). The relationship between teacher qualification and the quality of the early education and care environment. *Campbell Systematic Reviews.* DOI: 10.4073/ csr.2017.1 (http://campbellcollaboration.org/library).

National Institute of Early Education Research (NIEER). (2017). *Preschool Yearbook, 2016.* New Brunswick, NJ: Rutgers University.

National Institute of Early Education Research (NIEER). (2016). *Preschool Yearbook, 2015.* New Brunswick, NJ: Rutgers University.

Park, M., O'Toole, A. & Katsiaficas, C. (2017). *Dual Language Learners: A National Demographic and Policy Profile.* Washington, DC: Migration Policy Institute.

Puma, M., Bell, S., Cook, R. et al. (2012, October). *Third Grade Follow-Up to the Head Start Impact Study: Final Report.* Washington, DC: Office of Planning, Research and Evaluation, Administration for Children and Families, US Department of Health and Human Services. www.acf.hhs.gov/sites/default/ files/opre/head_start_report.pdf

Ramey, C. T. & Ramey, S. L. (1998). Early intervention and early experience. *American Psychologist, 53,* 109–120.

Reynolds, A. J. (2000). *Success in Early Intervention: The Chicago Child–Parent Centers.* Lincoln: University of Nebraska Press.

Reynolds, A. J. & Ou, S. (2011). Paths of effects from preschool to adult well-being: A confirmatory analysis of the Child–Parent Center Program. *Child Development*, 82 (2), 555–582.

Reynolds, A. J., Ou, S. & Topitzes, J. (2004). Paths of effects of early childhood intervention on educational attainment and juvenile arrest: a confirmatory analysis of the Chicago Child–Parent Centers. *Child Development*, 75(5), 1299–1328.

Reynolds, A. J., Temple, J. A., White, B. A., Ou, S. & Robertson, D. L. (2011). Age-26 cost–benefit analysis of the Child–Parent Center education program. *Child Development*, 82, 782–804.

Reynolds, A. J., Temple, J. A., Ou, S. Arteaga, I. A. & White, B. A. B. (2011). School-based early childhood education and age-28 well-being: effects by timing, dosage, and subgroups. *Science*, 333(6040), 360–364.

Reynolds, A. J., Magnuson, K. & Ou, S. (2010). PK-3 programs and practices: A review of research. *Children and Youth Services Review*, 32, 1121–1131.

Reynolds, A. J., Hayakawa, M., Ou, S. et al. (2017). Scaling and sustaining effective early childhood programs through school–family–community collaboration. *Child Development*, 88(5), 1453–1465.

Reynolds, A. J., Ou, S., & Temple, J. A. (2018). A multi-component, preschool to 3rd grade preventive intervention and educational attainment at 35 years of age. JAMA Pediatrics, 172(3), 247–256.

Reynolds, A. J. & Temple, J. A. (2008). Cost-effective early childhood development programs from preschool through third grade, *Annual Review of Clinical Psychology*, 4, 109–139.

Richmond, J. B. (1997). Head Start, A retrospective view: The founders; Section 3: The early administrators, in E. Zigler & J. Valentine (Eds.), *Project Head Start: A Legacy of the War on Poverty* (2nd ed.). Alexandria, VA: National Head Start Association, pp. 120–128.

Schweinhart, L. J., Montie, J., Xiang, Z., Barnett, W. S., Belfield, C. R. & Nores, M. (2005). *Lifetime Effects: The High/Scope Perry Preschool Study through Age 40* (No. 14). Ypsilanti, MI: High/Scope Educational Research Foundation.

Schweinhart, L. J., Barnes, H. V. & Weikart, D. P. (1993). *Significant Benefits: The High/Scope Perry Preschool Study at Age 27*. Ypsilanti, MI: High/Scope Press.

Seitz, V., Apfel, N. H., Rosenbaum, L. K. & Zigler, E. (1983). Long-term effects of Projects Head Start and Follow Through: The New Haven Project. In Consortium for Longitudinal Studies (Ed.), *As the Twig Is Bent . . . Lasting Effects of Preschool Programs*. Hillsdale, NJ: Erlbaum, pp. 299–332.

Siraj, I. & Mayo, A. (2014). *Social Class and Educational Inequality: The Impact of Parents and Schools*. Cambridge: Cambridge University Press.

Takanishi, R. (2016). *First Things First! Creating the New American Primary School*. New York, NY: Teachers College Press.

Takanishi, R. & Kauerz, K. (2008). PK inclusion: Getting serious about a P–16 education system. *Phi Delta Kappan*, 89(7), 480–487.

Temple, J. A. & Reynolds, A. J. (2015). Using benefit–cost analysis to scale up early childhood programs through Pay for Success financing. *Journal of Benefit–Cost Analysis*, 6(3), 628–653.

US Department of Education. (2017). *Digest of Education Statistics, 2016* (Table 202.30). Washington, DC: US Department of Education.

US Department of Education. (2016). *Digest of Education Statistics, 2015* (Table 202.30). Washington, DC: US Department of Education.

US General Accounting Office. (1999). *Education and Care: Early Childhood Programs and Services for Low-Income Families* (Report No. GAO/HEHS-00–11). Washington, DC: US General Accounting Office.

Zigler, E., Gilliam, W. S. & Jones, S. M. (Eds.). (2006). *A Vision for Universal Preschool Education*. New York, NY: Cambridge University Press.

Zigler, E. & Styfco, S. J. (1993). *Head Start and Beyond: A National Plan for Extended Childhood Intervention*. New Haven, CT: Yale University Press.

Zigler, E. & Trickett, P. K. (1978). IQ, social competence, and the evaluation of early childhood intervention programs. *American Psychologist, 33,* 789–798.

Part I

Program Dosage and Quality

2 Synthesis of Preschool Dosage
How Quantity, Quality, and Content Impact Child Outcomes

Barbara A. Wasik and Emily K. Snell

Introduction

In recent years, increased attention has been paid to preschool as a means of addressing the significant achievement gap that exists between children in poverty and their more advantaged peers (Duncan & Murnane, 2011; Heckman, 2006; Yoshikawa, Weiland, Brooks-Gunn et al., 2013). However, preschool is expensive, and the nature of the debate has shifted from whether federal, state, and local monies should support early childhood learning to the specifics of for whom, how much, and what programs should offer. Therefore, understanding the amount, or dosage, of preschool needed to achieve positive outcomes in young children and to increase their school readiness is critical as policymakers and educators try to balance funding challenges while attempting to increase access to early education. However, the issue of dosage cannot be addressed independently from considerations about the content of the preschool classroom because the two factors are intricately related. In order to inform the discussion of *how much* preschool is effective, we need to understand *how much of what* is needed in order to unpack what the key components of an effective preschool experience are for young children.

This chapter provides a brief overview of dosage and how it is currently used in implementation science. We then present the current research on preschool and dosage. Next, we review the research that is cited as support for preschool as an effective early intervention strategy to help close the achievement gap. We pay particular attention to both the content of the interventions and the dosage to help understand what is known about the effect of various aspects of preschool on child outcomes. Finally, we address the policy and research issues related to our findings.

History and Background of Dosage

The dosage of early childhood programs was less frequently discussed prior to the 1990s. In the last decade or two, however, increased attention

31

paid to implementation science and the development of evidence-based interventions has motivated some researchers to provide more careful attention to, and measurement and reporting of, various aspects of interventions, from content to dosage (Durlak & DuPre, 2008; Fixsen, Naoom, Blase et al., 2005).

Since increased dosage of an intervention often translates into higher intervention costs, understanding the dosage at which an intervention produces positive impacts also has substantial implications for developing cost-effective interventions (Karoly, 2012). Without considering dosage more carefully both in research and practice, we can neither account for how much intervention participants actually receive, nor fully understand the best delivery mechanisms for that intervention; nor can we measure its true costs or benefits at the individual, familial, or societal level (Halle, Metz & Martinez-Beck, 2013). Thus, understanding dosage is essential to advancing research, practice, and policy in the early childhood care and education field.

Dosage: Defining Key Concepts

We start with a brief overview of commonly used terminology (see also Wasik, Mattera, Lloyd & Boller, 2013). *Dosage* historically was used in the medical field, as far back as the Greek physician Galen, to refer to the quantity or amount of medicine. In early childhood education, dosage is often used more broadly to refer to years of preschool, or hours per day (usually half- or full-day). But the scientific origins of the term dosage belie its lack of precision when used in the early childhood field; in some studies, "full-day preschool" might refer to the six-hour school-year calendar, while in other contexts (e.g., studies of child care), preschool might only be considered full-day if it is available eight or ten hours a day, all year. In this chapter, we argue that to add precision to the debate over early childhood education, it is important to consider the various elements that make up dosage, including session duration (e.g., half-day vs. full school-day vs. full child care coverage), frequency (e.g., 3 vs. 5 days a week during the school year), and duration (e.g., one vs. two school years). If information is available on all these elements, it is possible to calculate the *cumulative dosage* of a program (cumulative dosage = session duration × frequency × intervention duration or length of program enrollment).

It can also be important to consider the dosage of specific elements of an intervention, program, or curriculum. For example, a pre-kindergarten curriculum that requires 30 minutes of specific literacy activities per day for one school year would have a cumulative intended dosage at the child level of 5,400 minutes (30 minutes multiplied by 5 days multiplied by 36 weeks). For all aspects of dosage, it is critical to distinguish between the *dosage intended, dosage offered,* and *dosage received.*

Less frequently examined in the empirical literature is the *intensity* of an intervention and *threshold dosage. Intensity* of an intervention is another term that is sometimes used to describe the "strength" or the rate of exposure of an intervention, which might include elements of frequency, session duration, and intervention duration. In addition, it may also be used to describe how much of a particular component of an intervention is delivered within each session. A *threshold* dose is used to describe a specific dosage level at which an intervention affects outcomes. For example, a study may find that children only need to attend one year of preschool to achieve needed outcomes, and that an additional year does not add additional benefits.

Evidence on Preschool Dosage

Overall, research suggests that more participation in center-based pre-school education is associated with increased kindergarten readiness, especially for low-income children. Below, we examine how this functions within the various aspects of dosage, including session duration, frequency, duration, cumulative dosage, intended vs. offered and received dosage, intensity, and threshold dosage.

Session duration: Non-experimental work has suggested that full-day programs offer some benefits to children over part-day programs. For example, Reynolds, Richardson, Hayakawa et al. (2014) examined the impact of length of day by comparing children who attended part-day vs. full-day in Chicago Child–Parent Centers; they found significant improvements in children's socio-emotional development, language and math skills, and physical health for full-day children relative to children in the part-day program. A non-experimental analysis of the effects of different centers in the Head Start Impact Study (Walters, 2015) found that full-day programs boosted cognitive achievement by 0.14 SD above those in half-day programs. Recent experimental work by Gibbs (2014) in a sample of Indiana districts found that full-day kindergarten, relative to half-day, improved literacy skills by approximately 0.3 SD, with Hispanic students and students who began the year with low literacy skills experiencing the largest gains. These findings imply that more time in school might be especially beneficial for children who are farthest behind, decreasing the early achievement gap and potentially improving students' outcomes later in life.

There is some evidence, however, that if the quality of the full-day program is subpar, greater dosage (full-day) might not only have positive effects (Magnuson, Meyers, Rhum & Waldfogel, 2004; Robin, Frede & Barnett, 2006), but negative effects, as has been suggested by the NICHD study (Vandell, Belsky, Burchinal et al., 2010), which found evidence that more hours in child care (30+ hours a week) was associated with increased risk of behavioral problems.

Frequency: Most public preschool programs that have been evaluated are 5-day per week programs; however, some states or localities offer preschool programs that have fewer days. As far as we are aware, there have been no systematic evaluations of the effects of frequency of early childhood education programming.

Duration: The aspect of dosage that has been most frequently tested is duration. Most work suggests that at-risk children who attend more preschool or child care tend to enter kindergarten better prepared, especially on academic measures, although effects may dissipate over time (Loeb, Bridges, Bassok et al., 2007; Skibbe, Connor, Morrison & Jewkes, 2011). A large, international meta-analysis (Nores & Barnett, 2010) also found that programs lasting 1–3 years had somewhat larger effect sizes compared to those of less than one year (i.e., 0.3 versus 0.2).

A recent long-term follow-up of participants in Child–Parent Centers (Arteaga, Humpage, Reynolds & Temple, 2014) used propensity score weighting to compare groups of children attending preschool for two years versus those who attended for only one, and found that the two-year group was significantly less likely to receive special education, be abused or neglected, or to commit crimes, although differences in academic or cognitive outcomes were not found.

Cumulative dosage: We are unaware of any research that attempts to quantify the effect of cumulative dosage of preschool programs.

Dosage intended, offered, and received: Research has suggested that the intended dosage of an intervention is almost always more than what is actually received (Durlak & DuPre, 2008). This can occur at the program level, when state funding is delayed and school starts late (or a day is canceled each week), or at the family level (if children miss school due to illness or other reasons). For example, in Washington DC, more than one-quarter of Head Start students enrolled in public schools miss more than 10 percent of school days (Dubay & Holla, 2015); similarly, in

Chicago, half of 3-year-olds and one-third of 4-year-olds miss more than 10 percent of school days (Ehrlich, Gwynne, Pareja et al., 2013). The Chicago researchers also noted that children's preschool absences predicted long-term attendance problems and poor achievement.

Intensity of intervention: The effect of the intensity of early childhood interventions is less often studied, beyond examination of half-day vs. full-day programs. A limited number of studies have examined the intensity of specific activities offered in an educational program, and their findings suggest that increased intensity and/or more sessions do not always lead to better outcomes for children. For example, researchers studying print referencing compared more versus fewer references to print within sessions and found that a lower intensity of print referencing was associated with larger effects (McGinty, Breit-Smith, Fan et al., 2011). Overall, however, the effect of the intensity of most programs or curricula is relatively unknown, perhaps because other aspects of pre-school content and dosage are often endogenous with respect to intensity.

Threshold dosage: When comparing the marginal effect of two years versus one year of preschool, it appears that the incremental effect of attending a first year of preschool is generally greater in magnitude than that of a second year for children's short- and long-term outcomes (Arteaga et al., 2014; Reynolds, Temple, Ou et al., 2011; Wen, Leow, Hahs-Vaughn et al., 2012). Relatedly, Jenkins, Farkas, Duncan, Burchinal & Vandell (2015) found that children who attended Head Start at age 3, and then moved to public pre-K at age 4, had better outcomes than those who attended Head Start for two years. The authors speculate that this could be in part because children might "max out" on a particular program's curriculum, especially if that curriculum was not designed for the widely varying needs of children across multiple age groups. Their finding also supports the idea that the interaction of dosage and content is important to consider when examining the effect of preschool, and preschool dosage, on children's outcomes.

Defining High-Quality Preschool: Dosage and Content

In reviewing preschool programs, we observed that the term "high-quality" was used frequently in describing curricula, yet a description of high quality and data to substantiate the basis for labeling it "high quality" was typically not provided. We will briefly discuss the issue of high quality as it relates to dosage and content.

Definitions of "high quality" frequently address dosage as it relates to amount of time children spend in class and the ratio of children to adults in the classroom. For example, the US Department of Education's definition of high-quality preschool used in the 2014 Preschool Development Grants competition includes three points pertinent to dosage: high-quality preschools are full-day, have class sizes of 20, and a staff ratio of 10 to 1. Full-day is clearly related to the dosage or amount of experience. Class size and a small staff ratio is related to dosage in that the intention is that, by decreasing the number of children adults need to attend to, the amount of adult interaction increases. Although increased time and potential opportunities to interact is important, we return to an earlier point about dosage and content being intertwined: increases in time and adult child contact is only as effective as the quality and content of the interactions.

While the Department of Education's definition states that high-quality preschools include "developmentally appropriate, culturally and linguistically responsive instruction and evidence-based curricula, and learning environments that are aligned with the State Early Learning and Development Standards," suggesting that high-quality preschools implement content that is researched-based and that will result in positive child outcomes, there is little information about specific content in this definition.

Yet research is available that can specifically inform content. Early childhood research on language and literacy, for example, unequivocally shows that developing children's oral language and vocabulary is critical to future success in learning to read (Dickinson & Porche, 2011). In addition, children's language experiences from birth to preschool, especially relating to their vocabulary learning, set a critical foundation for children's success in science and mathematics (LeFevre, Fast, Skwarchuk et al., 2010) and in building positive relationships with peers (Menting, Van Lier & Koot, 2011). Therefore, high-quality preschool classrooms must include content designed to develop children's language and vocabulary skills.

Although there may be many approaches to providing rich language and literacy experiences to young children as reflected in various curricula, there is a consensus based on research that focusing on language and vocabulary is critical. However, less is known from research about what dosage of language and literacy experiences is needed to achieve positive outcomes in young children, especially those most at risk. Attention to dosage of the curricula or specific parts of a curriculum in research studies is mostly nonexistent. For example, there is no research examining the amount of quality interaction children need with teachers daily or weekly in order to increase their language skills. Similarly, little is known about the number of times children need to hear a word in order to learn to use the word in a meaningful way. In a recent review of book reading and vocabulary that we conducted, we identified from the research literature the number of exposures to a word children needed to have in order to learn the word. Of the 36 studies reviewed, only ten studies provided a count of the total number of exposures children had to the words they were being taught (Wasik, Hindman & Snell, 2016). Although attention to dosage at this level may seem irrelevant and/or result in an overly prescribed curriculum, information about dosage and how it relates to specific curriculum content could provide teachers with valuable information to help inform and improve instruction.

In reviewing the curricula in the following sections, we will report on dosage and curricula content to help inform what we know about effective preschool interventions. We will also note the attention to language and vocabulary, if any, given the research evidence.

Review of the Content and Dosage of Studies of the Effects of Adding Preschool

The following is a review of the research that has examined the effectiveness of preschool on child outcomes. We included eight large-scale studies (see Table 2.1) that have been used as evidence for the effectiveness of preschool (Yoshikawa et al., 2013). Specifically, we examine the dosage and content of the curriculum offered during the additional years as a means of trying to unpack what children experienced in these interventions to inform the discussion about how much of what is effective to improve child outcomes.

Three issues are important to note as we examine these studies in light of dosage and content. One important issue is that although several of the curricula examined in these studies are currently used in many preschool classrooms, the actual content of the curriculum may have changed significantly since the evaluation was conducted. This is important when we consider the impact of an intervention and how it is related to both dosage and content. We make note of the differences when applicable. The second issue, which is related to the first, is that the field's definition of curriculum has changed since the 1960s (or even 1990s), evolving from suggested frameworks and philosophical approaches to specific detailed lesson plans to be implemented with fidelity. We discuss each study's curricula in the context of current descriptions of curricula and provide as much detail as is available about what children experienced in the preschool classrooms. The third important issue is understanding the studies in their historical context, which informs our understanding of dosage and content. In the initial studies conducted in

Table 2.1 *Intended dosage and content of exemplar preschool programs*

Preschool Program	Intended Dosage	Content
Abbott	6-hour, 180-day, with additional wrap-around services; 1-year and 2-year programs	Variable
Abecederian	5 hours a day, 5 days a week, 50 weeks a year, 5 years+	Program curriculum; focused on language and cognitive development
Boston Preschool	Full-day, 1 academic year	OWL and Building Blocks, along with other district initiatives
Chicago Child Care Center	Originally half-day preschool expanded to full-day; 5 days a week; academic year + 6-week summer program; 1 or 2 years	EARLY program
Head Start Impact Study	Mix of half-day and full-day programs; primarily academic year; 1 year of Head Start	Majority were HighScope and Creative Curriculum
Oklahoma (Tulsa) Pre-K	Full- and half-day programs, academic year, 1 year	Variable
Perry Preschool	2.5 hours a day, 5 days a week, 8 months per year, two years	High/Scope Model and home visits
Tennessee Voluntary Pre-K	Minimum of 5.5 hours a day, 180 days a year, for one year	Variable

the 1960s and 1970s, attention to dosage was in terms of the presence or absence of preschool and the ratio of adults to children. Issues concerning fidelity of implementation and other factors related to implementation science were not discussed in educational research at that time, and we do not intend our discussion to be an anachronistic criticism of the research.

The Abbott Study

The Abbott Preschool Program was created as a result of the New Jersey Supreme Court's 1998 *Abbott* v. *Burke* case finding that children in economically disadvantaged districts must have access to high-quality early childhood programs (Frede et al., 2007). The National Institute for Early Education Research (NIEER) conducted a regression disconti-nuity design (RDD) longitudinal study to determine if the learning gains found in early research at kindergarten entry continued into elementary school. The RDD results show that substantial gains in learning and development occurred in language, literacy, and mathematics, with gains largely sustained during the kindergarten year (see Frede, Jung, Barnett et al., 2007 for the detailed report).

Curriculum: It is difficult to discern what curriculum was used in the Abbott Preschool Study and if there were differential effects depending on the specific curriculum used. In the 2014 state report, the curriculum in the Abbott Preschool program is described as "developmentally appropriate curriculum, aligned with the New Jersey CCCS and elementary school reforms." Further documentation suggests that High/Scope is being used in many Abbott schools (Lerner, 2014). In addition, a relatively small percentage of Abbott schools use Curiosity Corner, which is part of Success for All.

Dosage: A maximum class size of 15 was mandated by the Abbott decision. Abbott preschool classrooms combine a US Department of Education (DOE)-funded six-hour, 180-day component with a US Department of Human Services (DHS)-funded wrap-around program that provides daily before- and after-care and summer programs. In total, the full-day, full-year program is available 10 hours per day, 245 days a year. Data also revealed that children who attend Abbott preschools for two years at both age 3 and 4 significantly outperform at kindergarten those who attended for only one year at 4 years of age or did not attend at all (Frede & Barnett, 2011; Frede, Barnett, Jung et al., 2010).

Abecedarian Project

The Abecedarian Project, developed by researchers from the Frank Porter Graham Center at the University of North Carolina, provided low-income children with early childhood education. The initial study of the Abecedarian Project (Ramey & Campbell, 1984) found that the preschool intervention group scored significantly higher than the control group on several cognitive measures, including vocabulary, intelligence, and memory. Similar findings were documented in additional studies (Burchinal, Lee & Ramey, 1989; Martin, Ramey & Ramey, 1990). Researchers monitored children's progress over time with follow-up studies through age 35.

Curriculum: The Abecedarian project content is described as an approach that combines teaching and learning enrichment strategies for use in early childhood education settings comprised of four key elements: 1) learning games, 2) conversational reading, 3) language priority, and 4) enriched care giving. Each child had an individualized "prescription of educational games" incorporated into the day. These activities focused on social, emotional, and cognitive areas of development but were described as providing particular emphasis on language.

Dosage: Children in the intervention group attended a center-based program with teacher:child ratios that ranged from 1:3 for infants/toddlers to 1:6 for older children. The center operated 7:30 a.m. to 5:30 p.m., 5 days per week, and 50 weeks out of the year, with free transportation available. Individual child attendance is not available. Controls received the same medical and nutrition support that the intervention group received. We have not been able to determine the number, if any, of the children in the control group who attended preschool.

The Boston Preschool Project

Boston Public Schools, in collaboration with researchers from the Harvard Graduate School of Education, implemented and evaluated a research-based high-quality preschool program. Findings from a RDD indicated that the program had moderate-to-large impacts on children's language, literacy, numeracy, and mathematics skills, and small impacts on children's executive functioning and a measure of emotion recognition (Weiland & Yoshikawa, 2013). Some impacts were considerably larger for some subgroups. Curriculum fidelity measures indicated moderate to good fidelity.

Curriculum: A research-based literacy curriculum, Opening the World of Learning (OWL^{TM}) (Schickedanz, Dickinson & Schools, 2005) was implemented with some modifications. A research-based math curriculum, Real Math Building Blocks: Pre-K (Clements & Sarama, 2007) was also implemented. Teachers received training in Building Blocks (average of 6 days) and OWL (average of 7 days) with 2–3 days of training offered before school started and the remaining days during the school year. Each preschool teacher also received weekly or biweekly classroom coaching for (1 coach per 10 classrooms for three years).

Dosage: Full-day pre-kindergarten was offered to all children. The adult:child ratio was reported to be about 1:10. We were unable to discern what percentage of the day the OWL and Building Blocks curriculum was intended to be implemented, or in practice implemented.

Chicago Child–Parent Center

The Chicago Child–Parent Center (CPC) program is a center-based early intervention designed to provide high-quality early intervention services to both children and their families. An important goal of the project was to provide services to the family, with the expectation that working with the family would impact the child. The results reported in Reynolds, Temple, Robertson & Mann (2001) indicate that, overall, students enrolled in CPC had higher rates of graduation and lower rates of special education, criminal justice involvement, and child maltreatment.

Curriculum: Child–Parent Center curriculum has focused on the acquisition of basic knowledge and skills in language arts and math through a relatively structured but diverse set of learning experiences (e.g., whole class, small groups, individualized activities, field trips). The cognitive domains of the activities are described in three main areas: 1) body image and gross motor skills; 2) perceptual-motor and arithmetic skills; and 3) language. Most of the activities are implemented in small groups of four or five children.

Dosage: The amount of preschool offered by the CPC has changed over the years. In the Reynolds et al. (2001) study, the dosage generally consisted of half-day preschool at ages 3 to 4 years, half- or full-day kindergarten, and school-age services in linked elementary schools at ages 6 to 9 years. More recently, many (but not all) CPC children attend full-day preschool and kindergarten (Reynolds et al., 2014).

Head Start Impact Study: Although several studies have been conducted on the effects of Head Start, the Head Start Impact Study (HSIS) (Puma, Bell, Cook et al., 2012) is the only large-scale, randomized control trial (RCT) of Head Start. The evaluation found significant benefits for Head Start children across multiple domains, particularly for 3-year-old children. By the end of first and third grade, however, few significant differences remained (Puma et al., 2012).

Curriculum: In the HSIS, sites were asked to report the curriculum that they used; most Head Start sites did use a particular curriculum, mostly HighScope or Creative Curriculum. We note, however, that the HighScope curriculum implemented in this study is not the exact same curriculum implemented in the HighScope study reviewed above. In addition, HighScope and the Creative Curriculum are not systematic curricula that guide teachers in implementing specific lessons with learning objectives. Instead, these curricula suggest specific routines (such as *Plan–Do–Review* in High/Scope), or a philosophy or framework about teaching (such as an emphasis on approaches to learning and on room arrangements) rather than explicit guided support of math and literacy content.

Dosage: There is considerable variability in the dosage reported in the

HSIS in terms of full- versus half-day, and variation in number of months attending, from 8 months to year-round programs. Bloom and Weiland (2015) examined the effects of dosage and quality in the HSIS, noting that children with higher-than-average program dosage, and sites with higher concentrations of such children, experienced larger-than-average program effects. Overall, they found variation in Head Start programs in terms of dosage and classroom quality.

High/Scope Perry Preschool Project

The High/Scope Perry Preschool Study began in the mid-1960s. (For a comprehensive review of the project, see Schweinhart, Montie, Xiang et al., 2005.) Findings from a study following an early cohort of children indicated that children who received the High/Scope early intervention performed significantly better on intellectual and language tests starting after their first year of schooling until age 7, and general school achievement and literacy was also greater through age 14. Long-term employment, family, and criminal justice outcomes at ages 27 and 40 were found to be consistently better in the program condition (Schweinhart et al., 2005). Although there are many similarities, the current HighScope program – currently implemented in 19 percent of all Head Start programs (Aikens, Hulsey, Moiduddin et al., 2011) – is not the same content that was evaluated in the High/Scope Perry Preschool Study. (See their website for details about the current program content.) In a related study, the High/Scope Preschool Curriculum Comparison study (Schweinhart & Weikart, 1997a, 1997b), which immediately followed the High/Scope Perry Preschool study, examined the impact of various curricula for a similar population of children and found long-term impacts on emotional and behavioral outcomes.

Curriculum: HighScope is defined by its developers as "a flexible framework and can be used across all settings, ages and abilities" and is not a specified curriculum. The content of the HighScope program that was evaluated was designed to support children's self-initiated learning activities along with small-group and large-group activities. No specific details regarding content of lessons or lesson plans are provided. Although small groups do provide opportunities for greater adult and child interactions, there is no indication that there was an emphasis on vocabulary or language development.

Dosage: Children in the intervention condition received classroom instruction from October through May at the ages of 3 and 4, with 2.5 hours of daily in-class instruction followed by 1.5-hour teacher visits to their homes weekly. Children were offered two years of preschool, and children in the study, on average, attended 1.2 years of the Perry Preschool. The program ratio was 4 teachers for 20 to 25 children. There is no specific mention of the amount of literacy and language activities provided.

Oklahoma (Tulsa) Pre-K Study

The Oklahoma Pre-K Study measured the effects of Oklahoma's universal early childhood 4-year-old program on entering kindergartners' academic skills. Findings from the Tulsa-located evaluation revealed that children in the Tulsa pre-K program were 9 months ahead of their peers in measures of reading, 7 months ahead in writing, and 5 months ahead in math (Gormley, Phillips & Gayer, 2008).

Curriculum: The curriculum used in the Tulsa Pre-K study varied. It is reported that some teachers created their own curriculum and others borrowed from such standardized curricula as Curiosity Corner, the Waterford Early Learning Program, Integrated Thematic Instruction, Creative Curriculum, and Direct Instruction. Yet, the specific curriculum used in each classroom is not reported, although Tulsa pre-K teachers scored higher on instructional quality and spent more time on reading and math (Gormley et al., 2008).

Dosage: Full- and half-day programs were offered. No differences were reported for children attending full- vs. half-day programs. Class size was limited to 20 with a child:staff ratio of 10 to 1. We are unaware of any attendance data.

Tennessee Voluntary Pre-K Program

The Tennessee Voluntary Pre-K (TN-NPK) Initiative was designed to assess the effectiveness of preschool in Tennessee. The study includes a RCT and a RDD. The RCT was implemented in a limited number of schools with more applicants than seats in the pre-K program (Lipsey, Hofer, Dong et al., 2013). The results of the RCT indicate that children who participated in TN-VPK significantly outperformed the children who did not attend TN-VPK at the end of the VPK year on all of the direct assessment scales examined, with modest effect sizes ranging from 0.28 to 0.42. Compared to results from HSIS, effects were somewhat larger for literacy but not for mathematics. When the Tennessee results are compared to estimates from some other recent studies of public pre-K, they appear less robust. For example, studies of pre-K in Boston,

Oklahoma, and New Jersey (all three will be discussed below) find larger impacts on literacy and much larger effects on math.

Curriculum: Tennessee's VPK and Head Start programs chose curricula from an approved list that are described as "research-based, reliable, age-appropriate and aligned with the TN Early Learning Developmental Standards." In reviewing the list of the programs, with the exception of OWL, the programs listed have not shown evidence of effectiveness.

Dosage: The Tennessee program ran for a minimum of 5.5 hours per day, exclusive of nap time, for a minimum of 180 days per year within a calendar that includes 200 working days of 7.5 hours for teaching staff, with an adult:student ratio no smaller than 1:10 and a small class size maximum of 20. There are no data reported in the range of child attendance.

Summary of Curriculum Dosage and Content

The data from the review of these studies suggest several important findings. With the exception of the Boston Study, we found it challenging, in this initial review of programs that have been cited as evidence for the effectiveness of preschool on child outcomes, to find documentation of the actual content that was used in the intervention. This is important, as lack of information makes it difficult to unpack what is effective in order to scale up what works. For example, in the Oklahoma study, it is reported that a variety of curricula were used across the classrooms. Yet, if the Tulsa study is to be replicated, is the important factor that the children attended preschool or is it that the classrooms were found to devote more classroom time to reading and math than their counterparts, activities that research suggests are important for increasing child-outcomes? Although all programs refer to the curricula implemented as "high quality," less is known about the actual content children were exposed to during the day. This makes it very difficult to discuss impact of dosage and to identify the necessary and sufficient characteristics that are needed to replicate the intervention. Critical information about the nature and quality of experiences children were exposed to is unknown, making it difficult to conclude how much is needed for preschool to be effective. Again, this brings to light the importance of documenting both content and dosage in evaluation research.

Review of Research on Preschool Curricula

To complete the discussion about the importance of the content and dosage of preschool programs in relation to child outcomes, it is relevant to discuss what is known about research on preschool curricula.

To date, the Preschool Curriculum Evaluation Research (PCER, 2008) program is the most comprehensive evaluation of the efficacy of commonly used preschool curricula. The goal of PCER was to conduct a rigorous, systematic evaluation of preschool curricula by supporting small-scale efficacy evaluations of curricula widely used in preschools. Fourteen curricula were evaluated using a common assessment protocol and a randomized experimental design. For a complete review of the study design, curricula, measures and analysis, see the PCER report (2008). In sum, the findings indicated that only two of the 14 intervention curricula had impacts on the student-level outcomes for the pre-kindergarten year. DLM Early Childhood Express^{TM} supplemented with Open Court Reading Pre-K positively affected reading, phonological awareness, and language in pre-kindergarten and kindergarten. Pre-K mathematics supplemented with DLM Early Childhood Express^{TM} math software curricula positively affected mathematics in pre-kindergarten.

The PCER evaluation reported limited information on dosage. In the report, very little information is provided about what teachers were asked to do in the interventions. The report documents information about required dosage for only four curricula, although it is possible that things were more specified in training materials for the other curricula. The report notes that Early Literacy and Learning Model (ELLM) required one hour of daily literacy instruction; Literacy Express and DLM Early Childhood Express^{TM} supplemented with Open Court Reading Pre-K required 3–4 small group activities a week (although the time was not reported); PreK Math required small-group math activities for 20 minutes, twice per week; and Project Approach required 45–60 minutes daily in small group investigations.

An interesting point about the PCER findings is that, with the exception of Curiosity Corner, which was implemented in select preschools in the Abbott study, none of the curricula evaluated were implemented in any of the preschool studies evaluating the overall impact of preschool on young children.

Summary

When tested using rigorous designs, preschool curricula that are widely used (as compared to locally developed curricula) have small-sized effects. Our brief review suggests that this could be due to the fact that the most commonly used curricula tend to have little guidance for teachers (either described in the curricula or through training) on aspects of *dosage* (frequency, duration, or intensity) or *content* regarding activities that research suggests are most effective at boosting language, literacy, and mathematics learning in early childhood. For example, in the domain of language, Neuman and Dwyer's work (2009) suggests that many commonly used preschool curricula do not include specific instruction on the best ways to support language and vocabulary development. It has also been well documented that preschool teachers spend little time on mathematics, and that work has also shown that teachers lack knowledge and understanding about evidence-based mathematics content (Ginsburg, Boyd & Sun Lee, 2008; National Research Council [NRC], 2009). And, even when curricula might include content that would bolster learning, there is very little on-the-ground, ongoing professional development or coaching to help teachers implement with fidelity and at the most effective frequency and duration. The important message that should not be lost in these findings is that perhaps if the content of the preschool experience were more aligned with research-based content, specifically addressing children's language and literacy skills, and early mathematical foundations, the effects of a year of preschool might be larger and translate into longer-term impacts.

Research and Policy Recommendations for Sustaining Early Childhood Gains through Dosage and Content

The following are research and policy recommendations to help inform the field and to support the expansion of research-based, high-quality preschool for young children so that early childhood gains can be sustained, the achievement gap can be diminished, and all children can be successful in school. With regard to research, the following recommendations are:

• *Examine dosage as a variable in research.* We must unpack critical components of evidence-based interventions, both dosage and content, so we can communicate with educators about what to do, how much to do, and how often to do it. In addition, it is important to understand precisely what is being implemented in classrooms in order to effectively interpret findings. To do this, researchers must include fidelity measures that detail the specifics of the program and curriculum implementation, as well as specific dosage characteristics, including session duration, frequency, intensity, and duration. Including all these elements will also help establish the total cumulative dosage associated with the intervention, allow for more accurate cost–benefit calculations, and elucidate what dosage is required to effectively sustain children's learning gains over the school year and beyond. Reports should also include the ratio of children to staff to help unpack how much of the intervention individual children may be getting.

• *Define high-quality preschool in terms of content and dosage.* Researchers must develop a research-based definition of high-quality preschool that specifically outlines the quality and quantity of experiences children need to improve long-term outcomes in literacy, math and social/emotional issues.

• *Include teachers and parents in discussions about research questions and findings.* It seems naïve to be developing interventions without input about feasibility and alignment without feedback and cooperation from teachers and parents.

The following are policy recommendations:

• *Curricula need a strong foundation in language and vocabulary.* Not all preschool is equal. Adding a year of preschool to children's educational experience without attention to the curricula content will not result in gains that are sustained over time. The research documenting the importance of developing language and vocabulary skills during the early years is rigorous and unequivocal. The challenge is to train teachers to effectively provide a language-rich classroom for young children that supports development of children's skills across linguistic, literacy, mathematics, and science domains.

• *Invest in teacher training.* An effective, research-based curriculum is only effective if it is implemented as intended with fidelity (Durlak & DuPre, 2008). Teachers need to be trained to implement any program, and new programs must come with funding for training. For gains to be sustained, similar attention must be given to implementing effective, research-based education throughout the elementary years and beyond.

• *Give vulnerable populations priority access to preschool.* With limited resources and funds, the data clearly support the differential effects of preschool on high-poverty children. Funding for these populations should take priority.

References

Aikens, N., Hulsey, L. K., Moiduddin, E. et al. (2011). *Data Tables for FACES 2009 Head Start Children, Families, and Programs*. OPRE Report 2011–33b. Washington, DC: OPRE, ACF, U.S. DHHS.

Arteaga, I., Humpage, S., Reynolds, A. J. & Temple, J. A. (2014). One year of preschool or two: is it important for adult outcomes? *Economics of Education Review*, 40, 221–237.

Barnett, W. S. (2011). Effectiveness of early educational intervention. *Science*, 333(6045), 975–978.

Bloom, H. S. & Weiland, C. (2015). *Quantifying Variation in Head Start Effects on Young Children's Cognitive and Socio-Emotional Skills Using Data from the National Head Start Impact Study*. New York, NY: MDRC.

Burchinal, M., Lee, M. & Ramey, C. (1989). Type of day-care and preschool intellectual development in disadvantaged children. *Child Development*, 60, 128–137.

Clements, D. H. & Sarama, J. (2007). Effects of a preschool mathematics curriculum: summative research on the Building Blocks project. *Journal for Research in Mathematics Education*, 38(2), 136–163.

Dickinson, D. K. & Porche, M. (2011). Relationship between language experiences in preschool classrooms and children's kindergarten and fourth grade language and reading abilities. *Child Development*, 82(3), 870–886.

Dubay, L. & Holla, N. (2015). *Absenteeism in DC Public Schools Early Education Program*. Washington, DC: The Urban Institute.

Duncan, G. J. & Murnane, R. J. (2011). *Whither Opportunity? Rising Inequality, Schools, and Children's Life Chances*, New York, NY: Russell Sage Foundation.

Durlak, J. A. & DuPre, E. P. (2008). Implementation matters: a review of research on the influence of implementation on program outcomes and the factors affecting implementation. *American Journal of Community Psychology*, 41, 327–350.

Ehrlich, S., Gwynne, J., Pareja, A. & Allensworth, E. (2013). *Preschool Attendance in Chicago Public Schools: Relationships with Learning Outcomes and Reasons for Absences*. Chicago, IL: The University of Chicago Consortium on Chicago School Research.

Fixsen, D., Naoom, S., Blase, K., Friedman, R. & Wallace, F. (2005). *Implementation Research: A Synthesis of the Literature*. Tampa, FL: Florida Mental Health Institute, National Implementation Research Network. (FMHI Publication No. 231).

Frede, E. C. & Barnett, W. S. (2011). New Jersey's Abbott pre-K program: A model for the nation, in E. Zigler, W. Gilliam & W. S. Barnett (Eds.), *The Pre-K Debates: Current Controversies and Issues* (pp. 191–196). Baltimore, MD: Brookes Publishing.

Frede, E. C., Barnett, W. S., Jung, K., Lamy, C. E. & Figueras, A. (2010). Abbott Preschool Program Longitudinal Effects Study (APPLES): Year one findings, in A. J. Reynolds, A. J. Rolnick, M. M. Englund & J. A. Temple (Eds.), *Childhood Programs and Practices in the First Decade of Life* (pp. 214–231). New York, NY: Cambridge University Press.

Frede, E., Jung, K., Barnett, W. S., Lamy, C. E. & Figueras, A. (2007). The Abbott preschool program longitudinal effects study (APPLES). New Brunswick, NJ: National Institute for Early Education Research.

Gibbs, C. (2014). *Experimental evidence on early intervention: the impact of full-day kindergarten*. Frank Batten School of Leadership and Public Policy Working Paper (2014–04).

Ginsburg, H. P., Boyd, J. & Sun Lee, J. (2008). Mathematics education for young children: what it is and how to promote it. *Social Policy Report*, 22 (1), 1–23.

Gormley, W. T., Phillips, D. & Gayer, T. (2008). Preschool programs can boost school readiness. *Science*, 320(5884), 1723–1724.

Halle, T., Metz, A. & Martinez-Beck, I. (Eds.), (2013). *Applying Implementation Science in Early Childhood Programs and Systems*. Paul H. Brookes Publishing Company.

Heckman, J. J. (2006). Skill formation and the economics of investing in disadvantaged children. *Science*, 312(5782), 1900–1902.

Jenkins, J., Farkas, G., Duncan, G. J., Burchinal, M. & Vandell, D. L. (2015). Head Start at ages 3 and 4 versus Head Start followed by state pre-K: Which is more effective? *Educational Evaluation and Policy Analysis*, 38(1), 88–112.

Karoly, L. A. (2012). Toward standardization of benefit–cost analysis of early childhood interventions. *Journal of Benefit–Cost Analysis*, 3(01), 1–45.

Keys, T. D., Farkas, G., Burchinal, M. R., et al. (2013). Preschool center quality and school readiness: quality effects and variation by demographic and child characteristics. *Child Development*, 84(4), 1171–1190.

LeFevre, J.-A., Fast, L., Skwarchuk, S.-L. et al. (2010). Pathways to mathematics: longitudinal predictors of performance. *Child Development*, 81 (6), 1753–1767.

Lerner, S. (2014). The Abbott District's Fortunate Few. *The American Prospect*, Jan. 16.

Lipsey, M. W., Hofer, K. G., Dong, N., Farran, D. C., & Bilbrey, C. (2013). *Evaluation of the Tennessee Voluntary Prekindergarten Program: Kindergarten and First Grade Follow-Up Results from the Randomized Control Design (Research Report)*. Nashville, TN: Vanderbilt University, Peabody Research Institute.

Loeb, S., Bridges, M., Bassok, D., Fuller, B. & Rumberger, R. (2007). How much is too much? The influence of preschool centers on children's cognitive and social development. *Economics of Education Review*, 26, 52–66.

Magnuson, K., Meyers, M., Rhum, C. & Waldfogel, J. (2004). Inequality in preschool education and school readiness. *American Educational Research Journal*, 41(1), 115–157.

Martin, S. L., Ramey, C. T. & Ramey, S. (1990). The prevention of intellectual impairment in children of impoverished families: findings of a randomized trial of educational day care. *American Journal of Public Health*, 80(7), 844–847.

McGinty, A. S., Breit-Smith, A., Fan, X., Justice, L. M. & Kaderavek, J. N. (2011). Does intensity matter? Preschoolers' print knowledge development within a classroom-based intervention. *Early Childhood Research Quarterly*, 26 (3), 255–267.

Menting, B., Van Lier, P. A. C. & Koot, H. M. (2011). Language skills, peer rejection, and the development of externalizing behavior from kindergarten to fourth grade. *Journal of Child Psychology and Psychiatry*, 52(1), 72–79.

National Research Council (NRC). (2009). *Mathematics Learning in Early Childhood: Paths toward Excellence and Equity.* Washington, DC: National Academies Press.

Neuman, S. B. & Dwyer, J. (2009). Missing in action: vocabulary instruction in pre-K. *The Reading Teacher*, 62(5), 384–392.

Nores, M. & Barnett, W. S. (2010). Benefits of early childhood interventions across the world: (Under) Investing in the very young. *Economics of Education Review*, 29(2), 271–282.

Preschool Curriculum Evaluation Research Consortium. (2008). *Effects of Preschool Curriculum Programs on School Readiness: Report from the Preschool Curriculum Evaluation Research Initiative* (NCER 2008–2009). Washington, DC: US Department of Education, Institute of Education Sciences.

Puma, M., Bell, S., Cook, R. et al. (2012). *Third Grade Follow-Up to the Head Start Impact Study: Final Report.* OPRE Report 2012–45. Administration for Children & Families.

Ramey, C. T. & Campbell, F. A. (1984). Preventive education for high-risk children: Cognitive consequences of the Carolina Abecedarian Project. *American Journal of Mental Deficiency*, 88(5): 515–523.

Reynolds, A. J., Richardson, B. A., Hayakawa, M. et al. (2014). Association of a full-day vs part-day preschool intervention with school readiness, attendance, and parent involvement. *JAMA*, 312(20), 2126–2134.

Reynolds, A. J., Temple, J. A., Ou, S.-R., Arteaga, I. A. & White, B. A. B. (2011). School-based early childhood education and age-28 well-being: Effects by timing, dosage, and subgroups. *Science*, 333, 360–364.

Reynolds, A. J., Temple, J. A., Robertson, D. L. & Mann, E. A. (2001). Long-term effects of an early childhood intervention on educational achievement and juvenile arrest: A 15-year follow-up of low-income children in public schools. *JAMA*, 285(18), 2339–2346.

Robin, K., Frede, E. & Barnett, W. S. (2006). *Is More Better? The Effects of Full-Day vs. Half-Day Preschool on Early School Achievement.* New Brunswick, NJ: Rutgers University, National Institute for Early Education Research.

Schickedanz, J., Dickinson, D. & Schools, C. M. (2005). *Opening the World of Learning.* Iowa City, IA: Pearson.

Schweinhart, L. J., Montie, J., Xiang, Z., Barnett, W. S., Belfield, C. R., & Nores M. (2005). *Lifetime effects: The High/Scope Perry Preschool Study through Age 40.* Ypsilanti, MI. Available at: http://works.bepress.com/william_barnett/3/.

Schweinhart, L. J. & Weikart, D. P. (1997a). *Lasting Differences: The High/Scope Pre-School Curriculum Comparison Study through Age 23.* Ypsilanti, MI: High/Scope Press.

Schweinhart, L. J. & Weikart, D. P. (1997b). The High/Scope preschool curriculum comparison study through age 23. *Early Childhood Research Quarterly*, 12, 117–143.

Skibbe, L. E., Connor, C. M., Morrison, F. J. & Jewkes, A. M. (2011). Schooling effects on preschoolers' self-regulation, early literacy, and language growth. *Early Childhood Research Quarterly*, 26(1), 42–49.

Vandell, D. L., Belsky, J., Burchinal, M., Steinberg, L. & Vandergrift, N. (2010). Do effects of early child care extend to age 15 years? Results from the NICHD Study of Early Child Care and Youth Development. *Child Development*, 81(3), 737–756.

Walters, C. R. (2015). Inputs in the production of early childhood human capital: evidence from Head Start. *American Economic Journal: Applied Economics*, 7(4), 76–102.

Wasik, B. A., Mattera, S. K., Lloyd, C. M. & Boller, K. (2013). *Intervention Dosage in Early Childhood Care and Education*: It's Complicated (OPRE Research Brief OPRE 2013–15). Washington, DC: Office of Planning, Research and Evaluation, Administration for Children and Families, US Department of Health and Human Services.

Wasik, B. A., Hindman, A. H. & Snell, E. K. (2016). Book reading and vocabulary development: a systematic review. *Early Childhood Research Quarterly*, 37, 39–57.

Weiland, C. & Yoshikawa, H. (2013). Impacts of a prekindergarten program on children's mathematics, language, literacy, executive function, and emotional skills. *Child Development*, 84(6), 2112–2130.

Wen, X., Leow, C., Hahs-Vaughn, D. L., Korfmacher, J. & Marcus, S. M. (2012). Are two years better than one year? A propensity score analysis of the impact of Head Start program duration on children's school performance in kindergarten. *Early Childhood Research Quarterly*, 27, 684–694.

Yoshikawa, H., Weiland, C., Brooks-Gunn, J. et al. (2013). *Investing in Our Future: The Evidence Base on Preschool Education*. New York, NY: Foundation for Child Development.

3   Teacher Influences and Program Effectiveness in Early Childhood Education

Gregory Camilli

Four kinds of influence on intellectual outcomes in early education are considered in this chapter: the effects of teaching quality; the effects of teacher qualifications; teacher effects; and program interventions intended to improve child outcomes. While these influences are conceptually distinct, they work in unison (or perhaps disharmony) in the context of operational programs and interventions. For this reason, it is important to consider how they are related. Positive program outcomes have been obtained in a number of comparative evaluations and experiments, both previously and recently (see the review of Barnett, 2008; Weiland & Yoshikawa, 2013), and these would appear at first to be mediated through teachers. Positive effects ensuing from interventions constitute at least weak support for the proposition that teacher effects can be intentionally produced. If instructional and care quality are associated positively with cognitive outcomes, then it would also seem that the effect of quality must be mediated through teachers and caregivers. However, as observed by Phillips, Lipsey, Dodge, et al. (2017):

> Despite our certainty that these early education programs caused these outcomes, we do not know what it was precisely about these programs that produced positive outcomes nearly 20 years later. What was it about the experiences provided by these programs that, apparently, put children on such a positive developmental trajectory? This is the "black box" question that scientists are now actively exploring. (pp. 19–20)

Accordingly, empirical support for highly plausible claims about the positive effects of teaching is presently weak.

There has been a great deal of work in quality measures (Mashburn, Pianta, Hamre, et al., 2008), but global measures of quality may not be targeted sufficiently well to particular cognitive outcomes of interest such as word recognition or pre-mathematics skills. As observed by Farran (2017):

Many of the characteristics identified in this paper as important can be found in individual items on all of these scales, but most summaries of their use find them disappointing in their ability to capture quality. (p. 48)

In this paper, the effects of teaching quality and teacher qualifications on cognitive outcomes are of central interest. In particular, outcomes of interest are more achievement-oriented than intelligence-based constructs. This distinction is important because teachers can and do teach skills, while general cognition has a more complex origin. This should not be taken as advice to ignore intelligence, but rather that achievement is an important outcome and should be a distinct focus of early education policies.

Program implementation is often submerged in an official description of the intervention or interventions, referred to below as a program *label* for convenient reference. Yet this is precisely where causal mechanisms lurk. Consider a study (National Institute of Child Health and Development & Duncan, 2003) in which the data from the National Institute of Child Health and Development (NICHD) Early Child Care Research Network study (2002) were reanalyzed. A range of controls was used, and models with the most complete controls for selection and specification error revealed effect sizes in the range $d = 0.04 - 0.08$ for a 1 SD increment in observed child care quality sustained between 24 and 54 months of age (and slightly higher for at-risk children). Another variable in Duncan's study, "Percentage Center Care," was observed to have a larger effect. This variable was constructed as follows:

- Telephone interviews were conducted with mothers on 16 occasions at 3—4-month intervals.
- One type of care that mothers reported was the number of occasions on which children of 24–54 months old received care in a center.
- This variable was converted to a proportion ranging from 0% to 100%.

When entered as a variable predicting outcomes in regression analyses, a relatively large effect size of $d = 0.27$ (for cognitive outcomes) resulted, which is 4–5 times larger than the corresponding effect for child quality. The question arises then of just what this variable might indicate, and Duncan provided the following explanation:

Although our primary focus has been on ORCE-based quality impacts, it is important to point out that time in center-based child care in the third and fourth years of life had the most consistently significant associations with both cognitive and achievement outcomes across all of our various models. Our most complete models produced effect size estimates for spending all versus none of this developmental period in center-based care ranged from .09 to .27 for cognitive outcomes and .22 to .33 for achievement outcomes. (p. 1470)

The much greater intensity and duration of these treatments, as well as their target population of at-risk children, are the most likely explanations for their larger effect sizes. In addition, the effect sizes in these randomized experimental studies may be more precise because extensive covariates are not needed to adjust for potential selection bias. (p. 1471)

While it is tempting to consider this effect size a measure of "dosage," there are various ways to define dosage and there are various ways in which dosage can interact with quality (Wasik, Mattera, Lloyd & Boller 2013). The effect of "Percentage Center Care" could also mean that unobserved activities not directly related to child care quality are influencing cognitive development, or it might mean that the cognitive functioning of some children is enhanced by limiting exposure to out-of-center environmental factors like second-hand smoke, lead paint, or nutritional deficits. But these explanations are essentially grasping at straws for the practical purpose of designing interventions because the actual causal mechanisms are unknown. They are unobserved to statisticians and data analysts, and they may not be systematically recorded by program staff who observe program activities directly. In either case, the result is the same: the impact pathways are ineffectively described by predictor variables that are intended to describe or explain the effect of an intervention.

Many studies have shown positive and significant treatment-of-the-treated (TOT) effects. This means that analysts can estimate the impact of a program for children who actually received the program, but not necessarily for children who were originally assigned to the treatment and control conditions. In terms of program evaluation, a number of successful programs have been identified in the literature. However, TOT effects are not equivalent to intent-to-treat (ITT) effects. The ITT estimate of program effect describes the effect of *assignment* to treatment or comparison condition. The ITT label is thus related to expected returns of intentional policies; in turn, this makes it more relevant to policy makers. Obtaining the ITT estimate requires a greater degree of control (through data collection and preventing attrition). To some degree the lack of control can be compensated through rigorous statistical modeling (like NICHD & Duncan, 2003) to broaden the policy relevance of TOT effects.

Even so, a number of essential problems remain. First, estimating causal effects is much less difficult that identifying causal mechanisms. Second, it is possible that causal mechanisms once identified may not be easily leveraged or maintained outside the framework of an experiment. Third, if a causal mechanism cannot be identified, then even well-estimated ITT effects may not generalize to other contexts (or these extrapolations may be inconsistent). If the experimental effect is interpreted primarily in terms of the treatment label, interactions between those mechanisms and environmental characteristics may not be recognized. For example, suppose a treatment is designed to improve early learning through caregiver–child interactions, but the focus on achievement is implicitly carried out through local interpretation of curriculum and instruction standards. In turn, this may result in unintended implementation across program sites, but the implementation may also vary in unknown ways across treatment and comparison groups within a site. As noted by Barnett (2017):

> as the Planned Variation Head Start and Follow-Through studies revealed, there is considerable variation within curriculum models and substantial overlap across models that adds to the difficulty of drawing conclusions about what is more effective generally. If the alternatives and their counterfactuals are not clearly defined, or if they vary (perhaps necessarily) with local context, it is difficult to draw useful general conclusions for policy and practice. (p. 69)

Certainly, some of this variability can be avoided by design, but this is easier said than done in situations in which implementing placebo treatment in the control groups is undesirable if not unethical.

Michael Scriven (1981) wrote that "evaluation is usually supposed to serve decision making, and decision making is choosing between alternatives, and if evaluation does not look at the comparative merits of the alternatives, it is not serving decision making" (p. 137). Ignoring or failing to recognize those relative "merits" may create interpretive hazards for decision-makers. For example, according to a What Works Clearinghouse report (Mathematica Policy Research, 2015):

> Head Start was found to have potentially positive effects on general reading achievement and no discernible effects on mathematics achievement and social-emotional development for 3- and 4-year-old children. (p. 1)

> [C]hildren were randomly selected from the applicant pool of each program and then randomly assigned either to be offered Head Start or to be in the comparison group. Parents of children in the comparison group were free to enroll their children in any program other than the Head Start programs in the study (or to not enroll them in any program). *Consequently, children in the comparison group experienced diverse types of early care and education settings ranging from parent-only care to programs that were similar in type and services to Head Start.* [emphasis added] (p. 16)

A formal way to characterize this issue is to observe that there may be substantial endogeneity of causal mechanisms within a treatment group, and this endogeneity gets absorbed, for lack of a better term, into the treatment. In simple terms, one could say that the treatment is an umbrella for a number of influences on outcomes, and some of these influences may be highly interactive. Comparison groups are likewise umbrellas for myriad influences.

A less fancy way to call attention to this issue is to ask, "What the heck is happening inside the experimental groupings?" as Murnane & Willet (2010) explained:

Randomized experiments and quasi-experiments typically provide estimates of the total effect of a policy intervention on one or more outcomes, not the effects of the intervention holding constant the levels of other inputs. (p. 31)

Another example from outside early education served to highlight this idea. Murnane and Willet considered policies to increase the schooling options available to children from poor families to have significant promise. In this regard, the authors cited an interesting study by the Abdul Latif Jameel Poverty Action Lab (J-PAL). In rural India, teacher absenteeism is a significant problem. A school might consist of one classroom, and teacher absence requires the school to be closed on that day. Nongovernmental organizations (NGO) often train teachers who typically have a high school education, but are paid on short-term contracts at low rates of pay.

An experiment was designed for the NGO Seva Mandir to estimate the effect of basing teacher pay on the number of days actually taught, rather than the typical flat monthly contract. The control group was paid a base salary, and the treatment group a base salary for 20 days with rewards/fines for attendance/nonattendance. Teachers were counted as present based on tamper-proof classroom cameras. To be counted as present, two photos of a teacher were required five hours apart on a given day, with a minimum number of students. Teachers in the experimental and control groups received a base salary of Rs1000 per month (then about $23). Experiment group teachers then received a 50 rupees ($ ₹ $)/day increment (then about $1.15) for days attended in excess of the 20 days, and they received a ₹50/day fine for each cumulative day less than 20. The maximum salary in the treatment group was capped at ₹1300, and the maximum fine was capped at ₹500. More detail is given in Duflo and Hanna (2006).

From the 27-month experiment, a 21% decrease in absenteeism was found (42% absenteeism in the control versus 21% in the treatment group). The program was reported to be a success with respect to this outcome, but some ambiguity remained regarding endogeneity. Assuming that schools were open 6 days a week, a teaching month would be about 26 days, leading to the maximum ₹1300 possible in the treatment group. Yet the actual average salary in the treatment group was about ₹1000: *about the same as that for the comparison group*. This seems to indicate that the number of teaching days increased but also that the incentives and fines cancelled out. It is interesting to speculate on the cost function that would account for this unusual finding. At the same time, a deeper understanding of the causal mechanisms would be required for creating a sustainable program for reducing absenteeism.

Estimating effects is something that quantitative researchers can do well, but proficiency in causal inference is often downplayed, perhaps because contextual reasoning is messy, laborious, and is aided by training in qualitative methods. Estimating causal effects is valuable, but estimation is the easy part. Presumably, the wisdom inherent in the experimental manipulation goes partway in determining the causes of those effects; but, as seen in the J-PAL study, human responses to treatment are often vastly more complex than either prior descriptions of treatment or even protocols for assessing program implementation. Fidelity to the treatment label is often less complete than expected while experimental arrangements are highly interactive across contexts. Without an adequate understanding of this diversity of influence, the capacity to design effective programs is limited.

This is also one reason that a program evaluation may be ineffective in identifying key factors leading to improved learning outcomes. Treatments may bundle a number of services to children that are also implicit in comparison groups. While it is appropriate to compare a treatment to an alternative (or competitor) from a policy perspective, this may not be sufficient to identify the most powerful influences on child outcomes. Likewise, NICHD and Duncan (2003) demonstrated that examining the relationship of teaching quality to learning outcomes may be insufficient in itself for detecting the presence of other important moderators that are malleable in program design.

Getting the Endogeneity Out: Examples

A number of issues are considered below that generally relate to the notion of endogeneity. There are effects ensuing from both programs and interventions, and the effect of these influences can often be detected with well-designed analysis. The next step is not so easy. In particular, the causes of many of the important effects are not well recognized in early childhood education. But this is not an uncommon result in education. These same issues are frequently encountered in K–12 education, and have also emerged in higher education. Nonetheless, the goal below is to provide some examples of endogeneity program writ large with respect to four types of effects on cognitive outcomes in early childhood education:

the effects of teaching quality, the effects of teacher qualifications, teacher effects, and the effects of program interventions. The focus is on cognitive outcomes oriented toward achievement, but this choice is not intended to diminish the role of other cognitive outcomes or noncognitive outcomes.

There is an important distinction between teaching influences and teacher effects. Teacher effects, like other causal effects, can be isolated despite a lack of understanding of the mechanism by which teachers affect student outcomes. Using teacher quality to predict an outcome is an attempt to estimate the effect as well as to identify the causal mechanism. Statistical models exist that permit teacher effects to be isolated and estimated despite hidden mechanisms. Because of the overlapping constructs of these two types of effect, both are considered in the following sections. In addition, the effect of a program intervention is also loosely related to teacher influences such as training or coaching. In professional development, for example, the idea is to improve teaching quality and thereby positively impact child outcomes indirectly. Program effects are considered in the section following teacher influences. The four kinds of effect described below are part and parcel of most explicit early childhood education policies.

Influences of Teachers

Teachers have an unarguable impact on the learning of children. Yet after this acknowldgement, there is a lot of uncertainty both of the mechanisms of better teaching, and how malleable those mechanisms are through initial teacher preparation and professional development. In any case, however, measurement instruments are necessary to assess teaching quality prior to relating assessed differences in quality to differences in child outcomes. This section begins with an illustration of measurement issues before tackling teacher influences. Teacher effects are examined in the section immediately following measurement issues. A number of illustrations are based on the study by Araujo, Carneiro, Cruz-Aguayo & Schady (2016), who conducted a study in Ecuador in which they assigned students entering kindergarten to teachers in 204 schools based on an *as-good-as-random* rule (a kind of systematic sampling).

Measurement Issues. A number of measures of teaching quality are available. One example is the Classroom Assessment Scoring System or CLASS (Pianta, La Paro & Hamre, 2008), which is targeted to three broad domains of interaction between children and teachers: emotional support, classroom organization, and instructional support. The last domain, which is of key interest in understanding student achievement, includes the dimensions of concept development, quality of feedback, and language modeling. Scoring the CLASS is performed at the dimension level using a seven-point scale. If achievement is of interest, then instructional support is arguably a more proximal influence than those represented by the other two dimensions. Yet the CLASS total score is sometimes used, rather than separate dimensional scores.

In their study of two cohorts of Ecuadoran children entering kindergarten in the 2012–13 and 2013–14 school years, Araujo et al. applied the CLASS to evaluate the effects of teacher quality on student achievement. Fortunately, Carneiro, Cruz-Aguayo, and Schady (2013) provided the correlation matrix (Table 3.2). Upon factor analyzing the intercorrelations between CLASS dimensions, the factor structure given in Table 3.1 below was derived:

This is about as clear an empirical factor structure as one ever sees. It was obtained using maximum likelihood factor analysis with an oblimin (oblique) transformation to simple structure. The three factors are correlated from $r = 0.39$–0.67, which might serve to bolster the argument that the dimensions of the CLASS should be collapsed into a single score. However, this argument is not convincing: the factors are distinct statistically in terms of the factor structure. It is also of interest here that the correlation is between Emotional Support and Instructional Support is $r = 0.67$. These dimensions may be correlated because they are related aspects of learning in early education setting. It may also signal that enthusiasm for learning is difficult to distinguish from the process of learning.

Table 3.1 *Factor pattern matrix for CLASS dimensions (highest loadings in bold)*

Domain	Dimension	F1	F2	F3
Emotional Support	Positive Climate	**.94**	0.01	0.03
	Negative Climate	**.36**	−0.19	0.30
	Teacher Sensitivity	**.86**	0.04	0.06
	Regard for student	**.63**	0.06	−0.15
	Behavior Manage	.05	−0.09	**0.84**
Classroom Organization	Productivity	−0.09	0.11	**0.85**
	Instr Learning Formats	0.30	0.12	**0.61**
	Concept Development	−0.02	**0.84**	0.05
Instructional Support	Quality Feedback	0.24	**0.63**	0.03
	Language Modeling	−0.02	**0.91**	−0.02

Table 3.2 *CLASS statistics from Table 6 of Carneiro et al. (2013).* *("Segments" refers to reliability between 20-minute video segments of teaching, and "Raters" to segment scores summed to rater)*

			Reliability Ratio	
CLASS Domains	Mean (1–7)	SD	Raters	Segments
Emotional Support	4.07	0.33	0.89	0.59
Classroom Organization	4.79	0.47	0.89	0.57
Instructional Support	**1.15**	**0.18**	**0.85**	**0.29**
Total CLASS Score	3.41	0.28	0.92	0.61

Digging into the psychometrics of the CLASS results (Carneiro et al., 2013), descriptive statistics for the three domain scores of the CLASS are given in Table 3.2. It can be seen that the CLASS scores for Instructional Support are highly compressed (low standard deviation) at the lower range across in the sample of teachers providing data for the reliability study. The reliability analysis also suggests there is much less inter-rater agreement in the area of Instructional Support, probably due to the lack of variability. For the purpose of finding quality effects on learning outcomes, the factor and reliability analyses provide scant rationale for aggregating across the dimensions of the CLASS. Aggregation may be suitable to describing very general effects of quality, but does not provide actionable results in designing preschool interventions or professional development aimed at increasing student achievement. The effects of instructional support (of which there appears to have been very little) are obscured by the CLASS total score which is primarily driven by the other dimensions.

Effects of Teaching Quality. After observing classroom teacher quality, Araujo et al. (2016) were able to determine that a 1 standard deviation (σ) increase in quality resulted in 0.13σ, 0.11σ, and 0.07σ higher test scores in language, math, and executive function, respectively. Araujo et al. only reported these effects for the total CLASS score. Yet, as indicated above, it is important to use the most proximal indicator possible for student achievement. Thus, the effect sizes for each domain should be reported separately. Unfortunately, Araujo et al. (2016) do not provide this information.

However, even by disaggregating the domains of the CLASS, the endogeneity issue is not easily resolved, unless it can be shown that some subscores reflect instructionally sensitive processes. Research for determining predictors of improvement on cognitive outcomes is an important priority.

But one more specification is crucial: in order to discover or construct instruments to describe effective practices, the question must be asked: "Effective for what outcome?" Quality measures predicting mathematics outcomes may be different from other kinds of achievement outcome. Burchinal, Vandergrift, Pianta & Mashburn (2010) noted the lack of attention in observational instruments to content-specific instructional strategies.

Araujo et al. found that a 1σ increase in CLASS score corresponds to about a 0.10σ increase in learning across outcome measures. This conclusion was obtained with two different approaches to estimation: an empirical Bayes method (multilevel modeling) similar to that of Kane & Staiger (2002) and Chetty et. al. (2011), and an instrumental variables approach based on using the AY 2011 CLASS scores as an instrument for AY 2012 CLASS scores. Araujo et al. estimated two other interesting effects. First, the cross-year, cross-subject correlations were notable. For example, $r = 0.37$ for math in year 1 and language in year 2. Accordingly, "It is the *same* teachers who have their children learn more math and more language year after year" (p. 26). It could also be argued that a correlation of 0.37 indicates a mild effect: only 10% of the variance in lagged teacher effect is in fact due to teachers.

Araujo et al. also concluded: "More broadly, our results are consistent with there being a single (or very low-dimensional) factor that drives the effectiveness of kindergarten teachers in all domains" (p. 26). Yet in the next section, "In the case of math … on average, children assigned to tenured teachers learn 0.10 standard deviations more than those assigned to contract teachers." This finding is not consistent with the claim that that the causal mechanisms of teacher effects are "low dimensional." The effect of teacher experience (inexperienced v. tenured) on achievement is as large as the quality effect, so perhaps this provides some clue to salient instructional mechanisms. In general, however, teacher characteristics tend not to correlate with teacher quality, and this leads to ineffective personnel policy decisions such as teacher reassignment or retirement (voluntary or involuntary).

Effects of Teacher Qualifications. A key question in early childhood care and education (ECE) is the extent to which classroom and student outcomes can be increased by raising teacher education requirements. The current policy debate, framed by state-funded preschool initiatives, is focused on teacher qualifications and, in particular, whether or not preschool teachers should have a bachelor's degree. Kelley & Camilli (2007) examined in a meta-analysis a set of 32 mostly quasi-experiments and correlational studies. They found and effect size of

$d = 0.15$ for having a bachelor's degree versus lower levels of qualification, and an average association of $r = 0.22$ between educational level and child outcomes in correlational studies. In contrast, Early, Maxwell, Burchinal et al. (2007) reported no significant relationship in their analysis of seven studies. However, across the seven studies, there were 27 comparisons of bachelor yes–no, and 19/27 comparisons favored teachers with a bachelor degree.

A more recent study by Gong (2015) used the techniques of Ordinary Least Squares (OLS) linear regression with rich controls, propensity score matching, and instrumental variables to examine this issue. Though results varied by methodological approach, Gong concluded that

Overall, there are some positive effects of having a teacher with a B.A. identified on some of the child development outcomes at age 4 (e.g., some robust evidence of positive B.A. effects on early reading and math); still, the evidence is not very strong, given the inconsistency of the findings across models and the negative effect of the B.A. on parent-reported social competence in the OLS and PSM models. (p. 200)

Given these results, an answer to the question of whether there are effects of a bachelor's degree on children's outcomes is a resounding *maybe*. But there should be no joy in the glass-is-half-full interpretation if the observed effects of teacher qualifications are small and inconsistent (Barnett, 2017). Qualifications seem to be necessary but are not sufficient for effective programming.

Teacher effects. There is a growing literature on teacher effects in early education. A number of studies have examined potential instructional effects. Two policy-related questions are the extent to which teacher effects exist, and, if they do exist, whether these effects are associated with teacher credentials such as baccalaureates or ECE certificates. The work of Araujo et al. (2016) is useful for illustrating the difficulties of searching for interpretable teacher effects on cognitive outcomes. They showed that, as a backdrop, their study on the effects of quality showed there was little evidence that instructional support actually occurred. Yet they also found "substantial" classroom effects (highest performing teacher v. lowest performing teacher): 0.26σ for language, 0.22σ for mathematics, and 0.17σ for executing function. Recall that the 0.10σ quality effect noted above (using CLASS) meant that a 1σ increase in quality results in a 0.10σ increase in achievement. The highest–lowest difference seems to indicate a very wide gap for teaching capacity within schools (especially given the good-as-random assignment rule). It would seem that, on average, huge teacher influences on achievement are not captured by the CLASS – and this is probably true of any extant observational measure. Thus, the teacher effects are somewhat mysteriously related to what teachers actually do in the classroom.

Teachers effects obtained through value-added modeling are weakly associated with observational quality and other teacher background variables. This is a widespread finding not limited to preschool. In recent surveys of the literature, Hanushek & Rivkin (2006, 2012) documented substantial heterogeneity in the effects of teachers on students in the United States. In ten studies, they found that a 1σ increase in teaching quality raises mathematics outcomes by an average of 0.17σ and reading by 0.13σ. They also demonstrated the determinants of teacher effectiveness are unobserved: characteristics of teachers such as education, experience, test scores, or salary, are poor predictors of student learning in the value-added sense. Teacher effects nonetheless appear to be estimated reliably (Bacher-Hicks, Kane & Staiger, 2014). Konstantoploulos & Chung (2011, p. 1561) showed, using the Tennessee STAR data, that teacher effects in the early grades persist through third grade, especially in reading: "students who are taught by effective teachers at the 85th percentile of the teacher effectiveness distribution in three consecutive grades (e.g., kindergarten, first, and second grade) would experience achievement increases of about one-third of a SD in reading."

Surveys of the literature from developing countries (Glewwe, Hanushek, Humpage & Ravina, 2011; Kremer, Brannen & Glennerster, 2013; and Kremer & Holla, 2009) reached similar conclusions. This led Araujo et al. (2014, p. 35) to be "somewhat pessimistic about such screening tests, at least for teachers of young (kindergarten) children." This situation can be likened to one in astrophysics: the gravity effects of dark matter can be observed, but the mechanism (dark matter) is unknown. Teacher influences on cognition also remain somewhat mysterious. There is some interesting research on this topic on older students by Lavy, Paserman & Scholosser (2011). They showed that a classroom effect can be confounded with a teacher effect: namely, the proportion of low-ability peers can negatively affect student performance by reducing the level of pedagogical practices and the quality of classroom interactions. Muñoz, Scoskie & French (2013) carried out a study of fourth grade teachers. A sampling of their findings indicated that more- versus less-effective teachers in the area of reading reported a higher priority on maintaining a physically and emotionally safe environment for students, having high expectations, and higher-order skills. Less-effective versus more-effective teachers placed higher priority on implementing and planning instruction and on monitoring student progress. It should also be noted that these are self-reported priorities, and it is not clear how strongly self-reported and actual behaviors would agree. However, the difference between more-effective versus less-effective teachers was minimal.

The correlations between observational measures of instruction and teacher effects in the form of value-added scores are typically and disturbingly low. Value-added scores may reflect the capacity of teachers, but substantial controversy remains (Rothstein, 2014; Chetty, Friedman & Rockoff, 2014; Rothstein, 2017). Currently, value-added scores do not provide practical guidance for designing early educational programs. To say there are better teachers and worse teachers, and better teachers teach more effectively, is a trivial observation unless an effective policy tool can be constructed from this information. For example, it may be possible to reduce achievement gaps between schools if more effective teachers were reassigned to lower-performing schools or classrooms, but it is not clear how or if reassignment would work as an ongoing personnel policy. As noted by Rothstein (2015), bonus policies may have small effects on selection, while hiring and firing policies pay may have larger effects only if accompanied by substantial salary increases.

Program Interventions

A number of studies have documented substantial impacts of preschool intervention programs. This work is international in scope. For example, Rao, Sun, Wong et al. (2014) examined 111 relatively high-quality studies from 40 developing countries. They found an average effect size of $d = 0.34$. They also noted a correlation of $r = 0.35$ between the qualifications of direct-change agents (education at the tertiary level, paraprofessionals and professionals) and program effect.

In the USA a number of studies have demonstrated the beneficial effect of intervention (Burchinal et al., 2008; Howes et al., 2008; Mashburn et al., 2008). In a meta-analysis of US studies, Camilli, Vargas, Ryan & Barnett (2010) examined 123 comparative studies of early childhood interventions. Each study provided a number of contrasts, where a contrast is defined as the comparison of an intervention group of children with an alternative intervention or no intervention group. Across these studies they found that interventions that employed a nontreated comparison group resulted in an average effect size of $d = 0.23$, but interventions compared to an *alternative* intervention had an average effect size of $d = 0.07$. Thus, the alternative comparison does matter, and if the purpose is to create scalable interventions, one cannot avoid drilling down into the treatment label.

Camilli et al. coded the treatment and control group for (1) teacher-directed activities designed to teach information and develop skills, and

(2) whether services were provided in addition to ECE. The results were highly consistent. Pooling across control and alternative comparisons showed that the effects of directive instruction were positive ($d = 0.24$ and 0.29 for the treatment and comparison groups) and the effects of additional services was negative ($d = -0.47$ and -0.23 for the treatment and comparison groups). Regardless of the treatment label, other influences on cognitive development could be recognized beyond the treatment label. Yet these moderator effects were haphazardly distributed across treatment and comparison groups, and would have been invisible if one focused solely on the treatment label. In retrospect, these effects appear to be more important than the treatment per se. The effects of observed treatments tend to diminish over time, but these outcomes are concoctions of treatment effects as well as effect endogenous to treatment and control labels in intervention experiments.

Duncan and Magnuson (2013), in a meta-analysis of 84 studies, reached slightly different conclusions from Camilli et al. (2010). They found an overall treatment effect of $d = 0.25$, but with weighting (giving more influence to larger programs) the effect diminished to $d = 0.21$. They also examined a number of moderators such as experimental rigor, source of publication (peer reviewed journal v. other), and date of publication. With respect to time trends, Duncan and Magnuson (2013) were aware that "the counterfactual conditions for children in the control group in these studies have improved substantially" over time (p. 114). In contrast, Camilli et al. (2010) argued that the conditions in comparison groups vary substantially in the present. Using predictor variables relating to instructional support is precisely about the counterfactual conditions noted by Scriven (1981) and highlighted by Cronbach and Shapiro (1982). Often the impact of a meta-analysis on program design will be determined by the quality of the follow-up meta-regression. This is especially the case if the active moderator variables can be identified. It is possible the choice of moderators explains the difference between these two meta-analyses.

While Duncan and Magnuson (2013) found a fade-out effect of early intervention programs, Camilli et al. (2010) projected that small effects remained over a period of approximately 10 years. Vandell, Belsky, Burchinal, Steinberg & Vandergrift (2010) also estimated moderate effects of child care quality remained after 15 years. Konstantopoulos and Chung (2011) observed teacher effects in early grades persisted through third grade in reading and mathematics achievement. The latter finding is not the same as the persistence of program effects, but it does raise profound questions if effects of teachers can be shown to persist but not program effects. As noted by Phillips, Lipsey, Dodge et al. (2017), it is well known that some effects do persist:

> There is persuasive evidence from earlier small-scale programs like the Perry Preschool and Abecedarian programs that long-term impacts are possible under some circumstances. But the evidence that contemporary scaled up state or district pre-K programs can produce such impacts is not conclusive. The path ahead must combine well-documented program innovations at the state and district level with evaluation research of broader scope and greater rigor. (p. 27)

However, innovations investigated on a larger scale with greater rigor may not be sufficient unless they are combined with effective descriptions that lead to reproducibility. Cronbach and Shapiro (1982) recognized three levels of reproducibility and how innovations may evolve in this regard. Lykken (1968) noted that deliberate as well as unintended (and perhaps unobserved) procedures are undertaken in replications.

Overemphasis on internal validity in this complex situation may be avoidable by combining a range of research methodologies. This is illustrated in the study by Mendive, Weiland, Yoshikawa & Snow (2016). They carried out a study of implementation fidelity (IF) that complemented the randomized intervention study of Yoshikawa et al. (2015) in Chile. By videotaping and analyzing classroom practices, Mendive et al. (2016) found large impacts on the dosage of language and literacy instruction, but small (though significant) relationships between dosage and achievement outcomes. The experimental dosage (in minutes of instruction) tripled from baseline to end of kindergarten (10.8 to 30.8 minutes for an average of 94 minutes of video per class). Dosage in the control group doubled over the same period (9.3 to 21.6 minutes). Clearly the study of implementation fidelity provided important insights, but the relationship of dosage and adherence to impact was frustratingly low. Maxwell (2004) considered how qualitative methods can be used to assist causal explanation. Simultaneous policy studies might also be useful.

Measurement issues of the kind discussed above are also important in evaluating program effects. For example, Yoshikawa et al. (2015) examined cognitive impacts of a two-year professional development program for pre-kindergarten and kindergarten in Chile. No significant child cognitive outcomes were detected, yet positive effects were found for classroom quality in terms of emotional support and classroom organization (d = 0.38 and 0.43). Key moderators for cognitive outcomes may relate to the quality of instruction, but Yoshikawa et al. did not find a program improvement for instructional support ($d = 0.06$). However, this result would not be surprising if instructional support is minimal. Barnett (2012) wrote, "Controlled randomized trials that look at teacher quality might get us farther, but even these may not tell us what we really want to know, and they are few and far between in any case," which is the case in the studies conducted by Yoshikawa et al. (2015) and Araujo et al. (2016). While randomized experiments are becoming more prevalent, it is not clear that the critical moderators (or variance in the critical moderators) have been identified to the degree that would allow preschool interventions to be effectively scaled up.

A large-scale preschool intervention in Tennessee has the potential to shape the preschool debate, if not preschool policy. A randomized study carried out by Lipsey, Farran & Hofer (2015) examined the state's Voluntary Prekindergarten Program (TNVPK):

TN-VPK is a full-day prekindergarten program for four-year-old children expected to enter kindergarten the following school year. The program in each participating school district must meet standards set by the State Board of Education that require each classroom to have a teacher with a license in early childhood development and education, an adult–student ratio of no less than 1:10, a maximum class size of 20, and an approved age-appropriate curriculum. TN-VPK is an optional program focused on the neediest children in the state. (p. 1)

Because there were more applicants than seats available, an experiment was conducted to select children randomly. Those not selected were assigned to the control groups. Outcomes were then compared after the end of the pre-K school year. The treatment-on-the-treated (TOT) effect on the composite achievement measure was significant, with an effect size of $d = 0.32$. The largest outcomes were observed in the area of literacy, and effect sizes varied depending on the variables of mother education, and English as a second language. Among other results, the study found that the treatment effect did not persist to the end of kindergarten, and no continuing effects were observed in first grade.

Lipsey et al. (2015, p. 5) argued that because of this finding "we need to think carefully about what the next steps should be" and "It is apparent that the term pre-K or even 'high-quality' pre-K does not convey actionable information about what the critical elements of the program should be." The *label* of high-quality and associated subcategories do not yet convey elements of instructional support that lead to improved learning outcomes:

If we are to continue offering pre-K through the public school system, fundamental empirical work may be required to identify specific behaviors and instructional practices important for young children's development in that environment. (p. 41)

Though Camilli et al. (2010) did find short-term effects ($d = 0.21$) and longer-term effects ($d = 0.12$) of program interventions, it is clear that many prefer more recent estimates from randomized experiments. In any event, there is no disagreement that program effects tend to diminish over time.

An interesting pattern in the TN-VPK data is that effect sizes did not just diminish to zero by the end of third grade; they became negative. For example, in applied problems in mathematics, the effect sizes diminish by the progression from pre-K to third grade: $d = 0.17, 0.07, 0.04, -0.14$, and -0.21. This pattern above may be artifactual, due to an unrecognized selection effect or possibly to the particular method used for the imputation of missing data. Moreover, for teacher ratings of children (on the *Cooper–Farran Behavioral Rating Scales* and the *Academic Classroom and Behavior Record*), some sub-scores show an unexpected pattern of outcomes. Three subscales had positive effects for the start of kindergarten, negative effects at first grade, and near-zero subsequently.

Lipsey et al. (2015) did not comment on these findings, but it appears there is more to be learned from the data. Their results have been already widely cited, and it is important to see if they hold up under alternative estimation strategies. In studies like this, it would be very interesting to see a variable like Duncan's "Percentage Center Care" in the regression of outcomes on program and background variables. In any case, the teachers in Tennessee may have been similar to those in the Chile or Ecuador studies in the area of instructional services. In this regard, Lipsey et al. (2015) refers to an insightful comment by Fuhs, Farran & Nesbitt (2013):

If we are to continue offering pre-K through the public school system, fundamental empirical work may be required to identify specific behaviors and instructional practices important for young children's development in that environment. For example, a recent study involving 60 pre-K classrooms in elementary schools demonstrated that the emotional tone, quality of instruction, and level of child involvement in math and literacy activities were significant factors in predicting gains in self-regulation over the year.

When the literature on teacher effects begins to cohere with the literature on teaching quality, it will be more likely that programmatic preschool effects can be reliably obtained at scale. Yet even if program benefits do not persist, there are nonetheless short-term benefits to children. There is no doubt that programs can be designed that lead to higher levels of functioning. The critical question is how to design an environment at scale in which they persist.

In a recent regression discontinuity study of a pre-K intervention in Boston, Weiland & Yoshikawa (2013) found large effects at kindergarten entry for early reading and numeracy skill ($d = 0.44$ to 0.62) and smaller effects for executive function ($d = 0.21$ to 0.28). The impacts were larger for children from lower-income families and Latino children. Scores for the CLASS instructional support subscale were much higher than typically found (4.30 on a scale of 1–7). This suggests that a stronger focus on instruction is critical for positive impact, but Weiland, Ulvestad, Sachs & Yoshikawa (2013) concluded that the CLASS subscales had little or no relationship with student gains. Moreover, the program implemented in Boston public schools included a range of features from political to financial support. It is not clear which, or which combination, is central to improvement. Moreover, as noted by Jenkins & Duncan (2017), neither the sustained impact of this program has been determined nor its potential replicability to other sites.

Conclusions

In this chapter, there has been no attempt to provide an overview of the literature in studies of teacher effectiveness in early childhood education. Rather, the goal was to illustrate issues that have arisen in the last decade of research. The easiest conclusion to draw is that more research is necessary. The second easiest conclusion is that until we can "get the endogeneity out," selection through hiring and firing is the tangible solution on the table. Neither approach inspires confidence. The first option is not actionable, and the second involves many unknowns about personnel pools, personnel policy, and workforce development.

It is both ironic and remarkable that effective programs have been, and continue to be, designed that have substantial impact on child outcomes, yet the disagreement that exists concerns how large the effect is and how long it persists, not whether it exists. Understanding the impact of teachers remains an obstacle to further progress, but work goes on in the present in operational programs that demonstrably benefit the achievement of children. Yet cracking the black box of teacher effects may not occur before astrophysicists discover the nature of dark matter. Psychometric advances in assessing student outcomes as well as quality measures of classrooms and teachers may ultimately have a payoff. It is surprising how little of modern psychometric theory has been applied in early childhood research.

References

Araujo, M. C., Carneiro, P., Cruz-Aguayo, Y. & Schady, N. (2016). Teacher quality and learning outcomes in kindergarten. *Quarterly Journal of Economics*, 131, 1415–1453.

Bacher-Hicks, A., Kane, T. J. & Staiger, D.O. (2014). *Validating Teacher Effect Estimates Using Changes in Teacher Assignments in Los Angeles*. (NBER Working Paper No. 20657). Cambridge, MA: National Bureau of Economic Research.

Barnett, W. S. (2017). Challenges to scaling up effective pre-kindergarten programs, in D. Phillips, M. Lipsey, K. Dodge et al. (Eds.), *The Current State of Scientific Knowledge on Pre-Kindergarten Effects* (pp. 67–74). Washington, DC: Brookings Institution.

Barnett, W. S. (2012, February 10). The pre-K debates: what the research says about teacher quality. *Preschool Matters* (NIEER blog).

Barnett, W. S. (2008). Preschool education and its lasting effects: Research and policy implications. *EPRU Policy Brief*. Boulder and Tempe: Education and the Public Interest Center & Education and Policy Research Unit.

Burchinal, M., Howes, C., Pianta, R. et al. (2008). Predicting child outcomes at the end of kindergarten from the quality of pre-kindergarten teacher-child interactions and instruction. *Applied Developmental Science*, 12, 140–153.

Burchinal, M., Vandergrift, N., Pianta, R. & Mashburn, A. (2010). Threshold analysis of association between child care quality and child outcomes for low-income children in pre-kindergarten programs. *Early Childhood Research Quarterly*, 25, 166–176.

Camilli, G., Vargas, S., Ryan, S. & Barnett, W. S. (2010). Meta-analysis of the effects of early education interventions on cognitive and social development. *Teachers College Record*, 112(3), Article 15440.

Carneiro, P., Cruz-Aguayo, Y., & Schady, N. (2013). Can better teachers compensate for early deficits? Evidence from a randomized experiment in Ecuador. Downloaded 10–15–2018 from http://www.cedlas-er.org/sites/defau lt/files/cer_ien_activity_files/schady.pdf

Chetty, R., Friedman, J., Hilger, N., Saez, E., Schanzenbach, D. & Yagan, D. (2011). How does your kindergarten classroom affect your earnings? Evidence from Project STAR. *Quarterly Journal of Economics*, 126, 1593–1660.

Chetty, R., Friedman, J. N. & Rockoff, J. E. (2014). Response to Rothstein (2014), "Revisiting the Impacts of Teachers." Downloaded on July 25, 2017 from http://obs.rc.fas.harvard.edu/chetty/Rothstein_response.pdf.

Cronbach, L. J. & Shapiro, K. (1982). *Designing Evaluations of Educational and Social Programs* (1st edn, A Joint publication in the Jossey-Bass series in social and behavioral science & in higher education). San Francisco, CA: Jossey-Bass.

Duflo, E., Hanna, R. & Ryan, S. P. 2012. Incentives work: getting teachers to come to school. *American Economic Review*, 102(4), 1241–1278.

Duncan, G. J. & Magnuson, K. (2013). Investing in preschool programs. *Journal of Economic Perspectives*, 27, 109–132.

Early, D. M., Maxwell, K. L., Burchinal, M. et al. (2007). Teachers' education, classroom quality, and young children's academic skills: Results from seven studies of preschool programs. *Child Development*, 78, 558–580.

Farran, D. C. (2017). Characteristics of pre-kindergarten programs that drive positive outcomes, in D. Phillips, M. Lipsey, K. Dodge et al. (Eds.), *The Current State of Scientific Knowledge on Pre-Kindergarten Effects* (pp. 45–50). Washington, DC: Brookings Institution.

Fuhs, M. W., Farran, D. C. & Nesbitt, K. T. (2013). Preschool classroom processes as predictors of children's cognitive self-regulation skills development. *School Psychology Quarterly*, 28, 347–359.

Glewwe, P., Hanushek, E., Humpage, S. & Ravina, R. (2011). School resources and educational outcomes in developing countries: a review of the literature from 1990 to 2010. NBER Working Paper No. 17554.

Gong, Xin (2015). *Does Having a Preschool Teacher with a Bachelor's Degree Matter for Children's Development Outcomes?* Unpublished Doctoral Thesis, Columbia University.

Hanushek, E. & Rivkin, S. (2012). The distribution of teacher quality and implications for policy. *Annual Review of Economics*, 4, 131–57.

Hanushek, E. & Rivkin, S. (2006). Teacher quality, in E. Hanushek & F. Welch (Eds.), *Handbook of the Economics of Education*, Vol. 2 (pp. 1051–1078). Amsterdam: North Holland.

Howes, C., Burchinal, M., Pianta, R. et al. (2008). Ready to learn? Children's pre-academic achievement in pre-kindergarten programs. *Early Childhood Research Quarterly*, 23, 27–50.

Jenkins, J. M. & Duncan, G. J. (2017). Characteristics of pre-kindergarten that drive positive outcomes, in D. Phillips, M. Lipsey, K. Dodge et al. (Eds.), *The Current State of Scientific Knowledge on Pre-Kindergarten Effects* (pp. 45–50). Washington, DC: Brookings Institution.

Jennings, J. L. & DiPrete, T. A. (2010). Teacher effects on social and behavioral skills in early elementary school. *Sociology of Education*, 83, 135–139.

Kane, T. J. & Staiger, D. O. (2002). The promise and pitfalls of using imprecise school accountability measures. *Journal of Economic Perspectives*, 16, 91–114.

Kelley, P. & Camilli, G. (2007). The impact of teacher education on outcomes in center-based education programs: A meta-analysis. NIEER Working Paper.

Konstantopoulos, S. & Chung, V. (2011). Teacher effects in early grades: evidence from a randomized study. *Teachers College Record*, 113, 1541–1565.

Konstantopoulos, S. & Chung, V. (2011). The persistence of teacher effects in elementary grades. *American Educational Research Journal*, 48(2), 361–386.

Kremer, M., Brannen, C. & Glennerster, R. (2013). The challenge of education and learning in the developing world. *Science*, 340, 297–300.

Kremer, M. & Holla, A. (2009). Improving education in the developing world: what have we learned from randomized evaluations? *Annual Review of Economics*, 1, 513–42.

Lavy, V., Paserman, M. D. & Schlosser, A. (2011). Inside the black box of ability peer effects: evidence from variation in the proportion of low achievers in the classroom. *The Economic Journal*, 122, 208–237.

Lipsey, M. W., Farran, D. C. & Hofer, K. G. (2015). *A Randomized Control Trial of the Effects of a Statewide Voluntary Prekindergarten Program on Children's Skills and Behaviors through Third Grade* (Research Report). Nashville, TN: Vanderbilt University, Peabody Research Institute.

Lykken, D. T. (1968). Statistical significance in psychological research. *Psychological Bulletin*, 70, 151–159.

Mashburn, A., Pianta, R., Hamre, B. et al. (2008). Measures of classroom quality in prekindergarten and children's development of academic, language, and social skills. *Child Development*, 79, 732–49.

Mathematica Policy Research. (2015). *Head Start*. Washington, DC: Institute of Educational Sciences, What Works Clearinghouse.

Maxwell, J. A. (2004). Using qualitative methods for causal explanation. *Field Methods*, 16, 243–264.

Mendive, S., Weiland, C., Yoshikawa, H. & Snow, C. E. (2016). Opening the black box: Intervention fidelity in a randomized trial of a preschool teacher professional development program in Chile. *Journal of Educational Psychology*, 108, 135–145.

Muñoz, M. A., Scoskie, J. R. & French, D. L. (2013). Investigating the "black box" of effective teaching: the relationship between teachers' perception and student achievement in a large urban district. Educational Assessment. *Evaluation and Accountability*, 25, 205–230.

Murnane, R. J. & Willet, J. B. (2010). *Methods Matter: Improving Causal Inference in Educational and Social Science Research*. New York, NY: Oxford University Press.

National Institute of Child Health and Human Development Early Child Care Research Network & Duncan, G. J. (2003). Modeling the impacts of child care quality on children's preschool cognitive development. *Child Development*, 74, 1454–1475.

Phillips, D., Lipsey, M., Dodge, K. et al. (2017). *The Current State of Scientific Knowledge on Pre-Kindergarten Effects*. Washington, DC: Brookings Institution.

Pianta, R. C., La Paro, K. & Hamre, B. K. (2008). *Classroom Assessment Scoring System (CLASS)*. Baltimore, MD: Paul H. Brookes.

Rao, N., Sun, J., Wong, J. M. S. et al. (2014). Early childhood development and cognitive development in developing countries. Report available from http://r4d.dfid.gov.uk/ or http://eppi.ioe.ac.uk/.

Rothstein, J. (2017). Supplement to "Revisiting the impacts of teachers." Available July 24, 2017 from https://eml.berkeley.edu/~jrothst/CFR/.

Rothstein, J. (2015). Teacher quality when supply matters. *American Economic Review*, 105, 100–130.

Rothstein, J. (2014). Revisiting the impacts of teachers. Available July 24, 2017 from https://eml.berkeley.edu/~jrothst/CFR/.

Scriven, M. (1981). Product evaluation, in N. L. Smith (Ed.), *New Techniques for Evaluation* (pp. 121–166). Beverly Hills, CA: Sage.

Vandell, D. L., Belsky, J., Burchinal, M., Steinberg, L. & Vandergrift, N. (2010). Do effects of early child care extend to age 15 years? Results from the NICHD study of early child care and youth development. *Child Development*, 81, 737–756.

Wasik, B. A., Mattera, S. K., Lloyd, C. M. & Boller, K. (2013). *Intervention Dosage in Early Childhood Care and Education: It's Complicated (OPRE Research Brief OPRE 2013–15)*. Washington, DC: Office of Planning, Research and

Evaluation, Administration for Children and Families, US Department of Health and Human Services.

Weiland, C., Ulvestad, K., Sachs, J. & Yoshikawa, H. (2013). Associations between classroom quality and children's vocabulary and executive function skills in an urban public prekindergarten program. *Early Childhood Research Quarterly*, 28, 199–209.

Weiland, C. & Yoshikawa, H. (2013). Impacts of a pre-kindergarten program on children's mathematics, language, literacy, executive function, and emotional skills. *Child Development*, 84, 2112–2130.

Yoshikawa, H., Leyva, D., Snow, C. E. et al. (2015). Experimental impacts of a teacher professional development program in Chile on preschool classroom quality and child outcomes. *Developmental Psychology*, 51, 309–322.

4   Boosting School Readiness with Preschool Curricula

Tutrang Nguyen, Greg J. Duncan, and Jade M. Jenkins

High-quality early childhood education (ECE) programs can improve children's school readiness and future academic success (Karoly, Kilburn & Cannon, 2005; Magnuson, Ruhm & Waldfogel, 2007; Duncan & Magnuson, 2013), particularly for children from low-income backgrounds who are more likely to enter school with fewer early academic skills than their higher-income peers (Barnett, 2011; Ramey & Ramey, 2006; Schweinhart, 2006). One of the reasons why high-quality ECE programs such as Head Start and some state-funded prekindergarten programs may be so effective at promoting school readiness is because they require the use of a curriculum. A curriculum can contribute to important aspects of classroom quality in ECE because it provides a framework to guide teacher and child interactions and activities (Klein & Knitzer, 2006; NAEYC & NAECS/SDE, 2003). This chapter describes the various kinds of preschool curricula and provides evidence on their relative effectiveness.

Types of Curricula

In general, curricula set goals for children's knowledge and skill development in an early learning setting, and they support educators' plans for providing the day-to-day learning experiences to cultivate those skills through daily lesson plans, materials, and other pedagogical tools (Goffin & Williams, 1994; Ritchie & Willer, 2008). There are also a number of dimensions across which curricula differ: philosophies, materials, the role of the teacher (i.e., directing versus observing child activities), modality (e.g., small or large group setting), classroom organization and design, and the use of child assessment. Most programs, such as Head Start, require that grantees use a curriculum that provides enriching experiences across the multiple domains of children's development (e.g., health, social-emotional, academic), known as "whole-child" curricula. State pre-K programs typically choose their own curricula, but their choices may be limited by preapproved lists from accrediting bodies and state agencies (Clifford & Crawford, 2009). But such lists are not often discriminating: a survey of state education agencies revealed that states have fairly loose requirements for pre-K curricular decisions (e.g., "research-based" curricula, without a clear definition), with vague guidelines for inclusion such as alignment to state early learning standards (Clements, 2007; Dahlin & Squires, 2016).

The vast majority of preschool curricula are created by researchers, practitioners, or publishers, and then marketed, sold, and distributed to practitioners by publishers. Other forms of curricula are developed less formally by preschool teachers and center directors themselves. Many states allow ECE providers to develop their own lesson plans or curricula rather than purchasing a published curriculum. We refer to these curricula as "locally-developed," but they may include components of various published curricula. We focus this review on two broad categories of curricula: "whole-child" and more targeted, skill-specific curricula.

We present in Table 4.1 the types of curricula used by state pre-K and Head Start programs, based on a recent nationally representative survey of child care providers (National Survey of Early Care and Education, 2012; Jenkins & Duncan, 2017). These data reveal that among pre-K centers, 41 percent use a whole-child curriculum; 25 percent use another comprehensive curriculum or a skill-specific curriculum (focusing on math or literacy); and 34 percent use no curriculum at all, or one that was locally developed. Whole-child approaches dominate preschool program curricula choices, in part because Head Start program standards require centers to adopt them. In addition, whole-child curricula reflect the standards for early childhood education put forth by the National Association for the Education of Young Children, the leading professional and accrediting organization for early educators (Copple & Bredekamp, 2009). Not surprisingly, 73 percent of Head Start centers use a whole-child curriculum, and another 20 percent use a different comprehensive or skill-specific curriculum. Many centers receiving subsidies through the Child Care and Development Fund program use them as well. In the following sections, we describe how these two broad types of curricula – whole-child and skill-specific – differ in their approach and, subsequently, in their comparative impacts on children's school readiness.

Table 4.1 *Curricula used in Head Start, pre-K, and other state and locally funded programs*

Curriculum	Pre-K	Head Start	CCDF Recipients
WHOLE-CHILD CURRICULA (subtotal)	41%	73%	31%
Creative Curriculum	32	55	25
HighScope	7	17	4
Montessori	2	1	2
OTHER PUBLISHED CURRICULA (including math and literacy curricula)	25%	20%	18%
OTHER APPROACHES (subtotal)	34%	7%	51%
"A curriculum we developed ourselves"	12	2	20
Did not use a curriculum	22	5	31
Total	100%	100%	100%

Source: The National Survey of Early Care and Education.

Notes: Total calculations by curricula type are shown in shaded rows and denoted by percentage signs. These figures are a sum of the unshaded calculations, which break down the total number of centers reporting a specific curricula package/approach (i.e., Creative Curriculum is a type of whole-child curricula, and is used by 32% of the pre-K programs in the sample). Figures are based on program director responses to survey questions about curriculum. We designated child care providers as state pre-K programs based on survey questions regarding sponsorship and tuition payments. We defined state pre-K programs as providers that were sponsored by the state or local government or unspecified Head Start or pre-K, AND answered "yes" to one of the following questions: (1) whether tuitions were paid by local government (e.g., pre-K paid for by local school board or other local agency, grants from county government) (2) whether tuitions were paid for by state government (vouchers/certificates, state contracts, transportation, pre-K funds, grants from state agencies). The "CCDF recipients" calculations also come from the NSECE. Centers were identified as subsidy recipients if the center director answered "yes" to the item, "funders pay him/her for vouchers or subsidies to specific eligible parents." Note that the NSECE does not distinguish between primary vs. secondary curriculum use. Calculations are tabulated from items in the teacher or director survey asking, "Is a specific curriculum used for this group?" and if they answered yes, "What is the name of the curriculum used?" The "Other Published Curricula" is a category created by NSECE and includes curricula like Bank Street, Preschool Paths, Reggio Emilila, and Galileo. NSECE did not collect data on primary and secondary curriculum, if more than one curriculum was in use. "CCDF recipients" is not a mutually exclusive category, and includes pre-K and Head Start centers in these calculations. This is because childcare centers are not restricted from offering both programs (e.g., Head Start recipients are eligible for, and often also enroll in, CCDF subsidy programs, which allows parents to cover hours for wrap-around care). We thank Jennifer Duer for tabulating these data.

Whole-Child Curricula

As the national data illustrate, whole-child are the most commonly used curricula in ECE programs. Such curricula are sometimes termed "global" or "constructivist" because they typically take a constructivist approach to development, emphasizing child-centered active learning cultivated by strategically arranging the classroom environment to promote individual and interactive discovery (DeVries & Kohlberg, 1987; Piaget, 1976; Weikart & Schweinhart, 1987). Rather than explicitly targeting developmental domains such as early math skills, whole-child curricula seek to promote learning by encouraging children to interact independently with the equipment, materials and other children in the classroom environment. In this framework, the teacher supports and encourage children's play explorations within the classroom setting. Montessori schools are famous for their whole-child approach. The Perry Preschool program was based on a version of the whole-child HighScope curriculum that is still used today (Belfield, Nores, Barnett & Schweinhart, 2006; Schweinhart, 2005).

Implementing this careful balance of teacher-supported, child-directed learning effectively takes considerable skill on the part of teachers using whole-child curricula. Each child engages with components of the classroom environment in his or her own way, and the teacher's task is to support or "scaffold" learning for everyone with just the right amount of input; not so little that the child fails to learn, but not so directed that the teacher's instruction reduces a child's interest in a task. Perhaps the most difficult goal of whole-child curricula is that the sequence of teacher's inputs should promote *cumulative* development of academic or social-emotional skills over the course of the pre-K year.

National data also show that Creative Curriculum is the most widely used whole-child curriculum in both pre-K and Head Start classrooms (Jenkins & Duncan, 2017). The Department of Education's What Works Clearinghouse (2013) describes Creative Curriculum as "designed to foster development of the whole child through teacher-led, small and large group activities centered around 11 interest areas (blocks, dramatic play, toys and games, art, library, discovery, sand and water, music and movement, cooking, computers, and outdoors). The curriculum provides teachers with detailed information on child development, classroom organization, teaching strategies, and engaging families in the learning process." Creative Curriculum, much like the other whole-child curricula, allocates a large proportion of the preschool day to child free-choice time (Fuligni, Howes, Huang, Hong & Lara-Cinisomo, 2012).

Skill-Specific Curricula

An alternative, or sometimes complement, to whole-child curricula are skill-specific (sometimes called "academically targeted") curricula. Skill-specific curricula have become increasingly popular, stemming from a greater focus on improving children's academic achievement as well as evidence that exposure to explicit learning opportunities may enhance the effectiveness of early childhood programs (Clements & Sarama, 2007; Hamre, Downer, Kilday & McGuire, 2008; PCER, 2008).

Supporters of skill-specific curricula argue that preschool children benefit most from sequenced, explicit instruction focused on specific academic (e.g., literacy or math) or social-emotional (e.g., self-regulation or problem-solving) skills and provided in the context of play and exploration (Wasik & Hindman, 2011). These curricula can supplement a classroom's regular curriculum, which could be a whole-child or locally-developed curriculum. For example, the Building Blocks pre-K math curriculum adds roughly 15–20 minutes of daily math activities to an existing classroom curriculum (Clements & Sarama, 2008).

The focus on specific academic skills often prompt researchers and practitioners to conflate the content-specific curricular approach with highly teacher-controlled, direct instruction methods, such as large-group worksheet-based academic activities, that have been linked with stress and reduced motivation in preschool children (Stipek, Feiler, Daniels & Milburn, 1995; Elkind, 1986). Far from the "drill and kill" methods justifiably admonished by developmentalists, successful evidence-based, skill-focused curricula are grounded in a sound developmental framework and embed learning in playful preschool activities, including storybook reading, games, art, and discovery activities that are conducted in both small- and large-group contexts. In contrast to the whole-child approaches, these curricula provide teachers with lesson plans to follow in which playful activities are strategically organized to present children with learning opportunities that are focused, sequential, and cumulative.

Investments in Curricula

Table 4.2 shows the average annual costs for some of the most widely used preschool curricula. Such investments are substantial; the average price of a whole-child curriculum is in the order of $2,000 per classroom per year. Moreover, these estimates do not include the additional

Table 4.2 *Publishers and costs of widely used curricula packages in preschool programs*

Curriculum	Publisher	Description	Annual Cost Per Classroom
Creative Curriculum	Teaching Strategies, Inc.	The Creative Curriculum® for Preschool focuses on project-based investigations as a means for children to apply skills. The curriculum is designed to foster development of the whole child through teacher-led, small and large group activities centered around 11 interest areas. The curriculum provides teachers with details on child development, classroom organization, teaching strategies, and engaging families in the learning process.	$2149
HighScope	HighScope Educational Research Foundation	HighScope® is based on the idea that children and adults learn best through hands-on experiences with people, materials, events, and ideas. Each individual program consists of a system of teaching practices, curriculum content areas for each topic and age group, assessment tools, and a training model.	$1150
Scholastic Big Day for PreK	Scholastic	Big Day for PreK® is organized into eight themes and includes five key elements of success: big experiences, meaningful conversations, best children's literature and nonfiction, innovative technology, and comprehensive program.	$2900
DLM Early Childhood Express	McGraw-Hill	The DLM Early Childhood Express® is based on the idea that children learn best by connecting what they know with what they learn. The curriculum uses eight themed units to incorporate this philosophy into daily instruction.	$4108
High Reach Learning	Carson-Dellosa Publishing Group	HighReach Learning® is a project-based curriculum organized by topic. The curriculum that includes a four-step planning process, which guides teachers in how to include children in the learning process. Additionally, family communication materials are included.	$1125

Notes: Per-classroom estimates are approximated from the cost of purchasing the curriculum teacher's manual or equivalent (in 2015), and the baseline set of materials required to implement the curriculum. Publishers offer different sets of materials and thus costs will vary by publisher and curriculum.

professional development activities that are often strongly recommended by publishers to implement the curricula with fidelity, and the costs of supplemental materials. The Head Start program alone has over 50,000 classrooms, driving the total costs of such policies into the tens of millions of dollars (Office of Head Start, 2010). Given the wide array of curricular choices available and the government expenditures for the curricula required in public preschool, it is of considerable policy interest to determine how curricula impact children's learning and development, and the types of curricula that are most effective at promoting the multiple domains of school readiness.

How Effective Are Preschool Curricula?

If a key purpose of preschool programs is to promote the school readiness of their students, it is important to know whether preschool curricula contribute to the development of children's concrete literacy and numeracy skills, such as knowing letters and numbers, self-regulation skills such as the ability to sit still and engage in the material being taught, and behaviors such as the ability to get along with teachers and fellow students. By far the biggest gaps in these kinds of capacities between kindergarteners from low- and higher-income families relate to achievement. Math and literacy skills of low-income children are a full year behind those of high-income children at the time of kindergarten entry, and these gaps do not diminish by the time the children reach eighth grade (Duncan & Murnane, 2011). When scored with a similar metric, gaps in self-regulatory "approaches to learning" skills are about half as large as achievement gaps, and behavior gaps are about one-quarter the size of gaps in academic skills. Effective curricular interventions have the potential to boost the quality of instruction and the nature of teacher-child interactions in preschool classrooms and, subsequently, close the income gap in these school readiness skills.

Impacts on Academic Skills

Beginning with whole-child curricula, the modal choice of preschool programs, it may be surprising that there exists almost no high-quality evidence of their influence on children's early academic skills. The only evidence for HighScope's effectiveness comes from the Perry Preschool Study that included a small sample of children in the 1960s with conditions (e.g., few learning activities in home and few center-based care alternatives) for comparison-group children that no longer apply to ECE today (Belfield et al., 2006; PCER, 2008; Schweinhart, 2005). No positive empirical support exists for Creative Curriculum and it has not demonstrated effectiveness based on rigorous What Works Clearinghouse standards (US Department of Education, 2013) despite its popularity in preschool classrooms. Only recently have researchers begun to question the conventional wisdom of whole-child curricula (see Jenkins, Auger, Nguyen & Wu, 2017; Jenkins & Duncan, 2017).

One comprehensive study used five samples of preschool children to examine whether differences existed across popular whole-child curricular packages in terms of preschool classrooms' academic activities and overall quality, and in children's school readiness outcomes (Jenkins et al., 2017). Results from this study indicate that children in classrooms using the Scholastic curriculum performed significantly better on academic and social-emotional outcomes, but it did not replicate across datasets. Surprisingly, the study also found that when a teacher reported using any published whole-child curriculum, the quality and academic activities of these classrooms were not distinguishable from classrooms where teachers reported using no published curriculum. This highlights that although we invest a substantial portion of public and private preschool dollars in whole-child curricula, we have very little evidence that such investments yield any return for children's development.

With respect to skill-specific curricula, there is some evidence that children who are in classrooms that implement this type of curriculum during preschool show moderate to large improvements in the targeted content domain (Clements & Sarama, 2008; Diamond, Barnett, Thomas & Munro, 2007; Jenkins et al., 2018; PCER, 2008; Weiland & Yoshikawa, 2013). For example, children who receive a literacy-targeted curriculum show improvements in their literacy and language skills (Justice et al., 2010; Lonigan, Farver, Philips & Clancy-Menchetti, 2011). Similar gains are also observed in the case of a preschool math curriculum, with children exposed to this curriculum demonstrating larger gains in their math skills compared with children who received the business-as-usual curriculum (Clements & Sarama, 2007, 2008).

Although there exists evidence of the effectiveness of skill-specific curricula on cultivating preschool children's academic development, very few evaluations compare across different types of content-specific curricula or between whole-child or locally developed curricula. To date, only one large-scale, systematic evaluation of curricula has been conducted. In the early 2000s, 12 grantees across the USA were funded by the Institute of Educational Sciences (IES) to study the effect of 14 preschool curricula on children's academic and social-emotional outcomes up to the end of kindergarten in the Preschool Curriculum Evaluation Research Initiative Study (PCER, 2008). The goal of the PCER study was to understand whether different widely available curricula, or specific features of these curricula, were beneficial in promoting children's learning and development during their preschool year at age 4. Of the 14 intervention curricula, ten focused on early language and literacy development, one focused on mathematics, and the other three focused on more general domains (Creative Curriculum, Project Approach, Project Construct).

The findings from the PCER study were largely null, although several analytic issues, such as low statistical power (because each curriculum was evaluated individually), have been cited to explain the lack of significant effects (PCER, 2008). However, two content-specific curricula (literacy and math) significantly affected children's reading and math outcomes at the end of preschool, with improvements in the targeted domain (i.e., math curricula affecting math outcomes). In a reanalysis of the PCER data, Jenkins et al. (2018) pooled the skill-specific curricula together and found that compared with the HighScope and Creative Curriculum found in most public preschool classrooms, skill-specific curricula increased children's outcomes in the targeted content domain.

Nguyen (2017) takes a much more comprehensive, meta-analytic approach to synthesizing the evaluation literature on preschool curricula. Drawing on 71 experimental and quasi-experimental studies published from 1990 to 2017, the study compares whole-child curricula with skill-specific curricula (literacy or math) to understand the impact on children's academic outcomes. Small to moderate effect sizes of targeted curricula relative to global curricula were found.

Figure 4.1 shows the impacts of various kinds of curricula on children's academic skills at the end of the program. Data are drawn from a variety of early childhood education settings, including not only pre-K but also Head Start and other kinds of programs. Impacts are expressed as fractions of a standard deviation. Since the kindergarten-entry gap between low- and high-income students amounts to a little over one standard deviation, the ".46" entry on the first bar means that the math curricula could close about 40 percent of the low-/high-income gap in math achievement.

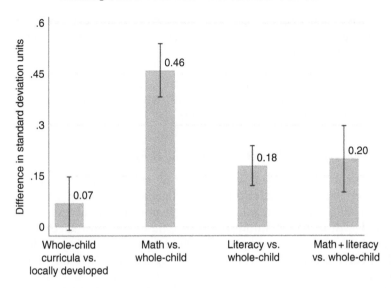

Figure 4.1 Impacts of various curricula on academic outcomes
Notes: Data are drawn from evaluations implemented in a variety of preschool settings, including pre-K and Head Start, and published between 1990 and 2017. Outcomes are not standardized across studies. Outcomes for the first and fourth bars are composite scores of math and literacy outcomes. The second bar includes only math outcomes. The third bar only includes literacy outcomes.

The relative performance of different kinds of curricula shown in Figure 4.1 is consistent with the general pattern of results found in other recent meta-analytic studies (Chambers, Cheung & Slavin, 2016; Jenkins et al., 2018; Wang, Firmender, Power & Byrnes, 2016). Math curricula are often quite successful at boosting math achievement relative to either a whole-child or locally-developed curriculum; literacy curricula are modestly successful at boosting literacy achievement relative to these same alternatives; and, on average, children exposed to whole-child curricula do not outperform children in classrooms where locally developed curricula are used. Note that these results, presented as averages, do mask important variation in impacts. For example, impacts for literacy curricula range from 0.71 standard deviations down to negative (although statistically insignificant) impact – in the case of two curricula.

The null results on whole-child curricula are remarkable, and confirm the overall lack of empirical support for the effectiveness of the two most widely used curricula in preschool programs, HighScope and Creative Curriculum. Despite their widespread use, existing evidence appears to indicate that whole-child curricula are no more effective at boosting school readiness than the assortment of activities that early childhood education centers develop on their own. If locally developed curricula are in fact equally as beneficial in promoting children's readiness for school, what is the value added by purchasing a whole-child curriculum?

Impacts on Social-Emotional Skills and Behaviors

Several recent experimental evaluations of supplemental curricula and teacher training modules directed at improving children's social-emotional skills and self-regulation have demonstrated success when compared with usual classroom practice. One of the most successful, Preschool PATHS, shows impacts on children's emotion knowledge, problem-solving skills, behavior, and self-regulation (Bierman et al., 2008; Morris et al., 2014). Researchers of the Head Start REDI intervention, which incorporates Preschool PATHS into a comprehensive, global classroom curriculum with a dual focus on improving children's language and emergent literacy skills, have also found similar impacts of the program up through the kindergarten year, with significant differences favoring children in the intervention classrooms on emotional understanding, social problem-solving, and reduced aggressive-disruptive behavior (Bierman et al., 2008, 2014). Other socioemotional-specific curricula, such as Tools of the Mind, do not have empirical support in terms of impacts on children's socioemotional skills (Barnett et al., 2008; Yoshikawa et al., 2013). Note that, on their own, whole-child curricula have not been shown to boost children's skills in either socioemotional or academic domains (PCER, 2008).

By devoting time and attention to academic skills, a common fear among developmentalists is that skill-focused curricula preclude full development of children's socioemotional capacities. But for the most part, such curricula generate impacts only in the developmental domain they target, such as math curricula affecting math skills, but not literacy or socioemotional skills. Importantly, developmentally appropriate skills-focused curricula do not appear to generate negative impacts children's development in socioemotional domains (Jenkins et al., 2018). In other words, preschool programs can provide important boosts to children's key academic skills with high-quality skill-focused curricula without sacrificing development in other social and self-regulatory domains.

If anything, better organized and sequenced instructional activities complemented by positive teacher–child interactions may work well to promote children's social-emotional development (Hamre, 2014). Future studies should consider the additive benefits of content-specific curricula with curricula focused on improving children's socioemotional skills.

Effective Preschool Curricula

Looking across strong evaluations of preschool curricula, we discuss a few and consider what insight they might provide regarding the nature of the relationship between targeted curricula and children's school readiness and what should be carefully thought about for future curricular interventions.

Building Blocks

The Building Blocks math curriculum is likely the most widely known study of skill-specific curricula. The reported impacts of the curriculum are substantial in some studies (Clements & Sarama, 2007, 2008; Clements et al., 2013), but null in others (Morris, Mattera & Maier, 2016). This variation is large, and many open questions remain about how successful curriculum interventions can be taken to scale to serve low-income children attending public preschool programs who stand to benefit from it the most and to whom many programs are targeted.

Building Blocks approaches children's mathematical learning as a series of research-based learning trajectories. The curriculum focuses on numeric/quantitative and geometric/spatial ideas and skills through sequenced, explicit activities. Building Blocks incorporates 30 weekly lesson plans through small group structures, computer activities, center-based learning, whole-group instruction, family letters, and teacher tracking of children's progress along the math trajectories. The intervention involved the training of the pre-K teachers in their own early math knowledge and in the curricular components, the coaching of those teachers throughout the study, the implementation of the curriculum in classrooms, the supplying of the classrooms with needed materials, and the evaluation of the classroom, teachers, and students involved.

The implementation of the Building Blocks curriculum led to large increases in mathematical knowledge of young children in several small studies (Clements & Sarama, 2007, 2008) with effect sizes ranging from 0.47 to 1.47 (Cohen's d). In the larger evaluation called the Technology-enhanced, Research-based, Instruction, Assessment, and Professional Development (TRIAD; Clements et al., 2013), consisting of 42 schools,

106 classrooms, and 1,375 preschoolers, was conducted to estimate the impact of this curricular intervention scaled up. Classrooms were initially randomized into one of three conditions. The first two conditions were either receiving the Building Blocks curriculum in pre-K or the business-as-usual curriculum (Where Bright Futures Begin or Opening the World of Learning). The third unique condition was the Building Blocks follow-through in which this group received the same pre-K intervention as the one-year-only Building Blocks condition, but also received additional Building Blocks instruction in kindergarten and first grade.

Implementation was primarily carried out through 13 professional development sessions offered to preschool teachers working in the treatment schools. These sessions emphasized both mathematical content and pedagogical strategies for teaching conceptually focused mathematics to young children. Schools assigned to the Building Blocks follow-through treatment received additional professional development for kindergarten and first grade teachers, and these sessions were designed to help early-grade teachers build on the math that children learned during the Building Blocks program in school.

Clements and colleagues found that the curriculum increased scores on the researcher-developed Research-based Elementary Math Assessment (REMA; Clements, Sarama & Liu, 2008) with an effect size of 0.72 (Hedge's *g*) and increased the quality and quantity of the mathematics environment and teaching in all treatment classrooms. Teachers achieved high levels of fidelity of implementation resulting in consistently higher scores in the intervention classes on the researcher-developed observation instrument, Classroom Observation of Early Mathematics – Environment and Teaching (COEMET; Clements & Sarama, 2007; Clements et al., 2011). Although the intervention was found to have large effects on children's math achievement at the end of pre-K, subsequent analyses found substantial fadeout of the average treatment effect after two years, especially in the absence of post-treatment instructional support (Clements et al., 2011, 2013).

Nevertheless, the treatment effect estimates of a targeted intervention such as Building Blocks suggest that a conceptually rich and intensive curriculum intervention can be brought to scale and produce impacts on the targeted content domain at the end of preschool. This could partly be explained by the intensity of the intervention for the teachers, as the intervention focused substantial effort on working with teachers to develop their understanding and effective use of all the tools of the curriculum. The intervention delivered approximately 75 hours of out-of-class teacher training as well as hours of mentoring in the classroom, which is substantially more than what is offered to most teachers in similar large-scale interventions (Borman et al., 2007). A total of 50 to 70 hours of professional development is consistent with prior research documenting what is necessary to achieve measurable effectiveness in curriculum studies? (Yoon, Duncan, Lee, Scarloss & Shapley, 2007). However, because the intervention comprised multiple components, Clements and colleagues were not able to independently determine which contributed to the reported impacts. Further, the authors were not able to disentangle the contribution of teachers' knowledge and use of the various aspects of the learning trajectories in the curriculum. Thus, whether the effectiveness of the Building Blocks curriculum comes from the considerable professional development from the treatment years is unclear. It is also unclear whether considerable professional development is necessary to achieve high-quality implementation of the curriculum. These remain topics of future research for curricula in ECE.

Given the large impacts of Building Blocks on children's outcomes, the curriculum was scaled up in New York City, but surprisingly, the preliminary impacts stand in contrast to the large effects of previously published studies of Building Blocks. Implementation of professional development and the curriculum model were reported to have been strong, and intervention teachers spent more time on math instruction, yet the intervention did not lead to stronger math skills for children at the end of the pre-K year. The evaluation reports insignificant effect sizes of 0.05 on the Early Childhood Longitudinal Study – Birth Cohort Math Assessment and 0.06 on the Woodcock–Johnson Applied Problems.

Literacy Express Preschool Curriculum

The Literacy Express Preschool Curriculum is another example of a cluster-randomized study of a skill-specific curriculum that led to moderate impacts (Lonigan, Clancy-Menchetti, Phillips, McDowell & Farver, 2005; Lonigan, Farver, Phillips, Clancy-Menchetti, 2011). In addition to concentrating on children's key literacy skills, Literacy Express also aimed to focus on teachers' professional development, both generally (i.e., key emergent literacy skills for children) and in support of the curriculum delivery and implementation. The curriculum was designed to be teacher-directed and incorporated a number of small-group activities that allowed for individualized instruction. As opposed to a highly scripted curriculum, teachers had flexibility in choosing a variety of small-group activities from the curriculum that they could then integrate into their classrooms. These small-group activities were sequenced into ten thematic units in order of the difficulty and complexity of the demands placed on children. Children also had the opportunity to engage in self-directed and self-initiated learning activities in centers and large-group activities that were also designed to support their language and literacy skills.

The Literacy Express teacher professional development was intensive, and the two treatment groups received different forms professional development. One treatment group received all of their professional development through workshops. The other group received their professional development through both workshops and weekly in-class mentoring visits by mentor teachers with a bachelor's degree or higher who were trained and supervised by the curriculum developers. These mentor teachers came once a week throughout the school year to coach the treatment classroom teacher. The control group teachers continued to use their existing curriculum, HighScope or Creative Curriculum, and they only received their usual professional development provided by their preschools.

Effect sizes for the use of the curriculum on children's outcomes ranged from 0.27 to 0.36 (Cohen's d). In classrooms where teachers received the workshops and mentoring, effect sizes ranged from 0.32 to 0.45, and for teachers who were assigned to only the workshops, effect sizes ranged from 0.20 to 0.40. The authors report that the most significant factor responsible for increases in children's early literacy skills was the curriculum itself. Compared with effect sizes for the Literacy Express impact, the effect sizes for professional development were much smaller and mostly insignificant on children's outcomes and measures of classroom quality.

A distinguishing feature in the evaluation of Literacy Express is that despite the skill-specific focus and number of teacher-directed small-group activities, treatment classrooms were rated as no more didactic in style than the control classrooms. Even more, treatment classrooms were significantly rated as more constructivist in style compared with the control classrooms. These results suggest that it is possible to have teacher-directed instructional interventions that include a higher level of focused and sequenced activities and small-group and individualized instruction while also still having content and teacher guidance that is developmentally appropriate for children. It may be the case that the intensity of Literacy Express – focus, explicitness, duration, and individualized instruction – led to these broad impacts of the curriculum. This was not studied in the evaluation, but future research should examine the intensity of the instructional activities in the curricula that are sufficient to substantially impact children's school readiness skills.

Integrated Curricular Approaches

Looking beyond individual curricula, an appealing policy approach to promoting school readiness is to integrate multiple skill-specific supplemental curricula for academic and behavioral skills and then focus on ensuring that it is implemented in classrooms as faithfully as possible. Classroom "quality" in this case is measured by the fidelity of the implementation of the curriculum. The Evidence-based Program for Integrated Curricula (EPIC) and the evaluation of the Boston Universal Pre-K Program are two examples of successful integrated curricular approaches.

Evidence-based Program for Integrated Curricula. EPIC was a comprehensive "playful learning" curriculum for children targeting math, language, literacy, and learning-related behaviors (Fantuzzo, Gadsden, McDermott, 2011) specifically for low-income children attending Head Start programs. The goal of EPIC was to systematically incorporate components of content, instruction, professional development, and repeated formative assessments within the existing expectations for delivery of Head Start services. Each of the eight curriculum units targeted a specific set of instructional objectives, resulting in intentional instruction of targeted skills that followed a developmental sequence. These instructional activities and methods were built into the daily classroom routine (e.g., large group, small group, transition time). Modules were developed to target children's positive learning-related behaviors and were integrated into the cognitive skills scope and sequence of EPIC. Curriculum-based assessments were completed by the teachers three times a year as part of routine implementation of the curriculum and were used to identify children's individual competencies and learning needs. Teachers also participated in intensive "learning communities" routinely throughout the year to share experiences and teaching strategies. This was done in different learning contexts for the teachers themselves: teaching teams, small groups, and large groups.

A rigorous experimental study of the EPIC curriculum in 70 Head Start classrooms found that it was effective, with greater impacts on math, literacy, and listening comprehension than the control curriculum. Effect sizes for these outcomes ranged from 0.17 to 0.22 (Cohen's *d*). That the EPIC curriculum produced significant, positive effects is remarkable given that the curriculum was developed in partnership with Head Start educators to meet the multiple mandates and standards for preschool programs at both the state and federal levels. This is no easy task, and many publicly-funded preschool programs may struggle to meet these requirements. In the case of curricula, some programs may decide to adopt commercially available products with little or no empirical evidence relying on the promise that it will meet all of the requirements. The EPIC evaluation calls for considering the "fit" between the curriculum intervention and the context that it would be operating within. Researchers should think carefully about the context and process variables when attempting to replicate successful curriculum interventions and bringing them to scale.

Boston Universal Pre-K Program. The highly successful Boston Universal Pre-K Program also uses an integrated approach. System leaders developed a highly scripted play-based pre-K curriculum by combining proven literacy (Opening a World of Learning) and math (Building Blocks) curricula in ways that also promoted social skills. The academic components focused on concept development, the use of multiple methods and materials to promote children's learning, and on a variety of activities to encourage analysis, reasoning and problem-solving (Weiland & Yoshikawa, 2013). Pre-K classrooms were embedded in existing public schools and taught by credentialed teachers who received extensive professional development training and ongoing coaching to ensure that they understood the curriculum and were able to implement it effectively.

A regression-discontinuity evaluation of the Boston pre-K program showed large impacts on vocabulary, math and reading at the end of the pre-K year, with effect sizes ranging from 0.45 to 0.62 standard deviations (Weiland & Yoshikawa, 2013). They also found smaller but still noteworthy impacts on two elements of executive function: working memory and inhibitory control, ranging from 0.21 to 0.28 standard deviations. The follow-up evaluation of the Boston pre-K program through elementary school is in progress. replicable at scale in child care providers outside the public school systems serving predominantly low-income children.

These integrated curriculum approaches are promising, as they allow preschool teachers to focus on improving children's readings for school across multiple domains – such as language, literacy, mathematics, and social-emotional skills. However, it is premature to view this model as the gold standard approach. The EPIC and Boston models need to be evaluated using a strong design that can track impacts on child outcomes during elementary school. Most importantly, this approach must be replicable at scale in other types of preschool settings.

Key Features of Effective Curricula

Closing the preschool achievement gap will involve promoting curricula-guided teacher practices at scale. The success of this scale-up depends greatly on providing teachers with the professional development and other supports that can help them more effectively promote early literacy, math, and social-emotional skills in the context of real-world preschool classrooms (Klein & Knitzer, 2006). Across the curricular interventions reviewed here, the amount of instruction and support preschool teachers receive for the curricula and the overall fidelity of implementation were the two common features that emerged as key ingredients for improving classrooms experiences and child outcomes in preschool. Below, we discuss these two features in greater detail.

Implementation Fidelity

Implementing a curriculum can be challenging, and programs often must train and mentor teachers to implement the chosen curriculum faithfully; however, we cannot expect that each teacher will implement a curriculum identically across classrooms (Justice, Mashburn, Hamre & Pianta, 2008). Research suggests that even with adequate organizational support and training, the quality and quantity of curriculum implementation varies widely across classrooms (Domitrovich & Greenberg, 2000; Dusenbury, Brannigan, Hansen, Walsh & Falco, 2005; Pankratz et al., 2006). Curricula packages provide supports for teachers to individualize instruction for children within a classroom, but it is unclear whether teachers use these resources and adjust their instruction accordingly.

Studies from K–12 curricular research (see O'Donnell, 2008, for a review) as well as school-based prevention programs (Greenberg, Domitrovich, Gracyk & Zins, 2005) suggest that curricula implemented without a high degree of fidelity will fail to produce the intended benefits. Researchers have recognized the importance of implementation fidelity for decades in the evaluation of interventions, yet there is surprisingly little empirical research examining issues of implementation fidelity within the ECE literature (see Clements & Sarama, 2008; Mishara & Ystgaard, 2006; Zvoch, Letourneau & Parker, 2007). By knowing the strength of an intervention as it was actually delivered researchers can better understand how varying levels of implementation can help interpret intervention effectiveness. However, implementation fidelity is largely unmeasured in ECE studies. Indeed, the PCER study (2008) did not include measures of teacher implementation fidelity in its consideration of moderators of child outcomes. This is a primary example of the field's relative inattention to fidelity as an influential component of the impacts of curricula on child outcomes.

It is possible that curricula implementation fidelity could be a moderator of child outcomes. Fidelity is one of several essential measures used to ensure that outcomes of interest could indeed be related to the delivery of a treatment. In other words, if researchers cannot confirm that essential elements of a curriculum intervention were delivered as intended, then positive outcomes cannot be attributed to the treatment.

There exist several reasons why a curriculum may not impact children's outcomes. One may be that the intervention was not being implemented to the degree that the curriculum developers originally intended. Alternatively, the lack of effects may have occurred because teachers adequately implemented a curriculum that was ineffective at increasing children's language and literacy skills. Or, it is also possible that a lack of effects could have resulted from less than ideal levels of implementation in that teachers failed to deliver the critical elements of the curriculum necessary to increase children's skills.

Measurement of implementation fidelity for curricular programs and interventions is a fruitful area for future studies as it can help researchers explain why an intervention did or did not produce the expected results. Further, there is a considerable need for more research on factors that enhance or relate to adequate implementation of curricular programs and lead to effective classroom practices and child outcomes. In most evaluation studies involving real-world classrooms, curricula implementation may fall short of what curricula designers judge to be adequate. The policy infrastructure surrounding curricular requirements would therefore also need to involve on-site assistance and/or extensive training opportunities for child care providers if proven curricula are to be effective at scale (Lieber et al., 2009).

Teacher Supports

Another aspect of curriculum effectiveness, which is also related to implementation fidelity, is the kinds of supports that can be provided to teachers. Supports such as professional development and coaching are thought to be key to educational reform (Sarama, DiBiase, Clements & Spitler, 2004), with increases in teacher professional development and in-service education linked to improvements in classroom quality and children's development (Bowman, Donovan & Burns, 2001; Neuman & Cunningham, 2009; Pianta, Barnett, Burchinal & Thorrnburg, 2009; Powell, Diamond, Burchinal & Koehler, 2010). In the evaluation of the Boston Pre-K program, researchers hypothesized that the support for teachers and use of a highly structured curriculum was central to the program's positive effects on children's school readiness skills (Weiland & Yoshikawa, 2013).

Supports for teachers may come as part of the activity prescribed by the curriculum itself, such as the use of scripting which embeds these types of instructional conversations into the activity plans. However, teacher adherence to the lesson scripts are not necessarily associated with curriculum efficacy. Therefore, curriculum developers and preschool program administrators need to attend to other ways to support teachers' use of these practices. These supports may include intensive and ongoing training for teachers so that they are familiar with the curriculum itself and the training of coaches, the general skill-specific content covered, and know how to implement it as intended. There is now ample research suggesting that such supports are amenable to change if the supports provided to teachers are fairly intensive and ongoing (Caswell & He, 2008; Dickinson & Caswell, 2007; Domitrovich et al., 2009; Landry, Swank, Smith, Assel & Gunnewig, 2006; Pence, Justice & Wiggins, 2008). For example, Kinzie and colleagues (2014) showed for the My Teaching Partner – Math/Science curriculum that students whose teachers had professional development supports showed greater mathematics achievement at the end of treatment compared with students whose teachers did not have the supports. Supports for these teachers came in the form of two monthly workshops, access to online supports for the curriculum, video-based observation and time for reflection, a one-day summer workshop, and seven 2.5-hour teacher workshops. Similarly, the Building Blocks math curriculum provided teachers with 16 hours of personalized classroom observation and coaching twice a month (Clements & Sarama, 2008). These findings suggest the importance of ongoing support and professional development to ensure that teachers implement high-quality curricula effectively. Overall, curricula may be much more beneficial to children's school readiness skills if teachers are provided adequate supports and development opportunities to fully implement the curricular activities.

Conclusion

Given the large, persistent, and consequential gaps in literacy and numeracy between high- and low-income children when they enter kindergarten, perhaps the most important policy goal of preschool and other publicly supported early childhood education programs should be to boost early achievement skills and promote the socioemotional behaviors that support these skills. Federal, state and local policy can influence the effectiveness of preschool programs by prescribing curricula. Focusing on the whole-child approach of free play and social growth is not enough. It is possible to create early learning environments for children that include more powerful skill-specific instructional curricula than are typically found in early childhood education. The large investments in curricula and supports for preschool programs makes it necessary that we get the developmental and academic content right in order to promote school readiness for our most at-risk preschoolers.

Our review of the evidence highlights that curricular supplements focused on specific school readiness skills are more successful at boosting these skills than are widely used whole-child curricula. Recent data show no advantages in improving academic skills from popular whole-child curricula such as Creative Curriculum, compared with a "usual practice" curricular approach developed by the teacher or district themselves. These results lead us to question the policy wisdom of prioritizing whole-child curricula. Both the whole-child HighScope and Creative Curriculum now offer additional intensive skill-specific segments as add-ons to the primary curriculum, but these have yet to be assessed in rigorous impact evaluations (Yoshikawa et al., 2013). While it is conceivable that some kind of effective global, whole-child curriculum will be developed, there is currently no strong evidence to support these curricula as they currently exist. In the absence of such evidence, it may be best to focus more attention on assessing and implementing proven skill-focused curricula and move away from the comparatively ineffective whole-child approach.

References

Barnett, W. S. (2011). Effectiveness of educational intervention. *Science*, 333 (6045), 975–978. DOI: 1.1126/science.1204534

Barnett, W. S., Jung, K., Yarosz, D. J. et al. (2008). Educational effects of the Tools of the Mind curriculum: a randomized trial. *Early Childhood Research Quarterly*, 23(3), 299–313.

Belfield, C. R., Nores, M., Barnett, W. S. & Schweinhart, L. J. (2006). The High/Scope Perry Preschool Program. *Journal of Human Resources*, XLI (1), 162–19.

Bierman, K. L., Domitrovich, C. E., Nix, R. L. et al. (2008). Promoting Academic and Social-Emotional School Readiness: The Head Start REDI Program. *Child Development*, 79(6), 1802–1817. DOI: 1.1111/j.1467–8624.2008.01227.x

Bierman, K. L., Nix, R. L., Heinrichs, B. S. et al. (2014). Effects of Head Start REDI on children's outcomes 1 year later in different kindergarten contexts. *Child Development*, 85(1), 140–159. DOI: 1.1111/cdev.12117

Borman, G. D., Slavin, R. E., Cheung, A. C., Chamberlain, A. A., Madden, N. A. & Chambers, B. (2007). Final reading outcomes of the national randomized field trial of Success for All. *American Educational Research Journal*, 44(3), 701–731.

Bowman, B. T., Donovan, M. S. & Burns, M. S. (Eds.) (2001). *Eager to Learn: Educating Our Preschoolers*. Washington, DC: National Academy Press.

Caswell, L. & He, Y. (2008). *Promoting Children's Early Language and Literacy Development in Contexts of Early Educational Intervention and Care: A Review of the Impact of Federally Funded Research Initiatives on Young Children's School Readiness*. Washington, DC: US Department of Health and Human Services.

Chambers, B., Cheung, A. C. & Slavin, R. E. (2016). Literacy and language outcomes of comprehensive and developmental-constructivist approaches to early childhood education: a systematic review. *Educational Research Review*, 18, 88–111.

Clements, D. H. (2007). Curriculum research: toward a framework for "research-based curricula." *Journal for Research in Mathematics Education*, 38(1), 35–70.

Clements, D. H. & Sarama, J. (2007). Effects of a preschool mathematics curriculum: summative research on the Building Blocks project. *Journal for Research in Mathematics Education*, 38(2), 136–163.

Clements, D. & Sarama, J. (2008). Experimental evaluation of the effects of a research-based preschool mathematics curriculum. *American Educational Research Journal*, 45(2), 443–494. DOI: 1.3102/0002831207312908

Clements, D. H., Sarama, J. H. & Liu, X. H. (2008). Development of a measure of early mathematics achievement using the Rasch model: the research-based early maths assessment. *Educational Psychology*, 28(4), 457–482.

Clements, D. H., Sarama, J., Spitler, M. E., Lange, A. A. & Wolfe, C. B. (2011). Mathematics learned by young children in an intervention based on learning trajectories: a large-scale cluster randomized trial. *Journal for Research in Mathematics Education*, 42(2), 127–166.

Clements, D. H., Sarama, J., Wolfe, C. B. & Spitler, M. E. (2013). Longitudinal evaluation of a scale-up model for teaching mathematics with trajectories and technologies persistence of effects in the third year. *American Educational Research Journal*, 50(4), 812–850.

Clifford, R. M., Barbarin, O. A., Chang, F. et al. (2005). What is pre-kindergarten? Characteristics of public pre-kindergarten programs. *Applied Developmental Science*, 9(3), 126–143.

Clifford, R. M. & Crawford, G. M. (Eds.). (2009). *Beginning School: US Policies in International Perspective*. New York, NY: Teachers College Press.

Copple, C. & Bredekamp, S. (2009). *Developmentally Appropriate Practice in Early Childhood Programs Service Children from Birth through Age 8* (3rd edn). Washington, DC: National Association for the Education of Young Children.

Dahlin, M. & Squires, J. H. (2016). *State Pre-K Approved Curricula*. New Brunswick, NJ: National Institute for Early Education Research, Rutgers University.

DeVries, R. & Kohlberg, L. (1987). *Programs of Early Education: The Constructivist View*: White Plains, NY: Longman.

Diamond, A., Barnett, W. S., Thomas, J. & Munro, S. (2007). Preschool program improves cognitive control. *Science*, 318(5855), 1387–1388. DOI: 1.1126/science.1151148

Dickinson, D. K. & Caswell, L. (2007). Building support for language and early literacy in preschool classrooms through in-service professional development: Effects of the Literacy Environment Enrichment Program (LEEP). *Early Childhood Research Quarterly*, 22(2), 243–260.

Domitrovich, C. E., Gest, S. D., Gill, S., Bierman, K. L., Welsh, J. A. & Jones, D. (2009). Fostering high-quality teaching with an enriched curriculum and professional development support: The Head Start REDI program. *American Educational Research Journal*, 46(2), 567–597.

Domitrovich, C. E. & Greenberg, M. T. (2000). The study of implementation: current findings from effective programs that prevent mental disorders in school-aged children. *Journal of Educational and Psychological Consultation*, 11 (2), 193–221.

Duncan, G. J. & Magnuson, K. (2013). Investing in Preschool Programs. *The Journal of Economic Perspectives*, 27(2), 109–132. DOI: 1.1257/ jep.27.2.109

Duncan, G. J. & Murnane, R. J. (Eds.), (2011). *Whither Opportunity? Rising Inequality Schools, and Children's Life Chances*, Russell Sage Foundation.

Dusenbury, L., Brannigan, R., Hansen, W. B., Walsh, J. & Falco, M. (2005). Quality of implementation: developing measures crucial to understanding the diffusion of preventive interventions. *Health Education Research*, 20(3), 308–313.

Elkind, D. (1986). Formal education and early childhood education: an essential difference. *Phi Delta Kappan*, 67(9), 631–636.

Fuligni, A. S., Howes, C., Huang, Y., Hong, S. S. & Lara-Cinisomo, S. (2012). Activity settings and daily routines in preschool classrooms: diverse experiences in early learning settings for low-income children. *Early Childhood Research Quarterly*, 27(2), 198–209.

Greenberg, M. T., Domitrovich, C. E., Graczyk, P. A. & Zins, J. E. (2005). The study of implementation in school-based preventive interventions: theory, research, and practice. *Promotion of Mental Health and Prevention of Mental and Behavioral Disorders* (Volume 3). Rockville, MD: Center for Mental Health Services, Substance Abuse and Mental Health Services Administration (DHHS).

Goffin, S. G. & Williams, C. (1994). *Curriculum Models and Early Childhood Education: Appraising the Relationship*. New York, NY: Merrill.

Hamre, B. K. (2014). Teachers' daily interactions with children: an essential ingredient in effective early childhood programs. *Child Development Perspectives*, 8(4), 223–230.

Hamre, B. K., Downer, J. T., Kilday, C. R. & McGuire, P. (2008). Effective teaching practices for early childhood mathematics. White paper prepared for the National Research Council.

Jenkins, J. M., Auger, A., Nguyen, T. & Wu, Y. (2017). Distinctions without a difference? Preschool curricula and children's development. Working paper. Irvine Network for Interventions in Development, Irvine, CA: University of California.

Jenkins, J. M. & Duncan, G. J. (2017). Do pre-kindergarten curricula matter? in Philips, D. A., Lipsey, M. W., Dodge, K. A. et al. (Eds.), *Puzzling It Out: The Current State of Scientific Knowledge on Pre-Kindergarten Effects*. Washington, DC: The Brookings Institution.

Jenkins, J. M., Duncan, G. J., Auger, A., Bitler, M., Domina, T. & Burchinal, M. (2018). Boosting School Readiness: Should Preschool Teachers Target Skills or the Whole Child? *Economics of Education Review*, 65, 107–125.

Justice, L. M., Mashburn, A. J., Hamre, B. K. & Pianta, R. C. (2008). Quality of language and literacy instruction in preschool classrooms serving at-risk pupils. *Early Childhood Research Quarterly*, 23(1), 51–68.

Justice, L. M., McGinty, A. S., Cabell, S. Q., Kilday, C. R., Knighton, K. & Huffman, G.(2010). Language and literacy curriculum supplement for preschoolers who are academically at risk: a feasibility study. *Language, Speech & Hearing Services in Schools*, 41(2), 161–178.

Karoly, L. A., Kilburn, M. R. & Cannon, J. S. (2005). *Early Childhood Interventions: Proven Results, Future Promise*. Santa Monica, CA: RAND Corporation.

Kinzie, M. B., Whittaker, J. V., Williford, A. P. et al. (2014). MyTeachingPartner-Math/Science pre-kindergarten curricula and teacher supports: associations with children's mathematics and science learning. *Early Childhood Research Quarterly*, 29(4), 586–599.

Klein, L. & Knitzer, J. (2006). *Effective Preschool Curricula and Teaching Strategies*. National Center for Children in Poverty. Retrieved from www.nccp.org/publi cations/pdf/text_668.pdf.

Landry, S. H., Swank, P. R., Smith, K. E., Assel, M. A. & Gunnewig, S. B. (2006). Enhancing early literacy skills for preschool children bringing a professional development model to scale. *Journal of Learning Disabilities*, 39 (4), 306–324.

Lieber, J., Butera, G., Hanson, M. et al. (2009). Factors that influence the implementation of a new preschool curriculum: implications for professional development. *Early Education and Development*, 20(3), 456–481.

Lonigan, C. J., Clancy-Menchetti, J., Phillips, B. M., McDowell, K. & Farver, J. M. (2005). *Literacy Express: A Preschool Curriculum*. Tallahassee, FL: Literacy Express.

Lonigan, C. J., Farver, J. M., Phillips, B. M. & Clancy-Menchetti, J. (2011). Promoting the development of preschool children's emergent literacy skills: a randomized evaluation of a literacy-focused curriculum and two professional development models. *Reading and Writing*, 24(3), 305–337.

Magnuson, K. A., Ruhm, C. & Waldfogel, J. (2007). Does prekindergarten improve schoolpreparation and performance? *Economics of Education Review*, 26(1), 33–51.

Mishara, B. L. & Ystgaard, M. (2006). Effectiveness of a mental health promotion program to improve coping skills in young children: Zippy's Friends. *Early Childhood Research Quarterly*, 21(1), 110–123.

Morris, P., Mattera, S. K., Castells, N., Bangser, M., Bierman, K. & Raver, C. (2014). Impact Findings from the Head Start CARES Demonstration: National Evaluation of Three Approaches to Improving Preschoolers' Social and Emotional Competence. Executive Summary. OPRE Report 2014–44. MDRC.

Morris, P. A., Mattera, S. K. & Maier, M. F. (2016). Making Pre-K Count: Improving Math Instruction in New York City. MDRC.

National Association for the Education of Young Children (NAEYC) and National Association of Early Childhood Specialists in State Departments of Education (NAECS/SDE). (2003). *Early childhood curriculum, assessment, and program evaluation: Building an effective, accountable system in programs for children birth through age 8.* Retrieved from www.naeyc.org/about/positions/pdf/CAPEexpand.pdf.

Neuman, S. B. & Cunningham, L. (2009). The impact of professional development and coaching on early language and literacy instructional practices. *American Educational Research Journal*, 46(2), 532–566.

Nguyen, T. (2017). Impacts of Targeted and Global Preschool Curricula on Children's School Readiness: A Meta-Analytic Review. Working paper. Irvine Network for Interventions in Development, Irvine, CA: University of California.

NSECE Project Team (National Opinion Research Center). National Survey of Early Care and Education (NSECE). (2012). ICPSR35519-v9. Ann Arbor, MI: Inter-University Consortium for Political and Social Research [distributor], September 27, 2017. https://doi.org/10.3886/ICPSR35519.v9

Pence, K. L., Justice, L. M. & Wiggins, A. K. (2008). Preschool teachers' fidelity in implementing a comprehensive language-rich curriculum. *Language, Speech, and Hearing Services in Schools*, 39(3), 329–341.

Pianta, R. C., Barnett, W. S., Burchinal, M. & Thornburg, K. R. (2009). The effects of preschool education what we know, how public policy is or is not aligned with the evidence base, and what we need to know. *Psychological Science in the Public Interest*, 10(2), 49–88.

Powell, D. R., Diamond, K. E., Burchinal, M. R. & Koehler, M. J. (2010). Effects of an early literacy professional development intervention on Head Start teachers and children. *Journal of Educational Psychology*, 102(2), 299.

O'Donnell, C. L. (2008). Defining, conceptualizing, and measuring fidelity of implementation and its relationship to outcomes in K–12 curriculum intervention research. *Review of Educational Research*, 78(1), 33–84.

Office of Head Start. (2010). Head Start Program Fact Sheet Fiscal Year 2010. Retrieved from http://eclkc.ohs.acf.hhs.gov/hslc/data/factsheets/fHeadStart Progr.htm

Pankratz, M. M., Jackson-Newsom, J., Giles, S. M., Ringwalt, C. L., Bliss, K. & Bell, M. L. (2006). Implementation fidelity in a teacher-led alcohol use prevention curriculum. *Journal of Drug Education*, 36(4), 317–333.

Preschool Curriculum Evaluation Research Consortium. (2008). *Effects of Preschool Curriculum Programs on School Readiness*. (NCER 2008–2009.) Washington, DC: National Center for Education Research, Institute for Education Sciences, US Department of Education.

Piaget, J. (1976). *Piaget's Theory*. New York, NY: Springer.

Ramey, C. T. & Ramey, S. L. (2006). Early learning and school readiness: can early intervention make a difference? in Watt, N. F., Ayoub, C., Bradley, R. H., Puma, J. E. & LeBoeuf A. (Eds.), *The Crisis in Youth Mental Health* (pp. 291–318). Westport, CT: Praeger.

Ritchie, S. & Willer, B. (2008) *Curriculum: A Guide to the NAEYC Early Childhood Program Standard and Related Accreditation Criteria*. Washington, DC: National Association for the Education of Young Children.

Sarama, J., DiBiase, A. M., Clements, D. H. & Spitler, M. E. (2004). The professional development challenge in preschool mathematics. Engaging young children in mathematics, *Standards for Early Childhood Mathematics Education*, 415–446.

Schweinhart, L. J. (2005). *Lifetime Effects: The High/Scope Perry Preschool Study through Age 40*. Ypsilanti, MI: High/Scope Educational Research Foundation.

Schweinhart, L. J. (2006). The High/Scope approach: evidence that participatory learning in early childhood contributes to human development, in Watt, N. F., Ayoub, C., Bradley, R. H., Puma, J. E. & LeBoeuf, W. A. (Eds.), *The Crisis in Youth Mental Health* (pp. 207–227). Westport, CT: Praeger.

Stipek, D., Feiler, R., Daniels, D. & Milburn, S. (1995). Effects of different instructional approaches on young children's achievement and motivation. *Child Development*, 66(1), 209–223.

US Department of Education. (2013). Early childhood education intervention report: The Creative Curriculum for Preschool, Fourth Edition. Institute of Education Sciences, What Works Clearinghouse.

Wang, A. H., Firmender, J. M., Power, J. R. & Byrnes, J. P. (2016). Understanding the program effectiveness of early mathematics interventions for prekindergarten and kindergarten environments: a meta-analytic review. *Early Education and Development*, 27(5), 692–713.

Wasik, B. A. & Hindman, A. H. (2011). Improving vocabulary and pre-literacy skills of at-risk preschoolers through teacher professional development. *Journal of Educational Psychology*, 103(2), 455–469.

Weikart, D. P. & Schweinhart, L. (1987). The High/Scope cognitively oriented curriculum in early education, in Roopnarine, J. L. & Johnson, J. E. (Eds.), *Approaches to Early Childhood Education* (pp. 253–268). New York, NY: Merill/Macmillan.

Weiland, C. & Yoshikawa, H. (2013). Impacts of a prekindergarten program on children's mathematics, language, literacy, executive function, and emotional skills. *Child Development*, 84(6), 2112–2130.

Yoon, K. S., Duncan, T., Lee, S. W. Y., Scarloss, B. & Shapley, K. L. (2007). *Reviewing the Evidence on How Teacher Professional Development Affects Student Achievement. Issues & Answers*. REL 2007-No. 033. Regional Educational Laboratory Southwest (NJ1).

Yoshikawa, H., Weiland, C., Brooks-Gunn, J. et al. (2013). *Investing in our future: The evidence base on preschool education*. New York, NY: Foundation for Child Development, Society for Research in Child Development

Zvoch, K., Letourneau, L. E. & Parker, R. P. (2007). A multilevel multisite outcomes-by-implementation evaluation of an early childhood literacy model. *American Journal of Evaluation*, 28(2), 132–15.

5   What Can We Learn from State-of-the-Art Early Childhood Education Programs?

Beth Meloy, Madelyn Gardner, Marjorie Wechsler, and David Kirp

Introduction: Learning from Effective Pre-K Programs

For the last half century, iconic programs such as Perry Preschool and the Abecedarian Project have been the calling card of early childhood interventions. Model programs like these provide important lessons – most notably that early childhood education has the potential to make a lasting impact on young children. Yet, newer programs implemented on a much larger scale and funded through public dollars are perhaps even more compelling. In recent years, well-crafted state and city early education programs have demonstrated that they, too, have the potential to produce enduring cognitive and non-cognitive benefits for children (Yoshikawa et al., 2013; Phillips et al., 2017; Duncan & Magnuson, 2013; Yoshikawa, Weiland & Brooks-Gunn, 2016; Karoly & Auger, 2016).

This chapter explores the lessons these programs can offer about how to ensure early childhood interventions lead to sustained impacts.

The substantial body of research on programs that succeed in preparing children for school, as well as professional standards for early education, identify important elements of preschool quality (Wechsler, Melnick, Maier & Bishop, 2016; NAEYC, 2017). These include:

- **A strong program structure** that facilitates opportunities to learn through sufficient time in the program, small class sizes, and low adult: child ratios.
- **Engaging and meaningful learning experiences** supported by comprehensive early learning standards and curricula and appropriate child assessments. These standards, curricula, and assessments address cognitive, social-emotional, and physical growth, are developmentally appropriate, and are effectively implemented.
- **A highly skilled and well-supported workforce**, developed through a strong teacher preparation pipeline leading to qualifications that ensure knowledge of early childhood, as well as ongoing supports for teachers, such as coaching and mentoring.

- **Comprehensive services for children and families**, including supports for healthy cognitive, social-emotional, and physical development and meaningful family engagement (Bierman & Morris, 2017).
- **Continuous quality improvement** through program assessments that consider both program structure and classroom interactions and that generate information used to hone program and teacher practices. This process of quality improvement is often supported by a quality rating and improvement system.

These research-based elements work together to help create a dynamic, engaging learning environment that supports child development. Research also suggests that investments in the years before and after preschool may be a key to sustaining the gains of effective preschool programs. Thus, in this chapter, we explore an additional element of quality:

- **An early learning continuum** from birth to third grade that builds from year to year and is developmentally appropriate for each age.

But what does it take to design and implement these elements well so that preschool programs support children's learning and healthy development and deliver benefits that last into elementary school and beyond? This chapter offers rich descriptions from proven programs to illustrate the intensity and depth of high-quality programming needed to produce meaningful benefits.

In this chapter, we draw on the experiences of six programs:

- The Child–Parent Centers
- Michigan's Great Start Readiness Program
- New Jersey's Abbott Preschool Program
- North Carolina's Smart Start and NC Pre-K programs
- Oklahoma's universal 4-year-old program
- Washington State Early Childhood Education and Assistance program

These six programs differ in their approaches to implementing high-quality preschool. The Child–Parent Centers started as an intensive pilot program that over time has been brought to scale in several urban districts. The remaining pre-K programs in Michigan, New Jersey, North Carolina, Oklahoma, and Washington operate statewide.

The programs differ, too, with regard to their size, whether they offer one year of preschool or two, and which children are eligible to attend. Oklahoma offers universal preschool – available to all 4-year-olds regardless of a child's circumstances. Each of the other programs is designed to serve children experiencing some dimension of risk. Child–Parent Centers and New Jersey's preschool program serve children living in an area of concentrated poverty regardless of their families' own income. The state pre-K programs in North Carolina, Washington, and Michigan

Table 5.1 *Overview of highlighted programs*

Program	Year Started	Annual Enrollment	Eligibility	Sustained Gains Observed
Child–Parent Centers [i]	1967	8,000 children	Targeted to 3- and 4-year-olds living in Title I school attendance areas	Participants had better performance on math and reading achievement tests in 9th grade; higher rates of high school graduation; lower rates of remedial education, child maltreatment, and juvenile arrest into adulthood than a comparison group of similar children who did not participate.
Michigan Great Start Readiness Program [ii]	1985	38,000 children	Targeted to 4-year-olds with family incomes below 250% of the federal poverty level	At end of high school, GSRP participants had lower grade retention rates and higher graduation rates than a comparison group of similar children who did not participate.
New Jersey Abbott Preschool Program [iii]	1999	43,500 children	Universal for 3- and 4-year-olds in state's lowest income districts	In fifth grade, observed gains in reading and math achievement; reductions in special education placements and grade retention.
North Carolina Smart Start and NC Pre-K [iv]	1993 (Smart Start) 2001 (NC Pre-K)	30,000 children (NC Pre-K)	NC Pre-K: Targeted to 4-year-olds in families with incomes below 75% of the state median income Smart Start: Universal access to early childhood system support for families with 0–5-year-olds	By third grade, reduced likelihood of special education placements (Smart Start and NC Pre-K combined) for children in counties with the largest investments in these services, and by third grade reduced gap in reading and math test scores between children in low-income and high-income families (NC Pre-K).

Table 5.1 (*cont.*)

Program	Year Started	Annual Enrollment	Eligibility	Sustained Gains Observed
Oklahoma's universal 4-year old program [v]	1998	41,000 children	Universal for 4-year-olds	In third grade, better performance on math achievement tests than similar children who did not attend the program.
Washington Early Childhood Education and Assistance program [vi]	1985	10,000 children	Targeted to 3- and 4-year-olds in families with incomes below 110% of the federal poverty level	Through fifth grade, better performance on reading and math achievement tests than similar children who did not attend the program.

i. Number of children estimated to be served by the Child–Parent Centers Investing in Innovation expansion when fully scaled. Reynolds, A. (2016). Gains reported from Reynolds, et al. (2011) and Reynolds, et al. (2001).
ii. Michigan's Center for Educational Performance and Information (2016). Early childhood count, all ISDs, GSRP/Head Start blend and GSRP, all ISDs (2014–15) [Data file]. Schweinhart et al. (2012).
iii. Barnett et al. (2016), Barnett et al. (2013).
iv. Unpublished data from the North Carolina Department of Health and Human Services, Division of Child Development and Early Education (personal communication, February 25, 2016). Muschkin et al. (2015); North Carolina Department of Public Instruction (2011).
v. Barnett et al. (2016), Hill et al. (2015).
vi. Washington Department of Early Learning (n.d.). ECEAP outcomes 2014–15. Retrieved from www.del.wa.gov/publications/eceap/docs/ECEAP_Outcomes_2014–15.pdf. Bania et al. (2014).

enroll children based on the circumstances of the children and their families. Despite these differences, each has substantial evidence indicating greater academic achievement that persists into elementary school, and in some cases, into high school, as well as other benefits such as less grade retention and higher graduation rates.

We selected these six programs because each has been evaluated and found to produce observable benefits for children through at least third grade. We recognize, however, that there are other many other programs that already meet this criterion or whose in-progress evaluations suggest that they will.

In presenting the myriad approaches taken by this set of diverse programs, this chapter underscores that there is no single best approach to early education. There are numerous ways to combine these elements as long as they are designed to be high quality and are implemented in a manner that creates meaningful early learning environments. The goal of this chapter is to give life to the elements of quality programs – a strong program design, engaging and meaningful learning experiences, a highly skilled and well-supported workforce, comprehensive services for children and families, continuous quality improvement, and an early learning continuum – and inspire policymakers and practitioners to implement these elements in a way that works for the children and families they serve.

A Strong Program Structure

Effective preschool programs have basic structural elements including small class sizes and low adult:child ratios that facilitate supportive and engaging learning experiences (Wechsler, Melnick, Maier & Bishop, 2016). Having fewer students and more staff in a classroom creates opportunities for engaging interactions between teachers and children. Although there is little research on the optimal number of children and teachers in a classroom, early childhood professional standards such as those used to determine national accreditation (NAEYC, 2017) suggest that preschool programs should limit class sizes to 20 children with an adult:child ratio of 1:10 (Barnett, Schulman & Shore, 2004).

Further, many successful programs ensure children have enough learning time by offering full-day, year-round or multi-year preschool. Research shows that more daily instructional time can yield bigger benefits for children (Wasik & Snell, 2015). While some programs that offer relatively less instructional time have shown strong results (e.g., the state preschool programs in Washington and Michigan), most highly effective programs provide extended preschool schedules. Oklahoma's universal

4-year-old program and New Jersey's Abbott Preschool program provide illustrations of these decisions in practice.

Oklahoma's Universal 4-Year-Old Program   Through Oklahoma's universal 4-year-old program, the state offers a year of pre-K to any age-eligible child, regardless of family income.[1] Though the program only requires participating schools to offer a half day of preschool (2.5 hours), many choose to offer school-day programs (6 hours). In some cases, districts also work with local partners to arrange extended-day care to meet the need of working parents (Barnett et al., 2016). As a result, most pre-K participants (84 percent) attend a full-day program. Regardless of the length of the program day, state pre-K programs run for 5 days a week during the school year. As in other states with effective programs, Oklahoma requires pre-K classrooms to adhere to class sizes and ratios established by professional standards (NAEYC, 2017): classes are limited to 20 children, with an adult:child ratio of 1:10 (Barnett et al., 2016).

New Jersey's Abbott Preschool Program   New Jersey's Abbott Preschool program offers two years of voluntary preschool to young children living in the state's poorest school districts. In these districts, all 3- and 4-year-old children are eligible to attend full-day pre-K, which meets at least 6 hours per day, during the school year. Some children also receive wraparound care that extends services to up to 10 hours per day – enough to cover full-time parent work schedules – throughout the calendar year (Barnett, Jung, Youn & Frede, 2013). The pre-K program also adheres to other structural standards associated with successful programs. Class sizes are capped at 15 children and each class is taught by a certified teacher and assistant, a ratio that exceeds the guidelines set by professional standards (Wechsler, Melnick, Maier & Bishop, 2016). These basic structural elements create a foundation for other program elements, including comprehensive curricula and extensive teacher supports, to construct quality learning experiences for children.

Engaging and Meaningful Learning Experiences

Providing preschool children with rich and engaging learning experiences requires intentional instruction guided by explicit expectations for what children should know and be able to do by the end of the program. In many cases these expectations are outlined in state- or program-wide

---

[1] All but three of Oklahoma's 516 school districts offer pre-K for 4-year-olds (Barnett et al., 2016).

early learning standards, the best of which reflect the comprehensive body of research that describes how children learn. They set expectations linked to school success, acknowledge that children's developmental trajectories vary from skill to skill, and provide teachers with adequate information to support every child's progress wherever their skills fall (Wechsler, Melnick, Maier & Bishop, 2016).

The implementation of a developmentally appropriate curriculum is also critical to supporting young children's learning. These curricula emphasize guided learning opportunities that are language-rich and hands-on and that combine teacher-directed and child-initiated activities. Most are play-based, with activities designed to leverage children's natural curiosity, since research shows that students who initiate activities or engage in play and exploration to satisfy their own questions are better able to master skills (Yoshikawa et al., 2013). Programs may rely on a single comprehensive curriculum or combine curricula to ensure teachers have the instructional scaffolding they need to support child progress in every developmental domain.

Relatedly, well-planned and effective child assessments allow teachers to track children's social-emotional, academic, and physical development by collecting observational data on a range of skills (Landry, Anthony, Swank & Montesque-Bailey, 2009; Snow, Van Hemel & The Committee on Developmental Outcomes and Assessments for Young Children, 2008). For example, a teacher might note whether a child seeks out playmates in the classroom as an indicator of social-emotional skills, or observe a child attempting hopscotch for evidence of physical development. Teachers can then use these data to plan instruction tailored to students' strengths and needs and ensure all students are mastering the skills that will prepare them to succeed in school. The Michigan Great Start Readiness Program (GSRP) offers a particularly strong example of aligned standards, curricula, and assessments in action.

Michigan Great Start Readiness Program   Michigan's Great Start Readiness Program fosters program quality through clear, integrated standards, and expectations for learning. The program, which is targeted to low-income preschoolers and those with other risk factors, requires the use of aligned curricula and formative assessments to ensure instruction scaffolds child progress toward established standards, intentionally guiding children through progressively more challenging lessons to build their conceptual understanding.

Michigan was at the forefront of setting learning standards for early education. In 1971, Michigan's State Board of Education approved "Preprimary Objectives" to describe the learning and development expected for preschool- and kindergarten-age children in the affective, psychomotor, and cognitive domains, and which were first used to help identify children with special needs. Attention to the importance of standards has continued over the years (Wechsler et al., 2016). The most recent iteration of these early learning standards was approved in 2013 and establishes early learning expectations for 3- and 4-year-old children in nine domains of development, including language and literacy, math, science, and social-emotional and physical health. Michigan's early learning standards guide teachers by describing indicators of progress toward each expectation and providing teaching strategies to ensure the classroom environment, teacher–child interactions, and learning experiences all support that progress (Michigan State Board of Education, 2005).

For example, one expectation specified in the social, emotional, and physical development domain of Michigan's early learning standards is that "children develop and exhibit a healthy sense of self." The standards provide several indicators for understanding whether children meet this expectation such as children "demonstrate growing confidence in expressing their feelings, needs and opinions." Finally, the early learning standards suggest that programs provide "an environment where [children] feel safe expressing their feelings" and that teachers "model sensitivity, sincerity and empathy with children and other adults" to support children in meeting the expectation (Michigan State Board of Education, 2005).

To guide programs in curriculum selection, the Michigan Department of Education provides a list of curricula which are research-based, align with the state's early learning standards, and provide a sequence of play-centered activities that support children's development across a comprehensive range of developmental domains. By means of these curricula, children learn through hands-on explorations (e.g., at sensory tables or in outdoor play spaces) rather than by listening to a teacher explain ideas. The state further assists programs in selecting a curriculum by providing a set of guiding questions about the curriculum's scope and sequence, materials, learning experiences, and activities, such as:

- Are elements of the curriculum clearly based on research about the development of young children? Has research demonstrated the effectiveness of the curriculum model in improving outcomes or results for children?
- Are both scope and sequence included in the design? Is there evidence that the curriculum is tied to children's developmental progress?
- Does the daily routine support a balance between adult-initiated and child-initiated activities? Does the curriculum encourage teachers to

plan topics of investigation based on the interests of the children? (Michigan Department of Education, n.d.).

The Michigan Department of Education also emphasizes the importance of child assessment for informing instruction in preschool classrooms. State preschool programs use an ongoing observational assessment in the classroom that asks teachers to observe children's learning and behavior over the course of the year and document their progress toward specific learning goals aligned with the state's early learning standards (Michigan State Board of Education, 2005). For example, a teacher might observe a child who drew a picture of his family and then told a story about the picture, and document her reflections on the interaction using the assessment. This process of observation and documentation helps teachers see the connections between the activity and the many skills that children need to develop – from the fine motor skills associated with drawing a picture to the language and social emotional skills associated with telling a story. Systematically tracking children's progress in this way enables teachers to adjust classroom instruction and programs to fine-tune design and implementation throughout the year to improve children's outcomes.

A Highly Skilled and Well-Supported Workforce

Investing in educators is critical to building an effective early learning program. Strong program features – from the physical space to the curriculum – only matter if teachers know how to engage young learners and support their development using those tools. Studies have found that it is important for teachers to have knowledge about child development and instruction for young children, including knowledge that is specific to the age group they will teach (Bueno, Darling-Hammond & Gonzales, 2008). A strong teacher preparation pipeline can help ensure a sufficient supply of qualified teachers; adequate compensation and/or salary supplements for early learning providers also can help attract high-quality candidates. Efforts in Oklahoma and North Carolina illustrate how to build a highly skilled workforce.

Strong early education systems also support teachers throughout their career by providing coaching and mentoring. While research has yet to uncover the precise formula for successful coaching, direct observation paired with individualized feedback from a mentor has been linked to improved student–teacher interactions, less teacher burnout, and increased teacher retention (Aikens & Akers, 2011; Boller et al., 2010). Coaching and mentorship programs are integral to many programs that show strong results, and in New Jersey, a focus on building a personnel system through observation, feedback, and discussion has been key to supporting highly qualified and knowledgeable educators.

Oklahoma's Universal 4-Year-Old Program   Oklahoma has long been a pioneer in state-supported early learning efforts and has developed a reputation for excellence in publicly funded pre-kindergarten. Part of the state's success is due to its high-quality work-force, fostered by a requirement that lead teachers have a bachelor's degree with certification in early childhood. Prospective preschool tea-chers can meet this requirement by completing a teacher education program at one of 20 approved Oklahoma colleges and universities and then passing two certification examinations through the Oklahoma Commission for Teacher Preparation: the Oklahoma Professional Teaching Examination (PK–8): Early Childhood and the Oklahoma Subject Area Test: Early Childhood Education (Oklahoma State Department of Education, n.d.). This requirement reflects a strong com-mitment to ensuring all preschool teachers have the knowledge and skills to provide individualized learning experiences that are developmentally appropriate for each child.

High standards for lead preschool teachers are paired with teacher compensation that is commensurate with K–12 teachers. Nationwide, K–12 compensation parity for preschool teachers is far from the norm. In fact, the median salary for preschool teachers is approximately half that of kindergarten and elementary school teachers, and between 2009 and 2013, 34 percent of pre-K teachers relied on public assistance to meet the needs of their own families (Whitebook, McLean & Austin, 2016). Oklahoma preschool teachers are paid comparatively better. In Tulsa, one of the state's largest cities, first-year pre-K teachers with bachelor's degrees earned $32,900 in 2016, and those with the most experience earned $47,630. That same year, the national average salary for preschool teachers was a mere $27,130 (US Bureau of Labor Statistics, 2016).

Pay parity in Oklahoma is funded by the permanent inclusion of pre-K in the state's school aid formula. In other words, districts receive state funding for each 4-year-old attending preschool, just as they do for each student in kindergarten through twelfth grade, and these funds allow for higher teacher salaries. Increasing teacher compensation in concert with strong qualifications has allowed Oklahoma to build a more stable, highly qualified early childhood workforce to support an effective early child-hood program.

North Carolina's NC Pre-KProgram[2]   Even before the inception of the NC Pre-K program, North Carolina had begun to invest substantial resources into building its early childhood workforce through two nationally recognized programs that offered higher education scholarships and wage subsidies to early childhood educators. As a result, North Carolina was poised to set high standards for teachers in its pre-K program – a bachelor's degree and a birth-through-kindergarten teaching license. This license qualifies early educators to teach in preschool or kindergarten classrooms, and requires the same amount of training as any other K–12 teaching license in the state. For North Carolina, the key to implementing this ambitious requirement lay in pairing financial supports and training opportunities with flexibility in the timeline for teachers to obtain the requisite degrees.

For the first decade of the NC Pre-K program, lead teachers were allowed to work on a bachelor's degree and birth-through-kindergarten licensure while remaining in the classroom. The gradual rollout of qualification requirements for NC Pre-K teachers was supported by investments in the Teacher Education And Compensation Helps (T.E.A.C.H.) program. T.E.A.C.H. provides scholarships to help early care professionals pursue degrees in early childhood education (T.E.A.C.H. Early Childhood® North Carolina Scholarship Program, n.d.). Articulation agreements among North Carolina universities enable educators who already hold an associate's degree in early childhood education to transfer those credits toward the first two years of coursework for a bachelor's degree in the same field.

There are also scholarships available for teachers working to acquire the specialized birth-through-kindergarten teaching license. All teachers who hold a birth-through-kindergarten license receive mentoring and evaluation on a regular basis, with especially intensive support during their first three years in the classroom. Teachers at public school sites receive support from their local school district, while teachers at private child care and Head Start sites receive support directly from the state.

To further incentivize continued education and address compensation, each educator who completes a T.E.A.C.H.-sponsored program receives a predetermined raise or bonus paid for by his or her employer. In return, participants agree to stay at their current jobs or in the early care field for six months to a year, depending on the scholarship program.

New Jersey's Abbott Preschool Program   New Jersey's Abbott preschool program has focused on developing an effective personnel system – one that supports teachers and leaders for the benefit of pre-K

---

[2] *Adapted from Wechsler et al., 2016*

students. In designing the program, state administrators recognized that a high-quality system is supported by leaders who are expert in early care and education and professional development and who use data to inform decisions within a continuous improvement cycle. The state invested in the development of administrator capacity from the start. Initially, the early learning expertise of newly appointed supervisors and coaches across the districts ranged from none (e.g., former high school assistant principals) to long-time early childhood professionals (e.g., former Head Start education directors). To support the development of preschool leaders, the New Jersey Department of Education held monthly early childhood supervisor meetings to discuss new initiatives and share in problem-solving. These informal professional learning communities encouraged leaders to learn from each other (Frede, 2016).

The New Jersey Department of Education also offers intensive professional development opportunities that ensure teachers can measure child progress toward desired outcomes and implement curricula to support that progress. Coaching is an integral aspect of the state's professional development system for early educators. Coaches in Abbott preschool classrooms must have a bachelor's degree and teacher certification; at least three years of experience teaching in preschool programs; and experience providing professional development, implementing developmentally-appropriate curricula, and using performance-based assessments. Coaches have a maximum caseload of 20 preschool classrooms to allow them to visit classrooms on a regular basis to observe and provide feedback to teachers. Their responsibilities range from administering classroom evaluations to providing individualized follow-up support that reflects each teacher's level of development. Program quality assessments at the classroom level direct the focus of coaching for each teacher by identifying areas in need of improvement. Coaches also plan small group meetings for teachers who demonstrate similar needs to discuss challenges and identify strategies to improve (New Jersey Department of Education, 2015).

Well-Supported Teachers in an Abbott Preschool Classroom

Classrooms at the Eugenio Maria de Hostos Center for Early Childhood Education in Union City, New Jersey, offer a window into the benefits of the state's investments. Art plasters the walls, plants hang from the ceiling, and materials stowed in every nook seize a child's imagination. At any given time, small groups of 3- and 4-year-olds may be found designing paper clothing, while others are painting, giving their pictures titles in a mix of English and

Spanish. Children peer at insects through a microscope and explain what they see, while others listen as the teacher's aide reads a book aloud in the poet's corner, or pretend to do each other's hair in the "beauty salon." As children play, the teacher circulates, engaging in dozens of mini-lessons as she converses with groups solving puzzles, examining insects, and building cardboard chairs.

Few of the teachers in Union City have glittering resumes, but they receive many supports from the school system, including coaching by master instructors, time to share classroom successes and failures with other teachers, and frequent evaluations coupled with detailed, what-to-do-in-the-future feedback. What's happening in all of Union City's preschools is essentially the same – high quality preschool experiences are supported by a sizeable infusion of pre-K dollars and paired with an understanding that in order to make preschool not just a place for play, but a center for learning, teachers are key.

Adapted from Kirp, D. (2012). Kids first: Five big ideas for transforming children's lives and America's future. Public Affairs.

Like other efforts to support the workforce among successful programs, the New Jersey professional development system was not established quickly; instead, it was developed steadily with consistent attention to improvement. The lasting benefits for the children who participate are proof that it was worth the effort.

Comprehensive Services for Children and Families

High-quality early education programs strive to address the needs of both the children and the families they serve. Providing robust wrap-around services to meet the comprehensive needs of children and families is a strategy pioneered by Head Start, the federal preschool program for low-income children. This comprehensive approach is particularly important because many publicly-funded preschool programs target vulnerable children who may not otherwise have access to the services they need. (Yoshikawa et al., 2013; Barnett, 2010). For example, in addition to providing activities that stimulate children's development in language, literacy, and math, programs might offer meals and health check-ups so that children's more basic needs are met and they are ready to learn.

Effective programs also foster strong linkages between home, school, and community – a process known as family engagement (Wechsler, Melnick, Maier & Bishop, 2016). Effective family engagement strategies acknowledge the role that parents play as their children's first teachers and celebrate the cultures of all families. Programs may encourage frequent parent visits to school, provide home visits to build relationships between parents and teachers, or offer parent classes to support parenting skills and knowledge of child development. Teachers and other staff in strong family engagement programs often work collaboratively with families to set goals not just for children but for parents, too – such as getting a GED or completing college coursework – and then offer referrals or provide direct services to achieve those goals. (Henderson & Mapp, 2002; Halgunseth, Peterson, Stark & Moodie, 2009). Strong program–family partnerships – characterized by trust, shared values, ongoing communication, mutual respect, and attention to children's well-being (Caspe & Lopez, 2006) – have been linked to greater academic motivation, grade promotion, and social-emotional skills among young children, including those from diverse ethnic and socioeconomic backgrounds (Christenson, 2000; Mantzicopoulos, 2003; McWayne, Hampton, Fantuzzo, Cohen & Sekino, 2004). Each of the programs in this chapter provides some degree of support services for children and families, but Washington's state pre-K program and the Child–Parent Centers offer particularly intensive illustrations of this element.

Washington Early Childhood Education and Assistance Program[3]   A defining feature of Washington's state preschool program is that it was designed to address the multifaceted needs of the children it serves, rather than focusing singularly on academic readiness for school. To meet children's needs, Washington's pre-K, like Head Start, provides access to comprehensive health, nutrition, and family support services, in addition to preschool education. The program serves children in families with incomes below 110 percent of the federal poverty level – among the most economically disadvantaged families in the state.

Extensive wraparound services have been integral to the program since its inception. Through the program, health advocates provide both well-child and dental exams for children, sometimes in the classroom, and connect them to medical and dental providers for follow-up and ongoing care. In this way, the program serves as a gateway to medical services for families, many of whom previously lacked access. These services are critical for early prevention. For example, some treatable hearing or vision challenges can cause permanent damage if not diagnosed and addressed, and may also inhibit children's ability to meaningfully engage in classroom activities.

The program also serves as a bridge to other community resources that are available outside of the normal instructional day, such as referrals for housing or legal services. Similarly, if a parent wants to advance professionally, the state pre-K program may help them find a relevant education

---

[3] *Adapted from Wechsler, Melnick, Maier & Bishop, 2016*

or training program. To support this menu of services, each state pre-K site is staffed with both a health advocate and a family support worker. Nutrition and mental health consultants are also on hand to advise staff and parents about children's specific needs.

The state pre-K program is also designed to promote ongoing family engagement and support. Teachers meet with families to discuss their child's development and school readiness at least three times throughout the year. Together, teachers and families set goals, discuss progress toward meeting those goals, and identify community resources to support reaching them. Many programs run parent education classes, too, on topics like child development or advocacy skills. End of year surveys suggest that these services make families more familiar with community resources and strategies to support their child behaviorally and academically and ensure that parents feel like full partners in the education of their children.

Child–Parent Centers   As the name suggests, the Child–Parent Center model acknowledges family members as key partners in supporting each child's learning, development, and readiness for school. Parent involvement is one of the primary goals of the Child–Parent Center program. The program's approach to parental involvement also prioritizes strong school–community connections and support for parents' educational, career, and personal development (Hayakawa & Reynolds, 2016).

Every Child–Parent Center site offers an extensive, menu-based program of activities designed specifically for these purposes. In addition to encouraging parents to visit or volunteer in their child's classroom regularly, programs recommend parents be involved at home through activities such as reading, cooking, or play (Reynolds, Hayakawa, Candee & Englund, 2016). Every center has a parent resource room where parents can socialize with each other, meet with program staff, or attend parent classes that cover topics ranging from GED preparation and sewing to child nutrition and strategies for reading to children (Kirp, 2007). Parent involvement activities are offered at various times of the day and week to facilitate parent participation. Ongoing communication through home visits, phone calls, calendars, and newsletters helps inform families of these opportunities and offers another forum for strengthening school–family connections (Reynolds, Hayakawa, Candee & Englund, 2016).

To support this intensive family engagement, each Child–Parent Center has a team of staff dedicated specifically to the task. Each pre-K site has a parent resource teacher who leads the effort to get to know families through one-on-one meetings and needs assessments and designs programming to support parent involvement at school and at home. Each pre-K site also has a school–community representative that focuses on reinforcing broader school–community connections, in addition to supporting the implementation of parent involvement activities. These representatives lead outreach and enrollment efforts, troubleshoot barriers to school attendance, and help connect children and families in need of health services or other supports to community service agencies. As with other components of the Child–Parent Center model, this commitment to educational collaboration with families extends beyond preschool into the early elementary years; elementary schools attended by Child–Parent Center participants have a liaison whose role is similar to that of a parent resource teacher (Reynolds, Hayakawa, Candee & Englund, 2016).

Investing in families is an essential part of the Child–Parent Center program. The depth of this investment, exemplified by the program's commitment of substantial staff time and resources, reflects the model's philosophy that parent involvement and family stability is crucial for creating a positive learning environment for children.

Continuous Quality Improvement

High-quality early learning programs can be developed and sustained when they are part of systems that assess the quality of care they offer, incentivize providers to improve the quality, and support providers in their improvement efforts. In recent years, many states have adopted quality rating and improvement systems (QRISs) to accomplish these goals.

QRIS frameworks identify elements of quality on which programs are assessed and establish tiers or levels that identify progressively higher benchmarks. Traditionally, the elements of quality in a QRIS include class sizes and adult:child ratios, teacher qualifications and the amount of professional development teachers receive, and the use of an evidence-based curriculum and assessment system. Responding to recent research on the importance of teaching practices that support meaningful learning experiences (Mashburn et al., 2008), many states have incorporated measures of the learning environment and teacher–child interactions. For instance, some QRIS frameworks include direct observations of instructional quality or the emotional climate of the classroom, since these measures are directly linked to child outcomes.

How programs ascend in a QRIS framework depends upon how a state assigns ratings. In some states, achieving a higher tier of quality requires programs to meet a higher standard across every element in the framework. Other states award points for a program's performance on each quality benchmark and sum the total to assign a quality rating. Often, states use licensing standards as the lowest tier or minimum benchmark to receive points (US Department of Health and Human Services, n.d.).

QRISs further establish an infrastructure for supporting and incentiviz-ing program quality improvement. That support can take the form of technical assistance, such as on-site coaching; financial incentives for programs that hire better trained teachers; or workforce supports, like scholarships and wage subsidies for teachers who pursue advanced degrees (The Build Initiative & Child Trends, 2016). Finally, QRISs disseminate information about program quality, which parents can use to choose programs with higher quality ratings. In this way, public ratings encourage a constant feedback loop that further incentivizes programs to continue to improve.

Michigan and North Carolina have both invested significant resources into QRIS implementation to ensure high quality and continuous improvement across their preschool programs.

Michigan's Great Start to Quality   In 2011, Michigan developed the Great Start to Quality program, a five-star QRIS for all programs in the state's early care and education system. While participation for most providers is voluntary, Michigan requires programs to maintain a three-star rating or higher to be eligible for state preschool funding.

All programs that participate in the QRIS must complete an online self-assessment that asks about their program design and implementation in five areas: family and community partnerships, administration and man-agement, environment, curriculum and instruction, and staff qualifica-tions and professional development. The survey collects information on more than 40 different program quality indicators across the five cate-gories. Michigan's QRIS assigns ratings based on points, so there is no one set of features that defines programs of a certain star level. Instead, programs earn credit for various elements and the cumulative number of points earned out of 50 determines their ratings. This system offers programs multiple ways to raise their ratings. For example, under envir-onment, programs can earn two points for operating in a space free of environmental risks, or two points for having smaller groups and better adult:child ratios than required by licensing. Programs that do both can earn all four points (Great Start to Quality, 2016).

An assessment specialist validates the self-assessment surveys for a random selection of all programs, as well as all programs that rate themselves as four- or five-star. Programs that receive a validated four- or five-star rating are also directly observed by an approved rater to assess the environment and the quality of teacher–child interactions. The on-site assessments are specific to the type of care the program provides with separate assessment tools for center-based infant and toddler care, center-based preschool care, and family child care. These on-site assessments are unannounced and involve a 3- to 6-hour observation period, depending on program length (Great Start to Quality, 2017). The information from these assessments is used to assign either a four- or a five-star rating to each program.

In addition to clearly defined quality criteria and a process for monitoring programs, Michigan's QRIS offers a variety of benefits to participating providers that incentivize and support quality improvement. Specifically, participants have access to support in four areas: a lending library of materials and guidance, professional development and training, financial assistance, and coaching and consultation services. The type and intensity of support available in each of these areas depends upon the star rating of the program and other eligibility criteria, such as accepting state funds for preschool or childcare. For example, participating providers that care for children receiving child care assistance from the state are eligible for higher reimbursement rates, tiered according to the star rating they receive (Great Start to Quality, 2017).

For Michigan's state preschool providers, the coaching and consultation services they receive through the state's QRIS have been especially important for quality improvement. All state preschool programs work with an early childhood specialist, who leads the teaching teams and supports continuous improvement efforts. These specialists have graduate degrees in early childhood education or child development and at least five years of relevant job experience. The early childhood specialist provides curriculum training and visits classrooms on a monthly basis to support and mentor teaching teams.

At the beginning of the school year, the early childhood specialist conducts a baseline quality assessment and then coaches teachers on areas that need improvement, such as adult–child interactions, learning environment, daily routine, curriculum planning and assessment, and parent involvement. Three times during the school year, the early childhood specialist runs data analysis team meetings where the participants discuss challenges identified through the data and the early childhood specialist provides teaching teams with strategies for improvement. For example, teachers struggling with classroom management might be given strategies for addressing – and then preventing – challenging behaviors in the classroom. Finally, the early childhood specialist conducts a follow-up assessment in the spring and submits those data to the state (adapted from Wechsler et al., 2016).

Through this integrated system of standards, assessment, and support, Michigan's QRIS contributes to high-quality preschool statewide.

North Carolina's Star-Rated License System
North Carolina's Star-Rated License system – in operation since 1999 – is one of the oldest QRISs in the nation. Recent research has confirmed a link between the implementation of the North Carolina QRIS and the quality of care provided in early childhood programs across the state (Bassok, Dee & Latham, 2017). In North Carolina, QRIS participation is mandatory for all licensed programs, including child care, state-funded preschool, and Head Start (Johnson-Staub, 2011). A rating of one star means that a program meets North Carolina's minimum licensing standards for child care. Programs that meet higher standards can apply for a two- to five-star license.

North Carolina's QRIS rates quality in two key areas: program standards and staff education. To determine their quality ratings, programs are awarded one to 15 points in each of these two areas based upon the quality indicators they meet. Programs can also earn a bonus "quality point" for exceeding the highest standard in any given category.

Program standards include structural factors such as adult:child ratio and sufficient space for activities, as well as metrics associated with children's classroom experiences, such as the quality of the learning environment and teacher–child interactions. For example, classrooms that offer a variety of learning centers, ranging from dramatic play props to art materials, musical instruments to sand tables, earn more points than classrooms without them (adapted from Wechsler, et al., 2016). Likewise, teachers in high-scoring classrooms encourage communication and use language to support children's conceptual development.[4]

The QRIS awards staff education points based on the proportion of lead teachers with certain levels of qualifications, with different requirements for center-based and home-based programs. For example, the QRIS requires that programs achieve the following in order to award its highest score for staff qualifications:

- The administrator has the top-level NC Administration Credential or equivalent;
- 75% of lead teachers have at least an associate's degree in early childhood;

---

[4] See http://ers.fpg.unc.edu/c-overview-subscales-and-items-ecers-r for an overview of the subscales and items of the ECERS-R rating scale, and www.nj.gov/education/ece/check ups/checklist.pdf for a more detailed ECERS-R classroom quality checklist.

- 50% of teachers have completed their NC Early Childhood Credential or equivalent, and have additional coursework; and
- school-age staff have completed school-age coursework, Basic School Age Training, and have experience working with school-age children.

NC Pre-K classrooms all reach this benchmark because other state regulations require them to meet even higher standards: state preschool lead teachers must have a BA degree and birth-through-kindergarten teaching license.

North Carolina's QRIS ties its star ratings to clear financial incentives, especially for providers that receive state funds to care for low-income children. For example, after a six-month grace period, providers who receive state child care subsidies must maintain at least a three-star license and state preschool providers must maintain a four- or five-star license to receive State funds. Further, the QRIS allows the state to reimburse higher quality centers at a higher rate. As of 2016, a five-star child care center in Mecklenburg County receives a 63 percent higher reimbursement rate than a provider offering one-star care in the same community (North Carolina Department of Health and Human Services, Division of Child Care and Early Education, 2016). This higher rate helps to offset the cost of paying better-educated teachers or purchasing additional classroom materials.

Finally, North Carolina has invested in communicating quality information to parents and boosting parent understanding of the importance of high-quality care. In addition to an online portal that allows parents to access information about a program's star rating, North Carolina has launched several statewide public information campaigns. These parent education efforts give child care providers an added incentive to pursue a higher star rating.

A Five-Star Classroom

Brown's Early Learning School in Durham offers child care and NC Pre-K in a five-star rated center. With one class of 18 children and three teachers, Brown's maintains an exceptionally low adult:child ratio that allows for ample attention to each student. The classroom itself offers an array of language-rich and hands-on activities, and children get to choose how to spend their hands-on learning time. At the water table, budding scientists can see whether objects float or sink, while in another part of the room a teacher helps children label drawings about their homes and families for a class book. A small desk in the corner holds three little pig figurines. The class recently read the classic fairy tale, and now, students can quietly practice retelling the story on their own, using the pigs as props. Teachers circulate between all the centers, asking questions and introducing new vocabulary. Soon it is circle time. As a soothing song plays, students begin to put their activities away and wander over to the carpet. They move at different rates, but they all know where they are going and what they need to do by the end of the song. The teachers have established a clear routine to transition from one activity to another, and have left ample time for students to prepare for the next activity. As the students settle on the carpet, they are ready to continue learning.

Adapted from Wechsler, M., Kirp, D., Ali, T. T. et al. (2016). The Road to High-Quality Early Learning: Lessons from the States. *Palo Alto, CA: Learning Policy Institute.*

State administrators continue to push for improvements in the QRIS. As more child care centers (approximately 65 percent) are rated as four- or five-star programs, officials have recognized that there remains significant variation in quality among programs with the same rating, and that many providers at the top end of the system are ready for a greater challenge. If proposed changes are implemented, the new NC QRIS will improve consistency within the rating levels and place a greater emphasis on measuring the quality of teacher–child interactions (Wechsler et al., 2016).

An Early Learning Continuum

Building an aligned continuum of early learning opportunities from birth into the early elementary grades is key to creating lasting gains for children. Neuroscience research has demonstrated that very young children are rapidly developing key brain infrastructure (Harvard University Center on the Developing Child, n.d.) and interventions that affect children earlier than preschool are effective in supporting school readiness, child and maternal health, and positive parenting, among other outcomes (Shonkoff, Phillips & Educational Resources Information Center, 2000). Further, it is unreasonable to expect that children who attend high-quality preschool but then matriculate to under-resourced and often economically or racially segregated elementary schools, will continue to outperform their peers. Rather, recent evidence suggests that additional investments in elementary school can help sustain gains from preschool (Johnson & Jackson, 2017).

Supporting children and families during the first three years of life, through services such as paid parental leave, home visiting or quality child care, is the first step in the continuum. An aligned continuum also includes children's transitions between preschool and elementary school. Kindergarten teachers can visit preschool classrooms to meet future students and discuss developmental progress with pre-K teachers. This collaboration among teachers keeps children on a forward trajectory of learning. Pre-K and elementary school teachers who have joint professional development or meet to plan curricula can ensure that children leaving pre-K have the skills they need to succeed in elementary school and avoid duplication of content when children have already mastered important skills. Aligning standards and curricula across the early years ensures that expectations and content build on each other from one grade to the next without redundancy. This process supports a shared sense of what children should learn and when, and increases student engagement by providing students with the appropriate level of challenge and support.

The Child–Parent Centers and North Carolina's state early learning initiatives are relatively mature programs that illustrate a focus on building an early learning continuum.

North Carolina NC Pre-K and Smart Start (Adapted from Wechsler et al., 2016)   From the start, North Carolina invested in the birth-to-age-5 continuum – predating state pre-K by nearly a decade. In 1993, the state developed Smart Start, a network of 75 nonprofit agencies offering local service coordination for families and children from birth to age 5 in each of North Carolina's 100 counties. Smart Start agencies provide administrative oversight and strategic planning that bring each county's early childhood services together into a more central, accessible system to better and more efficiently meet the needs of families with young children. Investing in this birth-to-5 strategy has benefited children and communities in North Carolina. Evaluations of the ongoing work of Smart Start, both on its own and in combination with NC Pre-K, have documented positive impacts on child care quality, children's receipt of health services, and special education placement by third grade (Frank Porter Graham Child Development Institute, Smart Start Evaluation Team, 2003; Muschkin, Ladd & Dodge, 2015).

Decisions about how to invest Smart Start dollars are made largely at the local level by a partnership that includes parents, school district representatives, child care workers, and non-profit staff, among others. Depending on local priorities, Smart Start may support everything from subsidies for early educator wages, parenting classes and home visiting programs to the distribution of free books at well-child check-ups or book lending programs in pre-K classrooms. Though Smart Start programs commonly offer services that target at-risk children and families, such as partnering with Medicaid providers to offer developmental and health screenings, they also provide services that benefit the broader community, such as providing coaching for child care providers to improve the quality of care.

The development of the Smart Start initiative paved the way for NC Pre-K eight years later. In each of the state's counties, Smart Start partnerships play a crucial role in administering the pre-K program, either directly or through supplemental funding. Because the two initiatives represent complementary investments in the first five years of life, North Carolina has relatively strong alignment between birth-to-age-3 services and preschool.

Child–Parent Centers

Since its inception in 1967, the Child–Parent Center model has provided a preschool through third grade approach to early learning. To facilitate continuity and smooth student transitions throughout this span, Child–Parent Center pre-K programs are housed in or near the elementary schools that students will one day attend. The program also follows a sequenced, evidence-based curriculum that is aligned from preschool through third grade. Throughout early elementary school, the curriculum remains hands-on, with a special emphasis on language development (Human Capital Research Collaborative, 2016).

Each site employs a curriculum alignment liaison who works with school leadership to review curricular materials, learning standards, and assessments and advise decisions about curriculum choice from preschool to third grade. These staff also support collaboration among teachers and cross-grade meetings to discuss class content and strategies for bolstering student learning to facilitate strong implementation of the curriculum (Reynolds, Hayakawa, Candee & Englund, 2016). The curriculum is aligned across developmental domains, including academic skills and knowledge, social-emotional learning, and discipline.

The program's strong commitment to collaboration with families similarly extends into the early elementary years. Elementary schools attended by Child–Parent Center students have special liaisons that spend some of their time staying in touch with families, overseeing parent resource rooms, and offering connections to family support services. These representatives plan parent activities, and work with other school staff charged with parent engagement, such as Title I coordinators or leaders of school Parent–Teacher Associations (Human Capital Research Collaborative, n.d.; Reynolds, Hayakawa, Candee & Englund, 2016). To ensure that family engagement remains aligned throughout the preschool through third grade continuum, these staff work closely with their counterparts at Child–Parent Center preschools, with the goal of creating a seamless experience for children and families. In short, the

Child–Parent Center model is designed to ensure that many of the elements of quality described in this chapter are reflected in children's educational experiences through the third grade.

Lessons Learned from Successful Programs

What can we learn from descriptions of how these six effective preschool programs have implemented key elements of early education? The six programs reviewed in this chapter have each documented their success – the children that attend are not only more ready to start school than their peers, but their advantages last into elementary school and beyond. The descriptions of how these programs have been designed and implemented provide several overarching lessons for policymakers, program directors, preschool teachers and others seeking to replicate their success.

A holistic approach is essential to delivering high quality. The elements of quality described in this chapter are each supported by research that links them with effective instruction and child outcomes (Wechsler et al., 2016). The programs reviewed in this chapter are designed to include all or most of these elements of quality, in ways that go beyond a simple checklist of features. For example, effective programs not only set early learning standards, but also ensure that those standards intentionally address the whole child and reflect the science behind child development. Effective programs also acknowledge that even the best standards carry little weight if they are not aligned with curricula and assessments to create engaging and meaningful learning experiences in the classroom. Further, because even exceptional learning experiences will fall short if children are hungry or sick or families lack the resources to address their needs, these programs support comprehensive services to ensure children arrive ready to learn each day.

Effective implementation matters. The experiences children and families have in preschool programs – and the impact the program has on their lives – reflects the way a high-quality program is implemented. The best curriculum is useless if it sits on the shelf because teachers lack the training and ongoing support to utilize it, but programs that support teachers in implementing it have seen how these strategies can transform their classrooms. Requiring advanced teaching credentials means little if preparation programs are unaffordable or unavailable, so high-performing states have offered scholarships, mentoring, and other supports to aspiring pre-K teachers. States and municipalities that follow through with the supports and resources necessary to implement these types of core program elements well have demonstrated how combining features creates a program worth more than the sum of its parts.

Effective implementation of high quality requires significant investments. To most, the idea that a program must set high standards and then implement them with fidelity may seem obvious. And yet many early childhood programs are well designed but poorly implemented. One likely reason is limited resources. The elements of high quality described in this chapter – like compensation and support for a highly qualified workforce, a full program day that provides adequate learning time and supports parental work, family engagement that improves parent–child relationships and reduces familial stress by offering wraparound services – all come at a price. Indeed, the cost per child of the programs reviewed here ranges from $6,291 in Michigan to $12,664 in New Jersey, all of which exceed the average expenditure of $5,696 per child for preschool nationwide in 2016 (Barnett et al., 2016). Though these expenditures may seem daunting, it is important to remember that they are no more than, and often still below, K–12 per-pupil amounts. Furthermore, these expenditures are best considered wise investments because when early learning programs do lead to sustained benefits, the returns to society are substantial (Karoly & Auger, 2016).

Achieving high quality takes time. Many of the programs described in this chapter are the product of many years of intentional, gradual quality improvement. Implementing early childhood programs capable of producing sustained benefits for children and society is a complex undertaking. Further, large-scale preschool programs are often developed on the backs of prior efforts. For example, while requiring highly qualified educators is an excellent goal, substantial time and investment is needed to build a workforce. North Carolina recognized that a gradual roll-out of new qualification requirements, along with scholarships that supported existing educators in meeting them, was necessary to meet their goals. Likewise, shifting the culture of existing program practices and staff beliefs to better reflect research-based approaches requires adequate time to foster buy-in. Changing ideas about the appropriate role of the family in school or the importance of formative assessments can be particularly challenging if alternative ideas are relatively entrenched. Successful programs have taken an incremental, intentional approach to transforming program practices.

Early education extends beyond preschool. When it comes to sustaining gains, there is ample research to suggest that you must look beyond the preschool years. A year or two of even the highest quality preschool cannot inoculate children against the detrimental effects of impoverished communities and poor elementary or secondary schooling. While there is variation in the extent to which these six programs invest in the early elementary years or begin interventions prior to preschool, in every case decision-makers have acknowledged that pre-K alone is not enough. In some cases, such as the Child–Parent Centers and North Carolina Smart Start, investing in more than pre-K is inherent to their model. For other programs, allocating resources to extend their reach beyond the preschool year is a recent development. Nonetheless, each of these programs makes it clear that while the quality of early learning instruction is important for immediate child outcomes, sustained benefits requires far more comprehensive investments in children and their families.

There is no one best system of early education. Each of the programs reviewed in this chapter has achieved its success by implementing the elements of quality differently and with varying levels of intensity. Though future research may better articulate the precise mix of program elements – and the best approach to implementing those elements – to ensure sustained gains, policymakers can learn from the choices these programs make about which elements to focus their efforts and resources on, and how to implement them. Washington's state preschool program was modeled after Head Start, providing intensive and comprehensive services to the most vulnerable children, while the Child–Parent Centers built a preschool-to-third-grade instructional continuum that integrates the early childhood experience into the early elementary years. Oklahoma decided to provide one year of high-quality preschool universally, to all the state's 4-year olds, by joining the program with its K–12 system. Each of these models is different, both in what they provide and who they provide it to, but each delivers an early learning experience that benefits children.

Investing for Impact

Pre-K programs that consistently reach the high levels of quality described in this chapter have the potential to create lasting gains for children. While the elements of quality are well known, there is much to learn from these programs about how to craft and implement these elements in meaningful ways. Specifically, policymakers aiming for impact can invest in:

- Full-day, multi-year ECE programs so children have sufficient time to learn, and small class sizes and low teacher:child ratios, so children have more opportunities to engage with their teachers.
- The development and alignment of early learning standards and formative assessments that address children's social, emotional, and physical health to support engaging and meaningful learning experiences.
- Educator compensation so that early childhood teachers are paid comparably to K–12 teachers and job-embedded professional development supports such as in-class coaching to further develop educators' skills.
- Comprehensive services for children and families, especially hiring professionals who can directly provide or refer children and families to the resources and supports they need.
- A robust system of continuous quality improvement that incentivizes participation and provides high-leverage supports for program quality, such as coaching and mentoring.
- Linkages between birth to age 3, preschool, and elementary school, such as mechanisms for the coordination of early childhood programs and professionals who focus on these transitions.

These are key areas in which the highlighted programs invested, often concurrently. And in each case, the result has been a program that promotes healthy child development so that children enter elementary school ready to learn and continue to thrive into adolescence and adulthood.

These programs also illustrate that approaches to providing early learning can reasonably diverge to meet the needs and goals of individual communities. For policymakers looking to expand or enhance preschool, the context of their own states and communities should dictate where to focus first. However, creating preschool programs with meaningful and sustainable impacts requires investing in all of the elements of quality in a deep and consequential way.

References

Aikens, N. & Akers, L. (2011). *Background Review of Existing Literature on Coaching*. Washington, DC: Mathematica Policy Research.

Bania, N., Kay, N., Aos, S. & Pennucci, A. (2014). *Outcome Evaluation of Washington State's Early Childhood Education and Assistance Program*. Olympia, WA: Washington State Institute for Public Policy.

Barnett, W. S. (2010). Universal and targeted approaches to preschool education in the United States. *International Journal of Child Care and Education Policy*, 4 (1), 1–12.

Barnett, W. S., Friedman-Krauss, A. H., Weisenfeld, G. G., Horowitz, M., Kasmin, R. & Squires, J. H. (2016). *The State of Preschool Yearbook 2016*. New Brunswick, NJ: National Institute for Early Education Research.

Barnett, W. S., Jung, K., Youn, M. & Frede, E. (2013). *Abbott Preschool Program Longitudinal Effects Sudy: Fifth Grade Follow-Up*. Rutgers, NJ: National Institute for Early Education Research.

Barnett, W. S., Schulman, K. & Shore, R. (2004). *Class Size: What's the Best Fit?* New Brunswick, NJ: National Institute for Early Education.

Bassok, D., Dee, T. & Latham, S. (2017). The effects of accountability incentives in early childhood education. NBER Working Paper No. 23859. Cambridge, MA: National Bureau of Economic Research.

Bierman, K. L. & Morris, R. M. (2017). *Parent Engagement Practices Improve Outcomes in Preschool Children*. State College, PA: Edna Bennett Pierce Prevention Research Center, Pennsylvania State University.

Boller, K, Del Grosso, P., Blair, R. et al. (2010). *Seeds to Success Modified Field Test: Findings from the Outcomes and Implementation Studies*. Princeton, NJ: Mathematica Policy Research.

Bueno, M., Darling-Hammond, L. & Gonzales, D. (2008). *Preparing Teachers for Pre-K: What Policymakers Should Know and Be Able to Do*. Washington, DC: Pre-K Now.

Caspe, M. & Lopez, M. E. (2006). *Lessons from Family-Strengthening Interventions: Learning from Evidenced-Based Practice*. Cambridge, MA: Harvard Family Research Project.

Christenson, S. L. (2000). Families and schools: rights, responsibilities, resources, and relationships, in Pianta, R. C. & Cox, M. J. (Eds.), *The Transition to Kindergarten* (pp. 143–177). Baltimore, MD: Paul H. Brookes Publishing Co.

Duncan, G. J. & Magnuson, K. (2013). Investing in preschool programs. *Journal of Economic Perspectives*, 27(2), 109–132.

Frank Porter Graham Child Development Institute, Smart Start Evaluation Team. (2003). *Smart Start and preschool child care quality in NC: Change over time and relation to children's readiness*. DOI: http://fpg.unc.edu/sites/fpg.unc.e du/files/resources/reports-and-policy-briefs/FPG_SmartStart_SS-and-Prescho ol-Child-Care-Quality-in-NC-March2003.pdf

Frede, E. (2016). *New Jersey's Abbot Preschool Program: Building a High-Quality Personnel System*. Unpublished manuscript.

Great Start to Quality. (2016). *Great Start to Quality* Program Quality Indicators. Retrieved from Great Start to Quality: http://greatstarttoquality.org/sites/defa ult/files/Great%20Start%20to%20Quality%20Program%20Quality%20Indic ators.pdf

Great Start to Quality. (2017, September 29). *Great Start to Quality User Guide: Start to finish*. Retrieved from Great Start to Quality: http://greatstarttoquality .org/sites/default/files/GSQ%20User%20Guide.pdf

Halgunseth, L. C., Peterson, A., Stark, D. R. & Moodie, S. (2009). *Family Engagement, Diverse Families, and Early Childhood Education Programs: An Integrated Review of the Literature*. Washington, DC: National Association for the Education of Young Children.

Harvard University Center on the Developing Child. (n.d.). *Brain Architecture*. Retrieved from Center on the Developing Child Harvard University: https://developingchild.harvard.edu/science/key-concepts/brain-architecture

Hayakawa, M. & Reynolds, A. (2016). Strategies for scaling up: promoting parent involvement through family-school-community partnerships. *Voices of Urban Education*, 44, 45–52.

Henderson, A. T. & Mapp, K. L. (2002). *A New Wave of Evidence: The Impact of School, Family, and Community Connections on Student Achievement*. Austin, TX: National Center for Family & Community Connections with Schools Southwest Educational Development Laboratory.

Hill, C. J., Gormley, W. T. & Adelstein, S. (2015). Do the short-term effects of a high-quality preschool program persist? *Early Childhood Research Quarterly*, 32, 60–79.

Human Capital Research Collaborative. (2016). *CPC-P–3 Executive Summary*. Retrieved September 25, 2017, from CPC-P–3: http://cpcp3.org/uploads/4/1/9/1/4191814/executivesummaryforweb.pdf

Human Capital Research Collaborative. (n.d.). *Parent Involvement Liaison Responsibilities*. Retrieved September 25, 2017, from CPC-P–3: http://cpcp3.org/parent-involvement-liaison.html

Johnson, R. C. & Jackson, C. K. (2017). Reducing inequality through dynamic complementarity: Evidence from Head Start and public school spending. NBER Working Paper No. 23489. Cambridge, MA: National Bureau of Economic Research.

Johnson-Staub, C. (2011, September 14). *The Relationship between Licensing and QRIS: Challenges and Opportunities*. Retrieved from CLASP: www.clasp.org/sites/default/files/public/resources-and-publications/files/QRISandlicensing-NARA-091411-final.pdf

Karoly, L. A. & Auger, A. (2016). *Informing Investments in Preschool Quality and Access in Cincinnati*. Santa Monica, CA: RAND.

Kirp, D. (2007). *The Sandbox Investment: The Preschool Movement and Kids-First Politics*. Cambridge, MA: Harvard University Press.

Landry, S. H., Anthony, J. L., Swank, P. R. & Montesque-Bailey, P. (2009). Effectiveness of comprehensive professional development for teachers of at-risk preschoolers. *Journal of Educational Psychology*, 101(2), 448.

Mantzicopoulos, P. (2003). Flunking kindergarten after Head Start: an inquiry into the contribution of the contextual and individual variables. *Journal of Educational Psychology*, 95(2), 268–278.

Mashburn, A. J., Pianta, R. C., Barbarin, O. A. et al. (2008). Measures of classroom quality in prekindergarten and children's development of academic, language and social skills. *Child Development*, 79(3), 732–749.

McWayne, C., Hampton, V., Fantuzzo, J., Cohen, H. & Sekino, Y. (2004). A multivariate examination of parent involvement and the social and academic competencies of urban kindergarten children. *Psychology in the Schools*, 41(3), 363–377.

Michigan Department of Education. (n.d.). *Great Start Readiness Program Implementation Manual: Curriculum*. Retrieved from Michigan Department of

Education: http://www.michigan.gov/mde/0,4615,7-140-63533_50451-2173 13-,00.html.

Michigan State Board of Education. (2005). *Early Childhood Standards of Quality for Prekindergarten. Revised March 12, 2013.* Retrieved from State of Michigan: https://www.michigan.gov/documents/mde/ECSQ_OK_Approved_422339_7 .pdf

Muschkin, C. G., Ladd, H. F. & Dodge, K. A. (2015). Impact of North Carolina's early childhood initiatives on special education placements in third educational evaluation and policy analysis. *Educational Evaluation and Policy Analysis*, 37(4), 478–500.

NAEYC. (2017). *Early Learning Standards and Accreditation Criteria & Guidance for Assessment.* Retrieved from NAEYC: www.naeyc.org/academy/ standardsandcriteria

New Jersey Department of Education. (2015). *Early Childhood Education and Family Engagement.* New Jersey Department of Education. Retrieved from: www.nj.gov/education/ece/guide/impguidelines.pdf

North Carolina Department of Health and Human Services, Division of Child Care and Early Education. (2016, January 1). *Subsidized* Child Care Market Rates *for* Child Care Centers. North Carolina Division of Child Development and Early Education. Retrieved from: http://ncchildcare.nc.gov/pdf_forms/ce nter_market_rate_table_effective_01012016.pdf

North Carolina Department of Public Instruction, Office of Early Learning. (2011). *Evaluation of More at Four State Pre-Kindergarten: The First Ten Years.*

Oklahoma State Department of Education. (n.d.). *Teacher Certification.* Oklahoma State Department of Education. Retrieved from: http://sde.ok.gov /sde/teacher-certification

Phillips, D. A., Lipsey, M. W., Dodge, K. A. et al. (2017). *Puzzling It Out: The Current State of Scientific Knowledge on Pre-Kindergarten Effects, A Consensus Statement.* Washington, DC: The Brookings Institution.

Reynolds, A. J., Hayakawa, M., Candee, A. J. & Englund, M. M. (2016). *CPC-P–3 Program Manual.* Minneapolis, MN: Human Capital Research Collaborative.

Reynolds, A. (2016). Child–Parent Centers: an iconic pre-K to 3 model goes to scale. Unpublished manuscript.

Reynolds, A. J., Temple, J. A., Ou, S., Arteaga, I. A. & White, B. A. B. (2011). School-based early childhood education and age-28 well-being: effects by timing, dosage, and subgroups. *Science*, 333, July 15, 360–364.

Reynolds, A. J., Temple, J. A., Robertson, D. J. & Mann, E. A. (2001). Long-term effects of an early childhood intervention on educational achievement and juvenile arrest: a 15-year follow-up of low-income children in public schools. *Journal of the American Medical Association*, 285(18), 2339–2346.

Schweinhart, L. J., Xiang, Z., Daniel-Echols, M., Browning, K. & Wakabayashi, T. (2012). *Michigan Great Start Readiness Program Evaluation 2012: High School Graduation and Grade Retention Findings.* Ypsilanti, MI: HighScope Educational Research Foundation.

Shonkoff, J., Phillips, D. & Educational Resources Information Center. (2000). *From Neurons to Neighborhoods: The Science of Early Childhood Development.* Washington, DC: National Academy Press.

Snow, C., Van Hemel, S. & The Committee on Developmental Outcomes and Assessments for Young Children. (2008). *Early Childhood Assessment: Why, What and How.* Washington, DC: The National Academies Press.

T.E.A.C.H. Early Childhood® North Carolina Scholarship Program. (n.d.). Retrieved from Child Care Services Association (CCSA): www.childcareservi ces.org/ps/teach-nc

The Build Initiative & Child Trends. (2016). *A Catalog and Comparison of Quality Rating and Improvement Systems (QRIS).* Retrieved from QRIS Compendium: http://qriscompendium.org/

US Department of Health and Human Services. (n.d.). *QRIS Resource Guide.* US Department of Health and Human Services. Retrieved from: https://qris guide.acf.hhs.gov/index.cfm?do=qrisabout

US Bureau of Labor Statistics. (2016). *May 2016 State Occupational Employment and Wage Estimates, Oklahoma.* Retrieved from www.bls.gov/oes/current/oesok .htm.

Wasik, B. & Snell, E. (2015). *Synthesis of Preschool Dosage: Unpacking How Quantity, Quality and Content Impacts Child Outcomes.* Philadelphia, PA: Temple University.

Wechsler, M., Kirp, D., Ali, T. T. et al. (2016). *The Road to High-Quality Early Learning: Lessons from the States.* Palo Alto, CA: Learning Policy Institute.

Wechsler, M., Melnick, H., Maier, A. & Bishop, J. (2016). *The Building Blocks of High-Quality Early Education Programs.* Palo Alto, CA: Learning Policy Institute.

Whitebook, M., McLean, C. & Austin, L. J. (2016). *Early Childhood Workforce Index, 2016.* Berkeley, CA: Center for the Study of Child Care Employment, University of California.

Yoshikawa, H., Weiland, C. & Brooks-Gunn, J. (2016). When does preschool matter? *The Future of Children,* 26(2), 21–35. DOI: 10.1353/foc.2016.0010

Yoshikawa, H., Weiland, C., Brooks-Gunn, L., et al. (2013). *Investing in our future: The evidence base on preschool education.* Foundation for Child Development. Retrieved from http://fcd-us.org/resources/evidence-base -preschool.

Part II

Continuity from Preschool to Third Grade

6   Patterns of Experiences across Head Start and Kindergarten Classrooms That Promote Children's Development

Andrew J. Mashburn and Rita Yelverton

The Head Start program was created as part of President Lyndon B. Johnson's *War on Poverty* to provide educational, medical, dental, and mental health services to young children and families from economically disadvantaged backgrounds (Administration for Children and Families, 2012). Head Start began in the summer of 1965 as an 8-week program for children who were about to enter public schools, and over the past 50 years, the program has expanded the scope and intensity of its services (Styfco & Zigler, 2003). Currently, Head Start is the largest provider of publicly-funded, center-based early childhood education (ECE) programs in the United States, serving nearly 1 million 3-year-olds and 4-year-olds each year (Barnett et al., 2015).

In 1998, reauthorization of federal funding for Head Start by the US Congress came with a mandate that the US Department of Health and Human Services, the federal agency that administers the program, determine on a national level the impacts of Head Start on the children and families it serves (US Department of Health and Human Services, January 2010). An advisory committee on Head Start Research and Evaluation recommended a framework for studying the impacts of the program that included the following features: an experimental design involving random assignment of children to Head Start and Control groups; a nationally representative sample of Head Start classrooms; multiple child and parent outcomes; and assessments of these outcomes collected at multiple points in time (Advisory Committee on Head Start Research and Evaluation, 1999). These recommendations became the blueprint for the Head Start Impact Study (HSIS; Puma, Bell, Shapiro et al., 2001).

The HSIS began in fall 2002 within a nationally representative sample of 84 Head Start grantee/delegate agencies and included newly entering 3- and 4-year-old children. Children who signed up to attend Head Start centers within these grantees were randomly assigned – separately within each age group – to the *Head Start* condition that was offered access to the program or the *Control* condition that was not offered access to the program. Results from this study offer two conclusions about the impacts[1] of Head Start: (1) offering children access to Head Start had positive impacts on their academic skills (e.g., literacy, math, language) at the end of the Head Start year, and (2) these early advantages were no longer evident for most outcomes at the end of kindergarten (Puma, Bell, Cook et al., 2012).

This result, suggesting a "drop-off" or "fade-out" of the impacts of offering access to Head Start, may come as no surprise to some. A meta-analysis described by Duncan (2015) included 67 studies of the impacts of ECE programs published between 1960 and 2007. Results indicated that the average post-program impacts on academic outcomes had an effect size of 0.23, which diminished to 0.10 on follow-up assessments conducted within one year after the program ended. These overall effects are similar in magnitude to what was found for academic outcomes in the Head Start Impact Study at the end of the Head Start year and the end of the kindergarten year, respectively (Puma, et al., 2012). Nonetheless, results indicating a drop-off of the impacts of Head Start and other ECE programs are troubling to many in the ECE community – policy-makers, program administrators, and teachers – whose investments of resources to implement, expand, regulate, monitor, and improve ECE programs come with expectations that these investments will produce long-term benefits to the children and families served, which return economic benefits to society. As evident by the title of and topics within this edited volume, this issue of sustaining the gains of early childhood programs on children's long-term development is a foremost concern on the minds of ECE researchers, as well.

However, research to address questions about the maintenance of impacts of Head Start has been impeded by some conceptual difficulties attributed to the multiple processes that impact children's long-term

---

[1] The impacts of Head Start were tested within an Intent-to-Treat (ITT) framework that estimated the impacts of offering *access to* Head Start by comparing the developmental outcomes of children randomly assigned to Head Start and Control groups, without regard for the children's actual ECE experiences during the Head Start year. In the ITT estimates for 4-year-olds, the Head Start group comprised 77% of children who attended HS and 23% of children who attended a different care setting (other ECE center, parent care, other setting), and the Control group comprised 14% who attended Head Start, 35% who attended an ECE center, 40% in parent care, and 11% in another setting). Follow-up Impact-on-Treated (IOT) analyses corrected for "non-compliance" to study condition (i.e., no-shows – children assigned to HS who did not attend; and cross-overs – children assigned to control who attended Head Start) to estimate the impacts of *participating in* Head Start. Not surprisingly, the authors note that "most of the IOT estimates have effect sizes noticeably larger than corresponding ITT effect sizes, no matter what assumptions go into the IOT analyses" (Puma et al., 2010, p. 552).

development. More specifically, children's development not only depends upon the nature and quality of their experiences *within* Head Start and kindergarten classrooms, but there also may be patterns of experiences *across* these grades that contribute to children's long-term development. The purposes of this chapter are to: (1) elucidate some of the classroom processes affecting children's development from the beginning of Head Start until the end of kindergarten; (2) generate three sets of hypotheses about specific patterns of experiences across Head Start and kindergarten classrooms that contribute to children's long-term development; and (3) test one of these hypotheses – that consistent instructional practices across Head Start and kindergarten classrooms is positively associated with children's development during kindergarten.

Classroom Processes Affecting Children's Development from Head Start through Kindergarten

Understanding children's development from the beginning of Head Start at age 4 until the end of kindergarten is a complicated endeavor, for at least three reasons. First, multiple factors affecting children's development during this time must be considered, including attributes of the child him- or herself, the multiple settings within which the child spends time (e.g., home, Head Start classrooms, kindergarten classrooms), and the multiple administrative agencies (Head Start, state and district K–12) that support the home and classroom settings. Second, the child, settings, and agencies are all dynamic, such that they are each changing over the course of this time. This includes changes occurring within the child, and, in particular, the rapid neurological development in the prefrontal cortex that helps to facilitate the child's capacities to regulate his or her emotion and attention (Durston & Casey, 2006); changes in their classroom experiences (i.e., moving from Head Start to kindergarten); and changes in administrative agencies that support these classrooms (e.g., Head Start to federal, state and local Departments of Education).

Third, there are multiple processes that contribute to children's development of academic and social-emotional skills during these two years. One process involves the *quality of children's interactions* within their homes, ECE classrooms, and other primary settings wherein the child spends substantial time and has defined roles and relationships. For example, ecological and social interaction theories of development (e.g., Bronfenbrenner & Morris, 2006; Vygotsky, 1962) applied to preschool classrooms (Mashburn & Pianta, 2010) offer explanations for how children's development occurs *within* Head Start and kindergarten classrooms. Namely, learning and development occurs through the child's back-and-forth interactions with adults, peers, and learning materials that occur on a regular basis and over extended periods of time, are appropriate to the child's current ability, and become progressively more complex. More specifically, the quality of social interactions in classrooms that impact young children's development of academic and social-emotional has been described as comprising three domains: emotionally supportive interactions, well-organized interactions, and instructionally supportive interactions (Hamre et al., 2013). There is empirical support that that more emotionally supportive classroom interactions (e.g., positive climate, sensitivity toward children's emotional needs) were positively associated with children's development of social-emotional skills and more instructionally supportive classroom interactions (e.g., language modeling, concept development) were positively associated with children's development of literacy, math and language skills during the preschool year (Mashburn et al., 2008).

Processes affecting children's development from Head Start through kindergarten also involve the *nature of the instructional practices* that children experience within their classrooms. Instructional practices vary across ECE classrooms with regard to how much time is spent on academic instruction (e.g., math and literacy instruction), child-led activities (e.g., free-choice centers) and teacher-directed whole group activities (e.g., book readings, group lessons), and there is some empirical evidence suggesting that specific instructional practices in ECE classrooms are positively associated with children's development. For example, Ball and Blachman (1991) found that kindergarten instructional practices focused on phonemic segmentation and letter-sound combinations were positively associated with children's reading and spelling outcomes. Further, Claessens, Engel, and Curran (2014) found that greater exposure to *advanced* math and reading instruction in kindergarten was positively associated with academic skills; however, frequency of *basic* skills instruction was not associated with children's development.

In addition to those processes within classrooms described above, children's development from Head Start through the end of kindergarten is also affected by their patterns of experiences as they transition *across* Head Start and kindergarten classrooms. The child's transition from a Head Start to a kindergarten classroom may present abrupt shifts in the quality of their interactions with teachers, peers, and learning materials, and in the types of instructional experiences with regard to how classroom activities are structured and the amount of time spent on direct academic instruction. This shift in children's instructional experiences may be particularly abrupt today, as accountability pressure from the K–12 systems have trickled down to kindergarten classrooms; the result of which is "a heightened focus on academic skills and a reduction in opportunities for play" (Bassok, Latham & Rorem, 2015). As a result, the transition from Head Start to kindergarten very likely involves a shift from play-focused, child-centered experiences to more academically focused, adult-directed experiences, and for some children, this shift is more pronounced than for other children.

In theory, these shifts in experiences from Head Start to kindergarten classrooms may have implications for children's long-term development. For example, Dewey (1938) introduced the concept of *continuity of experience*, which posits that acquiring new knowledge involves a process of taking current knowledge from previous learning experiences and modifying it based on current experiences. Thus, the learner's prior experiences and current capacities are the starting place for developing new knowledge, and for teaching to be effective, it must build upon those prior experiences and current capacities to make learning more meaningful and effective (Dewey, 1938). Similarly, in this volume, Stipek (2015) discusses how and why continuity, and more specifically, the alignment of policy and classroom practices across grades, promotes children's development. From both of these perspectives, children's development is not only affected by the nature of their instructional experiences and quality of interactions within classrooms; children's development is also affected by the accumulation of experiences across grades, and more specifically, the extent to which the child's current learning experiences are attuned to the child's capabilities and are consistent with their prior experiences. As such, we postulate that the fade-out of impacts of Head Start and other early learning programs may be due, in part, to a mis-alignment in between the systems of Head Start and kindergarten.

Despite the theoretical warrant for the importance of considering children's experiences across Head Start and kindergarten classrooms, there is very little empirical research that examines if and how specific patterns of experiences across grades affect children's long-term development. In the next section, we briefly present three sets of hypotheses – Consistency, Developmentally Sequenced, and High Quality – regarding specific patterns of instructional experiences across Head Start and kindergarten classrooms that we postulate are positively associated with children's long-term development.

Hypotheses about Long-Term Development of Children Who Attended Head Start

Consistency Hypothesis. Developmental and education theory (e.g., Bronfenbrenner & Morris, 2006; Dewey, 1938) and research (e.g., Ansari

& Winsler, 2013; Curby, Brock, & Hamre, 2013) indicate that children's development is affected by the degree of stability and consistency in their experiences across time. This suggests that when a child transitions from a Head Start classroom into a kindergarten classroom, the child will more readily adapt to and succeed within kindergarten if his or her experiences in this new setting build upon his or her prior experiences and current capabilities. In contrast, if the child's instructional experiences in kindergarten do not have this continuity with the child's prior experiences in Head Start or their current capabilities, then the child may experience difficulty adjusting to these new demands. This may be evident by the child's difficulties regulating his or her attention and behavior in kindergarten classrooms, which has implications for the child's academic and social-emotional development during kindergarten. More specifically, we hypothesize that consistency in children's instructional experiences (i.e., focus on academic instruction, structure of activities) across Head Start and kindergarten classrooms positively impacts children's development during kindergarten.

Developmentally Sequenced Hypothesis. Social-interaction theories of cognitive development (e.g., Vygotsky, 1962) indicate that learning and development occur through interactions that are suited to the child's current ability and that become progressively more complex, extending the child's knowledge to a new level that is within their "zone of proximal development." This suggests that when instructional experiences are properly suited to the child's ability, there is a greater likelihood that the instruction will build upon the child's current base of knowledge. However, instruction that is not aligned with his or her ability – being either too simple or too advanced for the child's current capability – will not promote academic development.

From this theoretical perspective, we hypothesize the following regarding the amount of time children experience basic academic instruction in Head Start and kindergarten classrooms. Kindergarten classrooms that involve more frequent direct instruction of basic academic skills will have positive effects on development among children who have experienced less of this sort of instruction previously and presumably have not achieved these basic skills; as such, this instruction is more appropriate to the child's developmental level and likely to result in new knowledge. In contrast, among children who have previously experienced greater amounts of basic instruction in Head Start and presumably achieved levels of proficiency of these skills, frequent academic instruction in kindergarten is redundant and unlikely to result in any new literacy and math skills. Interestingly, this hypothesis competes with the Consistency Hypotheses regarding the optimal amounts of academic instruction in Head Start and kindergarten.

The Consistency Hypothesis posits that children benefit when the amounts of academic instruction are consistent across classrooms, whereas the Developmentally-Sequenced Hypothesis posits some optimal patterns (low basic skills instruction in Head Start to high basic skills instruction in kindergarten) and sub-optimal patterns (high basic skills instruction in Head Start to high basic skills instruction in kindergarten).

High Quality Hypothesis. As discussed earlier, the quality of children's social interactions with teachers and peers in classrooms, including the quality of emotional support, classroom organization, and instructional support (Hamre et al., 2013), have implications for children's development within each grade. Further, we hypothesize that as children move from Head Start to kindergarten classrooms, there is one optimal pattern of experiences related to the quality of social interactions across grades – moving from a high-quality Head Start classroom to a high-quality kindergarten classroom – and a single worst pattern of experiences – moving from a low-quality Head Start classroom to a low-quality kindergarten classroom.

In sum, children may experience profound shifts in their experiences when they move from a Head Start classroom to a kindergarten classroom. We hypothesize that there are some specific patterns of experiences across Head Start and kindergarten classrooms that may be optimal for promoting children's long-term outcomes – when instructional practices are consistent, when academic instruction builds upon the child's current knowledge base, and when social interactions are emotionally supportive, well organized, and instructionally supportive across both Head Start and kindergarten classrooms. In the next section, we conduct an empirical investigation of the Consistency Hypothesis by testing the extent to which consistent instructional practices across Head Start and kindergarten classrooms are associated with children's development of academic and social-emotional skills.

More specifically, we address the following research question among the sub-sample of children in the HSIS who attended both Head Start and kindergarten classrooms: *Do the effects of kindergarten instructional practices on children's academic and social-emotional development during kindergarten depend upon the instructional practices children experienced in Head Start?* We explore this question for two dimensions of instructional practices: (1) focus on academic instruction (i.e., time spent on literacy/language activities and math activities), and (2) structure of activities (i.e., time spent doing child-chosen activities and whole-group activities). We hypothesize that greater consistency in the degree to which instruction is focused on academic skills (time spent doing literacy/language activities and math activities) across Head Start and kindergarten class-rooms will positively impact children's development of literacy/language and math skills, respectively; and greater consistency in how activities are structured (amount of time spent doing child-chosen activities, whole group activities) across Head Start and kindergarten classrooms will positively impact children's development of social-emotional skills during kindergarten.

Method

Participants

Participants in this study were 975 children from the 4-year-old cohort of the Head Start Impact Study (Puma et al., 2012). This included any child who (1) attended Head Start regardless of whether they were assigned to the Head Start or the Control condition (recall that 14% of children randomly assigned to the Control group attended a Head Start program) and (2) had complete data for classroom experience measures in Head Start and kindergarten. Refer to the HSIS Technical Manual (Puma et al., 2010) for details about the sampling and recruitment of this nationally representative sample of Head Start grantees, children, and families, and for more detailed information about the measures, which are briefly described next.

Measures

Child, family and school characteristics. Parents were asked to complete a survey during the fall of children's Head Start year, which included questions about their child's race/ethnicity, primary language spoken at home, gender, and age, as well as the mother's education level, whether she was a teenager when she had the child, whether the child lives with both biological parents, whether the school is located in an urban setting, and whether the child attended a full-day kindergarten. Table 6.1 presents characteristics of children, families, and schools in the study, which are used as covariates in analyses that address the primary research questions about the consistency of classroom instructional practices.

Instructional practices in Head Start and Kindergarten classrooms. To assess two dimensions of instructional practices that children experienced in Head Start and kindergarten classrooms – focus on academic instruction and structure of activities – teachers completed self-report measures of the amount of time children experienced different types

Table 6.1 *Demographic characteristics of children, families, and schools*
(n = 975)

		Frequency	Percent
Child Gender			
	Male	496	51%
	Female	479	49%
Child Race			
	White/other	406	42%
	Black	329	34%
	Hispanic	240	25%
HSIS Study Condition			
	Treatment	563	57%
	Control	412	42%
Mother's Education Status			
	Less than high school	320	33%
	High school diploma	376	39%
	Beyond high school	279	29%
Mother's Marital Status			
	Never married	425	44%
	Currently married	381	39%
	Separated/Divorced/Widowed	169	17%
Teen Mother			
	Yes	158	16%
Urbanicity			
	Urban	808	83%
	Not urban	167	17%
Length of Head Start Day			
	Full day	643	66%
	Not full day	332	34%

of instructional practices in their classrooms during the year. Head Start teachers completed these surveys at the end of the Head Start year, and kindergarten teachers completed the surveys at the end of the kindergarten year. The amount of *time spent on literacy/language instruction* was assessed by asking teachers to respond to 12 questions that began with the following stem: "How often do you or someone else do each of the following reading and language activities with the children in your classroom?" Twelve different language and literacy practices were presented (e.g., "work on learning the names of the letters," "practice the sounds that letters make," "retell or make up stories"), and teachers responded on a 1 (never) to 6 (every day) Likert-type rating scale. Overall, the scale for the 12-item measure achieved adequate internal consistency reliability (Cronbach's alpha) among Head Start ($\alpha = 0.810$) and kindergarten teachers ($\alpha = 0.708$). To assess the amount of *time spent on mathematics instruction,* teachers responded to the question, "How often do children in your class do each of the following activities?" for each of eight math activities (e.g., "count out loud," "play math games," "use music to understand math ideas"). Teachers responded on a 1 (never) to 6 (every day) Likert-type rating scale, and overall, this scale showed adequate internal consistency reliability (Head Start: $\alpha = 0.812$; kindergarten: $\alpha = 0.792$).

Teachers also reported about two aspects related to how they structure activities in Head Start and kindergarten classrooms. More specifically, Teachers responded to the question, "How much time daily did children in your classroom spend on the following activities?: the *amount of time spent in whole-group activities* and the *amount of time spent on child-chosen activities.*" Teachers responded on a 1 (no time) to 6 (five hours or more) Likert-type scale for the amount of time "child chooses activities" and the amount of time "adult directs whole class/group activities."

Table 6.2 presents descriptive statistics and correlations within year and across years for the four measures of instructional practices in Head Start and kindergarten classrooms. On average, teachers reported that children experienced a high amount of literacy/language and math instruction in both Head Start and kindergarten – approximately 3–4 times per week – and there was considerable variation in the amount of time spent on literacy/language instruction, ranging from once or twice per week to every day. As was expected, there was an increase, on average, in the amount of time children spent on literacy/language instruction from Head Start ($M = 4.79$, $SD = 0.72$) to kindergarten ($M = 5.02$, $SD = 0.55$); however, it was not expected that the amount of time children spent on math instruction would decrease from Head Start ($M = 4.99$, $SD = 0.99$) to kindergarten ($M = 4.77$, $SD = 0.73$).

Head Start and kindergarten teachers reported that children experienced, on average, over one hour of child-chosen activities every day, and there was an expected decrease in the amount of time devoted to child-chosen activities from Head Start ($M = 3.45$, $SD = 1.03$) to kindergarten ($M = 3.04$, $SD = 1.08$). Similarly, the amount of time children spent in adult-directed whole-group activities increased from between 30 minutes and 1 hour in Head Start ($M = 2.60$, $SD = 0.91$) to over an hour in kindergarten ($M = 3.10$, $SD = 1.12$). Within Head Start and kindergarten classrooms, the correlation between the frequency of literacy/language instruction and math instruction was 0.65 and 0.44, respectively (see Table 6.2). Interestingly, the correlations between instructional experiences within Head Start and within kindergarten were very small (ranging from −0.04 to 0.06), illustrating the wide-ranging and idiosyncratic

Table 6.2 Descriptive statistics for and correlations between instructional practices in Head Start and kindergarten (n = 975)

	M	SD	n	1	2	3	4	5	6	7	8
1-HS-Time Spent on Lit/Lang Activities[1]	4.79	0.72	975	–							
2-HS-Time Spent on Math Activities[1]	4.99	0.75	975	.65	–						
3-HS-Time Spent on Child-Chosen Activities[2]	3.45	1.03	975	.15	.12	–					
4-HS-Time Spent on Whole Group Activities[2]	2.60	0.91	975	.08	.01	.12	–				
5-KG-Time Spent on Lit/Lang Activities[1]	5.02	0.55	975	.03	.01	-.01	.04	–			
6-KG-Time Spent on Math Activities[1]	4.77	0.73	975	.04	.01	.01	.06	.44	–		
7-KG-Time Spent on Child-Chosen Activities[2]	3.04	1.08	975	-.01	-.03	.01	.01	.03	.35	–	
8-KG-Time Spent on Whole Group Activities[2]	3.10	1.12	975	-.04	-.03	-.02	.04	.17	-.20	-.24	–

[1] 1=never, 2=once a month or less, 3=2–3 times per month, 4=once or twice per week, 5=3–4 times per week, 6=every day.
[2] 1=no time, 2=30 minutes or less, 3=1 hour, 4=2 hours, 5=3–4 hours, 6=5+ hours

patterns of instructional experiences that children have across Head Start and kindergarten classrooms.

Children's academic and social-emotional skills. To assess children's development of academic and social-emotional skills during kindergarten, a variety of methods (e.g., direct assessments, teacher-reports, and parent-report) were used at the end of Head Start and again at the end of kindergarten. Children's academic skills were assessed using the following direct assessments. An adapted version of the Peabody Picture Vocabulary Test (PPVT; Dunn, Dunn, & Dunn, 1997) assessed children's **Receptive Language** skills. In this test, assessors orally present a stimulus word to children, who must choose among four pictures to correctly identify the picture that matches the stimulus word. An adaptive, shortened version of the traditional PPVT was created via Item Response Theory for this study (see HSIS technical report, Puma et al., 2010). For this version of the test, all children completed 20 core items, after which children whose responses were close to the ceiling (17 items correct or more) or floor (11 items correct or fewer) completed an additional 10 items. To score the test, the HSIS used Marginal Maximum Likelihood (MML) estimation to estimate children's true ability score from a) their actual score on the test, and b) a "prior score" that estimated what a child's ability score might be in the absence of any data, in order to reduce error variance associated with the test's reliability (see HSIS technical report for details). After estimation, children's scores were standardized within age cohorts to have a mean of 100 and a standard deviation of 15.

Children's **Literacy** skills were assessed using the Letter-Word Identification subtest of the Woodcock–Johnson III test (Woodcock & Johnson, 1990). Children are asked to recognize and name letters and words, and their raw scores were converted to standardized scores ($M=100$; $SD=15$) that assess children's performance relative to others in their age group. Children's **Math** skills were assessed using the Applied Problems subtest of the Woodcock–Johnson III test. In this measure, children complete a series of basic mathematical problems, including items tapping children's ability to use basic mathematical operations (e.g., adding and subtracting) as well as other basic math skills (e.g., using a thermometer). Both scales have been positively linked to other measures of academic achievement in other samples (Woodcock & Johnson, 1990).

At the end of Head Start, and again at the end of kindergarten, parents and teachers completed surveys about their child's social-emotional skills at home and in the classroom, respectively. To assess children's **Social Skills and Positive Approaches to Learning**, parents completed a seven-item survey about their child's cooperative and empathetic behavior (e.g., "Comforts or helps others"), openness to new skills and challenges (e.g., "Likes to try new things"), and attitudes toward learning (e.g., "Enjoys learning"). Parents rated each item on a 0 ("not true") to 2 ("very true") scale. As has been found in prior studies, the score distributions on this scale were skewed such that most responses fell toward the top of the scale, indicating that most parents rate their children as high on all of the scale items; however, previous studies have found strong, predictive relations between this scale and other social-emotional outcomes as well as other child and family characteristics (Puma et al., 2010).

Parents were also asked to rate their children's **Problem Behaviors** using a fourteen-item scale. The items on this scale tapped children's aggressive behaviors (e.g., "Hits and fights with others"), inattentive and hyperactive behaviors (e.g., "Can't concentrate; can't pay attention for long"), and withdrawn behaviors (e.g., "Is unhappy, sad, or depressed"). Parents rated each item on a scale ranging from 0 ("not true") to 2 ("very true"). The overall scale ranged from 0 to 28, with lower scores representing fewer problem behaviors and higher scores representing more problem behaviors.

Children's **Classroom Aggression** was measured using the aggression subscale of the Adjustment Scales for Preschool Intervention (ASPI; Lutz, Fantuzzo & McDermott, 2002). In this scale, teachers are asked about each child's behaviors in a variety of common classroom situations. For example, teachers are presented with a classroom scenario (e.g., "How does this child cope with learning tasks?") and are asked to select any behavior that the student has engaged in for the past two months from a menu of options representing both typical and problem behaviors (e.g., the possible answers for the example scenario include "has a happy-go-lucky attitude to every problem," "charges in without taking time to think or following instructions," "approaches new tasks with caution, but tries," "won't even attempt it if he/she senses a difficulty," "likes the challenge of something difficult," and "cannot work up the energy to face anything new"). Teachers were able to select multiple child behaviors for each of 24 different scenarios, each with 6 possible responses. Of the 144 possible child behaviors identified through this scale, 22 items represented behaviors indicative of aggression (e.g., "starts fights in free play"; "has made unprovoked attacks on other children"). Raw scores were calculated by adding together the number of items checked for each student that loaded onto the aggression factor, and these raw scores were converted to t-scores based on the original ASPI standardization sample. Table 6.3 presents descriptive statistics for children's academic skills (receptive

Table 6.3 *Descriptive statistics for children's academic and social-emotional skills in Head Start and kindergarten (n = 975)*

	End of Head Start			End of Kindergarten		
	Mean	SD	n	Mean	SD	n
Receptive Language (PPVT)	91.5	10.2	801	92.6	12.3	757
Literacy (WJ-III)	89.2	13.6	805	99.4	14.9	757
Math (WJ-III)	93.2	13.3	803	96.8	14.0	757
Social Skills and Positive ATL (Parent)	12.5	1.69	809	12.7	1.56	783
Problem Behaviors (Parent)	6.00	3.58	809	5.31	3.69	783
Classroom Aggression (Teacher)	50.2	7.55	917	49.4	7.63	929

language, literacy, math) and children's social-emotional skills (social skills and approaches to learning, problem behaviors, and aggression) at the end of Head Start and at the end of kindergarten.

Analyses

Preliminary analyses examined direct associations between instructional practices in Head Start and kindergarten classrooms and children's academic and social-emotional outcomes during kindergarten. To do so, models were run in which each child outcome was regressed on children's instructional practices in Head Start and kindergarten classrooms, controlling for their baseline scores at the end of Head Start and a variety of child and family demographic characteristics. To address our primary research questions, we entered targeted interaction terms to this preliminary model. More specifically, for children's math development, we included an interaction term between time spent on math instruction in Head Start and time spent on math instruction in kindergarten; for children's literacy and language development, we included an interaction term between time spent on literacy/language instruction in Head Start and time spent on literacy/language instruction in kindergarten; for children's development of social-emotional skills, we included (separately) an interaction term between time spent on child-chosen activities in Head Start and in kindergarten, and an interaction term between time spent on whole-group activities in Head Start and in kindergarten. In general, these interaction terms test the extent to which the effect of kindergarten instructional practices on children's development during kindergarten depended upon children's instructional experiences during Head Start.

All analyses were conducted using R statistical analysis software (R Core Team, 2015). Tables 6.4 and 6.5 present results from analyses using list-wise deletion. There was a small amount of missing data for child outcome variables (the amount of missing data per outcome ranged from 5% to 22%), and an examination of these data showed that they met Missing at Random assumptions. Thus, we replicated the analyses using datasets in which missing values were imputed via Multiple Imputation techniques, and the results of these analyses were consistent with the results reported herein.

Results

In our preliminary analyses, we tested direct effects of instructional practices in Head Start and kindergarten classrooms on children's academic and social-emotional development during kindergarten. Results from these analyses are presented in Table 6.4 for academic outcomes and Table 6.5 for social-emotional outcomes (see Block 1, which includes these eight measures of instructional practices entered into the models). There were no significant associations ($p < 0.05$) found between any of the instructional practices and children's development of academic skills during kindergarten (Table 6.4). Thus, instructional practices in Head Start and in Kindergarten classrooms did not contribute, uniquely and independently, to children's language, literacy or math development during kindergarten. Children's development of social-emotional skills during kindergarten (Table 6.5) was positively associated with the frequency of literacy instruction they experienced; however, the patterns of these results are not intuitive. For example, more frequent literacy instruction in Head Start was negatively associated with children's development of social-emotional skills and positive approaches to learning ($B = -0.21$, $SE = 0.10$, $p < 0.05$) during kindergarten. More frequent literacy instruction in kindergarten was positively associated with teachers' reports of the child's classroom aggression ($B = 1.36$, $SE = 0.56$, $p < 0.05$) and negatively associated with parents' reports of the child's problem behaviors ($B = -0.59$, $SE = 0.25$, $p < 0.05$).

To evaluate the primary research questions about the consistency of children's experiences across Head Start and kindergarten classroom and children's development of academic skills during kindergarten (Table 6.4), interaction terms were added to the preliminary analyses. More specifically, for the two models examining children's development of receptive language skills and literacy skills during kindergarten, the

Table 6.4 *Classroom instructional practices and children's development of academic skills during kindergarten (n = 975)*

	Receptive Language			Literacy			Math		
	B	SE	p	B	SE	p	B	SE	p
Block 1: Direct Effects									
Instructional Practices in KG									
Time Spent on Lang/Lit	-0.01	0.67	0.983	-0.92	1.04	0.378	-1.04	0.94	0.267
Time Spent on Math	-0.26	0.52	0.623	0.60	0.81	0.463	0.39	0.73	0.598
Time Spent Child-Choice	-0.14	0.31	0.647	0.06	0.48	0.902	-0.06	0.44	0.890
Time Spent Whole-Group	-0.53	0.30	0.082	-0.34	0.47	0.478	0.20	0.43	0.639
Instructional Practices in HS									
Time Spent on Lang/Lit	0.40	0.56	0.471	0.05	0.87	0.953	-0.53	0.78	0.500
Time Spent on Math	-0.05	0.55	0.925	-1.02	0.85	0.231	0.57	0.77	0.457
Time Spent Child-Choice	0.43	0.31	0.162	-0.08	0.48	0.874	0.76	0.43	0.079
Time Spent Whole-Group	-0.34	0.34	0.324	0.59	0.54	0.271	0.20	0.48	0.683
Block 2: Interactions									
Lang/Lit KG × Lang/Lit HS	-1.09	0.78	0.160	-1.19	1.21	0.326	–	–	–
Math KG × Math HS	–	–	–	–	–	–	2.16	0.82	0.009

Notes: Block 1 includes Instructional Practices in KG and Instructional Practices in Head Start. Block 2 includes each interaction term entered separately. Analyses control for end of HS assessments, age, HSIS study condition, child lives with both biological parents, race/ethnicity, gender, maternal education, maternal marital status, teen mother, urban school, full day kindergarten.

Table 6.5 *Classroom instructional practices and children's development of social-emotional skills during kindergarten* (n = 975)

	Social Skills and Positive Approaches to Learning			Problem Behaviors			Aggression		
	B	SE	p	B	SE	p	B	SE	p
Block 1: Direct Effects									
Instructional Practices in KG									
Time Spent on Lang/Lit	-0.04	0.12	0.737	-0.59	0.25	0.020	1.36	0.56	0.016
Time Spent on Math	-0.01	0.09	0.871	0.32	0.20	0.110	-0.15	0.44	0.743
Time Spent Child-Choice	-0.07	0.05	0.191	-0.06	0.12	0.584	-0.15	0.26	0.570
Time Spent Whole-Group	-0.05	0.05	0.330	0.10	0.12	0.368	-0.04	0.25	0.864
Instructional Practices in HS									
Time Spent on Lang/Lit	-0.21	0.10	0.030	-0.16	0.21	0.460	0.13	0.48	0.781
Time Spent on Math	0.13	0.10	0.166	0.15	0.21	0.471	0.05	0.46	0.911
Time Spent Child-Choice	-0.03	0.05	0.551	-0.04	0.12	0.749	-0.30	0.26	0.243
Time Spent Whole-Group	0.04	0.06	0.557	-0.10	0.13	0.469	-0.12	0.29	0.694
Block 2: Interactions									
Child Choice KG × Choice HS	0.10	0.05	0.035	0.06	0.11	0.557	0.25	0.24	0.303
Whole Group KG × Whole HS	-0.07	0.05	0.188	0.07	0.12	0.568	-0.44	0.24	0.065

Notes: Block 1 includes Instructional Practices in KG and Instructional Practices in Head Start. Block 2 includes each interaction term entered separately. Analyses control for end of HS assessments, age, HSIS study condition, child lives with both biological parents, race/ethnicity, gender, maternal education, maternal marital status, teen mother, urban school, full day kindergarten following interaction term was added: frequency of literacy/language instruction in kindergarten × frequency of literacy/language instruction in Head Start. This resulting coefficient represents the extent to which the effects of more frequent literacy/language instruction in kindergarten on children's language or literacy development during kindergarten depended upon the frequency with which children experienced literacy/language instruction in their Head Start classrooms. Neither of these two interaction terms was statistically different from zero. For children's math development during kindergarten, we entered the interaction between the frequency of math instruction in kindergarten classrooms and the frequency of math instruction in Head Start classrooms. A statistically significant coefficient for this interaction was found (B = 2.19, SE = 0.82, p < 0.01).

We depict this interaction in Figure 6.1 using model-based estimates to generate math scores at the end of kindergarten for nine groups of children who had each different combination of low, medium, and high frequency of math instruction in Head Start and in kindergarten. To estimate these means, low was defined as one standard deviation below the mean, medium was defined as at the mean, and high was defined as one standard deviation above the mean. This interaction in Figure 6.1 illustrates that the association between math instruction in

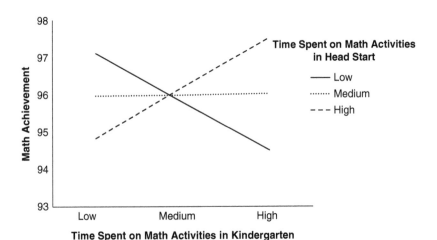

Figure 6.1 Consistency of math instruction across Head Start and kindergarten classrooms and children's development of math skills during kindergarten

kindergarten and children's development of math skills during the kindergarten year depended upon the frequency with which children experienced math instruction in Head Start.

More specifically, among children who experienced low frequency math instruction during Head Start, less frequent math instruction during kindergarten was positively associated with math skills at the end of kindergarten. In addition, among children who experienced high frequency math instruction during Head Start, more frequent math instruction during kindergarten was also positively associated with math skills at the end of kindergarten. This figure also indicates that highest math skills at the end of kindergarten were achieved by children who experienced low frequency math instruction across both grades (Mean = 97.1) and children who experienced high frequency math instruction across both grades (Mean = 97.5). In addition, the lowest math skills at the end of kindergarten were achieved by two groups of children: those who experienced high frequency math instruction in Head Start and low frequency math instruction in kindergarten (Mean = 94.8), and those who experienced low frequency math instruction in Head Start and high frequency math instruction in kindergarten (Mean = 94.5). These patterns of associations provide some evidence in support of the Consistency Hypothesis.

To evaluate the research questions related to children's development of social-emotional skills during kindergarten (Table 6.5), we entered the following two interaction terms separately for each of the three social-emotional outcomes: frequency of child-chosen activities in kindergarten × frequency of child-chosen activities in Head Start; and frequency of whole-group activities in kindergarten × frequency of whole-group activities in Head Start. A statistically significant coefficient was found for the interaction between the frequency of child-chosen activities in Head Start and kindergarten on children's development of social skills and positive approaches to learning during kindergarten ($B = 0.10$, SE = 0.05, $p < 0.05$). Figure 6.2 illustrates this interaction. Among children who spent more time doing child-chosen activities during Head Start, more frequent child-chosen activities in kindergarten was positively associated with children's development of social-skills and positive approaches to learning. In contrast, among children who spent less time doing child-chosen activities during Head Start, less frequent opportunities for child-chosen activities during kindergarten were also positively associated with development. Another coefficient – for the interaction between the frequency of whole-group activities in kindergarten and the frequency of whole-group activities in Head Start on children's classroom aggression – approached statistical significance ($B = -0.44$, SE = 0.24, $p = .065$). Figure 6.3 illustrates this interaction, which has a similar pattern to

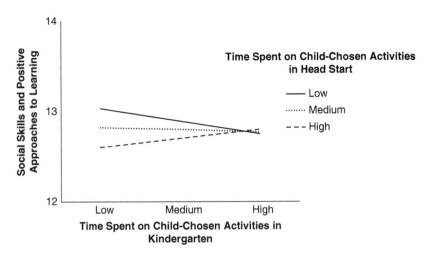

Figure 6.2 Consistency of child-chosen activities across Head Start and kindergarten classrooms and children's development of social skills during kindergarten

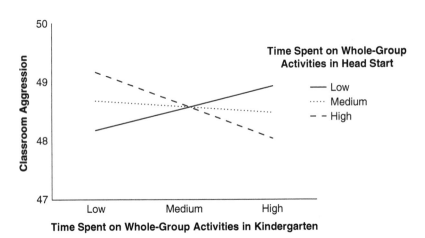

Figure 6.3 Consistency of whole-group activities across Head Start and kindergarten classrooms and children's development of aggression during kindergarten

Figures 6.1 and 6.2. More specifically, for children who experienced frequent whole-group activities in Head Start, more frequent whole group activities during kindergarten were associated with lower classroom aggression; similarly, for children who experienced less frequent whole-group activities in Head Start, less frequent whole group activities during kindergarten were also associated with lower classroom aggression. Both of these figures suggest that the children who experienced consistent instructional practices across Head Start and kindergarten made the greatest gains on social-emotional skills during kindergarten, while children who experienced inconsistent patterns in how activities were structured had the lowest gains in their social skills and approaches to learning and greatest gains in classroom aggression during kindergarten.

Discussion

Our empirical investigation into the Consistency Hypothesis among children in the 4-year-old cohort of the HSIS who attended Head Start and kindergarten classrooms provides some initial evidence that the combination of children's instructional practices across Head Start and kindergarten classrooms affects their development during kindergarten. Results indicate that, overall, instructional practices that children experienced during kindergarten (time spent on a literacy/language instruction, math instruction, whole-group activities, child-chosen activities) were not directly associated with their development of academic and social-emotional skills during kindergarten. However, the effects of these instructional practices on children's development depended upon children's previous instructional experiences during Head Start. More specifically, the pattern of results provides some initial evidence that consistency in the amount of math instruction across grades promotes math development during kindergarten, and consistency in how activities are structured (whole-group, child-chosen) across grades promotes positive development of social-emotional skills during kindergarten. This pattern of results was found for multiple child outcomes, including direct assessments of math, teacher-reports of classroom aggression, and parent-reports of social skills.

There are some notable limitations with this study related to its correlational design, which through the inclusion of covariates may not adequately account for other unmeasured factors that affect children's development during kindergarten. In addition, the measures of children's instructional experiences in Head Start and kindergarten are teacher-reported and reflect the perspectives of teachers, and thus may not directly comport with children's actual experiences. Further, the measure of the frequency of literacy/language instruction and math instruction had limited variability, due to the rating scale that truncated the most frequent response to "daily" and, therefore, did not capture variability in the number of hours and minutes of instruction per day.

Despite these limitations, these results provide initial empirical evidence that consistent instructional practices across Head Start and kindergarten classrooms is positively associated with children's development. Further empirical investigations are warranted, which include: extending the analyses with this sample to include first grade experiences and child outcomes, and third grade experiences and child outcomes; replicating these analyses with other samples; exploring other analytic approaches to investigate the consistency hypothesis; and exploring the two other sets of hypotheses regarding developmentally-sequenced and high-quality experiences across Head Start and kindergarten classrooms.

Just as ECE researchers in this volume and elsewhere are engaged in work to advance our understanding of children's long-term development and how to sustain the gains of the investments made in ECE programs, policymakers, program administrators, and teachers have been engaged in numerous efforts to implement strategies that support children and families amid the transition to kindergarten. For example, there is a long history of developing and implementing a wide-range of "transition" strategies that support children as they move into kindergarten (e.g., Kagan, Karnati, Friedlander & Tarrant, 2010). Strategies range from short-term, low-cost, and easy-to-implement practices, such as kindergarten open houses, phone calls, and home visits before the school year begins, which are intended to help children and families become acquainted with the new settings and establish relationships that open lines of communication between children, teachers, and parents.

Other strategies provide more intensive supports to children and families during the summer before the beginning of kindergarten as well as throughout the early elementary grades. For example, in 1990, the Head Start Bureau began implementing a large-scale transition program to provide a comprehensive set of supports to former Head Start children and their families during the first four years of elementary school (Kagan & Neuman, 1998), including parent involvement activities, educational enhancements for children, family social support services, and health and nutrition services (Ramey, Ramey, Phillips et al., 2000). Other types of transition strategies involve aligning standards, curriculum, instruction, and assessment from pre-kindergarten through third grade (Bogard & Takanishi, 2005), in order to support children's development by promoting experiences across grades that are consistent and effectively build upon the child's current capabilities (Kagan, Karnati, Friedlander & Tarrant, 2010).

In conclusion, children's transitions from Head Start into kindergarten bring changes in their instructional experiences. Among children in the Head Start Impact Study, this shift involved moving from Head Start classrooms into kindergarten classrooms wherein they spent more time on literacy/language instruction and in whole-group activities and less time in child-chosen activities (Table 6.2). We proposed that the magnitude of this shift in instructional practices that children experience upon entering kindergarten, which varies widely between children, has implications for their development of academic and social-emotional skills during kindergarten. Results from this study provide some empirical evidence that the consistency of instructional practices across Head Start and kindergarten classrooms is positively associated with children's development of math skills and social-emotional skills during kindergarten. Thus, strategies that effectively increase the consistency of instructional experiences when children move from Head Start into kindergarten classrooms can help sustain the gains in children's academic and social-emotional skills that were made during the Head Start year.

References

Administration for Children and Families. (2012). History of Head Start. Retrieved September 3, 2015, from: http://transition.acf.hhs.gov/programs/ohs/about/history-of-head-start

Advisory Committee on Head Start Research and Evaluation (1999). *Evaluating Head Start: A Recommended Framework for Studying the Impact of the Head Start Program*. Washington, DC: US Department of Health and Human Services.

Ansari, A. & Winsler, A. (2013). Stability and sequence of center-based and family childcare: links with low-income children's school readiness. *Children and Youth Services Review*, 35, 358–366. DOI: 10.1016/j.childyouth.2012.11.017

Ball, E. W. & Blachman, B. A. (1991). Does phoneme awareness training in kindergarten make a difference in early word recognition and developmental spelling? *Reading Research Quarterly*, 25, 49–66.

Barnett, W. S., Carolan, M. E., Squires, J. H., Clark Brown, K. & Horowitz, M. (2015). *The State of Preschool 2014*. The National Institute for Early Education Research.

Bassok, D., Latham, S. & Rorem, A. (2015). Is kindergarten the new first grade? EdPolicyWorks Working Paper Series, No. 20. Retrieved from: http://curry.virginia.edu/uploads/resourceLibrary/20_Bassok_Is_Kindergarten_The_New_First_Grade.pdf.

Bogard, K. & Takanishi, R. (2005). PK–3: An aligned and coordinated approach to education for children 3 to 8 years old. *SRCD Social Policy Reports*, 19 (3), 1–23.

Bronfenbrenner, U. & Morris, P. A. (2006). The Bioecological Model of Human Development, in *Handbook of Child Psychology (6th edn.): Vol 1, Theoretical Models of Human Development*. (pp. 793–828). Hoboken, NJ: John Wiley & Sons Inc.

Claessens, A., Engel, M. & Curran, C., (2014). Academic content, student learning, and the persistence of preschool effects. *American Educational Research Journal*, 51(2), 403–434.

Curby, T. W., Brock, L. L. & Hamre, B. K. (2013). Teachers' emotional support consistency predicts children's achievement gains and social skills. *Early Education and Development*, 24(3), 292–309. http://doi.org/10.1080/10409289 .2012.665760

Dewey, J. (1938). *Experience and Education*. New York, NY: Collier Books.

Duncan, G. (2015). Boosting school readiness with preschool curricula. Paper presentation at the 2015 Human Capital Research Collaborative National Invitational Conference. Minneapolis, MN.

Dunn, L. M., Dunn, L. L. & Dunn, D.M. (1997). *Peabody Picture and Vocabulary Test (PPVT)* (3rd edn.). Circle Pines, MN: American Guidance Service.

Durston, S. & Casey, B. J. (2006). What have we learned about cognitive development from neuroimaging? *Neuropsychologia*, 44(11), 2149–2157.

Hamre, B., Pianta, R., Downer, J. et al. (2013). Teaching through interactions: testing a developmental framework of teacher effectiveness in over 4,000 classrooms. *Elementary School Journal*, 113(4), 461–487.

Kagan, S. L., Karnati, R., Friedlander, J. & Tarrant, K., (2010). *A Compendium of Transition Initiatives in the Early Years: A Resource Guide to Alignment and Continuity Efforts in the United States and Other Countries*. New York, NY: National Center for Children and Families.

Kagan, S. L. & Neuman, M. J. (1998). Three decades of transition research: what does it tell us? *Elementary School Journal*, 98(4), 365–380.

Lutz, M. N., Fantuzzo, J. F. & McDermott, P. (2002). Contextually relevant assessment of the emotional and behavioral adjustment of low-income preschool children. *Early Childhood Research Quarterly*, 17, 338–355.

Mashburn, A. J. & Pianta, R. (2010). Opportunity in early education: Improving teacher-child interactions and child outcomes, in Reynolds, A., Rolnick, A., Englund, M. & Temple, J. (Eds.), *Childhood Programs and Practices in the First Decade of Life: A Human Capital Integration*. New York, NY: Cambridge University Press, pp. 243–265.

Mashburn, A. J., Pianta, R. C., Hamre, B. K. et al. (2008). Measures of classroom quality in prekindergarten and children's development of academic, language, and social skills. *Child Development*, 79(3), 732–749.

Puma, M., Bell, S. H., Cook, R. & Heid, C. (2010). *Head Start Impact Study: Technical Report*. Washington, DC: US Department of Health and Human Services, Administration for Children and Families.

Puma, M., Bell, S., Shapiro, G. et al. (2001). Building futures: The Head Start Impact Study Research Design Plan. Retrieved October 18, 2015. www.acf.hhs

.gov/programs/opre/resource/building-futures-the-head-start-impact-study-research-design-plan-updated.

Puma, M., Bell, S., Cook, R. et al. (2012). *Third Grade Follow-Up to the Head Start Impact Study Final Report.* OPRE Report no. 2012–45b. Washington, DC: US Department of Health and Human Services, Office of Planning, Research and Evaluation, Administration for Children and Families.

R Core Team. (2015). *R: A Language and Environment for Statistical Computing.* Vienna: R Foundation for Statistical Computing, www.R-project.org.

Ramey, S. L., Ramey, C. T., Phillips, M. M. et al. (2000). *Head Start Children's Entry into Public School: A Report on the National Head Start/Public School Early Childhood Transition Demonstration Study.* Birmingham, Al: Civitan International Research, University of Alabama at Birmingham.

Stipek, D. (2015). Quality and continuity in young children's educational experiences. Paper presentation at the 2015 Human Capital Research Collaborative National Invitational Conference. Minneapolis, MN.

Styfco, S. & Zigler, E. (2003). Early childhood programs for a new century. Reynolds, A., & Wang, M. (Eds.), *The Federal Commitment to Preschool Education: Lessons From and For Head Start* (pp. 3–33). Washington, DC: Child Welfare League of America, Inc.

US Department of Health and Human Services, Administration for Children and Families (January 2010). Head Start Impact Study. *Final Report.* Washington, DC.

Vygotsky, L. (1962). *Thought and Language.* Cambridge, MA: MIT Press.

Woodcock, R. W. & Johnson, M. B. (1990). *Woodcock–Johnson Psychoeducational Battery – Revised.* Allen, TX: DLM Teaching Resources.

7   Quality and Continuity in Young Children's Educational Experiences

Deborah J. Stipek

Introduction

Experts have proposed two likely explanations for the erosion of the advantages achieved in preschool during the early elementary grades: (1) the preschool "treatment" was not sufficiently strong, and (2) it was not followed up with high-quality educational opportunities in the early elementary grades. Supporting the first explanation is the observation that the preschool programs that have shown sustained effects (e.g., Abecedarian, Chicago Child–Parent Centers, Perry Preschool) were intense and unusually high in quality, including substantial parent involvement and well-trained teachers. Teachers in the Perry Preschool Program, for example, were certified to teach preschool, elementary, and special education (Schweinhart, Barnes & Weikart, 1993). Consistent with the second explanation is evidence that children in low-income communities attend elementary schools with fewer resources and relatively inexperienced teachers (Currie & Thomas, 2000; Peske & Haycock, 2006). Quality matters in both explanations. This chapter accordingly focuses on the issue of quality for preschool and the early elementary grades as well as strategies for achieving continuity in children's educational experience as they move from preschool into elementary school.

Quality of learning contexts is typically measured within classrooms. What transpires in the classroom, however, substantially depends on policies made beyond the classroom. For example, state standards and assessments, as well as district and school decisions about curriculum, affect the nature and quality of learning experiences in any given grade and the level of continuity across grades. Strategies to ensure and maintain the benefits of preschool therefore need to consider the larger ecology of schooling.

The first section provides a brief overview of evidence on the nature of high-quality instructional programs for preschool through third grade. This summary is followed by a discussion of policies outside of the classroom that affect the quality of children's learning experiences in the classroom. The final section focuses on the potential value of creating continuity in children's educational experience as they move from pre-school through the early elementary grades.

Program and Classroom Quality

This section focuses on the qualities of learning environments that are associated with positive student outcomes.

Social-Emotional Development

Social-emotional development is widely accepted as an important child outcome, both because it is associated with academic learning and because it is important in its own right. Social-emotional development typically includes prosocial skills (e.g., sharing, collaborating with peers) and the ability to develop close relationships, as well as the absence of externalizing behavior (acting out, aggression) and internalizing problems (withdrawn, depressed). Longitudinal studies suggest that aggression or externalizing behavior are stronger and more consistent negative predictors than are prosocial skills of academic learning (Duncan, Dowsett, Claessens, et al., 2007; Pagani, Archambault & Janosz, 2010) and other important outcomes, such as high school and college completion (Duncan & Magnuson, 2011).

Research has repeatedly demonstrated that children benefit from emotionally supportive and respectful learning environments (e.g., Hamre, 2014; Hamre & Pianta, 2005; Pianta, 1999; Rudasill, Gallagher & White, 2010), close caring relationships with teachers (Pianta, 1999; Sabol & Pianta, 2012), and classrooms that provide clear, consistent behavioral expectations (Emmer & Strough, 2001; Good & Grouws, 1977).

Synthesis reports have come to similar conclusions. In a report based on research by a National Academy of Science Panel (National Research Council (NRC), 2008), the following qualities of the social context of classrooms were deemed important (p. 158):
1. Affectionate, supportive, attentive, and respectful adults;
2. Explicit support for social skills;
3. Conversations about feelings;
4. Collaboration and cooperation opportunities;
5. Clear and developmentally appropriate rules; and
6. Use of redirection, positive reinforcement, encouragement, and explanations to minimize negative behavior.

Another synthesis of research and expert opinion adds to this list specific supports for children's social-emotion regulation and decision making (Hyson, Whittaker, Zaslow et al., 2011). These might include modeling and teaching specific strategies for self-calming (e.g., cuddling with a stuffed animal) and giving opportunities to choose among constrained options. The authors point out also that the organization of space and materials can foster or undermine positive social interactions and children's feeling of comfort. Crowded spaces and insufficient materials, for example, can encourage peer conflict.

Although research assessing the effects of cultural accommodations is sparse, most early childhood educators recommend practices that demonstrate respect for children's language and culture (see August & Shanahan, 2006; Espinosa, 2008; Goldenberg, Hicks & Lit, 2013). Examples are: learning and using words in the children's native language, showing an interest and appreciation for the children's culture, and creating a classroom environment (posters, picture books) that represents the children's culture.

Academic Skills

Academic outcomes are central to the purposes of schooling, and many studies have shown that academic skills at school entry predict skills through children's school careers (e.g., Duncan et al., 2007; Duncan & Magnuson, 2011). I focus on language, literacy and math because they are core competencies and central to most state accountability systems.

There is some resistance in the early childhood education field to teaching academic skills in preschool, based on concerns about developmental appropriateness and fear that it will crowd out opportunities for play and developing social-emotional skills. Efforts to design developmentally appropriate instruction for young children, however, have shown that academic skills instruction can be developmentally appropriate and integrate opportunities for children to develop social skills.

In general, research has shown that some amount of teacher-directed academic instruction is important to promote academic gains. One large recent study is illustrative. Fuller, Bein, Bridges, Kim & Rabe-Hesketh (2017) used a nationally representative data set (Early Childhood Longitudinal Study, Birth Cohort, ECLS-B) to examine the effects of the amount of time spent each week in preschool on academic activities (building oral language, pre-literacy skills, knowledge of math concepts). The children in the more academic preschools made substantially more academic gains, which persisted into kindergarten, with no observed negative effects on social skills. Similarly, the 2008 Preschool

Curriculum Evaluation Research Consortium, which assessed the effects of 14 preschool curriculum programs, found consistent effects on child outcomes for only two of the curricula, both of which involved direct instruction.

Although subject matter experts agree that children need some explicit, structured instruction, this can be implemented in a playful context and made meaningful and engaging for young children (Hirsh-Pasek, Golinkoff, Berk & Singer, 2009). Rhymes and songs can be used to help children recognize letters and letter–sound relationships. Games can be used to develop number sense and math operations. Books that are read to children and that children are given to read can be related to their interests, and vocabulary can be taught in the context of meaningful stories and exploration of the environment. Below is a summary of some of the instructional strategies that are widely considered both effective and appropriate for young children.

Language and literacy. Language skills form the foundation for literacy skills and have been shown to predict children's mastery of reading (Pressley, 2002). For both native English speakers and dual-language learners, native language skills predict the development of reading skills (August & Shanahan, 2006). "Emergent literacy" (an understanding that print represents spoken language, books are a source of information, and writing can be used to communicate words) also predicts later literacy skills (National Research Council [NRC], 1998). According to consensus reports (e.g., NRC, 1998), other important early literacy skills include:
1. Phonological awareness (including phonemic awareness);
2. Letter identification;
3. Word identification; and
4. Word, sentence, and passage comprehension.
In classrooms providing effective opportunities to develop language, teachers engage in conversations with children, provide activities that encourage conversation among children, and make explicit efforts to develop vocabulary and language skills in the context of meaningful activities. Engaging children in conversation is particularly critical for dual-language learners, who typically catch up with native English speakers in decoding skills but lag behind in vocabulary and comprehension.[1]

If English is the language of instruction, dual-language learners need special supports for developing English proficiency and gaining access to instruction in other areas. Comprehensible input is one recommended strategy (Krashen, 2003). Teachers facilitate children's understanding of

---

[1] See National Research Council (2010) for an extended discussion of addressing the needs of English language learners.

English by using visible referents, gestures, simplifying syntax, repeating and paraphrasing, speaking slowly and clearly, and checking often for comprehension. Teachers who speak children's native language can also use it to help children understand English (Goldenberg et al., 2013).

According to the National Research Council report on assessing young children (NRC, 2008), high-quality literacy learning opportunities at the preschool and kindergarten level include the following:

1. Children are being read to and given opportunities to read.
2. They engage in rhyming words.
3. They are taught initial sounds and letter–sound links, and spellings of common words are pointed out and practiced.
4. Their attention is called to functions and features of print.
5. They are given opportunities to dictate and write using invented spelling.

The NICHD-sponsored National Reading Panel (2000) report provides a synthesis of the research evidence on the most effective instructional strategies to support the development of reading skills in the early grades. In their report, the following strategies had strong empirical support:

1. Explicit teaching of phonemic awareness (the ability to focus on and manipulate phonemes in spoken words);
2. Systematic instruction related to phonics (letter–sound correspondences in creating words);
3. Guided oral reading with feedback to improve fluency;
4. Direct and indirect instruction designed to support vocabulary development (e.g., having students encounter new words often and in varying contexts); and
5. Explicit teaching of comprehension strategies (comprehension monitoring, graphic and semantic organizers, question answering, question generation, and summarization).

In contrast to the practices listed above, the panel found little evidence to support independent reading for young children who are learning to read. A recent meta-analysis provides further evidence for the value of some direct teaching (Chambers, Cheung & Slavin, 2016). They found substantially greater literacy skill gains in preschool programs using comprehensive approaches which included phonemic awareness, phonics, and other skills, along with child-initiated activities, than in developmental constructivist approaches that focused on child-initiated activities with little direct teaching of early literacy skills.

Research on dual-language learners indicates that learning to read in children's native language is often associated with higher reading skills in English than initially learning to read in English. Native language instruction also strengthens and maintains native language and literacy skills (Goldenberg et al., 2013).

Math. Math is typically given less attention in early childhood programs, but recent findings suggest that early math skills are important. First, as is true for literacy, there is a great deal of variation in children's math skills at school entry, and children who enter with relatively poor skills fall further behind as they advance through the grades in school (National Science Foundation, 2010). In two recent longitudinal studies of American and Canadian children, respectively, the achievement level in math at school entry predicted, as well or better than reading skills, both math and reading abilities several grades later (Duncan et al., 2007; Romano, Kohen, Babchishin & Pagani, 2010). In later studies, persistent problems in math over the elementary grades were a much stronger predictor than persistent problems in reading of both high school completion and college attendance (Duncan & Magnuson, 2011), and growth in math learning from 54 months through first grade was a strong predictor of math skills at age 15 years (Watts, Duncan, Siegler & Davis-Kean, 2014). Taken together, these findings suggest that developing math skills in preschool is important.

There is a fair amount of consensus about the math skills which are important to develop in the early grades (National Research Council, 2009). They fall into five strands: (1) number (including the sequence of number words, one-to-one correspondence, and cardinality) and relations (e.g., more/less); (2) operations (composition and decomposition of number); (3) algebraic thinking (sorting and classifying objects, observing patterns, predicting what comes next); (4) measurement and data (determining the attribute of objects to measure, selecting the units of measurement and using measuring tools); and (5) geometry (spatial reasoning and shape, e.g., recognition and naming, understanding of defining properties).

Early number skills have been shown to be a particularly strong predictor of later mathematics achievement (Bailey, Siegler & Geary, 2014; Jordan, Kaplan, Ramineni & Locuniak, 2009; Nguyen, Watts, Duncan et al., 2016). But all of the strands are considered important. Some researchers have demonstrated the importance of presenting these elements in a coherent sequence of topics and skills that is consistent with the logical and hierarchical structure of the content taught and with typical learning trajectories (Cai, Ding & Wang, 2013; Clements & Sarama, 2014; Ferrini-Mundy, Burrill & Schmidt, 2007).

The National Research Council (2009) report points out that math is often absent in preschool classrooms, and when it is present, it is embedded in activities in which the teaching of mathematics is secondary to play or learning goals related to other domains. Emerging research indicates that activities in which math is a supplementary activity rather than the primary focus are less effective in promoting children's math learning than activities focused on math learning as the primary goal. Dale Farran, for example, found a strong association between the amount of teacher-led math instruction in preschool and the gains children made in mathematics (Farran, Lipsey & Wilson, 2011).

The "math wars" (pitting traditional direct instruction against more reform-minded approaches that focus on understanding) continue, but there is a fair amount of agreement among experts about the essential qualities of effective math learning opportunities. No synthesis of effective math teaching strategies for young children has been conducted, as it has for reading. But a National Academy of Science panel that focused on early math learning (National Research Council, 2001) concluded that, whether focused on number, measurement, algebraic reasoning, or one of the other strands of mathematics, teachers should give children opportunities to develop (1) conceptual understanding (comprehension of mathematical concepts, operations, and relations); (2) procedural fluency (skill in carrying out procedures flexibly, accurately, efficiently, and appropriately); (3) strategic competence (ability to formulate, represent, and solve mathematical problems); (4) adaptive reasoning (capacity for logical thought, reflection, explanation and justification); and 5) productive dispositions (habitual inclination to see mathematics as sensible, useful, and worthwhile, coupled with a belief in diligence and one's own efficacy).

Stipek and Johnson (in press) summarized recommendations related to teaching strategies from recent documents published by national organizations that examined research in early childhood mathematics, including the NAEYC & NCTM Joint Position Statement (National Association for the Education of Young Children & National Council of Teachers of Mathematics, 2010), the National Research Council Committee on Early Childhood Mathematics (NRC, 2009), and the Institute for Education Sciences (IES) Practice Guide: Teaching Math to Young Children (Frye et al., 2013). According to their summary, teachers should:

1. Recognize and build from children's informal mathematical knowledge, as well as their linguistic, cultural, family, and community resources;
2. Support children to focus on, describe, and extend the mathematical opportunities present within everyday activities;

3. Intentionally devote time to engaging children in mathematics through planned mathematical activities, as well as through capitalizing on mathematical opportunities within play;
4. Integrate mathematics with other activities and other activities with mathematics;
5. Ground mathematics curriculum and teaching practices in research-based knowledge that details developmental progressions in number and operations, geometry, and measurement; and
6. Ensure that learning opportunities build on children's existing understanding by thoughtfully and continually assessing their mathematical knowledge, skills, and strategies.

Self-Regulation/Executive Functions

Recent research suggests the importance of self-regulation (both emotional and behavioral) and the executive functions required for self-regulation, including short-term memory, attention, and inhibitory control (similar to impulse control). It is during preschool and the early elementary grades that brain development supporting these skills is the most rapid (Luciana & Nelson, 1998). Studies have found that executive functions are highly predictive of social competencies, learning-related behavior, and academic achievement gains (see Obradovic, Portilla & Boyce, 2012). For example, working memory is necessary for children to remember what they want to say while waiting for a peer to finish talking in a social context as well as to hold numbers and steps in mind while working on a math problem. Attention is required to read another child's emotions and to process the teacher's directions for an academic task. And inhibitory control is needed by a child whose immediate inclination is to grab a toy from another child as well as to reflect before writing down or calling out the first answer that comes to mind.

A few educational programs have been designed specifically to help young children develop self-regulation and executive functions (see Bierman & Torres, 2016). Tools of the Mind is the best known. It is aimed at improving executive functions primarily in the context of scripted dramatic play. The program includes a set of activities that are designed to help children use private speech for self-regulation and to use external aids to support memory and attention (Barnett, Jung, Yarosz et al., 2008). The Chicago School Readiness Project implemented in Head Start programs (Raver, Jones, Li-Grining et al., 2011) and a preschool intervention by Tominey and McClelland (2011) also focus on the development of self-regulation and executive functions.

Although there is some evidence for the effectiveness of these programs, specific efforts to improve children's self-regulation skills and executive functions are relatively new and we can only speculate about the critical elements of successful programs. Fortunately, research is burgeoning in this area and we should be able to identify effective practices in the near future.

Motivation and Engagement

To gain anything from preschool or the early elementary grades, children need to be actively engaged. Engagement can be broadly defined in terms of three dimensions: emotional (e.g., enthusiasm, interest), intellectual (e.g., involving active thought, problem solving), and behavioral (sometimes referred to as "learning-related behavior," such as following teacher directions, paying attention, and completing work). Many longitudinal studies have demonstrated strong associations between learning-related behavior and academic skills (DiPerna, Lei & Reid, 2007; Galindo & Fuller, 2010; Nesbitt, Farran & Fuhs, 2015). Learning-related behavior has cognitive as well as social/motivational components. Maintaining attention on the teacher, for example, requires the cognitive capacity to resist distractions. Capacity, however, is not sufficient. Attending to the teacher or to a task also requires motivation – the *desire* to engage in teacher-sanctioned behavior, perhaps out of a wish to please the teacher, to avoid punishment, or because the task is intrinsically interesting. Engagement is also affected by students' goals and by their self-confidence and self-efficacy – whether they believe they can perform tasks and activities in the classroom. In brief, to exert effort, students need to *want* to engage and they need to believe they *can* engage effectively.

Qualities of educational settings have powerful effects on both students' capacity and desire to be engaged, and we know a great deal about the qualities of classroom instruction and activities that are most engaging for young children (Stipek, 2002; Wigfield & Wentzel, 2007). For example, the social-emotional climate of the classroom affects children's motivation and engagement as well as their social development. Children who feel excluded by peers and not cared for by adults can become preoccupied with their own emotional discomfort, which can undermine their involvement in both academic and social activities.

The nature of tasks is also important. Being asked to complete tasks that children do not have the prerequisite skills to do can undermine self-confidence, the belief that effort will pay off, and children are not likely to be motivated to complete tasks that don't make any sense to them.

In brief, extant research (see Stipek 2002, 2011; Ramey & Gambrell, 2013) suggests that the following qualities of instruction are important for fostering children's motivation and engagement:

1. Tasks are challenging – not beyond children's ability to grasp, but requiring some effort and learning;
2. Activities are personally meaningful – related to children's interests, experiences and culture;
3. Instruction provides opportunities for active involvement, including experimentation, analysis, and problem-solving;
4. Children have some discretion in choosing or completing tasks;
5. The focus is on learning and understanding rather than on getting correct answers or performing well relative to peers;
6. Evaluation is specific and constructive (provides guidance); errors are considered a natural part of learning and provide information that can be used to guide future efforts; and
7. Success is attributed to effort and persistence, not ability, and teachers consistently convey high but realistic expectations.

Family Communication and Involvement

There is substantial evidence on the value of children's primary caregivers being involved in children's learning and development (e.g., Pomerantz, Moorman & Cheung, 2012; for a review see Henderson & Mapp, 2002). Research on effective practices for promoting family involvement[2] suggests that caretakers are most likely to play productive roles in their children's education when

1. Teachers communicate regularly and thoroughly (covering all academic subjects, social-emotional development, behavior, etc.) with caregivers and listen attentively to their concerns and suggestions. Conversations can occur in informal contexts before and after school, in home visits, in formal parent–teacher conferences, and in phone calls.
2. Back-to-school events and programs are used to inform caregivers generally of the curriculum and to provide guidance on strategies they can use at home to support their children's development (e.g., on reading to children or managing difficult behavior).
3. Classroom newsletters and other materials are sent home to provide caregivers with information about current topics of instruction and suggestions for activities that they can engage in with their children to reinforce school learning.

[2] For more detailed suggestions see Caspe, 2005; www.hfrp.org/family-involvement.

4. Caregivers are made to feel welcome in the classroom, such as by being encouraged to volunteer or participate in special classroom events.

Continuity

There is indisputable evidence that high-quality preschool, as described above, is required for substantial and sustained benefits (Barnett, 2011) and that children benefit from high-quality teaching subsequent to pre-school. Indeed, Hanushek (2002) concluded from his analyses that the achievement gap could be closed by providing economically disadvantaged children three consecutive years of a highly effective teacher. Children whose quality preschool experience is followed by high quality instruction in the early elementary grades thus have an advantage over children whose quality preschool experience is followed by low-quality instruction in elementary school.

Quality counts at every grade, but many experts and policymakers claim that there are additional benefits to continuity[3] between preschool and the early elementary grades. Quality, then, needs to be conceptualized not just as the quality of instruction within a grade, but the continuity of educational experiences across grades.

Why might a lack of continuity result in a failure to achieve the expected long-lasting effects of preschool? Here are a few examples. If kindergarten teachers do not build on the gains children made in preschool and continue to advance in their skills, and instead teach material that children have already learned, children without the benefit of preschool will catch up. Significant and unnecessary changes in behavioral expectations or the nature of instruction likewise might disrupt children's continuous learning. Time for learning is reduced by the time needed to learn new routines and expectations. If parents are not invited or given opportunities to participate in elementary school, the habits and expectations of being involved in their children's education, developed in high-quality preschool, would not provide ongoing benefit for children.

Proponents of what is often referred to as "Pre-K–3" have written widely on the policies and practices that are important to achieving continuity in children's educational experiences so that the benefits of quality preschool are maintained and children continue to make gains in the early elementary grades. The focus has been on such elements as

---

[3] The terms "continuity," "alignment," "coherence," and others are used somewhat interchangeably in the literature. I use "continuity" here to denote alignment over time (across grades), and "alignment" to refer to coherence among policies and practices within a grade.

standards, assessments, curricula, and instructional strategies (Kauerz, 2006; Bogard & Takanishi, 2005; Graves, 2006; Takanishi, 2016).

The value of continuity from preschool through the early elementary grades is suggested by evidence that programs providing continuity in services and supports have produced particularly impressive long-term effects in child outcomes (see Reynolds, Magnuson & Ou, 2006). Otherwise, there is little empirical evidence for the benefits of continuity in policies and practices across grades, over and above the value of high-quality learning environments and the provision of services at every grade. Given the dearth of research, the discussion below is an analysis of what dimensions of policy and practice continuity are most likely to matter for children's learning and development.

Clearly, for children who are enrolled in low-quality preschool, the goal is *not* to create continuity by continuing ineffective practices throughout the early elementary grades. And no proponent of Pre-K–3 continuity suggests that children should engage in the same academic activities for several grades, or that 3- or 4-year-olds should have the same level of autonomy and responsibility as 8-year-olds. The important questions are: What kind of continuity across grades is beneficial? What should change in children's school experience? How should it change and what should remain the same? These issues are discussed below at various levels of policy and practice (see also Stipek, Clements, Coburn et al., 2017).

State Policies

What matters for children is what transpires in their classroom. But, as mentioned above, the larger educational policy context substantially affects children's experiences in the classroom. It is safe to assume, therefore, that some articulation between state policies at the preschool and elementary grades is necessary for continuity in classroom practices. If kindergarten teachers are expected to build on the competencies that children developed in preschool and to move them along a coherent continuum of skills, then kindergarten standards and assessments need to be aligned with preschool standards and assessments.

Apparently, failing to build on skills developed in preschool is common. Engel, Claessens & Finch (2013) found that, in a nationally representative sample, children had, prior to entering kindergarten, already mastered most of the mathematics concepts reportedly covered by teachers during that year. Moreover, coverage of this basic content, which most children had already learned, was negatively associated with student achievement gains at the end of kindergarten. Failing to give students an opportunity to build on skills they had developed in preschool appeared to cause them to plateau. Meanwhile, children who did not have the benefit of preschool, had time to catch up. Although it is not clear that the problem was misalignment of standards, it may have contributed to the problem.

In addition to leading to too much duplication between kindergarten and preschool, nonaligned standards can create gaps between what children are expected to learn in preschool and what they are expected to learn in kindergarten. Discontinuous standards could therefore also lead to instruction in preschool that does not prepare children for the academic demands of kindergarten and instruction in kindergarten that assumes skills that have not yet been developed.

Differences in relative weight given to different dimensions of development could also result in the early elementary grades failing to build on strides children made in preschool. For example, if literacy but not math skills are emphasized in the preschool standards, but they both figure prominently in standards for the early elementary grades, children may enter kindergarten well prepared to meet the elementary grade standards in literacy, but not at all in math.

Differential attention to social-emotional development may also undermine children's success in school. Currently, most states' preschool standards and assessments give relatively equal weight to social-emotional and academic development, whereas most elementary standards and assessments are focused entirely on academic skills. Given evidence that social-emotional skills support learning (see Durlak, Weissberg, Dymnicki et al., 2011; Payton, Weissberg, Durlak et al., 2008), the absence of standards and assessments related to social-emotional development in the elementary grades could contribute to fade out because teachers in elementary school are not capitalizing on whatever gains on this dimension children made in preschool.

Ideally, standards and assessments follow a clear developmental trajectory that is coherent with both the discipline and with the developing cognitive capacities of children moving from preschool through the early elementary grades. But having well-articulated standards across the grades is not sufficient to ensure instruction that helps children move from wherever they are in the learning trajectory to the next level. Teachers need to know the standards that come before and after their grade. Not all children who enter kindergarten will have met all of the preschool standards and teachers need to provide instruction that helps these children meet those standards before they tackle the kindergarten standards. By the same token, some children entering kindergarten will have already achieved the kindergarten standards and teachers need to provide instruction that allows them to continue to grow their skills beyond the expectations of kindergartners.

A more radical but arguably sensible policy might be to create one set of Pre-K–3 standards and assessments that acknowledges the diversity of skills that children bring to each grade. The goal would be for all children to achieve the high end of the standards by the end of third grade. The teachers' task would be to determine where each child is on these learning trajectories and provide learning opportunities designed to move him or her to the next level. Short of this ambitious change, at the very least standards should be aligned across grades, with teachers well informed of the previous and later grade standards, and understanding that instruction needs to be targeted at each child's current skill level, which may be at, above or below the grade-level standard.

District and School Policies

Standards and assessments used for accountability purposes are typically imposed by the state. District and school-level policies related to curricula, formative and summative assessments, and teacher professional development also affect children's learning experiences in the classroom. Although there is no empirical evidence demonstrating specifically that using the same curriculum and assessments or providing similar or the same professional development across preschool and the early elementary grades leads to better learning outcomes for children, there are reasons to expect advantages associated with this kind of continuity.

Using the same literacy, math or science curricula across grades should help teachers move students along a coherent trajectory of skill building, with new instruction building on previously developed skills. Curriculum continuity would also make it easier for teachers to return to material from the previous grade for students who had not mastered it, and to jump ahead to material in the next grade for students who had already mastered their current grade standards. The absence of meaningful curriculum connections across grades could lead to instruction that is either repetitious of the previous grade or skips important prerequisite skills and understandings.

Continuity in assessments allows teachers to assess children where they are in a learning trajectory that transcends the particular grade they are in so they can provide more appropriate learning experiences. If the kindergarten teachers in the study by Engel et al. (2013) had had easy access to their children's skill levels in math when they entered kindergarten, they might not have targeted instruction to skills most of their children had already mastered.

Tracking children's individual progress from preschool through third grade should help teachers plan instruction and develop interventions for children who have stalled in their progress. Having the data available is a first step, but teachers also need to be trained to effectively use data on individual children's skills to plan instruction. If teachers lack such skills, the data alone will not result in improved student learning. Tracking learning over time can also help administrators and teachers assess learning losses from spring to the next fall and develop strategies for helping parents support their children's learning over the summer.

Note, however, that the same curriculum can be implemented in classrooms in very different ways. Thus, even if the same curriculum is used in preschool through third grade, instruction could be discontinuous. Continuity in children's experience therefore requires support for teachers and opportunities for teachers to work collaboratively across grade levels.

All of the policies and practices described above are designed to create a seamless educational experience for children as they move from preschool through early elementary school. The next section focuses on continuity in the classroom practices that children experience directly.

Classroom

We know little about what aspects of instruction should be continuous and which should change. Some adjustment in teaching style is appropriate. For example, children should be given more independence and responsibility as they advance in age. But there are also ways in which a different approach to teaching could be disruptive. Consider math, for example. Learning could be undermined if children move from a classroom using a more progressive approach – in which manipulatives are used extensively, children work in pairs or groups and are encouraged to figure out their own strategies to solve problems, and understanding is stressed more than getting the right answer – to a more traditional approach, in which all activities involve paper and pencil, children work alone, and the teacher stresses a particular single strategy to get the right answer. These are very different approaches to teaching math and it could be confusing to children to shift suddenly from one approach to the other.

There may also be value in consistency in particular practices or routines (e.g., keeping daily journals, using a problem that children solve in their heads as a warm-up activity for math). This kind of consistency can give children a feeling of familiarity and self-confidence. Teaching strategies can be made increasingly complex so they are appropriate for children in preschool (e.g., dictating journal entries in preschool) and in later grades (doing their own writing). The complexity changes, but the task is familiar.

Continuity in classroom management strategies, as well, should make it easier for children to learn and follow the rules. Routines that support students' self-regulation, for example, such as practices designed to gain children's attention, transitions to go outside or eat lunch, and language (e.g., "crisscross applesauce") used in conversations about appropriate behavior may give children a sense of comfort and confidence, and reduce the time required to acquaint them with new practices and language. Changing the rules from year to year unnecessarily can be confusing and can require additional time away from instruction to teach children the new classroom rules.

Clearly children should be given increasing responsibility for self-regulation and managing tasks. Four-year-olds can be expected to put their materials away. Older children may be expected to identify and collect the materials they need, as well as put their materials back in their place. But the increased responsibility should come in small increments. To do this, teachers need to know what responsibilities children had in the previous grade so they can begin with what children are used to, and then slowly add responsibility and complexity.

Continuity in how schools involve parents may also be important (Takanishi, 2016). Parent involvement is stressed in high-quality pre-school. If parents are not actively invited to engage productively in their child's elementary schooling, the involvement they practiced in preschool may disappear. A failure to build in the elementary grades on what parents learned when their children were in preschool could thus contribute to the fading of the benefits of high-quality preschool. Consistency in the form in which schools and teachers inform parents may also be useful. For example, although the content of assessments will change as children develop new skills, the reporting formats can be similar and continuous. This facilitates parents' processing and understanding of their children's performance and needs, and it allows them to see progress across grades. Consistency in messages about parent involvement across preschool and the early elementary grades is also more likely to succeed in engaging parents than inconsistent messages about expectations.

Achieving continuity in practices – whether they concern instruction, management or communication to parents – requires communication among teachers from different grades. Opportunities for cross-grade collaboration and professional development may be the most important practice in achieving coherence and continuity across grades. For this to occur, dedicated and regular time needs to be made available for teachers at different grade levels to discuss standards, curriculum, instruction, assessment, management, communication, and connections with families, and any other topic that might affect the educational experience of their students.

Summary

Quality is typically assessed within grades. But continuity and coherence across grades most likely also contributes to the quality of children's experience and thus their learning. This chapter suggests ways in which a lack of continuity could undermine the overall quality of children's educational experience and contribute to the fading of the benefits of high-quality preschool.

Achieving the kind of continuity described here is difficult in the context of the typical organizational disconnect, especially between preschool and elementary grades. Preschool is often embedded in different institutional contexts (e.g., Head Start, state preschool) from elementary schools, with different funding sources and different regulations, and with different teacher certification requirements. Preschools and elementary schools are also often not located on the same campus, making collaboration among teachers at the different levels difficult. And in some states, there are substantial differences in the nature and quality of teachers' training.

Many districts and schools have made attempts to address these challenges and promote greater continuity (Valentino & Stipek, 2016). These efforts should be followed closely, documenting successful strategies, the challenges encountered, and the effects on classroom instruction and student learning. There is a strong research base supporting the description of quality educational contexts reviewed in the first section of this chapter. A similar research base is needed to answer the questions asked in the second section concerning continuity of policies and practices needed to sustain the benefits of high-quality preschool and promote children's learning and development.

References

August, D. & Shanahan, T. (2006). *Developing Literacy in Second-Language Learners*. Mahwah, NJ: Lawrence Erlbaum Associates.

Bailey, D. H., Siegler, R. S. & Geary, D. C. (2014). Early predictors of middle school fraction knowledge. *Developmental Science*, 17(5), 775–785. https://doi.org/10.1111/desc.12155

Barnett, S., Jung, K., Yarosz, D. et al. (2008). Educational effects of the tools of the mind curriculum: a randomized trial. *Early Childhood Research Quarterly*, 23, 299–313.

Barnett, S. W. (2011). Effectiveness of early education interventions. *Science,* 333, 975–978.

Bierman, K. & Torres, M. (2016). Promoting the development of executive functions through early education and prevention programs, in Griffin, J. A., Freund, L.S. & McCardle, P. (Eds.), *Executive Function in Preschool Age Children: Integrating Measurement, Neurodevelopment and Translational Research.* Washington, DC: American Psychological Association.

Bogard, K. & Takanishi, R. (2005). *PK–3: An aligned and coordinated approach to education for children 3 to 8 years old.* SRCD Social Policy Report.

Cai, J., Ding, M. & Wang, T. (2013). How do exemplary Chinese and U.S. mathematics teachers view instructional coherence? *Educational Studies in Mathematics,* 85(2), 265–280.

Caspe, M. (2005). A catalog of family process measures. The evaluation exchange: evaluating family involvement programs. *Harvard Family Research Project,* 10(4), 8–9.

Chambers, B., Cheung, A. & Slavin, T. (2016). Literacy and language outcomes of comprehensive and developmental-constructivist approaches to early childhood education: a systematic review. *Educational Research Review,* 18, 88–111.

Clements, D. H. & Sarama, J. (2014). *Learning and Teaching Early Math: The Learning Trajectories Approach* (2nd edn.). New York, NY: Routledge.

Currie, J. & Thomas, D. (2000). School quality and the longer-term effects of Head Start. *Journal of Human Resources,* 35(4), 755–774.

DiPerna, J. C., Lei, P. W. & Reid, E. E. (2007). Kindergarten predictors of mathematical growth in the primary grades: an investigation using the early childhood longitudinal study, kindergarten cohort. *Journal of Educational Psychology,* 99(2), 369–379.

Duncan, G. J., Dowsett, C. J., Claessens, A. et al. (2007). School readiness and later achievement. *Developmental Psychology,* 43(6),1428–1446.

Duncan, G. & Magnuson, K. (2011). The nature and impact of early achievement skills, attention skills, and behavior problems, in Duncan G. & Murnane, R. (Eds.), *Whither Opportunity: Rising Inequality, Schools, and Children's Life Chances* (pp. 47–69). New York, NY: Russell Sage.

Durlak, J., Weissberg, R., Dymnicki, A., Taylor, R. & Schellinger, K. (2011). The Impact of enhancing students' social and emotional learning: a meta-analysis of school-based universal interventions. *Child Development,* 82(1), 405–432.

Emmer, E. T. & Strough, L. (2001). Classroom management: a critical part of educational psychology, with implications for teacher education. *Educational Psychologist,* 36, 103–112.

Engel, M., Claessens, A. & Finch, M. (2013). Teaching students what they already know? The (Mis) Alignment between mathematics instructional content and student knowledge in kindergarten. *Educational Evaluation and Policy Analysis,* 35(2), 157–178.

Espinosa, L. (2008). *Challenging Common Myths about Young English Language Learners.* Policy Brief No. 8: Advancing PK–3. Foundation for Child

Development. Retrieved from http://fcd-us.org/sites/default/files/MythsOfTea chingELLsEspinosa.pdf

Farran, D., Lipsey, M. & Wilson, S. (2011). *Experimental evaluation of the Tools of the Mind Pre-K curriculum.* Working paper available online. Retrieved from http://peabody.vanderbilt.edu/Documents/pdf/PRI/Tools_Evaluation_Report .pdf

Ferrini-Mundy, J., Burrill, G. & Schmidt, W. H. (2007). Building teacher capacity for implementing curricular coherence: mathematics teacher professional development tasks. *Journal of Mathematics Teacher Education*, 10(4–6), 311–324.

Frye, D., Baroody, A. J., Burchinal, M. et al. (2013). *Teaching Math to Young Children: A Practice Guide.* Washington, DC: National Center for Education Evaluation and Regional Assistance (NCEE), Institute of Education Sciences (IES), US Department of Education. Retrieved from https://ies.ed.gov/ncee/ wwc/Docs/PracticeGuide/early_math_pg_111313.pdf

Fuller, B., Bein, E., Bridges, M., Kim, Y. & Rabe-Hesketh, S. (2017). Do academic preschools yield stronger benefits? Cognitive emphasis, dosage, and early learning. *Journal of Applied Developmental Psychology 52*, 1–11

Galindo, C. & Fuller, B. (2010). The social competence of Latino kindergartners and growth in mathematical understanding. *Developmental Psychology*, 46(3), 579–592.

Goldenberg, C., Hicks, J. & Lit, I. (2013). Teaching young English learners, in Reutzel, R. (Ed.), *Handbook of Research-Based Practice in Early Childhood Education* (pp. 140–160). New York, NY: Guilford Press.

Good, T. & Grouws, D. (1977). Teaching effects: a process-product study of fourth grade mathematics classrooms. *Journal of Teacher Education*, 28, 49–54.

Graves, B. (2006). PK–3: What is it and how do we know it works? *Foundation for Child Development Working Paper 4: Advancing PK–3*.

Hamre, B. (2014). Teachers' daily interactions with children: an essential ingredient in effective early childhood programs. *Child Development Perspectives*, 4, 223–230.

Hamre, B. K. & Pianta, R. C. (2005), Can instructional and emotional support in the first-grade classroom make a difference for children at risk of school failure? *Child Development*, 76, 949–967.

Hanushek, E. (2002). Teacher quality, in Izumi, L. T. and Evers, W. M. (Ed.), *Teacher Quality*. Stanford, CA: Hoover Institution Press, pp. 1–12.

Henderson, A. & Mapp, K. (2002). *A New Wave of Evidence: The Impact of School, Family and Community Connections on Student Achievement.* Austin, TX: Southwest Educational Development Laboratory. www.sedl.org/connections

Hirsh-Pasek, K., Golinkoff, R., Berk, L. & Singer, D. (2009). *A Mandate for Playful Learning in Preschool: Presenting the Evidence.* New York, NY: Oxford University Press.

Hyson, M., Whittaker, J., Zaslow, M. et al. (2011). Measuring the quality of environmental supports for young children's social and emotional competence, in Zaslow, M., Martinez-Beck, I., Tout, K. & Halle, T. (Eds.), *Quality Measurement in Early Childhood Settings* (pp. 105–134). Baltimore, MD: Paul Brookes Publishing Co.

Jordan, N. C., Kaplan, D., Ramineni, C. & Locuniak, M. N. (2009). Early math matters: kindergarten number competence and later mathematics outcomes. *Developmental Psychology*, 45(3), 850–867. https://doi.org/10.1037/a0014939

Kauerz, K. (2006). Ladders of learning: Fighting fade-out by advancing PK–3 alignment. New America Foundation Early Education Initiative, Issue Brief No. 3.

Krashen, S. (2003). *Explorations in Language Acquisition and Use*. Portsmouth: Heinemann.

Luciana, M. & Nelson, C. (1998). The functional emergence of prefrontally-guided working memory systems in four- to eight-year-old children. *Neuropsychologia*, 36, 273–293.

National Association for the Education of Young Children, & National Council of Teachers of Mathematics. (2010). *Early childhood mathematics: Promoting good beginnings* (Joint position statement). Washington, DC. Retrieved from www.naeyc.org/files/naeyc/file/positions/psmath.pdf

National Reading Panel (US) & National Institute of Child Health and Human Development (US). (2000). *Report of the National Reading Panel: Teaching Children to Read: An Evidence-Based Assessment of the Scientific Research Literature on Reading and Its Implications for Reading Instruction: Reports of the Subgroups*. Washington, DC: National Institute of Child Health and Human Development, National Institutes of Health.

National Research Council (US). (1998). *Preventing Reading Difficulties in Young Children*. Washington, DC: The National Academies Press.

National Research Council (US). (2001). *Adding It Up: Helping Children Learn Mathematics*. Washington, DC: The National Academies Press.

National Research Council (US). (2008). *Early Childhood Assessment: Why, What, and How*. Washington, DC: The National Academies Press.

National Research Council (US). (2009). *Mathematics learning in early childhood: paths toward excellence and equity*, in Cross, C., Woods, T. & Schweingruber, H. (Eds.), *Committee on Early Childhood Mathematics*. Washington, DC: The National Academies Press.

National Research Council (U.S.). (2010). *Language Diversity, School Learning, and Closing Achievement Gaps: A Workshop Summary*. Washington, DC: The National Academies Press.

National Science Foundation. (2010). *Science and Engineering Indicators*. Retrieved from www.nsf.gov/statistics/seind10/figures.htm.

Nesbitt, K., Farran, D. & Fuhs, M. (2015). Executive function skills and academic achievement gains in prekindergarten: Contributions of learning-related behaviors. *Developmental Psychology*, 51(7), 865–878.

Nguyen, T., Watts, T. W., Duncan, G. J. et al. (2016). Which preschool mathematics competencies are most predictive of fifth grade achievement? *Early Childhood Research Quarterly*, 36, 550–560.

Obradovic, J., Portilla, X. A. & Boyce, W. T. (2012). Executive functioning and developmental neuroscience, in Pianta, R. (Ed.), *Handbook of Early Childhood Education* (pp. 324–351). New York, NY: Guilford Press.

Pagani, C., Archambault, I. & Janosz, M. (2010). School readiness and later achievement: A French Canadian replication and extension. *Developmental Psychology*, 46, 984–994.

Payton, J., Weissberg, R., Durlak, J. et al. (2008). *The Positive Impact of Social and Emotional Learning for Kindergarten to Eighth-Grade Students: Findings from Three Scientific Reviews*. Chicago, IL: Collaborative for Academic, Social, and Emotional Learning.

Peske, H. G. & Haycock, K. (2006). *Teaching Inequality: How Poor and Minority Students Are Shortchanged on Teacher Quality*. Washington, DC: The Education Trust.

Pianta, R. (1999). *Enhancing Relationships Between Children and Teachers*. Washington, DC: American Psychological Association.

Pomerantz, E. M., Moorman, E. A. & Cheung, C. S. (2012). Parents' involvement in children's learning, in Harris, K. R., Graham, S., Urdan, T. C. et al. (Eds.), *APA Educational Psychology Handbook* (pp. 417–440). Washington, DC: American Psychological Association.

Preschool Curriculum Evaluation Research Consortium (2008). *Effects of Preschool Curriculum Programs on School Readiness Report from the Preschool Curriculum Evaluation Research Initiative*. Washington, DC: Institute for Education Sciences.

Pressley, M. (2002). Before reading instruction begins, in Pressley, M. (Ed.), *Reading Instruction That Works: The Case for Balanced Teaching* (2nd edn., pp. 90–133). New York, NY: Guilford.

Ramey, D. & Gambrell, L. (2013). Motivating and engaging children in early childhood settings, in Reutzel, R. (Ed.). *Handbook of Research-Based Practice in Early Childhood Education* (pp. 193–204). New York, NY: Guilford Press.

Raver, C. C., Jones, S. M., Li-Grining, C. P. et al. (2011). CSRP's impact on low-income preschoolers' pre-academic skills: Self-regulation as a mediating mechanism. *Child Development*, 82(1), 362–378.

Reynolds, A., Magnuson, K. & Ou, S. (2006). PK–3 education: programs and practices that work in children's first decade. *Foundation for Child Development Working Paper 6: Advancing PK–3*.

Romano, E., Kohen, D., Babchishin, L. & Pagani, L. S. (2010). School readiness and later achievement: replication and extension study using a nation-wide Canadian survey. *Developmental Psychology*, 46, 995–1007.

Rudasill, K., Gallagher, K. & White, J. (2010). Temperamental attention and activity, classroom emotional support, and academic achievement in third grade. *Journal of School Psychology*, 48, 113–134.

Sabol, T. & Pianta, R. (2012). Recent trends in research on teacher–child relationships. *Attachment and Human Development*, 14(3), 213–231.

Schweinhart, L., Barnes, H. & Weikart, D. (1993). Significant benefits: The High/Scope Perry preschool study through age 27 [Monograph]. High/Scope Educational Research Foundation, No. 10.

Stipek, D. (2002). *Motivation to Learn: Integrating Theory and Practice* (4th edn.). Needham Heights, MA: Allyn & Bacon.

Stipek, D. (2011). Classroom practices and children's motivation to learn, in Zigler, E., Gilliam, W. S. & Barnett, W. S. (Eds.), *The Pre-K Debates: Current*

Controversies & Issues (pp. 98–103). Baltimore, MA: Paul H. Brookes Publishing.

Stipek, D. & Johnson, N. (in press). Developmentally appropriate practice in early childhood education redefined: the case of math, in Graue, B., Levin, F. & Ryan, S. (Eds.), *Advancing Knowledge and Building Capacity for Early Childhood Research: Creating Synergies Among Segregated Scholarly Communities*. Washington, DC: American Education Research Association.

Stipek, D., Clements, D., Coburn, C., Franke, M. & Farran, D. (2017). PK–3: What does it mean for instruction? *SRCD Social Policy Report*, 30(2), 1–23.

Takanishi, R. (2016). *First Things First! Creating the New American Primary School*. New York, NY: Teachers College Press.

Tominey, S. & McClelland, M. (2011). Red light, purple light: Findings from a randomized trial using circle time games to improve behavioral self-regulation in preschool, *Early Education & Development*, 22, 489–519.

Valentino, R. & Stipek, D. (2016). *PreK–3 Alignment in California's Education System: Obstacles and Opportunities*. Stanford University: Policy Analysis for California Education.

Watts, T., Duncan, G., Siegler, R. & Davis-Kean, P. (2014). What's past is prologue: Relations between early mathematics knowledge and high school achievement. *Educational Researcher*, 43(7), 352–360.

Wigfield, A. & Wentzel, K. (2007). Introduction to motivation at school: Interventions that work. *Educational Psychologist*, 42(2), 191–196.

8 The Child–Parent Center Preschool-to-Third-Grade Program
A School Reform Model to Increase and Sustain Learning Gains at Scale

Arthur J. Reynolds

The increasing emphasis on supporting children's learning throughout the first decade of life is based on two unfortunate realities. First, the size of the achievement gap by family income is large and increasing. A single program or practice at any one phase is not enough to close the gap in any enduring way. In the 2015 National Assessment of Educational Progress, 20 percent of fourth-graders from low-income families (up to 185 percent of the poverty line) were proficient readers compared to 52 percent of students from higher-income families (NAEP, 2016). This 32-point gap, which has increased by a third over the past decade, indicates that, to be effective, prevention services must be proportionate to the identified need (Belfield & Levin, 2007; Braveman & Gottlieb, 2014; Takanishi, 2016).

A one- or two-year preschool program, even if high quality, can reduce this gap by only about a third (Barton & Coley, 2009; Reynolds et al., 2017). Early gaps in school readiness magnify over time and, in conjunction with post-program learning environments, contribute to disparities in achievement proficiency, school completion, and health behavior. To realistically address these challenges, multi-year and multi-component approaches that integrate services are needed.

The second unfortunate reality is that, despite the overall evidence of positive benefits for good-quality programs, impacts of early childhood programs vary substantially in magnitude, consistency, and duration. Too much variation in program quality is a major reason why, as is the fact that later education is not aligned to reinforce and bolster early learning gains (Camilli et al., 2010; Reynolds & Temple, 2008; Zigler, Gilliam & Jones, 2006). Even if large and sustained effects do occur as well as greater alignment of services, these programs are rarely scaled to entire populations.

Given the size of achievement disparities, the relatively modest levels of achievement proficiency of US students, and the limited reach of current programs, programs must be implemented that are longer in duration and more comprehensive in scope than existing approaches. They also must have the capacity to scale, since only a small fraction of education and prevention programs are ever scaled to the population level (O'Connell et al., 2009; Spoth et al., 2013).

Multi-level programs in the first decade of life can redress these trends. To increase scalability and sustainability, collaborative models of engagement are needed.

Chapter Focus

In this chapter, I review the Midwest Child–Parent Center Preschool-to-Third-Grade Program (CPC-P–3) as an approach for scaling and sustaining an evidence-based education program. Key elements, short- and longer-term impacts, and shared lessons for implementation at the neighborhood, district, and state levels are described. Supported by an Investing in Innovation Grant from the US Department of Education, the Chicago Longitudinal Study, and related projects, CPC-P–3 provides comprehensive education and family support services to children and parents in six Illinois, Minnesota, and Wisconsin school districts. Designed to accelerate achievement, socio-emotional learning, and parent involvement (HCRC, 2012; Reynolds et al., 2016), CPC-P–3 is a school reform model to engage schools and families, thereby facilitating scale up. This is illustrated with evidence from ongoing longitudinal studies, which support scaling at larger levels and key principles of effective collaboration.

Principles of School–Family–University Collaboration

As a school reform model, CPC-P–3 implements a set of core elements in elementary school or center-based sites to enhance student learning. CPC services through third grade can be completely co-located or as a partnership between centers and schools. The framework is a school–family–university collaboration model which emphasizes three principles: (a) shared ownership, (b) committed resources, and (c) progress monitoring for improvement (Reynolds et al., 2017).

In shared ownership, the major partners have an equal responsibility to plan, implement, manage, and improve the program. Rather than the usual approach in which an externally developed (e.g., university-based) program is adopted without modification, a shared ownership model distributes the responsibility to ensure effective implementation, thereby strengthening the commitment from all partners to work together in achieving common goals. This is consistent with emerging collaborative stakeholder models of research (Frank, Basch & Selby, 2014). Shared ownership provides a foundation of trust necessary for scaling and sustaining programs. Families also have an active role by providing input and ideas about strategies to implement, and working collaboratively with teachers and staff to create and maintain a strong learning environment.

For committed resources, each partner makes key investments that are necessary for effective implementation. Resources include time, financial capital, and physical space. Although resources denote the "stake" that each partner has in an initiative, the increased commitment that goes along with investment can facilitate scale-up and sustainability. Alternative financing options that are used, such as matching grants, blended funding, and leveraging, increase the capacity and feasibility of further expansion. Given shared ownership, staff collaboration in fulfilling roles and responsibilities is further enhanced, which also increases efficiency.

Progress monitoring for improvement addresses how well programs are meeting their short- and intermediate-term goals. This ongoing formative evaluation is essential for continuous improvement. Measuring and reporting the extent of implementation fidelity enables timely adjustment of program strategies and activities to the needs of participants and partners alike. This is especially important in comprehensive programs in which responses to intervention have large variability. The use of data and evidence, and sharing these among partners, reinforce the importance of meeting milestones and standards. The tools that are routinized also help ensure that the quality of the program can be maintained as scaling occurs.

Midwest Child–Parent Center Expansion Program

The CPC program began in 1967 in inner-city Chicago. This was made possible by funding from Title I of the Elementary and Secondary School Act of 1965, which provided grants to school districts serving high proportions of low-income children. The goal of the Act was to "Employ imaginative thinking and new approaches to meet the educational needs of poor children" (US Senate, 1967; p. 1455). The Chicago Public School District was the first school system to use these funds for preschool and thereby established CPC as the second oldest (after Head Start) federally funded preschool. Although CPC began as a comprehensive preschool program, children received continuing services in kindergarten and the early grades the following year, resulting in the P–3 program that exists today. The program was designed as a response to three major problems facing Chicago's west side neighborhoods: low rates of attendance, family disengagement with schools, and low student achievement.

The conceptual foundations of the program derive from ecological, risk/protection, and human capital theories (Bronfenbrenner, 1989; Rutter & Rutter, 1993), in which well-being is a product of proximal and distal influences at multiple levels of contexts (individual, family, school, community) experienced during the entire early childhood period (ages 3 to 9). The program's focus on the quality and continuity of learning environments indicates that optimal development can be promoted through enriched experiences and settings co-created by children, families, and schools. Due to discontinuities in instructional support and philosophy between early childhood and school age settings, improvements in the integration and alignment of services during this important ecological transition can improve children's levels of readiness for kindergarten that are sustained over the elementary grades (Takanishi, 2016; Takanishi & Kauerz, 2008; Zigler & Styfco, 1993). Increased teacher preparation and ongoing resource support reinforce instructional improvements (Manning et al., 2017).

In the current expansion, each CPC-P–3 site provides a dynamic support system. Comprehensive education and family support services are provided. Under the direction of a leadership team at each site and in collaboration with the Principal, CPC-P–3 enhances school readiness skills, increases early school achievement, and promotes parent involvement. It is a stand-alone school or center in which all children receive services. Sites implement a set of six core elements following the program guidelines and requirements specified in the manual (HCRC, 2012; Reynolds et al., 2016). All teachers, staff, and children participate as well as staff hired to reduce class sizes, and provide program leadership, professional development, and family engagement. For historical comparisons of the program, see Reynolds et al. (2016) and Reynolds (2012).

The program expansion and scale-up is guided by six major goals: (1) Implement the CPC model with high levels of quality following key elements of effectiveness; (2) Assess the quality of implementation of the preschool, kindergarten, and first- to third-grade components by context and participant characteristics; (3) Evaluate the impact of the CPC program from preschool to third grade using a rigorous and multi-faceted design; (4) Assess the impact of the CPC program by child, family, and program characteristics; (5) Determine the cost-effectiveness of the program over preschool to third grade; and (6) Implement a sustainability plan to facilitate program expansion in additional settings.

The CPC's Head Teacher (HT) or Director works under the leadership of the elementary school Principal. HTs are the administrative leads for the program and manage implementation, provide coaching and supervision to staff, and help establish expectations of performance. The Parent Resource Teacher (PRT) directs the CPC's parent resource room and family services, and outreach activities are organized by the School–Community Representative (SCR). Health services are coordinated between the preschool and elementary grades. Liaisons work with the HT and PRT to provide alignment of curriculum and parent involvement activities.

After preschool participation at ages 3 and/or 4 in small classes with student:teacher ratios of 17:2, the K–3 component provides reduced class sizes (maximum of 25), teacher aides for each class, continued parent involvement opportunities, and enriched classroom environments for strengthening language and literacy, math, science, and social-emotional skills. Site mentors from HCRC also work with leadership and staff to ensure effective implementation. Curricular and performance monitoring are integrated within a robust professional development system of school facilitators and online supports.

In order to enhance shared ownership and school-wide integration of P–3 services, the Midwest CPC expansion conceptualizes the program as a school reform model led by the principal. Figure 8.1 shows the continuity principle of implementation and Figure 8.2 the organizational structure, in which the CPC head teacher, in concert with the principal and other coordinators, implements all program elements. Children's learning is supported by the family within the context of the school and community. The system of services is mutually beneficial to all partners and builds shared ownership, committed resources, and progress monitoring for improvement.

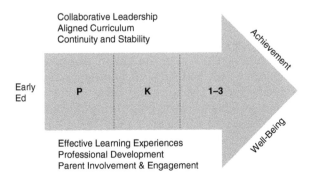

Figure 8.1 Child–Parent Center Preschool to Third Grade Conceptualization

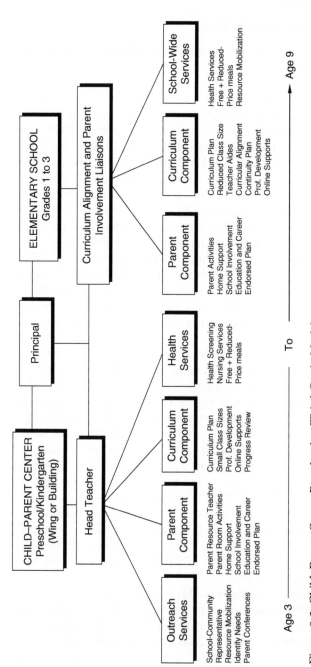

Figure 8.2 Child–Parent Center Preschool to Third Grade Model

CHILD–PARENT CENTER
Preschool/Kindergarten
(Wing or Building)

Principal

ELEMENTARY SCHOOL
Grades 1 to 3

Head Teacher

Curriculum Alignment and Parent
Involvement Liaisons

Outreach
Services

School-Community
Representative
Resource Mobilization
Identify Needs
Parent Conferences

Parent
Component

Parent Resource Teacher
Parent Room Activities
Home Support
School Involvement
Education and Career
Endorsed Plan

Curriculum
Component

Curriculum Plan
Small Class Sizes
Prof. Development
Online Supports
Progress Review

Health
Services

Health Screening
Nursing Services
Free + Reduced-
Price meals

Parent
Component

Parent Activities
Home Support
School Involvement
Education and Career
Endorsed Plan

Curriculum
Component

Curriculum Plan
Reduced Class Size
Teacher Aides
Curricular Alignment
Continuity Plan
Prof. Development
Online Supports

School-Wide
Services

Health Services
Free + Reduced-
Price meals
Resource Mobilization

Age 3 ———— To ———— → Age 9

CPC-P-3 as School Reform

Given the historic focus on specific elements of reform, including curriculum enhancement and small classes (Reynolds, Magnuson & Ou, 2010), newer comprehensive approaches for promoting effective school transitions may not only have larger effects on child development but also provide a greater likelihood that gains will be sustained. To date, key principles of effective school improvement developed in the 1970s have not been successfully utilized in early childhood programs and their follow-on efforts (Reynolds et al., 2017; Zigler & Styfco, 1993; Zigler & Trickett, 1978). Among these are principal leadership, school climate and high expectations of performance, and engaged learning communities (Rury, 2016; Takanishi & Kauerz, 2008). These principles have been incorporated in school reform with positive results, most notably the 5 Essentials framework of effective leaders, ambitious instruction, involved families, supportive environment, and collaborative teachers (Bryk, Sebring, Allensworth, Lupescu & Easton, 2010). Although developed independently within the context of early childhood programs, the six core elements of CPC are consistent with the 5 Essentials, and they provide a strategy of school improvement that can promote well-being and achievement.

Figure 8.1 shows the continuity inherent in CPC-P-3 in its equal emphasis on preschool, kindergarten, and the early grades. Preschool or early education provides the foundation and the next few grades build on this to promote achievement and well-being for children and parents. The figure also illustrates the inherent tension between the early timing of intervention versus duration of services. One is the early timing versus the developmental continuity in learning. CPC-P-3 represents both, but a major focus of dissemination will be the importance of continuity in learning for children to benefit most and for the achievement gap to be realistically closed (see Figure 8.2).

As shown, there are six core elements that are described as follows:

1. **Collaborative leadership team.** A leadership team is run by the HT in collaboration with the principal. The HT ensures that all elements are effectively implemented. The PRT, SCR, and other staff work together to support the system.

2. **Effective learning experiences.** Ensure mastery in core learning domains (e.g., literacy and language, math, science, socio-emotional) through small classes, diverse and engaged instruction, and increased time through full-day preschool and kindergarten classes. For example, preschool and K–3 classes are limited to 17 and 25, respectively, with assistants in each.

3. **Aligned curriculum.** Organize a sequence of evidence-based curricula and instructional practices that address multiple domains of child development within a balanced, activity-based approach. A curriculum alignment plan is developed with the principal is and updated annually.

4. **Parent involvement and engagement.** Comprehensive menu-based services are led by the PRT and SCR, including multifaceted activities and opportunities to engage families.

5. **Professional development system.** Online professional development and on-site follow-up support is integrated for classroom and program applications. Among the topics covered by the modules are oral language, thinking skills, movement, inquiry, and socio-emotional learning.

6. **Continuity and stability:** Preschool to third grade services, through co-located or close-by centers, incorporate comprehensive service delivery and year-to-year consistency for children and families. Instructional and family support services are integrated across grades.

The strength of the model lies in the synergy of all six elements working together, with across-element coordination a strong design feature. These are key to producing long-term impacts on children's educational progress, socio-emotional development, and well-being.

Figure 8.3 shows a more detailed program structure and operations for the six key elements to promote well-being, which includes achievement, performance, parent involvement, and health. Beginning with a strong foundation at ages 3 and 4, children participate in small classes through third grade and each class has an assistant for at least half of the day. The learning environment created by the principal and CPC head teacher provides an integrated context for improved achievement and sustained gains. Transitions from year to year are supported by the parent involvement team, site mentors, and school staff, who share instructional approaches across grades for the benefit of children and families. A curriculum alignment plan and parent involvement plan are developed each year to guide implementation and program improvement. Professional development includes on-line teaching modules and on-site coaching and review of instructional practices to support a balance of teacher- and child-initiated instructional practices. Outreach services, including home visits and workshops, are through the parent resource room, as the parent resource teacher and school–community representative develop a menu-based system that is informed by a family needs assessment.

Table 8.1 provides a description of how each of the program elements contributes to the three core principles of collaboration.

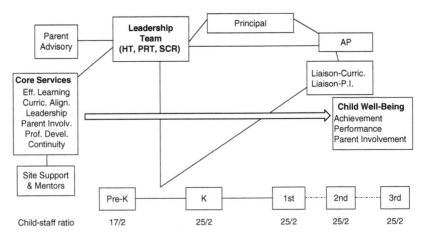

Figure 8.3 Child–Parent Center Structure, Key Elements, and Outcomes
HT = Head Teacher, PRT = Parent Resource Teacher, SCR = School-
Community Representative, AP = Assistant Principal, and P.I. = Parent
Involvement.

The collaborative leadership team of the principal and HT help
establish the learning environment of shared ownership among the
partners, which provides opportunities for CPC staff to serve children
and families in all facets of the program. The principal's increased
commitment to the program, including participation in institutes and
decisions to increase school resources to P–3, is a significant advance
from the original program. This results in not only greater implementation fidelity but increased resource investments by the partners,
who see the benefits of improved learning environment. The greater
attention to progress monitoring by the leadership team increases
fidelity to program principles and accountability.

Other program elements contribute in similar ways to the collaboration
and shared ownership, resource commitments, and progress monitoring,
and provide a foundation for scaling. In effective learning experiences, for
example, the implementation of full-day preschool in small classes emphasizes a balance of teacher-directed and child-initiated instruction for promoting strong learning gains (Reynolds et al., 2016). This is
complemented by increased alignment of instruction across grades, in
which a curriculum alignment plan is developed, and grade level meetings
and coaching visits are frequent. As a consequence, sustained gains of early
education are more likely to occur.

Table 8.1 *Midwest Child–Parent Center expansion core elements and collaboration*

Core program element	Shared ownership	Committed resources	Progress monitoring	Evidence of impact
Collaborative Leadership Team	Create a positive learning environment	Hire leadership team for implementation	Ensure that instructional and family services are effective	Increased fidelity of implementation; increased principal support to teachers, staff
Effective Learning Experiences	Small classes and balance of instructional activities	Provide matching funds to open new classrooms	Classroom Activity Report tool; observation of instruction tool; teacher checklists	Full-day preschool increased readiness skills and attendance; increased engagement in learning.
Aligned Curriculum	Provide coordinated instruction across grades	Implement new curricula to enhance learning	Annual curriculum alignment plan; observation of across-grade coordination	Increased child-initiated instruction linked to greater learning gains
Parent Involvement and Engagement	Establish a menu-based system of services	Increase staff time to work with parents and family members	Parent involvement logs; annual parent involvement plan	Program linked to increased parent involvement in school
Professional Development	Create a professional learning community	Hire coaches and mentors to improve teaching	Checklist of fidelity; facilitation and review of teaching	Increased time in math instruction and in child-initiated activities
Continuity and Stability	Ensure consistency and predictability in learning	Increase classroom supports (e.g., assistants)	Determine percentage of students who remain in the program over time	Participating families have lower mobility

Implementation Examples for Increasing and Sustaining Effects

Although CPC has a distinguished history, expansion beyond Chicago has been a major need. This is addressed by the Midwest expansion. At the time of the expansion in 2012, only the preschool component of the program was being implemented in just ten of the original sites. On the basis of the accumulated evidence, the Chicago district and others expressed interest in not only re-establishing the P–3 elements but enhancing the program so that it could be effective in a variety of community contexts. Working with Chicago's leadership and others, the HCRC team developed a comprehensive plan that integrated six core elements that was implemented under a school reform model consistent with the US Department of Education's Office of Innovation.

Program elements were modified and strengthened to address large demographic changes at both the societal level (e.g., increasing numbers of single-parent households and working mothers of young children) and program level (e.g., more diverse populations of children and families, new geographic locations).

Children's participation in CPC-P–3 is expected to promote enduring positive impacts for three major reasons: (a) a longer duration of participation can produce greater and more foundational changes in school achievement and performance; (b) the program encourages stability and predictability in learning environments; and (c) it is implemented during the transition to school, a critical phase of development in which continuing services can accelerate learning and reduce the likelihood of drop-off effects (Reynolds, Magnuson & Ou, 2010). Studies of preschool impact show that the length of gains is a function of program quality, magnitude of initial effect, timing and duration, and subsequent school quality (Camilli et al., 2010; Currie & Thomas, 2000; Englund et al., 2014). We describe three examples of how CPC-P3 is strengthening impacts in ways that are scalable and that overcome earlier limitations.

Collaborative Leadership and Effective Learning

As a school reform model, CPC-P–3 has a collaborative leadership structure in which the principal and staff establish a positive learning environment for students and families. Principals develop a CPC leadership team and support key program elements through matching funding (e.g., open full-day preschool, hire teaching assistants and outreach staff), and facilitate cross-grade curriculum and parent involvement activities.

During the planning stages, the HCRC team worked with each principal to develop an implementation plan for a smooth roll-out in each school. One of the main recommendations by principals and head teachers was to open full-day preschool classrooms in the first year (fall 2012). This was based in large part on feedback from parents that they wanted their children in full-day preschool due to the incompatibility between their work schedules and the school's existing part-day program. The added challenge of coordinating care and education for the other part of the day was a major concern. Some parents went so far as to indicate that they would not enroll their child in the center unless there was a full-day option. In addition to parents' demands, principals also believed full-day preschool would improve school readiness skills and the successful transition to the kindergarten and the elementary grades.

Full-day preschool, however, was not part of the CPC expansion design and consequently significant changes were needed. HCRC and the principals agreed that if schools contributed at least 25 percent of the added cost for opening a full-day classroom, HCRC would match the remainder. Eleven of the 16 schools agreed to do this, with the contributions ranging from 25 percent to 100 percent. HCRC reallocated funding to cover these costs. Twenty-three full-day classrooms were opened in fall 2012. This was the first time in these schools that principals directly funded preschool classrooms out of their own budgets. This process also supported key elements of shared ownership and committed resources (see Table 8.1). Our partnership with schools in opening full-day preschool classrooms led to the district financially sustaining and expanding them the following year. Other districts also opened full-day classes. CPC leadership positions also were sustained.

Menu-based System of Parent Involvement and Engagement

While the importance of parent involvement in children's school success has been well documented (Jeynes, 2007; Reynolds, 2012; See & Gorard, 2015), daily schedules and demands, school climate, and the lack of necessary school resources often prevent parents from fully engaging in family support activities (e.g., workshops, home visits). Through collaborations with principals, school staff, family members, and the community, we developed a menu-based system of parent involvement that overcomes these barriers by offering a comprehensive program tailored to the educational and career needs of families. Parents choose among a range of events activities in which to participate and agree to be involved at least 2.5 hours per week (Reynolds et al., 2016).

The goals of family engagement are to (a) implement a menu-based program that addresses family needs while strengthening the school-family partnership, (b) sustain parent involvement in children's education, and (c) enhance support for educational attainment, career opportunities, and personal development through the following topics and activities: a supportive home environment, healthy child and family development, parent education, career, and personal development. Each site has a parent resource room to host events and serve as a center for parents to visit throughout the day. The PRT works collaboratively with the HT and the school principal to engage families throughout the school-based parent program (see also Table 8.1).

School–family–community relationships are especially important in the CPC model. The role of the SCR is to help lead these efforts. Usually residing in the community, this para-professional staff member recruits families, informs them of programming, works toward increasing and maintaining child and parent attendance, and conducts home visits. These home visits are an opportunity to foster positive school and community relations by better understanding the obstacles impacting a family's ability to participate in events. Given the need for home visits and monitoring attendance, SCRs became full-time positions in the first year.

A needs assessment is conducted at the beginning of the year to avoid planning events that do not match the identified needs of families. The available resources in the community are assessed through asset mapping. These are integral components of the Parent Involvement Plan. In collaboration, the HTs, PRTs and Parent Involvement Liaisons (K–3) develop activities at each center to promote involvement and engagement. Parent involvement logs (an electronic documentation system) are maintained for progress monitoring. Given the needs assessment results and the increased time of the SCR, parent involvement logs showed that CPC families in year 1 participated in an average of 12.4 school events compared to 2.7 for the comparison group (Reynolds et al., 2017). This difference was maintained the following year.

Family support behavior is one of five mechanisms through which CPC participation affects well-being (Reynolds, 2012). Benefits will accrue to the extent that participation enhances parenting skills, attitudes and expectations, and involvement in children's education (Hayakawa et al., 2013; Ou & Reynolds, 2010). Parent involvement in school and parent expectations for achievement have been found to improve well-being by increasing children's learning time, enhancing children's motivation and school commitment, and increasing expectations for attainment and success (Hayakawa et al., 2013). They also improve social support and parenting skills, which reduce social isolation and the risk of child maltreatment. Meta-analyses of family and two-generation interventions as well as parenting behaviors (Jeynes, 2007; Sweet & Applebaum, 2004) show that involvement and monitoring link to higher achievement and delinquency prevention.

Progress Monitoring for Improving Instruction

Monitoring ensures that learning is optimized for all students. It is not only for accountability but essential to improvement. Based on site visits, interviews, and a review of data collected for each element, we assessed each school's fidelity of implementation in meeting requirements. The scale for each element and overall ranged from 1 (few requirements met) to 5 (almost all). The overall average rating of implementation fidelity for year 1 across the six program elements was 3.9 or moderately high. The highest was continuity and stability (4.2) and the lowest aligned curriculum (3.3). Parent involvement was in the moderate range (3.9). Across the six elements, 75 percent of sites met the moderate-to-high fidelity standard defined as a rating of 3.5 or higher. In year 2, the overall fidelity rating improved to 4.1 with collaborative leadership, parent involvement, and professional development rated highest. In years 3 and 4, overall fidelity averaged 4.0.

CPC classrooms are expected to utilize a variety of instructional strategies to maintain a balance of teacher-directed and child-initiated activities at a ratio no higher than 65/35. The Classroom Activity Report (CAR) was developed by HCRC to monitor classroom progress in meeting this requirement. This tool documents the organization and implementation of instructional activities (i.e., percentage of time during the day devoted to math, language and literacy activities, science, and social-emotional activities). Classroom teachers complete the CAR on a regular basis. HCRC staff review the submitted CARs and provide feedback. This promotes a collaborative approach to program fidelity and helps schools identify gaps and design new instructional strategies. We have found that learning gains in preschool and kindergarten are linked to the degree to which child-initiated instruction activities are implemented.

Table 8.2 provides an example of how the CAR can be used as a progress monitoring tool for improving learning outcomes. Although the distribution of instructional time was similar in full-day and part-day classes, the number of hours of total instructional time was nearly 2.5 times greater in full-day classes (984 vs. 417). This increase was proportionate across instructional domains and activities. For example, the number of hours

Table 8.2 *Percentage of time in instructional activities by Chicago full-day and part-day classes*

Instruction	Mean Percentage Time, Hours, and Percent Change			
Type of Activity	Part-Day (n = 76)	Full-Day (n = 21)	Increased hours in full-day classes	Percent change over part-day classes
Language & Literacy	48.9 (9.9)	48.1 (6.1)	269	232
Math	18.9 (5.7)	19.3 (3.2)	111	241
Social-Emotional	7.8 (4.1)	8.8 (3.5)	54	264
Science	8.1 (3.0)	8.4 (2.5)	49	244
Teacher-Directed vs. Child-Initiated				
Language & Literacy				
Teacher-Directed	50.5 (13.8)	52.4 (12.1)	145	241
Child-Initiated	49.5 (13.8)	47.6 (12.1)	124	225
Math				
Teacher-Directed	49.6 (11.8)	50.6 (12.0)	57	246
Child-Initiated	50.4 (11.8)	49.4 (12.2)	54	235
Science				
Teacher-Directed	43.1 (15.7)	53.1 (15.0)	29	293
Child-Initiated	56.2 (16.6)	46.2 (16.3)	20	205
Mean hours of total instruction for year	417	984	567	236

Note. Data are teacher reports for 16 sites in Chicago. Two full-day classrooms out of 23 did not report time use. Standard deviations are in parentheses. Due to omitting the category "other," percentage time in instruction activity does not add up to 100%.

in child-initiated literacy activities increased to 225 in full-day from 101 in part-day (increase of 124 hours) to 225. These data were used by schools and the district to determine if and how the additional hours were productively spent. One district asked that full-day classrooms be added, while another planned to open them the following year.

Based in part on the increased instructional time and the content distribution documented by CAR, one district began to offer full-day preschool and strengthened their curriculum alignment between preschool and the early grades. Teacher collaboration across grades also increased. The CAR, along with an observational assessment called the Classroom Learning Activities Checklist, provides valuable information for improving the quality of experiences in the classroom. Independent observations of program and comparison sites on this assessment indicated that 76 percent of CPC preschool classrooms were rated moderately high to high in task orientation and engagement, a key program focus. 43 percent of comparison classrooms had this rating. This advantage persisted into kindergarten and the early grades. The balance of instruction was consistent with program principles.

CPC Impacts over Time

The positive effects of CPC are well documented. I summarize findings from the Chicago Longitudinal Study (CLS; Reynolds, 2012) and the initial implementation of the Midwest CPC expansion.

CLS. This study has tracked a CPC and comparison cohort born in 1979–80 and provides the most extensive evidence of impacts. It was also the basis of the Midwest CPC expansion. In a quasi-experimental design, 989 3- and 4-year-olds from low-income families who participated in 20 CPCs in the mid 1980s were compared to 550 children of the same age who enrolled in the usual early childhood programs in five randomly selected schools. A broad range of measures of well-being have been collected over three decades with over 90 percent sample recovery. These include school readiness and achievement, remedial education, educational attainment, involvement in the criminal justice system, and economic well-being. Program participation was from P–3 and followed the CPC elements. Study characteristics and findings are described in Table 8.3.

Based on a variety of regression, latent-variable, and propensity score analyses, CPC preschool participation was found to be associated with higher school readiness, higher reading and math achievement, reduced grade retention, reduced special education placement, and higher rates of high school completion (Reynolds, 2012). CPC–P–3 has shown similar patterns of gains with the exception of high school completion by age 21. Significant differences were detected in later in the 20s, however (Reynolds et al., 2011a).

Figure 8.4 shows the pattern of gains and effect sizes in reading achievement for the CPC preschool component from kindergarten through age 15. Developmental standard scores on the Iowa Tests of Basic Skills are shown and effect sizes in standard deviation units. The latter are across the bottom of the figure. Values are adjusted for child and family background characteristics as well as participation in CPC school-age services. A standard deviation of 0.20 is generally considered practically significant and signifies an improvement in performance of roughly 3 months (a third of a school year). Positive and significant effect sizes were sustained from kindergarten entrance to the end of ninth grade (age 15).

Table 8.3 *Child–Parent Center estimates for school readiness, parent involvement, and achievement in two studies*

Study characteristics	Midwest Longitudinal Expansion Project			Chicago Longitudinal Study
	Chicago	Saint Paul	Total	
Preschool years	2012–2013	2012–2013	2012–2013	1983–1985
Research design	Quasi-experimental, school-level propensity scores	Quasi-experimental,		Quasi-experimental, matched groups
Program, Control participants	1724, 906	215, 87	1993, 993	989, 550
Control group enrolled in pre-K (%)	100	100	100	15%
African American/Hispanic/Asian (%)	64/34/0	30/14/31	60/32/3	93/7/0
Assessment	TS-GOLD	PALS		ITBS composite
Time of assessment	End of pre-K	End of pre-K	End of pre-K	Beginning of K
Average class size/level of fidelity	17/high	17/high	17/high	17/high
School readiness effect size (SD units)	48	38	47	63
Higher dosage (full-day/2 years)	65	n/a	40	71
Lower dosage (part-day/1 year)	32	38	33	36
Parent involvement effect size	39	20	37	46
Time of assessment	End of PreK	N/A		First grade
Education outcomes effect size (SD or %)				
Third grade reading achievement				28 (pre-K), 0.60 (pre-K–3)
Eighth grade reading achievement				30, 0.35
Special education by age 18				14.4% vs. 24.6%, 13.5% vs. 20.7%
Grade retention by age 15				23.0% vs. 38.4%, 21.9% vs. 32.3%
High school completion by age 21				61.9% vs. 51.4%, 59.4% vs. 57.2%

Note. Midwest CPC Chicago sample size is enrolled 3- and 4-year-olds. Saint Paul sample size is enrolled 4-year-olds for whom the school district provided data. Evanston and McLean County (Normal, IL) districts were excluded due to lack of available data. Chicago Longitudinal Study sample size is an age cohort of children who enrolled at age 3 and/or 4. TS-GOLD = Teaching Strategies Gold Assessment, Total Score. PALS = Phonological Awareness Literacy Screening (Upper-Case Alphabet Recognition). ITBS = Iowa Tests of Basic Skills cognitive composite. The quasi-experimental designs are propensity-score matching at the school level (i.e., achievement, family income, race/ethnicity) and matched groups based on demographic similarity and participation in district intervention. For dosage, Midwest CPC is full-day/part-day; CLS is 2 years versus 1 year for part-day. SD = standard deviation units.

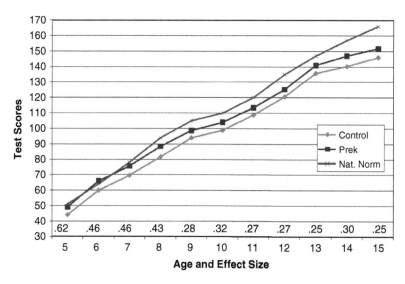

Figure 8.4 Reading growth to age 15

The large initial impact of roughly two-thirds of a standard deviation (based on a composite heavily weighted on literacy and language) was maintained at slightly lower levels through second grade and then stabilized in the range of 0.25 to 0.32 from middle childhood to adolescence. That the standard deviation increases with age naturally leads to a reduction in effect size. This is due to variability in learning opportunities and experiences as children develop. Since the sum total of experience and learning increases with age, the contribution of preschool experience to this total would be expected to decline in relative terms as children grow.

By age 21, the CPC preschool program is found to be associated with a higher rate of high school completion and a lower rate of juvenile arrest (Ou & Reynolds, 2006; Reynolds, Temple, Robertson, & Mann, 2001). Children participating in CPC-P–3 (4 to 6 years of participation from preschool to second or third grade) were found to have higher academic achievement when compared with children receiving only the preschool or follow-on programs (Conrad & Eash, 1983). CPC-P–3 participation was associated with lower rates of school remedial services and delinquency (Reynolds et al., 2001, 2011a; see Table 8.3).

Figure 8.5 shows the growth in reading achievement from kindergarten entry (age 5) to fourth grade (age 10) for the CPC-P–3 group that participated in 4 to 6 years of intervention (to second or third grade) compared to the CPC group that only completed preschool and

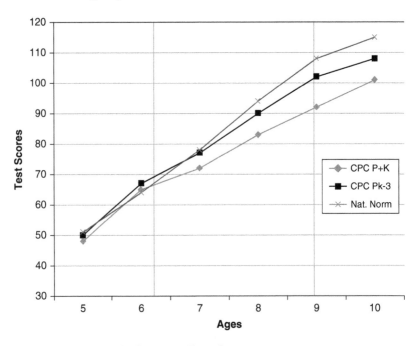

Figure 8.5 CPC-P–3 reading advantage

kindergarten. Scores are developmental standard scores on the Iowa Tests of Basic Skills and are adjusted from baseline child and family background characteristics (Reynolds, 1994, 2012). Although growth during the kindergarten year was similar between groups and at/above national norms, the CPC-P–3 group experienced greater growth between first and fourth grades. This translates to about a 6-month gain above and beyond preschool and kindergarten participation (Reynolds & Temple, 1998; Reynolds et al., 2011a). This advantage in performance reduced the gap with the national average by about 75 percent, even though the average performance of the CPC-P–3 group was not quite to the national average. That the program increased reading achievement to this extent is impressive given the high levels of economic and disadvantage growing up. CPC families reside in the highest poverty neighborhoods in Chicago, which are among the most extreme in the nation (Reynolds, 2012).

Midwest CPC-P–3 expansion. The expansion project assesses the impact and generalizability of the program model. Initial findings are similar to those in the CLS and indicate the benefits of the six core elements and services (see also Table 8.1). In the expansion project, the

CPC cohort included 2,364 CPC participants in 26 sites and 1,212 comparison participants from propensity-score matched schools in four districts of various sizes who enrolled in the usual preschool with no coordinated school-age programs (Reynolds et al., 2014, 2016). The groups are being followed to third grade with school achievement and parent involvement as the primary outcomes. The sample is more geographically and ethnically diverse compared to the CLS, which was in inner-city Chicago with over 90% of children African American. In the Midwest CPC, 53% are African American with 32% Hispanic, 7% White, and 5% Asian.

Controlling for baseline performance and child and family background characteristics, the mean effect size for school readiness skills at the end of preschool for Midwest CPC participants in Chicago (based on the Teaching Strategies Gold total score) and Saint Paul (based on PALS alphabet recognition) was 0.47 standard deviations (Table 8.3). The effect size for school readiness in the CLS was 0.63 standard deviations. Most of the control group in the CLS, however, was not enrolled in preschool, whereas in the Midwest CPC they were enrolled in state/ district pre-K or Head Start. Effects for parent involvement in school (teacher ratings) in the Midwest CPC was 0.33 standard deviations compared to 0.46 in the earlier study. These consistent effects indicate the continued feasibility and effectiveness of the program across contexts. Analyses of K–3 impacts are currently underway.

Finally, because full-day preschool was introduced in the CPC expansion to increase learning time, we found that relative to part-day, full-day participation was associated with significantly higher school readiness skills in language, math, and socio-emotional development (ES = 0.33), higher average daily attendance (ES = 0.30), and lower rates of chronic absences (ES = −0.45; Reynolds et al., 2014). Nevertheless, both part-day and full-day CPC were associated with significantly higher school readiness skills than comparison participants in the usual part-day preschool (ESs = 0.32 to 0.71; Table 8.3). The impact of dosage in the CLS was similar to the expansion as the 2-year group in part-day classes had greater school readiness skills than the 1-year group, but both significantly outperformed the matched comparison (Reynolds et al., 2011a).

The Midwest expansion findings led to an expansion of full-day preschool the following year, the introduction of full-day in another district, and plans to do so in a third district. Overall, the findings from both studies show the benefits of the CPC program and the advantages of the principles of shared ownership, committed resources, and progress monitoring.

Scaling and Financing through Pay for Success

Given the low rate of success in scaling evidence-based programs, new approaches to financing have been developed. One of the most prominent is called Social Impact Bonds or "Pay for Success." In a Pay for Success (PFS) approach, private investors and/or philanthropic organizations loan funds to public sector jurisdictions (e.g., school districts, cities, counties) to expand evidence-based or very promising programs (GAO, 2015; Temple & Reynolds, 2015). To the extent that these services are found to generate cost savings to the public sector, a state or local government is obligated to make payments to the investors based on the estimated cost savings. Economic evaluation is crucial in both determining the suitability of intervention programs to be financed in this manner and in determining the "success" payments. This approach can promote a shift from costly treatment-based interventions consuming ever larger portions of public budgets to proactive, preventive interventions that save more dollars than they cost.

PFS illustrates the role of shared ownership and committed resources in program expansion. Through a PFS initiative with the City of Chicago, the Midwest CPC has begun further expansion in the Chicago Public Schools. In this financing structure, Goldman Sachs, Northern Trust, and the J. B. & M. K. Pritzker Family Foundation provided $17 million in loans for the operational costs of new classrooms, which will serve an additional 2,600 children over four years (HCRC, 2014). The City will repay the loans only if the program improves outcomes as determined by an independent evaluation.

The CPC program under the Midwest expansion was selected for two major reasons. First, the expansion of CPC already underway was showing strong initial findings and school principals and the district were committed to the program. This was demonstrated by their increased funding and growing collaboration with the university. Second, the program had a long track record of effectiveness in promoting student success and in reducing the need for remediation. Two cost–benefit analyses documented that at an average cost per child of $8,512 (2012) for preschool, benefits exceed costs by a factor of 7 to 10 (Reynolds et al., 2002, 2011b). P–3 services showed similar returns.

A large percentage of the economic return was savings in special education, juvenile court, and child welfare. For example, the annual cost per child of special education services is over $15,000 above and beyond regular instruction. The majority of this cost is covered by the school district. Given the direct relationship between the city and the school district, the focus of the PFS was special education savings.

The CPC PFS initiative began implementation in February 2015 for an initial cohort of over 350 children in six sites. Five of them are existing schools in the CPC expansion. Annual evaluation results have been reported since 2016. Success payments of $2,900 were paid to the investor in 2017 for each child who was ready for kindergarten. Success payments of $9,100 were paid starting the next year for each CPC child who avoided special education as compared to the matched control group of children without CPC participation. Next, success payments of $750 may be made for each child proficient in literacy in third grade. Rates of special education will be tracked through high school. School readiness for each 4-year-old is defined as the percentage of children performing at or above the national average at the end of the year on five of six subscales of the Teaching Strategies Gold Assessment System (Lambert, Kim & Burts, 2013). The payment structure is based on the long-term evidence that CPC improves school achievement and reduces the need for special education by up to 41 percent or nearly a year of services (Reynolds et al., 2002).

Although the major advantage of PFS is the capacity for program expansion when existing public resources are not available, two limitations are notable. First, the success of the initiative is largely dependent on the selected program. Those having a track record, such as CPC or others with existing evidence of economic returns, are most reassuring to investors. Second, as a new type of financing, the success metrics of PFS so far rest on one jurisdiction of savings – special education or the justice system. Comprehensive programs having many sources of savings require multi-jurisdiction contracts. These are very challenging to complete and have not been completed to date. In CPC, for example, there are criminal justice system and child welfare savings, but because they are administered through counties, it was not feasible to secure partnership agreements. Consequently, PFS contracts may underestimate the possible savings.

Overall, PFS has helped scale CPC and can facilitate similar efforts in other districts. It provides a new avenue for leveraging resources in evidence-based programs. Private investment contributed to an initiative can also be combined with public resources to create a public–private approach to scaling, which then can be modified over time as public resources increase.

Implications for Creating, Increasing, and Sustaining Gains

The expansion of CPC-P–3 is based on a school reform approach to program improvement within a collaborative structure of partners. Through shared ownership, committed resources, and progress monitoring for improvement, the program is more likely to be scaled effectively and sustained in ways that continually produce benefits to children and families in school success and engaged parenting. This approach effectively bridges the historically large divide between early education and school-age services (Bogard & Takanishi, 2005; Takanishi, 2016; Ziger & Styfo, 1993). Successful implementation of CPC has yielded strong benefits so far in increasing school readiness skills, improving attendance, and in strengthening parental involvement in children's education. These positive benefits have led to further scale up through an innovative Pay for Success initiative in Chicago that will substantially increase enrollment in the coming years. Cost savings in special education and remediation are expected to be consistent with prior studies.

Buy-in from partners at every level of the school community – school leaders and staff, children, and families, and local partners – is critical to successful CPC expansion and prevention programs in general (Takanishi & Kauerz, 2008). The principle of shared ownership means that program and school decisions result from reciprocal dialogue among partners (Boyd & Crowson, 1993). Such a climate of collaboration helps ensure that benefits are sustained and that progress toward scaling is successful.

Based on development, implementation, and evaluation of the CPC-P–3 expansion, there are a number of lessons and implications for increasing and sustaining early learning gains in all programs. The essential principle is that by establishing and maintaining a comprehensive system of supports from preschool through third grade, achievement levels can be optimized and achievement gaps realistically closed.

1. **Principal leadership is essential for good implementation and positive effects on students.** In working directly with principals, the implementation team established a strong partnership with schools. Principals felt a shared ownership of the program. As a result, they prioritized program continuity and key elements over P–3 and directly financed key elements of the program: full-day pre-K, classroom assistants, and outreach staff. This support was essential in promoting a positive learning climate for students, families, and teachers necessary for sustained learning gains. Analysis of implementation data indicated that the collaborative leadership team was integral to the success of other program elements. Increased investment in principal preparation and professional learning about the design and impact of P–3 approaches is needed. Ongoing opportunities to engage principals in the key elements of P–3 programs are also warranted.

2. **Systems of support must be comprehensive and include family services.** CPC is a comprehensive school reform model of six core elements covering leadership, instructional support, school–family

relations, and continuity. This level of coverage is consistent with school reform strategies (Takanishi, 2016; Zigler & Styfco, 1993). Each site leadership team of Head Teacher, Parent Resource Teacher, and School–Community Representative as well as the Curriculum and Parent Involvement Liaisons play key roles. Alignment of services across P–3 has been instrumental for creating a strong learning climate. The extent to which each of the program elements contributes to short- and longer-term effects is an important next-step question.

3. **Menu-based system of parent involvement enables schools to tailor services more effectively.** Under this new framework, the parent involvement team increased the focus on home visits, check-ins with parents on attendance, and workshops ranging from English Language Learning and computer classes to career and GED training. CPC families had higher involvement through at least first grade. As shown in previous studies (Reynolds et al., 2011a), parent involvement is a key reason why CPC has sustained effects on later achievement, school completion, and lower need for remediation and treatment.

4. **P–3 can improve levels of student, family, and teacher engagement at multiple levels.** As a comprehensive support system to promote a strong climate for participation, P–3 reforms can not only increase student-level attendance and reduce chronic absenteeism but help at the school level as well. Prior to the introduction of CPC-P–3 in 2012–13, CPCs had the lowest average daily attendance of all Chicago district preschool programs. This was due in part to the centers being located in the highest poverty areas. After the first year of Midwest CPC, they had the highest rate (including tuition-based pre-K). The introduction of full-day programs and the comprehensive set of services contributed (Reynolds et al., 2014). These benefits carried over to the later grades. K–2 school-level attendance gains were 50 percent higher in CPC schools than in comparison schools. This is likely to be attributed to the established learning climate. P–3 strategies that are comprehensive in scope are more likely to affect the larger climate than reforms that are more narrowly focused on curriculum or professional development.

5. **Progress monitoring leads to program improvements and better P–3 alignment.** The evidence indicates that regular documentation of implementation of elements helps ensure that adherence to evidence-based elements is occurring. Because of such fidelity checks, changes can be made regularly and in a timely manner. This promotes better program effectiveness. Four tools were developed in the expansion to promote monitoring for improvement: observational assessment, brief teacher activity reports, and annual curriculum and parent involvement plans. The observational assessment measures classroom task orientation and

student engagement. CPC classes were observed to have significantly higher levels of task orientation than comparison classes. These results enhance instruction and professional development. This ongoing process of monitoring for program improvement is beneficial for all types of programs yet most monitoring is for accountability, and is not frequent or in-depth enough to encourage program improvement. Greater comprehensive in monitoring requires additional resources for implementation and should be a built-in part of program management at the school level.

In conclusion, the findings of the implementation and impacts of CPC-P–3 provide a strong foundation for increased investment in scale-up and expansion efforts, especially in communities and schools serving large proportions of at-risk children. Readiness for dissemination occurs when programs have strong evidence and there is a system of services to support expansion and provide consultation. This is now available in the CPC program and can facilitate further scale-up to promote increased achievement.

References

Barton, P. E., Coley, R. J. (2009). *Parsing the Achievement Gap II. Policy Information Report*. Princeton, NJ: ETS.

Belfield, C. R. & Levin, H. M., (Eds.) (2007). *The Price We Pay: Economic and Social Consequences of Inadequate Education*. Washington, DC: Brookings Institution.

Bogard, K. & Takanishi, R. (2005). PK–3: An Aligned and Coordinated Approach to Education for Children 3 to 8 years old. *Social Policy Report*, XIX, No. III. Washington, DC: Society for Research in Child Developmena.

Boyd, W. L., & Crowson, R. L. (1993). Coordinated services for children: designing arks for storms and seas unknown. *American Journal of Education*, 101, 140–179.

Braveman, P. & Gottlieb, L. (2014). The social determinants of health: it's time to consider the causes of the causes. *Public Health Reports*, 129 (Suppl. 2), 19–31.

Bronfenbrenner, U. (1989). Ecological systems theory. *Annals of Child Development*, 6, 187–249.

Bryk, A. S., Sebring, P. B., Allensworth, E., Luppescu, S. & Easton, J. Q. (2010). *Organizing Schools for Improvement: Lessons from Chicago*. Chicago, IL: University of Chicago Press.

Camilli, G., Vargas, S., Ryan, S. & Barnett, W. S. (2010). Meta-analysis of the effects of early education interventions on cognitive and social development. *Teachers College Record*, 112(3), 579–620.

Conrad, K. J. & Eash, M. J. (1983). Measuring implementation and multiple outcomes in a Child–Parent Center compensatory education program. *American Educational Research Journal*, 20, 221–236.

Currie, J., & Thomas, D. (2000). School quality and the longer-term effects of Head Start. *The Journal of Human Resources*, 35(4), 755–774.

Englund, M. M., White, B., Reynolds, A. J., Schweinhart, L. J. and Campbell, F. A. (2014). Health outcomes of early childhood interventions: A 3-study analysis, in A. J. Reynolds et al. (Eds.), *Health and Education in Early Childhood: Predictors, Interventions, and Policies*. New York, NY: Cambridge.

Frank, L., Basch, E. & Selby, J. V. (2014). The PCORI perspective on patient-centered outcomes research. *Journal of the American Medical Association*, 312(15), 1513–1514.

Government Accountability Office. (2015). *Pay for Success: Collaboration among Federal Agencies Would Be Helpful as Governments Explore New Financing Mechanisms* (GAO-15-646). Washington, DC.

Hayakawa, M., Englund, M. M., Warner-Richter, M. N. & Reynolds, A. J. (2013). The longitudinal process of early parent involvement on student achievement: a path analysis. *National Head Start Association Dialog*, 16, 103–126.

Human Capital Research Collaborative. (2012). *Program Requirement and Guidelines, Midwest Expansion of the Child–Parent Center Program, Preschool to Third Grade*. Minneapolis, MI: Human Capital Research Collaborative. http://humancapitalrc.org/midwestcpc.

Human Capital Research Collaborative. (2014). *Chicago's Social Impact Bonds for Child–Parent Centers Expands a Proven School Reform Model*. Minneapolis, MI: University of Minnesota. https://humancapitalrc.org/~/media/files/news/sib_chicago_summary.pdf?la=en.

Jeynes, W. H. (2007). The relationship between parental involvement and urban secondary school student academic achievement. *Urban Education*, 41(1), 82–110.

Lambert, R., Kim, D. & Burts, D. (2013). *Technical Manual for the Teaching Strategies Gold Assessment System (2nd edn.)*. CEME Technical Report. Center for Educational Measurement & Evaluation, Charlotte: University of North Carolina.

Manning, M., Garvis, S., Fleming, C. & Wong, G. T. W. (2017, January). The relationship between teacher qualification and the quality of the early education and care environment. *Campbell Systematic Reviews*. DOI: 10.4073/csr.2017.1 (http://campbellcollaboration.org/library).

National Assessment of Educational Progress. (2016). *The Nation's Report Card: 2015*. Washington, DC: US Department of Education, National Center for Education Statistics.

O'Connell, M. E, Boat, T. & Warner, K. E. (Eds.). (2009). *Preventing Mental, Emotional, and Behavioral Disorders among Young People: Progress and Possibilities*. National Research Council. Washington, DC: National Academy Press.

Ou, S. & Reynolds, A. J. (2006). School-age services: Programs that extend the benefits of early care and education services, in Groark, C. J. et al. (Eds.), *Evidence-Based Programs, Practices, and Policies for Early Childhood Care and Education* (pp. 114–134). Thousand Oaks, CA: Corwin Press.

Reynolds, A. J. (1994). Effects of a preschool plus follow-on intervention for children at risk. *Developmental Psychology*, 30, 787–804.

Reynolds, A. J. (2012). *Success in Early Intervention: The Chicago Child–Parent Centers*. Lincoln, NE: University of Nebraska Press (Reprinted from 2000).

Reynolds A. J., Hayakawa M, Candee, A. J. & Englund, M. M. (2016). *CPC-P–3 Program Manual: Child–Parent Center Preschool–3rd Grade Program*. Minneapolis, MI: University of Minnesota.

Reynolds, A. J., Hayakawa, M., Ou, S. et al. (2017). Scaling and sustaining effective early childhood programs through school-family-community collaboration. *Child Development*, 88(5), 1453–1465.

Reynolds, A. J., Magnuson, K. & Ou, S. (2010). PK-3 programs and practices: A review of research. *Children and Youth Services Review*, *32*, 1121–1131.

Reynolds A. J., Richardson, B. A., Hayakawa, M., et al. (2014). Association of a full-day versus part-day preschool intervention with school readiness, attendance, and parent involvement. *JAMA*, 312(20): 2126–2134.

Reynolds, A. J., Richardson, B. A., Hayakawa, M., et al. (2016). Multi-site expansion of an early childhood intervention and school readiness. *Pediatrics*, 137(7). doi: 10.1542/peds.2015-4587

Reynolds, A. J. & Temple, J. A. (2008). Cost-effective early childhood development programs from preschool through third grade, *Annual Review of Clinical Psychology*, 4, 109–139.

Reynolds, A. J. & Temple, J. A. (1998). Extended early childhood intervention and school achievement: Age 13 findings from the Chicago Longitudinal Study. *Child Development*, 69, 231–246.

Reynolds, A. J., Temple, J. A., Ou, S. Arteaga, I. A. & White, B. A. B. (2011a). School-based early childhood education and age-28 well-being: effects by timing, dosage, and subgroups. *Science*, 333(6040), 360–364.

Reynolds, A. J., Temple, J. A., Robertson, D. L. & Mann, E. A. (2001). Long-term effects of an early childhood intervention on educational achievement and juvenile arrest: a 15-year follow-up of low-income children in public schools. *Journal of the American Medical Association*, 285, 2339–2346.

Reynolds, A. J., Temple, J. A., Robertson, D. L. & Mann, E.A. (2002). Age 21 cost–benefit analysis of the Title I Chicago Child–Parent Centers. *Education Evaluation and Policy Analysis*, 24, 267–303.

Reynolds, A. J., Temple, J. A., White, B. A., Ou, S. & Robertson, D. L. (2011b). Age-26 cost–benefit analysis of the Child–Parent Center education program. *Child Development*, 82, 782–804.

Rury, J. L. (2016). *Education and Social Change: Contours in the History of American Schooling* (5th edn.). New York, NY: Routledge.

Rutter, M. & Rutter, M. (1993). *Developing Minds: Challenge and Continuity across the Life Span*. New York, NY: Basic Books.

See, B. H. & Gorard, S. (2015). The role of parents in young people's education – a critical review of the causal evidence. *Oxford Review of Education*, 41(3): 346–366.

Spoth, R., Rohrbach, L. A., et al. (2013). Addressing core challenges for the next generation of Type 2 translation research and systems: The translation science in population impact (TSci Impact) framework. *Prevention Science*, 14, 319–351.

Sweet, M. A. & Appelbaum, M. I. (2004). Is home visiting an effective strategy: a meta-analytic review of home visiting programs for families with young children. *Child Development*, 75, 1435–1456.

Takanishi, R. (2016). *First Things First! Creating the New American Primary School*. New York, NY: Teachers College Press.

Takanishi, R. & Kauerz, K. (2008). PK inclusion: getting serious about a P–16 education system. *Phi Delta Kappan*, 89(7), 480–487.

Temple, J. A. & Reynolds, A. J. (2015). Using benefit–cost analysis to scale up early childhood programs through Pay for Success financing. *Journal of Benefit–Cost Analysis*, 6(3), 628–653.

US Senate. (1967). *Elementary and Secondary Education Act of 1965* (Report No. 146, pp. 1146–1461). Washington, DC: Author.

Zigler, E., Gilliam, W. S. & Jones, S. M. (2006). *A Vision for Universal Preschool Education*. New York, NY: Cambridge University Press.

Zigler, E. & Styfco, S. J. (1993). *Head Start and Beyond: A National Plan for Extended Childhood Intervention*. New Haven, CT: Yale University Press.

Zigler, E. & Trickett, P. K. (1978). IQ, social competence, and the evaluation of early childhood intervention programs. *American Psychologist*, 33, 789–798.

Acknowledgments

Portions of this chapter were adapted from an earlier version of Reynolds et al. (2017) and the CPC-P–3 program manual (Reynolds et al., 2016). Preparation of this paper was supported by the US Department of Education Office of Innovation (No. U411B110098), the National Institute of Child Health and Human Development (No. HD034294), and the Bill & Melinda Gates Foundation (No. OPP1173152).

9 State Policies That Support Children's Literacy through Pre-K–Third Grade Education

Laura Bornfreund and Abbie Lieberman

Introduction

The first eight years of children's learning experiences lay the critical cognitive, social, and emotional foundations on which the entirety of their future education rests. Children who do not have these in place by age 8 are at high risk of later educational failure and negative life outcomes. Fortunately, aligned, high-quality early education programs can narrow opportunity and achievement gaps while also raising the achievement and accelerating the developmental progression of all students.

Yet access to high-quality birth-to-third grade early education remains rare in the United States. Early childhood education programs are delivered through a patchwork of school-based, non-school-based, and home-based providers, many of questionable quality. The early education workforce is similarly variable in both quality and credentialing. For instance, most states require just a high school diploma for teachers of infants and toddlers. This is also true for pre-K teachers working in non-school settings and for directors of child care centers. Finally, all too often, infant, toddler, and pre-K programs feed into elementary schools led by principals who have limited experience with early education. As a result, many of their K–3 classrooms feature inconsistent instruction and learning environments that are ill-suited to meet youngsters' needs.

Based on estimates from the National Institute for Early Education Research's *The State of Preschool 2014*, only about 42 percent of 4-year-olds and 15 percent of 3-year-olds are served by public pre-K programs, including special education and the federal Head Start program (Barnett, Carolan, Squires, Clarke Brown & Horowitz, 2015). Those enrollment figures do not account for the quality of programs in which children are enrolled. Even children who benefit from high-quality pre-K may lose the benefits of these programs when they continue into elementary schools where curriculum, instructional interventions, professional development, and assessments are not necessarily aligned with their pre-K experiences.

This fragmented system has produced dismal outcomes for children. Based on data from the National Assessment of Educational Progress (NAEP), known as "the nation's report card," just 42 percent of all American children read at or above the proficient level at fourth grade (National Center for Educational Statistics, 2013, p. 7). For children from low-income families, the percentage plummets to less than 20 percent (Guernsey, Bornfreund, McCann & Williams, 2014). For dual-language learners (DLLs), fewer than 10 percent are meeting expectations. While there is not a nationally comparable measure of children's early reading skills, there are other worrisome data. According to seminal research by Betsy Hart and Todd Risley, children from families receiving public assistance hear as many as 30 million fewer words than their peers living in more affluent families (1995). Later studies have found disparities between young children from poor families and those from more well-off families as early as 18 months (Fernald, Marchman & Weisleder, 2013).

Improving Reading Outcomes

Students who have weak literacy skills at third grade face a series of potentially damaging short- and long-term consequences. Many will repeat a grade and some will drop out of school. Worse still, when they reach adulthood, their lack of a high school diploma makes it more likely that they will face incarceration and become dependent on social supports (Lesaux, 2010). To improve children's literacy skills and close opportunity and achievement gaps, federal, state, and local policymakers, along with other stakeholders, have centered on third grade as a pivotal point in academic and life trajectories.

The low percentage of American fourth-graders who are proficient readers is the result of economic, health, education, and other factors. One key variable is that too many state and local education agencies (LEAs) lack a seamless, coordinated, high-quality birth-through-third grade continuum of learning. Meanwhile, progress at the state and federal levels to build a strong early "learning staircase" has been mixed (Bornfreund, McCann, Williams & Guernsey, 2014, p. 3). The focus on early literacy must begin much before third grade; ideally, it should begin at birth.

Nonie Lesaux, professor of education at Harvard School of Education, has made the case that isolated, compartmentalized policy reforms are insufficient for making sure children are on track in the pre-K–third grade years (2013). A comprehensive approach to literacy includes attention to a wide range of components, including: teacher preparation and professional development; early identification of struggling students and intervention to support their success; comprehensive and shared assessments;

language-rich and engaging reading curricula; provision of pre-K and full-day kindergarten; and school–community–family partnerships.

In order to significantly improve children's literacy development as well as learning and development across domains, federal, states, and local education agencies need to take a comprehensive, coordinated, and connected pre-K–third grade approach and use a long-term vision for this developmental period to provide a high-quality early education for each and every child.

History of Pre-K–Third Grade Approaches

Pre-K–3 is not a new approach to early education. Its origins date to the 1960s and 1970s with the Johnson Administration's War on Poverty, which popularized the notion that education can lift Americans out of poverty. Head Start was created in 1965 to provide low-income families and their 4-year-old children with educational, health, and social services. However, a number of studies conducted over decades show that, although Head Start children displayed positive outcomes on early childhood metrics, academic gains fade during the first year of elementary school (Omwake, 1969; US Department of Health & Human Services, 2010). In 1967, President Johnson issued an executive order creating Project Follow Through, an effort to identify whole-school approaches to curriculum and instruction that maintained the academic gains children made in Head Start (Hirsch, Jr. et al., 2005). As with Head Start, Follow Through was locally run, which allowed each community to develop its own model for instruction to fit the needs of its students (Meyer, Gersten & Gutkin, 1983).[1]

The Chicago Child–Parent Center Education Program (CPC) also started in 1967 as a comprehensive early education program to support children from low-income families who were not served by Head Start (Reynolds, 2000; Sullivan, 1971). The program provides 3- and 4-year-olds with a full day of pre-K. Parent engagement, including regular volunteering in the classroom, is a major component of the program. The original program followed a pre-K–3 model and provided key program elements such as reduced class sizes, low teacher:student ratios, and parent involvement throughout the early elementary school grades. Rigorous evaluations have found that CPC participation increases kindergarten readiness, improves high school

---

[1] The program was evaluated from 1968 to 1977 and found structured models, such as direct instruction, to be most effective in sustaining basic academic skills. See: www.jstor.org/stable/1001315.

graduation rates, and reduces crime (Reynolds et al., 2016a; Reynolds et al., 2011). In 2011, researchers at the University of Minnesota received a five-year grant from the US Department of Education to begin expanding the CPC program across the Midwest (Nyhan, 2013, Reynolds et al., 2016b).

Two demonstration programs, developed in the following decades, provide useful insight into the potential value of investing in a pre-K–3 approach to early education. North Carolina's Abecedarian Project (started in 1972; Campbell et al., 2002) included some elements of a strong PreK–3 model. The experimental program provided full-time, year-round education and care to low-income African American children from birth to age 5. A small number of children received extended family support in the primary grades (Graves, 2006, Campbell et al., 2002). Those children had higher academic outcomes than children who only received support during pre-K (Graves, 2006).

From 1974 on, the federal government established multiple programs to foster collaboration across child development programs and improve transition into public elementary programs. These include Project Developmental Continuity, the Head Start Transition Project, and the National Transition Study in the 1980s (Kagan & Neuman, 1998). In 1990, Congress passed legislation to make the focus on transitions a more permanent part of Head Start's model. The National Head Start/Public School Early Childhood Transition Demonstration Projection allocated grants to programs to continue providing social and health services for children and families. Preliminary qualitative findings on this program showed families had more positive adjustments to school (Kagan & Neuman, 1998).

In part because of these early examples, pre-K–3 approaches have begun to take hold in communities across the country. For instance, New Jersey's full-day, high-quality Abbott preschool program, which is aligned with full-day kindergarten and the later grades, has been found to improve student achievement well into elementary school (Barnett et al., 2013). Additional states and localities with promising pre-K–3 initiatives underway include: Seattle Public Schools; Boston; Minneapolis and St. Paul; and Lansing, Michigan, which adopted the First School model to reorganize elementary schools into pre-K–3 campuses (Manship et al., 2016). This list is growing, as new districts and organizations are realizing the value of a coordinated pre-K–3 continuum and beyond. Obama Administration efforts, such as the Race to the Top–Early Learning Challenge, have supported the growth of pre-K–3 strategies.

As the pre-K–3 approach gains traction with policymakers and educators, experts are also moving the early education field toward a stronger understanding of how to maximize these strategies' effectiveness.

In 2013, Kristie Kauerz, of the University of Washington, and Julia Coffman, of the Center for Evaluation Innovation, released their *Framework for Planning, Implementing, and Evaluating PreK–3rd Grade Approaches*, targeted at schools, local education agencies, early learning programs, and community partners.

State Pre-K–Third Grade Policies that Support Children's Literacy Development

Effective early education policy approaches must combine targeted early literacy initiatives with policies that support, scaffold, and sequence children's learning and development through third grade. New America recently completed a project to capture the range of current policies in this space (Bornfreund, Cook, Lieberman & Williams, 2015). The effort synthesized 2011–15 data on states' pre-K–3 policies. It also sought to explore which of these policies help or hinder the ability of local education agencies, schools, and teachers to ensure that all children are on track to read on grade level by the end of third grade. The project covers seven areas: educators; standards, assessment, and data; equitable funding; state-funded pre-K; kindergarten; dual-language learners; and third grade reading laws.

These policy areas, discussed in more detail below, offer some insight into the kind of priorities state leaders are setting and the conditions they are putting in place for districts to meet students' educational and developmental needs, particularly when it comes to literacy development in from pre-K to third grade. It is by no means an exhaustive list of important policies.

Educators (Teachers and Leaders)

Educator quality is the primary in-school variable affecting students' academic and developmental growth (Weisberg, 2009). Students who have an ineffective teacher multiple years in a row are doomed to fall further and further behind (Chetty, Friedman & Rockoff, 2013). Unfortunately, children from low-income families and children of color are often assigned less effective or less experienced teachers (Murnane & Steele, 2007). Given what we know about the importance of meaningful interactions between students and teachers, this variation in quality is worrisome (Allen & Kelly, 2015).

Educator practice does not develop in a vacuum, however. It is shaped by each school's particular context. Effective school leaders set expectations for teachers, provide support, and ensure coordination and collaboration within and across grade levels.

Various state policies also shape educator effectiveness. Relevant policies include teacher preparation and licensing, principal preparation and licensure, and educator evaluation. For example, prospective teachers' coursework and experiences are driven by their state's definitions of the teaching licenses they are pursuing. Most states offer both 1) an early childhood teaching license that begins at birth or pre-K and typically extends into the early grades of elementary school and 2) an elementary teaching license that begins at kindergarten or first grade and typically extends through fifth or sixth grade. While both licenses prepare prospective teachers for early grade classrooms, preparation can look very different depending on the track they are pursuing. Early childhood teacher preparation programs tend to place more emphasis on child development, family engagement, integrated curriculum learning strategies, and early literacy development. Elementary teacher preparation programs tend to place more emphasis on classroom management, teaching strategies better suited for the later grades, and content areas beyond literacy (Bornfreund, 2011).

By providing an early childhood license, prospective teachers who know they want to teach in early-grade classrooms can specialize in the ways that young children learn and develop as well as benefit from practical experience by working with younger children. An early childhood degree program and teaching license provides a path for teachers of infants, toddlers, and preschoolers to develop necessary knowledge and expertise and have opportunities to advance. This is critically important in an era of rising credential requirements for the birth-to-5 educator workforce. It is becoming more common for a BA to be the minimum qualification for entry into the profession. Head Start already mandates that at least 50 percent of teachers have a bachelor's degree with an early childhood specialization; many state pre-K programs require the same. The recent Institute of Medicine report, *Transforming the Workforce for Children Birth through Age 8: A Unifying Foundation*, makes this a long-term goal for all lead teachers of children birth-to-8 (Allen & Kelly, 2015). According to the NIEER's State Pre-K Yearbook (Barnett, Carolan, Squires, Clarke Brown & Horowitz, 2015), 21 states and the District of Columbia require the lead teacher in a state-funded pre-K classroom to have a bachelor's degree, but not necessarily a teaching license, regardless of whether she or he teaches in a public school or non-public school setting.

Outside of public school settings, policies also need to pay attention to the adults who are working with young children. It is essential that those

Table 9.1 *Do states require ECE training and/or licensure for pre-K–third grade teachers?*

Requires lead teachers in all state-funded pre-K programs to have a BA in ECE regardless of setting	Has an early childhood education license (for example, but not limited to: birth-to-third grade or pre-K–3)	Requires K teachers to have an ECE license
AL, AK, DC, GA, IL, KY, LA, ME, MD, MI, MS, MO, NE, NV, NJ, NY, NC, OK, RI, TN, WV, WI	AL, AK, AZ, AR, CO, CT, DE, DC, FL, HI, ID, IL, IN, IA, KS, LA, MD, MA, MN, MO, NE, NV, NH, NJ, NM, NY, ND, OH, OK, OR, PA, RI, SC, SD, TN, VT, VA, WA, WI, WY	AZ, CT*, DC, IL**, LA, MD, MA, MO, NY, ND, OH, OK, PA, RI, SC

* ECE license only extends to K.
** In progress.
Adapted from: Barnett, W. S., Carolan, M. E., Squires, J. H., Clarke Brown, K. & Horowitz, M. (2015). *The State of Preschool 2014: State Preschool Yearbook*. New Brunswick, NJ: National Institute for Early Education Research; National Association for the Education of Young Children. (2014). State Profiles: Early Childhood Teacher Certification; Bornfreund, L., Cook, S., Lieberman, A. & Williams, C. (2015, November). *From Crawling to Walking: Ranking States on Birth–3rd Grade Policies That Support Strong Readers.* . Washington, DC: New America; Allen, L. R. & Kelly, B. B. (Eds.) (2015). *Transforming the Workforce for Children Birth through Age 8: A Unifying Foundation.* Washington, DC: The National Academies Press.

lead teachers, assistant teachers, and program leaders have an understanding of child development and how to foster nurturing relationships and quality interactions with infants, toddlers, and preschoolers. States can establish requirements through child care licensing to help ensure that teachers of children at these stages have at least some specific training. As of 2011, only 19 states and the District of Columbia required lead teachers in child care centers to have more than a high school diploma (NACCRRA, 2013, pp. 188–189). What is especially worrisome is that 17 states do not even require teachers of younger children in center-based settings to have a high school diploma or GED at all. And states all but ignore assistant teachers, who spend significant amounts of time with children in early childhood classrooms.

State policies for educators are not just about aligning licensure requirements with the ages of teachers' students. To help ensure that elementary school teachers are well prepared to teach reading, many states require – either through coursework requirements or program

Table 9.2 *For child care center licensing standards, what educational requirements do states require birth-to-5 educators to have?*

Require lead teachers have more than high school diploma	Require center directors have more than high school diploma	Require center directors have at least an AA in related field
CA, CO, CT, DE, DC, GA, HI, IL, MD, MA, MI, MN, NH, NJ, NY, PA, RI, VT, VA, WI	AL, AK, AZ, CA, CO, DE, DC, FL, GA, HI, IL, IN, IA, KS, LA, ME, MD, MA, MI, MN, MS, MO, NV, NH, NJ, NM, NY, ND, OH, OK, PA, RI, SD, TN, TX, UT, VT, VA, WA, WI, WY	DE, IN, PA

Note: New Jersey requires center directors to have at least a BA, but it does not have to be in a field related to early childhood education.
Adapted from: NACCRRA (Now Child Care Aware). (2013). We *can* do better: State child care center licensing. Arlington, VA.

Table 9.3 *How do states help to make sure prospective teachers are prepared to teach reading?*

Require elementary school teachers to have preparation in five essential components of reading instruction	Require elementary school teacher candidates to pass a reading pedagogy test	Require ECE teacher candidates to pass a reading pedagogy test
AL, AR, CA, CO, CT, FL, GA, ID, IN, LA, MD, MA, MI, MN, MS, MO, OH, OK, PA, TN, TX, VT, VA, WA, WV	AL, CA, CT, FL, IN, MA, MN, MS, NH, NM, NY, NC, OH, OK, TN, VT, VA, WV, WI	AL, CT, FL, IN, MA, MN, NH, NY, OK, TN, VA, WV, WI

Adapted from: National Council on Teacher Quality (2014, January). *2013 State Teacher Policy Yearbook: National Summary*. Washington, DC: NCTQ, p. 33).

standards – that preparation programs address five essential components of reading instruction: phonemic awareness, phonics, fluency, vocabulary, and comprehension. As of 2013, 25 states require teacher preparation programs to incorporate all five components (National Council on Teacher Quality, 2014, p. 33).

Once teachers are prepared and credentialed to teach in pre-K–3 classrooms, they need principals who can effectively support them, providing feedback that can improve their practice. To do this well, elementary school principals, who in many cases have never taught in an elementary school, need to understand early child development to know what appropriate, content-rich instruction looks like in the early grades, so they can provide the right support for pre-K and early grade teachers (National Association of Elementary School Principals, 2014; Mead, 2011).

Illinois is the only state that has made early childhood education a part of principal preparation. In 2010, the state redesigned accreditation for principal preparation programs, requiring that they offer early childhood content and field experiences to expose principals to pre-K–12 instructional activities. The state also intends to add early childhood content to its principal certification exam (NGA, 2013).

Five additional states (Iowa, Minnesota, New York, Oklahoma, and Vermont) require principals to have at least some coursework in child development as part of their school leadership preparation (Bornfreund et al., 2015). Coursework may seem like a natural policy target – requiring that principals receive instruction in child development topics might mean that they act on this knowledge – but simply imparting information does not mean it is acted on. The National Governors Association points out in a recent report that Illinois did not simply layer early childhood on top of existing principal preparation requirements. Rather, a goal of the change is to embed early education into administrator candidates' coursework, field experiences, and licensure processes (NGA, 2013).

Leadership is essential in the elementary school, and also in early childhood programs serving infants, toddlers, and preschoolers. Directors of these centers are responsible for meeting requirements set by the myriad agencies they may be regulated by including child care licensing, Head Start, and possibly state-funded pre-K. They are also responsible for engaging and communicating with families, observing and developing teachers, and selecting curricula, assessments, and developmental and educational programming. It is unreasonable to expect that someone with no specialized knowledge or training could do these things well. Yet six states require center directors to have only a high school diploma. Only three states require at least an associate's degree in a related field (NACCRRA, 2013). Very few states require more advanced training in either business management or instructional leadership.

Standards, Assessment, and Data

Aligned standards, assessment, and data are also key components of a strong pre-K–3 continuum. High-quality standards and aligned curricula across the domains of learning and development are essential for guiding curriculum and instruction. All states have standards for K–12 in at least English language arts (ELA), mathematics, science, and social studies. All states but two (South Dakota and Vermont) have early learning guidelines across multiple domains at least for pre-kindergarten. But while many states report having aligned their early learning guidelines with their K–12 ELA and math standards, there is reason to doubt whether this alignment is substantive enough to drive instruction in pre-K–3 classrooms (Bornfreund et al., 2014).

It is not enough to align state early learning guidelines with K–12 reading and math standards. Other developmental domains such as social-emotional learning should be included in standards for the early grades of elementary school. Studies have shown that students who have instruction in social-emotional learning have better academic performance and fewer negative behaviors than those who do not (Durlak, Weissberg, Dymnicki, Taylor & Schellinger, 2011). Several states include some social-emotional learning references in standards for various subject areas, but few have free-standing standards. According to a state survey conducted by the Collaborative for Academic, Social, and Emotional Learning, only six states (Idaho, Illinois, Kansas, Pennsylvania, Washington, and West Virginia) have free-standing social-emotional learning standards that include specific grade level indicators through at least third grade (CASEL, 2014).

To get a full picture of children's learning and development as measured by state standards, policymakers and educators need comprehensive assessments, including screening, and diagnostic, formative, and summative tools. Capturing these data from the early grades and children's experiences before they enter school is critical. Surprisingly, few states are able to do this fully, meaning basic questions about the children served with public dollars go unanswered (Early Childhood Data Collaborative, 2014).

Approximately half of children with developmental problems are not identified until they begin elementary school, even though intervening earlier is often more effective and more affordable in the long run. And while all children can experience developmental delays, low-income families and mothers with lower educational attainment are more likely to report developmental disabilities.

Both the CDC and the AAP recommend that all children be screened for developmental delays and disabilities at 9, 18, and either 24 or 30 months of age at well-child visits. Developmental screenings, however, do not necessarily need to be conducted by a physician; home visiting nurses, early educators, social workers, and even parents can screen children. Because of the significant percentage of children still not being identified early enough, and the fact that so many children are sent to child care, child care centers offer an ideal opportunity to reduce the numbers of children falling through the cracks.

Yet, no states require all licensed child care centers to conduct developmental screenings of children. Several states do, however, include screenings as an indicator in their quality rating and improvement systems. Delaware, for example, rates centers on the use of a developmental screener. Since Delaware provides higher reimbursement subsidies for higher-rated providers, the state's support for screeners has material backing.

Developmental screeners are just the first critical assessments in an effective PreK–3rd grade approach to early education. Without diagnostic, formative, and summative tools, it is not possible for teachers, schools, districts, and states to capture and analyze children's progress toward meeting standards. Early childhood assessments should include multiple domains of learning, including physical well-being, motor development, social and emotional development, approaches to learning, language and literacy development, cognitive development, and general knowledge (Snow & Van Hemel, 2008). Twenty-four states and the District of Columbia require that all state-funded pre-K programs use a multi-domain assessment of a child's learning and development (Bornfreund, Cook, Lieberman, Williams, 2015).

Many states are at varying stages of implementing kindergarten entry assessments (KEAs) with an eye toward gathering better data. These assessments are typically given within the first two months of the kindergarten year to gauge students' skills and knowledge as they enter their first year of traditional schooling. With incentives from the federal government through Race to the Top–Early Learning Challenge and the Enhanced Assessment Grant competition that focused on KEAs, many states are moving toward more multi-domain assessments. Sixteen states have fully implemented KEAs, and another 21 and the District of Columbia are planning, piloting, or implementing them in 2015–16. Beyond KEAs, few states have requirements or even provide recommendations on the kind of assessment that should be taking place in kindergarten, first, or second grade.

In recent years, states have made progress on developing more comprehensive and connected early childhood data systems – expanding their ability to link to other early childhood programs, other systems serving children, and K–12 longitudinal data systems. Around a quarter of states and the District of Columbia can link child-level data across the array of early childhood programs.

Table 9.4 *States that offer recommendations or have requirements for pre-K–third grade assessment*

Requires multi-domain pre-K assessment for all state-funded pre-K programs and gives recommendations on type of assessment used	States without a KEA in some stage of development or implementation	States currently providing recommendations or requirements for K–2 literacy and math assessment
AL, AK, AR, CA, CO, DE, DC, GA, IL, IA, KS, KY, LA, MA, MI, MO, NE, NM, NC, OH, OR, RI, VT, WA, WV	CO, ID, KS, LA, MI, MN, MT, NE, NH, SD, TN, UT, WY	AR, IN, KY, MI, OH, TN, TX,

Adapted from: Barnett, W. S., Carolan, M. E., Squires, J. H., Clarke Brown, K. & Horowitz, M. (2015). *The State of Preschool 2014: State Preschool Yearbook*. New Brunswick, NJ: National Institute for Early Education Research; Bornfreund, L., Cook, S., Lieberman, A. & Williams, C. (2015, November). *From Crawling to Walking: Ranking States on Birth–3rd Grade Policies That Support Strong Readers*. Washington, DC: New America

Table 9.5 *States that can link child-level data from early childhood programs to K–12 longitudinal data system*

Part C Early Intervention	Preschool Special Education	State Pre-K	State-subsidized Head Start	Federally Funded Head Start	Subsidized Child Care
CT, DE, DC, IA, KS, LA, MD, MN, MO, NE, OH, PA, WA, WI	AR, CT, DE, DC, FL, IL, IN, IA, KS, KY, LA, MD, MN, MS, MO, NE, NV, NJ, NM, OH, PA, RI, VA, WA, WI	AK, AR, CT, DC, FL, GA, IL, IA, KS, KY, LA, MD, MO, NE, NV, NJ, NM, OH, PA, SC, VA, WA, WI	AK, CT, DE, DC, MO, NJ, PA	AK, AR, DE, HI, IN, MS, MO, NJ, PA	AR, CT, DC, HI, IN, MD, MA, MS, PA, SC

Adapted from: Early Childhood Data Collaborative. (2014). 2013 state of states' early childhood data systems. Washington, DC: ECDC.

Twenty-nine states and the District of Columbia securely link data from at least some early childhood programs to the K–12 longitudinal system. Nine additional states are planning to link data in these systems at some point in the future (ECDC, 2014).

Only one state, Pennsylvania, is currently able to securely link child-level data from each early childhood program and connect all of those programs to the K–12 longitudinal data system (Early Childhood Data Collaborative, 2014). Information about a child's participation and experiences in child care, pre-K, or other programs can help state and local education agencies make decisions about current and future invest-ments in early education policies and programs. And these data can help kindergarten teachers be better prepared to meet the needs of the young-sters entering their classrooms.

Equitable Funding

Strong educators and solid standards, curriculum, data, and assess-ments require appropriate resources. According to the 4th edition of the School Funding Fairness report, *Is School Funding Fair? A National Report Card*, states' per-pupil expenditures in the K–12 system ranged from about $6,400 to $18,500 for 2012 (Baker, Sciarra & Farrie, 2015). State funding for education is generally distributed by formula. Many states use funding formulas that pro-vide money based on the number of pupils in a district. These formulas are sometimes weighted based on the number of students with disabilities, the number of students living in poverty, or the number of students who are English learners.

The School Funding Fairness report also looked at whether states send more dollars to districts with higher concentrations of students living in poverty. At the local level, the primary funding source is property tax, which means that schools serving the nation's most vulnerable children are often the least likely to have sufficient economic and non-economic resources to overcome the challenges they face (PreK Financing Overview, 2015). States can establish a formula that addresses these local inequalities. According to the analysis, in 2012, only 15 states had progressive funding distributions, meaning they provide higher-poverty districts (or schools) with more state resources. Meanwhile, 19 states had flat funding distributions, and 14 states had regressive funding distribu-tions (Baker, Sciarra & Farrie, 2015).

Stable and equitable funding is also important for pre-K. States fund pre-K in a variety of ways, from general funds to money generated through tobacco and lottery taxes. Sixteen states and the District of

Table 9.6 *Pre-K and K–12 funding in states*

States that fund at least one pre-K program through their school funding formula	States with a progressive funding distribution	States with a flat funding distribution	States with a regressive funding distribution
CO, CT, DC, IA, KS, ME, MD, MI, NE, NJ, NY, OK, RI, TX, VT, WV, WI	CT, DE, IN, LA, MA, MN, NE, NJ, NC, OH, OK, SD, TN, UT, WI	AZ, AR, CA, CO, FL, GA, ID, KS, KY, MI, MS, MT, NM, NY, OR, RI, SC, WA, WV	AL, IL, IA, ME, MD, MO, NV, NH, ND, PA, TX, VT, VA, WY

Adapted from: National Conference of State Legislatures. (2015). Funding Pre-K through the school funding formula; Baker, B. D., Sciarra, D. G. & Farrie, D. (2015). *Is School Funding Fair? A National Report Card* (4th edn.) Newark, NJ: Education Law Center.

Columbia pay for at least one of their state-funded pre-K programs through their core school funding formula, raising its profile by recognizing it as a part of children's core education and provides more reliable funding (National Conference of State Legislatures, 2015). Funding pre-K through these formulas can take a number of forms. Some states apply their K–12 funding formula to pre-K (creating a true *Pre*-K–12 system). Other states weight pre-K more heavily, recognizing that quality pre-K requires higher per-pupil costs. Some provide a basic per-pupil rate for pre-K and then supplement with additional money for children with special needs. Other states set a cap for pre-K funding in the formula.

Quality and Access in State-Funded Pre-K

If states and local education agencies are serious about improving children's chances of reading on grade level by the end of third grade, then they will focus on what happens before students enter kindergarten. Increased national awareness of pre-K's benefits for students has sparked efforts to expand access to public programs in several states and local communities. There are, however, big differences in the reach and quality of these programs. With limited state dollars to support early education, leaders often grapple with how to balance access and quality. There are quality indicators related to both a program's structure and process that should be in place to help ensure maximum benefits for children (Yoshikawa et al., 2013).

Access

Forty-one states and the District of Columbia have some type of state-funded pre-K program and three more are planning programs with the help of the federal government's Preschool Development Grant competition. As of 2015, just Idaho, New Hampshire, North Dakota, South Dakota, Utah, and Wyoming have no statewide programs. But even in those states, some local initiatives are underway. While the majority of states have programs, according to data collected by the National Institute for Early Education Research (2015), only nine and the District of Columbia serve more than 40 percent of 4-year-olds. Twenty-six states serve less than 20 percent of four-year-olds. Turning to 3-year-olds, only Vermont and the District of Columbia serve more than 25 percent of children. The District of Columbia is a strong example of broad access, providing pre-K for nearly 99 percent of 4-year-olds and 69 percent of 3-year-olds (Barnett et al., 2015).

Quality

In addition to the educational requirements for teachers and assistant teachers, states set other expectations for state-funded pre-K programs. Whether or not states require programs to follow state early learning standards, establish limits for child:teacher ratios, and conduct site visits of programs can provide some insight on the level of quality in those programs. Based on information collected by NIEER, states are offering varying levels of structural quality. All of the 41 states and the District of Columbia with established state-funded pre-K programs have comprehensive early learning standards. More than half of the states with pre-K programs report alignment with the Common Core State Standards for the early grades of elementary school. For pre-K classroom ratios, NIEER recommends a ratio of no more than 10 children per adult. Of the 42 states with established programs, 36 meet this benchmark. But when it comes to monitoring, only 29 states conduct site visits to programs. In many states, site visits include structured observations of classroom quality and documentation of children's learning. In others, visits are limited to reviews of program records (2015).

Provision of Full-Day Kindergarten

High-quality pre-K experiences are most impactful when followed by a strong, full-day kindergarten program to help sustain children's pre-K learning. Yet in 35 states, children are not required to attend kindergarten at all, much less for a full day (Workman, 2013). Five states do not require districts to provide kindergarten at all. To improve learning outcomes for all children, states must make quality in kindergarten a much bigger priority.

A strong full-day kindergarten program is a key component of the pre-K–3 continuum as it is the bridge of continuity in early elementary school. Some research shows that full-day kindergarten supports better academic outcomes than half-day kindergarten. Students who attend full-day also have better attendance in the primary grades and are less likely to be held back a grade or require remediation (Children's Defense Fund, 2014).

Surprisingly, many states fund only a half-day of kindergarten, and in some cases kindergarten is funded at a lower amount than first grade (Workman, 2013). This leaves districts that still want to offer a full-day kindergarten with the challenge of figuring out how to fund it. More than ten states allow districts to pass the cost onto families by charging tuition for full-day kindergarten. In many places, district leaders establish a sliding scale so that rates are based on family income. Still other states that may not require districts to offer full-day kindergarten fund it anyway. New Jersey and Wisconsin are two examples; this creates a financial incentive for districts to provide full-day kindergarten for all children even when it is not required for them to do so. Still, not requiring full-day kindergarten by law leaves it more vulnerable in challenging budget years.

Time alone, though, will not make a difference without solid, developmentally appropriate instruction and opportunities for learning. The difference between a half day and a full day is not just related to dosage, but also to how the time is structured. A full day should allow teachers to expand lessons beyond reading and math content and to provide time for child-directed learning, small-group activities, exploration and inquiry, and interactions between children – all of which are crucial in the early years of elementary school. While 11 states and the District of Columbia require that districts offer full-day kindergarten, "full day" is not necessarily equivalent to a full day in the first grade. Depending on the state, a full kindergarten day can range from about four to seven hours.

While all children can benefit from attending full-day kindergarten, it may be especially important for certain subgroups of children. Some research suggests that dual-language learners, for example, who attend full-day kindergarten do better on academic measures and are less likely to be retained in the early grades when compared to peers who attended only half-day programs (Cannon, Jacknowitz & Painter, 2011).

Table 9.7 *State provision of full-day pre-K and full-day kindergarten*

Require districts to offer full-day kindergarten	Allow districts to charge tuition for full-day kindergarten
AL, AR, DE, DC, LA, MD, MS, NC, OK, SC, TN, WV	AZ, CO, ID, IL, KS, MA, MO, NV, NH, NJ, OH, PA, WA

Adapted from: Barnett, W. S., Carolan, M. E., Squires, J. H., Clarke Brown, K. & Horowitz, M. (2015). *The State of Preschool 2014: State Preschool Yearbook*. New Brunswick, NJ: National Institute for Early Education Research; Bornfreund, L., Cook, S., Lieberman, A. & Williams, C. (2015). *From Crawling to Walking: Ranking States on Birth–3rd Grade Policies That Support Strong Readers*. Washington, DC: New America; Children's Defense Fund. (2013). Full-Day Kindergarten in the States.

Dual-Language Learners

Some demographers have estimated that by 2030, nearly 40 percent of American students will speak a language other than English at home (Thomas & Collier, 2002, p. 10). This population shift will be seen in schools most significantly in the early grades. Unfortunately, state policies governing dual-language learner (DLL) identification, linguistic supports, and reclassification into mainstream English classrooms are frequently misaligned with current research on students' academic needs.

Identifying and supporting DLLs as early as possible is important for their long-term success in both English and their other language. Yet only 15 states and the District of Columbia require state-funded pre-K programs to conduct screenings to identify children who are DLLs. While research is increasingly clear that the best way to support young DLLs' academic growth, linguistic development, and English acquisition is by providing ongoing home language support at school alongside English exposure, six states (Arkansas, California, Arizona, Massachusetts, New Hampshire, and Tennessee) endorse "English-Only" instruction in one form or another. Only 21 states have family engagement laws or regulations that make any mention of families that primarily speak another language at home (Belway, Duran & Spielberg, 2013).

As the English learner population continues to grow, it is increasingly likely that general classroom teachers will have students who need English acquisition support. General classroom teachers should be equipped with the knowledge and skills to provide DLLs with the linguistic support they need. Under federal law, local education agencies "must provide research-based professional development to any teachers, administrators, and staff who work with English language learners" (Education Commission of the States, 2014). Based on an analysis conducted by the Education

Commission, few states require specialized training for regular classroom teachers beyond what the federal government requires. States such as Indiana, New Mexico, Pennsylvania, and Virginia have made it a licensing requirement, meaning that prospective teachers are required to have course-work on methods for teaching English acquisition. And resources matter. The overwhelming majority of states provide some funding to help meet the needs of English language learners, but four do not (Millard, 2015).

Third Grade Reading Laws

Students' reading proficiency in third grade is an effective predictor of their future academic success. Because of this, 36 states and the District of Columbia have laws aimed at supporting third-grade reading success. But to date, these laws have focused more heavily on intervention rather than prevention. Further, they often consider language and literacy devel-opment only after children have entered kindergarten, even though research clearly shows that language and literacy development prior to kindergarten are critical for later academic success.

Florida was among the first states to pass legislation, in 2002, to improve third graders' reading proficiency and promote only those stu-dents scoring proficient on Florida's third grade reading assessments. By 2015, 36 states and the District of Columbia had followed Florida's lead passing similar laws aimed at improving students' third grade

Table 9.8 *State English learner policies*

Require state-funded pre-K programs to screen for dual-language learners	Have language instruction rules for state-funded pre-K programs	Mention of families that speak non-English language at home in family engagement laws or regs
AK, AR, CA, DE, DC, IL, ME, NJ, NY, OK, OR, RI, SC, TX, WA, WV	AK, AR, CA, DE, DC, GA, IL, IA, KY, LA, ME, MD, MI, MN, NE, NJ, NM, NY, OK, OR, SC, TX, WA, WI	AK, AZ, AR, CA, CT, FL, HI, ID, IL IN, MA, MN, NE, NJ, NM, NY, NC, RI, UT, WA, WI

Adapted from: Belway, S., Durán, M. & Spielberg, L. (2013). *State Laws on Family Engagement in Education.* Alexandria, VA: National PTA. Retrieved from www.pta.org/files/State_Laws_Report.pdf.
Barnett, W. S., Carolan, M. E., Squires, J. H., Clarke Brown, K. & Horowitz, M. (2015). *The State of Preschool 2014: State Preschool Yearbook.* New Brunswick, NJ: National Institute for Early Education Research; Bornfreund, L., Cook, S., Lieberman, A. & Williams, C. (2015). *From Crawling to Walking: Ranking States on Birth–3rd Grade Policies That Support Strong Readers.* Washington, DC: New America.

reading. Of the states with these laws, 18 and the District of Columbia include a requirement to retain students who do not score at proficient levels on the state's reading test (Workman, 2014).

The body of research on retention is somewhat clearer: it shows that retained students are generally no better off in the long-term. Several studies, in fact, show negative impacts for retained children (Jimerson, 2001). For instance, 19 studies included in a meta-analysis indicate that retention is associated with dropping out of high school. Additionally, retention is also expensive for local education agencies, making it a questionable policy.

Beyond retention, state third grade reading laws have much in common. Most, but not all, states with these laws require annual reading assessments in K–3. Five states require assessment before kindergarten. Most laws include a mix of intervention strategies. The majority require intervention before third grade for students identified as struggling readers. Interventions required or recommended include things like creating academic improvement plans, establishing home reading programs, tutoring or instruction outside of school hours, and providing summer school. Some states require or recommend that schools hire a reading specialist who can provide more intensive instruction to students and/or coaching for general classroom teachers. Twenty-five states and the District of Columbia require parents to be notified about their child's progress in reading (Workman, 2014).

Of the 18 states and the District of Columbia that do require retention, some specify certain actions that districts or schools must take to support students in their retained year or to allow for an alternate pathway for grade

Table 9.9 *State third-grade reading policies*

States with third grade reading laws	Require students to be retained if they do not attain a proficient score on the state's third grade reading test	Provide an opportunity for promotion if student participates in an intervention
AK, AZ, AR, CA, CO, CT, DE, DC, FL, GA, ID, IN, IA, KY, LA, MD, MN, MS, MO, NY, NC, ND, NM, NV, OH, OK, RI, SC, TN, TX, UT, VT, VA, WA, WV, WI, WY	AZ, AR, CA, CT, DC, FL, GA, IN, IA, MD, MS, MO, NV, NC, OH, OK, SC, TN, WA	AZ, CA, CT, DC, IN, IA, MD, MO, OH, OK, SC, TN, WA

Adapted from: Workman, E. (2014). *Third-Grade Reading Policies*. Denver, CO: Education Commission of the States. Retrieved from www.ecs.org/clearinghouse/01/16/44/11644.pdf.

promotion. It would make little sense to simply have students repeat a grade without making modifications that could help produce different results. Reflecting this idea, five states require that students who are held back have a different teacher. Eleven states and the District allow students to be promoted if they participate in an intervention such as summer school and 19 include exemptions, but these vary greatly across states. Most states provide for certain students to be exempt from retention. These laws do focus attention on third grade reading, but they alone will not ensure all children are on the path to being strong readers in third grade. That requires a more comprehensive approach to children's early education and development.

Implications for State Policy

Each of these policy areas is important on its own, but the most powerful impacts will take form when they are considered together. Policies exist in context. Investing in or addressing bits and pieces of a pre-K–3 approach will not result in sustained gains for all children. What is necessary is a coherent and connected set of policies that flow and fit together.

Most states are far from unified alignment. *From Crawling to Walking* shows that states are at very different levels of progress toward a set of strong pre-K–3 policies that establish promising conditions at the local level. Several states are tackling pieces of the pre-K–3 approach fairly well. But real progress will occur when states begin to knit those discrete policies together.

Equally important to the structure of state policy is how those policies are implemented by communities, public schools, and local education agencies. Understanding the implementation of these laws and how they do or do not fit together is an area for future research. State education agencies and other related entities as appropriate should work with experts and practitioners to help think through implementation; pilot initiatives in different communities; and evaluate the success, failure, and potential consequences of those efforts, establishing a feedback loop that will provide important information for making necessary changes.

Without coherent and connected pre-K–3 policies, it will be much harder to ensure that the gains children make in pre-K programs are sustained and built upon in kindergarten, the early grades, and beyond.

References

Allen, L. R. & Kelly, B. B. (Eds.). (2015). *Transforming the Workforce for Children Birth through Age 8: A Unifying Foundation*. Washington, DC: The National Academies Press.

Baker, B. D., Sciarra, D. G. & Farrie, D. (2015*). Is School Funding Fair? A National Report Card*. (4th edn.) Newark, NJ: Education Law Center.

Barnett, W. S., Carolan, M. E., Squires, J. H., Clarke Brown, K. & Horowitz, M. (2015). *The State of Preschool 2014: State Preschool Yearbook*. New Brunswick, NJ: National Institute for Early Education Research.

Barnett, W. S., Jung, K., Youn, M., & Frede, E. C. (2013). *Abbott Preschool program longitudinal effects study: Fifth grade follow-up*. New Brunswick, NJ: National Institute for Early Education Research, Rutgers University.

Belway, S., Durán, M. & Spielberg, L. (2013). *State Laws on Family Engagement in Education*. Alexandria, VA: National PTA.

Bornfreund, L. (2011). *Getting in Sync: Revamping Licensing and Preparation for Teachers in Pre-K, Kindergarten and the Early Grades*. Washington, DC: New America.

Bornfreund, L., McCann, C., Williams, C. & Guernsey, L. (2014). *Beyond Subprime Learning: Accelerating Progress in Early Education*. Washington, DC: New America.

Bornfreund, L., Cook, S., Lieberman, A. & Williams, C. (2015, November*). Scan of Birth-through-Third Grade Policies with a Focus on Literacy* (title). Washington, DC: New America.

Campbell, F. A., Ramey, C. T., Pungello, E. Sparling, J., & Miller-Johnson, S. (2002). Early childhood education: Young adult outcomes from the Abecedarian Project. *Applied Developmental Science*, 6(1), 42–57.

Cannon, J., Jacknowitz, A. & Painter, G. (2011). The effect of attending full-day kindergarten on English learner students. *Journal of Policy Analysis and Management*, 30(2), 297–309.

Chetty, R., Friedman, J. N. & Rockoff, J. E. (2013). *Measuring the Impacts of Teachers II: Teacher Value-Added and Student Outcomes in Adulthood*. Cambridge, MA: National Bureau of Economic Research.

Children's Defense Fund. (2014, June). The facts about full-day kindergarten. Retrieved from www.childrensdefense.org/library/data/the-facts-about-full-day .pdf.

Children's Defense Fund. (2013). Full-Day Kindergarten in the States. Retrieved from www.childrensdefense.org/library/data/state-data-repository/full-day-k/f ull-day-kindergarten-states-2012.html?referrer=https://www.google.com.

Collaborative for Academic, Social, and Emotional Learning (CASEL). (2014). Identifying K–12 standards for SEL in all 50 states.

Durlak, J. A., Weissberg, R. P., Dymnicki, A. B., Taylor, R. D. & Schellinger, K. B. (2011). The impact of enhancing students' social and emotional learning: a meta-analysis of school-based universal interventions. *Child Development*, 82(1), 405–432.

Early Childhood Data Collaborative. (2014, February). *2013 State of States' Early Childhood Data Systems*. Washington, DC: ECDC.

Education Commission of the States. (2014). 50-State Comparison: English Language Learners. Retrieved from www.ecs.org/english-language-learners/.

Fernald, A., Marchman, V. A. & Weisleder, A. (2013). SES differences in language processing skill and vocabulary are evident at 18 months. *Developmental Science*, 16, 234–248.

Graves, B. (2006). *PK–3: What Is It and How Do We Know It Works?* New York, NY: Foundation for Child Development.

Guernsey, L., Bornfreund, L., McCann, C. & Williams, C. (2014). *Subprime Learning: Early Education in America Since the Great Recession.* Washington, DC: New America.

Hart, B. & Risley, T. R. (1995). *Meaningful Differences in the Everyday Experience of Young American Children.* Baltimore, MD: P. H. Brookes.

Hirsch Jr., E. D., Apple, M. W. & Rochester, J. M. (2005). *Education Reform and Content: The Long View.* Brookings Papers on Education Policy, No. 8 (pp. 175–207). Washington, DC: Brookings Institution Press.

Jimerson, S. R. (2001). Meta-analysis of grade retention research: Implications for practice in the 21st century. *School Psychology Review*, 30(3), 420–437.

Kagan, S. L. & Neuman, M. J. (1998, March). Lessons from three decades of transition research *The Elementary School Journal*, 98(4), 365–379.

Kauerz, K. & Coffman, J. (2013, March). *Framework for Planning, Implementing, and Evaluating Pre-K–3rd Grade Approaches.* Seattle, WA: College of Education, Univ. of Washington.

Lesaux, N. K. (2010). *Turning the Page: Refocusing Massachusetts for Reading Success: Strategies for Improving Children's Language and Literacy Development, Birth to Age 9.* Boston, MA: Strategies for Children.

Lesaux, N. K. (2013). *PreK–3rd: Getting Literacy Instruction Right.* New York, NY: Foundation for Child Development.

Manship, K., Farber, J., Smith, C., & Drummond, K. (2016). *Case studies of schools implementing early elementary strategies: Preschool through third grade alignment and differentiated instruction.* Washington, DC: U. S. Department of Education, Office of Planning, Evaluation and Policy Development (Prepared by the American Institutes for Research, Washington, DC).

Mead, S. (2011). *PreK–3rd: Principals as Crucial Instructional Leaders.* New York, NY: Foundation for Child Development. Retrieved from http://fcd-us.org/sit es/default/files/FCD%20PrincipalsBrief7.pdf

Meyer, L. A., Gersten, R. M. & Gutkin, J. (1983, November). Direct instruction: a project follow through success story in an inner-city school. *The Elementary School Journal*, 84(2), 241–252.

Millard, M. (2015). *State Funding Mechanisms for English Language Learners.* Denver, CO: Education Commission of the States.

Murnane, R. J. & Steele, J. L. (2007). What is the problem? The challenge of providing effective teachers for all children. *The Future of Children*, 17(1), 15–43.

NACCRRA (Now Child Care Aware). (2013). *We Can Do Better: State Child Care Center Licensing, 2013 Update.* Arlington, VA.

National Association for the Education of Young Children. (2014). *State Profiles: Early Childhood Teacher Certification.*

National Association of Elementary School Principals. (2014). *Leading PreK–3 learning Communities: Competencies for Effective Principal Practice.* Alexandria, VA.

National Center for Educational Statistics. (2013). *A First Look: 2013 Mathematics and Reading: National Assessment of Educational Progress at Grades 4 and 8*. Washington, DC: US Department of Education.

National Conference of State Legislatures. (2015, April 24). *Funding Pre-K through the school funding formula*.

National Council on Teacher Quality. (2014, January). *2013 State Teacher Policy Yearbook: National Summary*. Washington, DC: NCTQ.

National Governors Association. (2013). *Leading for Early Success: Building School Principals' Capacity to Lead High-Quality Early Education*. Washington, DC: NGA.

Nyhan, P. (2013). i3 grant tests potential reach one country's oldest PreK–3rd programs. EdCentral blog, New America. www.newamerica.org/education-p olicy/edcentral.

Omwake, E. B. (1969, March). From the president. *Young Children*, 24(4), 194–195.

PreK–12 financing overview. (updated 2015, June 29). New America Atlas website. Retrieved from http://atlas.newamerica.org/school-finance

US Department of Health and Human Services, Administration for Children and Families. (2010, January). *Head Start Impact Study*. Final Report. Washington, DC.

Reynolds, A. J. (2000). *Success in early intervention: The Chicago Child-Parent Centers and youth through age 15*. Lincoln: University of Nebraska Press (Reprinted 2012).

Reynolds, A. J., Richardson, B. A., Hayakawa, M., Englund, M. M., & Ou, S. (2016a). Multi-site expansion of an early childhood intervention and school readiness. *Pediatrics*, 138(1). doi: e20154587.

Reynolds, A. J., Temple, J. A., White, B. A., Ou, S., & Robertson, D. L. (2011). Age-26 cost-benefit analysis of the Child-Parent Center education program. *Child Development*, 82, 782–804.

Reynolds, A. J., Hayakawa, M, Candee, A. J., Englund, M. M. (2016b). *CPC P-3 Program Manual: Child-Parent Center Preschool-3rd Grade Program*. Minneapolis: Human Capital Research Collaborative, University of Minnesota.

Snow, C. E. & Van Hemel, S. B. (Eds.) (2008). *Early Childhood Assessment: Why, What, and How*. Washington, DC: National Academies Press.

Sullivan, L. M. (1971). *Let us not underestimate the children*. Glenview, IL: Scott, Foreman.

Thomas, W. P. & Collier, V. P. (2002). *A National Study of School Effectiveness for Language Minority Students' Long-Term Academic Achievement*. Santa Cruz, CA: Center for Research on Education, Diversity and Excellence.

Weisberg, D. (2009). *The Widget Effect: Our National Failure to Acknowledge and Act on Differences in Teacher Effectiveness*. Brooklyn, NY: The New Teacher Project.

Workman, E. (2013, March). *Inequalities at the Starting Line: State Kindergarten Policies*. Denver, CO: Education Commission of the States.

Workman, E. (2014, December). *Third-Grade Reading Policies*. Denver, CO: Education Commission of the States.

Yoshikawa, H., Weiland, C., Brooks-Gunn, J. et al. (2013, October). *Investing in Our Future: The Evidence Base on Preschool Education*. New York, NY: Foundation for Child Development.

Part III

School and Family Processes of Impacts
over Time

10 School-Related and Family Processes Leading to Long-Term Intervention Effects

Arthur J. Reynolds, Suh-Ruu Ou, Christina F. Mondi, and Momoko Hayakawa

Growing evidence that early childhood experiences can improve adult well-being and reduce educational disparities has increased attention to the importance of prevention (Braveman & Gotlieb, 2014; Power, Kuh & Morton, 2013). Early disparities between high- and low-income groups are evident in school readiness skills, which increase substantially over time in rates of achievement proficiency, delinquency, and educational attainment (Braveman & Gotlieb, 2014; O'Connell, Boat & Warner, 2009). In this chapter, we review evidence for three major processes by which early childhood interventions (ECI) promote well-being and reduce problem behaviors. These are: (a) cognitive advantage; (b) family support behavior; and (c) school quality and support.

The accumulated research widely supports these processes as critical targets of prevention programs for children growing up in economically disadvantaged contexts. Our perspective on promoting well-being is informed by three decades of studying the Child–Parent Centers (CPC), a large-scale program providing comprehensive education and family services to low-income children from preschool to third grade. The CPCs' success in promoting well-being and high economic returns is documented in the Chicago Longitudinal Study (CLS), which has tracked 1,500 families into adulthood. We also draw on the accumulated life-course research on the benefits of primarily center-based ECIs, as well as contemporary programs and practices.

Consistent with prevention research, well-being is used to describe the multi-dimensional outcomes of ECI, including school achievement and

Reprinted by permission of John Wiley, Inc.: Processes of Early Childhood Intervention to Adult Well-Being (*Child Development*, 2017, Vol. 88(2), pp. 378–387 by A. J. Reynolds, S.-R. Ou, C. F. Mondi, and M. Hayakawa), modified to include three tables and figures from the appendices plus a few minor changes. Preparation was supported in part by the National Institute of Child Health and Human Development (Grant No. HD034294), the Office of Innovation, US Department of Education (Grant No. U411B110098), matching grants to the US Department of Education, and the National Science Foundation Graduate Student Fellowship Program.

attainment, socio-emotional development and mental health, and health behavior. We regard well-being as not just the absence of negative outcomes, but the presence of positive ones. Strengthening processes can promote lifelong good health, and reduce the risk of social, emotional, and behavioral problems (O'Connell et al., 2009; Braveman & Gotlieb, 2014). We use the term *process* to describe how ECI affects later well-being. Documenting processes or mechanisms can improve program design. Paths that are identified can contribute to improvement efforts. Understanding processes also can increase generalizability. If results across studies share a common process, expansion would be more likely to be successful. The terms intervention, prevention programs, and early childhood programs are used interchangeably.

Three Processes of Early Childhood Intervention Impacts

In recognition of the complex array of factors during and after program participation that account for long-term effects, research has increasingly emphasized examination of a comprehensive set of child-, family-, and school-related processes. This led to the development of the five-hypothesis model of intervention (5HM; Reynolds, 2012). Derived from the accumulated research on ECI over four decades, 5HM posits that effects are explained by indicators of five general paths of influence: cognitive-scholastic advantage (CA), family support behavior (FS), school quality and support (SS), motivational advantage (MA), and socio-emotional adjustment (SA).

Because the major purpose of ECI is to promote enduring effects into adulthood, the extent to which this pattern is observed will depend on the magnitude of effects on one or more of the processes. As shown in Figure 10.1, we emphasize the contributions of CA, FS, and SS due to their strong evidence as processes. The contributions of MA and SA are usually initiated by the other three. Space limitations also necessitate this focus (see Ou & Reynolds, 2010; Reynolds, 2012). To be valid explanations, paths must be independently associated with both program and outcome measures. The hypotheses could work in combination. For example, participation may affect parent involvement through early CA, just as parent involvement and CA may link directly to SS. Although substantial support exists for the independent and combined influence of the processes, the pattern is expected to vary depending on goals, program content (e.g., family- vs. center-based), and implementation fidelity. The summary of evidence for the three processes, which are not rank ordered, is followed by a review of findings from a variety of interventions.

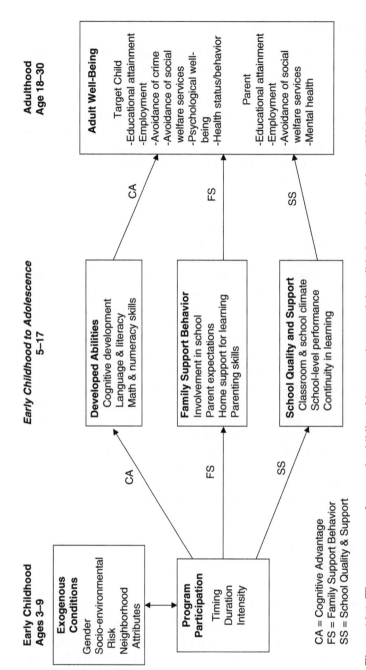

Figure 10.1 Three processes from early childhood intervention to adult well-being. Adapted from 5HM (Reynolds, 2012). Motivational advantage and socio-emotional adjustment also contribute to impacts.

Cognitive-Scholastic Advantage

Effective ECIs provide systematic, activity-based educational experiences that stimulate children's emerging cognitive, language, numeracy, and social skills. All of these skills are necessary for optimal school readiness. Decades of research have linked participation in effective ECIs to CA and reductions in the achievement gap among high-risk populations (Camilli et al., 2010; Reynolds, 2012, p. 19). CA promotes effective and smooth school transitions that provide cumulative advantages in adjustment and performance by enhancing later learning, increasing teacher expectations of performance, promoting school commitment and stability in learning environments, and avoiding the need for remediation. The cumulative benefits of CA was a key finding of the landmark multi-site Cornell Consortium for Longitudinal Studies (1983), in which participants in 11 ECI programs experienced increases in cognitive and school readiness skills by half a standard deviation (half a year gain over controls). This culminated in reduced remedial education and higher rates of school completion. Findings from the Abecedarian Project, HighScope/Perry Preschool, and CPC consistently show that participation is associated with CA and achievement (Campbell et al., 2002; Reynolds, 2012; Schweinhart et al., 2005). CA is also supported by ECI meta-analyses documenting mid- to long-term effects on achievement, socio-emotional learning and delinquency (Camilli et al., 2010; WSIPP, 2014).

In sum, graduates of high-quality ECIs tend to exhibit CA relative to non-participating peers. Upon school entry, they are more cognitively prepared, motivated, and confident in their ability to succeed. CA thus initiates a process of scholastic achievement and commitment, which has in turn been linked to well-being in other domains across the lifespan. For example, children with greater CA upon school entry have been found to exhibit higher levels of social competence and lower rates of problem behaviors, and are more likely to obtain high school diplomas, college degrees, and steady employment as adults (Power et al., 2003). Thus, the research in this area has increasingly affirmed that "doing well" in school is strongly predictive of "being well" – psychologically, physically, and financially – in both childhood and adulthood (Figure 10.1).

Family Support Behavior

The FS process indicates that longer-term effects of ECI will occur to the extent that participation enhances parenting skills, attitudes and expectations, and involvement in children's education (Ou & Reynolds, 2010; Reynolds et al., 2004). The main factors examined are parent involvement in school, parent expectations for achievement, and support for learning at home. Parenting behaviors lead to improved well-being (e.g., achievement) by increasing children's learning time directly (reading with parents, higher school attendance) or indirectly (parental monitoring), enhancing children's motivation and school commitment, and increasing expectations for attainment and success. They also improve social support and parenting skills, which reduce social isolation and the risk of child maltreatment. Meta-analyses of family interventions and parenting behaviors (Farrington & Welsh, 2007; Jeynes, 2007) show that involvement and monitoring link to higher achievement and delinquency prevention.

Previous CPC research supports the critical role of FS – and especially parent involvement – in promoting children's academic success and long-term well-being. Using longitudinal CPC data, Hayakawa and colleagues (2013) reported that parent involvement influenced continued achievement via two major pathways. First, early parent involvement predicted later parent involvement, such that parents who were highly involved in kindergarten were likely to continue their high levels of involvement throughout the elementary grades. Second, parent involvement in school influenced children's school motivation, which in turn impacted achievement. These results suggest that parents' sustained involvement across the elementary years initiates a cumulative process that continues to foster children's motivation and subsequent parent involvement, which both influence school achievement.

Further evidence on the importance of FS in fostering well-being comes from home visiting and parenting interventions, including Nurse–Family Partnership, Family Check-Up, and Parents as Teachers (PAT; Avellar & Supplee, 2013). In a large-scale PAT study, Zigler, Pfannenstiel & Seitz (2008) found that significant improvements in third-grade achievement for a state sample were initiated by parental home literacy and school readiness skills, both of which were further impacted by preschool participation. This suggests the reinforcing influences of FS and CA. Other parenting and home visiting programs generally support these findings (Avellar & Supplee, 2013; Sweet & Appelbaum, 2004), though mixed effects are also reported. The strongest impacts occur for high-need families at relatively high levels of dosage.

In another CPC study, FS, as measured by parent involvement in school and avoidance of later child maltreatment, was found to mediate the effects of preschool on educational attainment, crime, and health behaviors (Reynolds & Ou, 2011). Increased parent involvement in school led to greater school commitment and student achievement, which in turn reduced the incidence of child maltreatment. The generalizability of these results is supported by research from three different ECIs, each of which identified parent involvement as a contributing path from ECI to educational attainment (Abecedarian, Perry, CPC; Englund et al., 2014).

School Quality and Support

In this process, intervention effects are expected to persist as a function of attending schools of sufficient quality and enrichment. Key indicators of SS include aggregate achievement, student school stability, and school climate (Bogard & Takanishi, 2005; Reynolds et al., 2004; Kyriakides et al., 2013). SS provides the developmental continuity necessary to sustain preschool gains by increasing the duration, predictability, and stability of enriching post-program learning environments. Families are likely to value and seek out schools that match the quality and climate of children's preschool program (Reynolds, 2012). ECI gains are more sustained in the presence of this learning environment (Campbell et al., 2002; Englund et al., 2014; Reynolds et al., 2010a). Evidence indicates that attendance in schools with relatively high percentages of proficient achievers positively affects school climate, performance expectations, and peer norms (Jennings & Greenberg, 2009; Kyriakides et al., 2013; Pianta, 2005). School mobility, especially if frequent, creates learning discontinuities that hinders the maintenance of a positive and predictable environment (Takanishi & Kauerz, 2008). These discontinuities can be reduced and counteracted by ECI (Bogard & Takanishi, 2005; Reynolds, 2012).

Previous studies have indicated that the benefits of Head Start participation are more strongly sustained if participants attend more supportive and higher quality elementary schools (Currie & Thomas, 2000; Lee & Loeb, 1995; Redden et al., 2001). These results parallel studies showing that enhanced elementary-grade services (e.g., smaller classes and greater instructional time) add to and sustain the benefits of earlier intervention (Finn et al., 2010; Mashburn, 2015; Reynolds et al., 2010a). These links have also been corroborated in the findings for children attending CPCs. For example, continued enrollment in higher quality schools mediates the relation between participation and school achievement and attainment (Reynolds et al., 2010b; Reynolds & Ou, 2011).

School mobility is a negative indicator of the continuity in learning environments that has been frequently associated with lower school performance and higher levels of school dropout and behavioral problems (Han, 2014; Reynolds, Chen & Herbers, 2009). Recent studies have found that school mobility is associated with adjustment and mental health difficulties (Gruman et al., 2008), because it may break social ties that increases the risk of later problem behaviors.

Most prior studies indicate that frequent mobility is associated with lower school achievement and problem behaviors, and this impact holds after many individual and family differences are taken into account. Participation in high quality preschool promotes school stability and support (Bogard & Takanishi, 2005; Englund et al., 2014; Schweinhart et al., 2005), which helps maintain learning gains. Mobility has also been found to mediate preschool effects on early adult well-being (Englund et al., 2014; Reynolds et al., 2009, 2010b), as school-stable children are more likely to remain in better schools, avoid remediation, and delinquency.

In the next section, we describe the background and impacts of the CPC program and other ECIs that promote the three processes of influences. This is followed by a breakdown of the magnitude of the influence of the processes in accounting for effects on long-term well-being.

Effects of CPC Intervention

The CPC program opened in 1967 with funding from Title I of the Elementary and Secondary Education Act to counteract the negative effects of poverty on school success. The 25 CPCs were located in the highest poverty neighborhoods in Chicago, in which seven in ten families are low-income. Common problems were high rates of absenteeism and low achievement.

As the second oldest federally funded preschool program, CPC provides comprehensive educational and family support services to children within a developmentally appropriate ecological framework (Reynolds, 2012; Sullivan, 1971). The program is implemented in centers which are directed by a Head Teacher, a Parent-Resource Teacher, who manages the parent-resource room, and a School–Community Representative to connect families with health and social services. Core program principles include a school-based structure, a strong emphasis on literacy, the use of child-focused instructional approaches, and strengthening the family–school relationship. To maximize individual learning opportunities, preschool class sizes are small (average teacher:child ratio is 2:17). Comprehensive parent involvement included a variety of home- and school-based approaches. Services are provided from preschool to third grade.

Research on CPC effectiveness is based on many cohorts of graduates and a diverse set of studies, including the Chicago Longitudinal Study (CLS, 2005). The CLS is an ongoing prospective study of a complete cohort of 989 children who attended 20 CPCs, as well as a matched comparison group of 550 same-age children who attended publicly funded full-day kindergarten in five randomly selected schools. The groups were equivalent on child and family characteristics and many analyses assessing robustness (e.g., propensity-score and latent-variable approaches) support internal validity (Reynolds et al., 2011a; Reynolds & Ou, 2011). Over 90 percent of the groups have been followed successfully from kindergarten to adulthood. Evidence from CPC studies meet the rigorous standards of the What Works Clearinghouse and many other registries of effectiveness (Reynolds et al., 2011a; Reynolds & Temple, 2008).

The performance of CPC preschool participants consistently exceeded that of the comparison group on many indicators of well-being, from the beginning of kindergarten through early adulthood (see Table 10.1). Although effect sizes varied by outcome, most exceeded 0.20 standard deviations, which translate to substantial social benefits. As shown in Table 10.1, the program's initial effect on cognitive skills (ES = 0.63 SD) at age 5 contributed to a cumulative advantage on later well-being. Program-related reductions in special education placement (ES = −0.45 SD) and grade retention (ES = −0.37 SD) as well as lower rates of delinquency and crime are indicative of significant economic benefits. For example, by age 24 the preschool group had a 22% lower rate of felony arrest than the comparison group (16.5% vs. 21.1%, respectively). The educational and crime prevention benefits also carry over to mental health, as CPC graduates had lower rates of depressive symptoms in early adulthood (12.8% vs. 17.4%; ES = 0.20 SD or a 26% reduction). Beneficial effects were not detected for classroom adjustment, perceived competence, or overall college attendance (Reynolds, 2012; Ou & Reynolds, 2010).

Effects of Other ECIs

Although there is a large literature on the effects of ECIs, only a few studies have tracked participants into adulthood. We highlight studies examining the effects of five programs on school achievement, educational attainment, and crime prevention. They illustrate the three processes of long-term effects. Findings from the Abecedarian Project, Perry Preschool, and the Cornell Consortium show effect sizes on school achievement ranging from one-third to three-quarters of a standard deviation. These are consistent with the effect sizes of CPC and state prekindergarten programs (Camilli et al., 2010). A similar pattern of findings was found for high school completion and years of education (Reynolds &

Table 10.1 *Effects of preschool participation in the Child–Parent Centers*

Domain and Measure	Preschool Group (n = 950)	Comparison Group (n = 523)	Difference	Effect Size
School Achievement/Performance				
Average cognitive composite score – age 5	48.7	44.0	4.7*	0.63
Met national norm on cognitive composite – age 5, %	46.7	25.1	21.6*	0.59
Met national norm on reading achievement – age 14, %	35.0	22.0	13.0*	0.38
Child Maltreatment				
Any indicated abuse or neglect from ages 4 to 17, %	9.9	17.4	−7.5*	−0.35
Any out of home placement, %	5.2	8.5	−3.3*	−0.25
Juvenile Arrest by Age 18				
Petition to juvenile court, %	16.9	25.1	−8.2**	−0.29
No. of petitions to juvenile court	0.45	0.78	−0.33*	−0.30
Adult Crime by Age 26				
Any felony arrest, %	13.3	17.8	−4.5*	−0.19
No. of felony arrests	0.32	0.44	−0.12*	−0.21
Health and Mental Health				
Reported any depression symptom, %	12.8	17.4	−4.6+	−0.20
Substance misuse, %	14.3	18.8	−4.5*	−0.19
Daily tobacco use, %	17.9	22.1	−4.2	−0.15

* $p \leq 0.05$. Effect sizes are in standard deviations. Dichotomous outcomes were converted using the probit transformation. Sample sizes vary by outcome. National norm is for the Iowa Tests of Basic Skills. The sample sizes for adult crime by age 26 are provided. Coefficients are from linear, probit, or negative binomial regression analysis. Coefficients are adjusted for the eight indicators of preprogram risk status, gender, race/ethnicity, child welfare history, and a dummy-coded variable for missing data on risk status. Sample comparisons are based on published studies whenever possible.

Temple, 2008). Perry Preschool, a panel study of Head Start (Garces et al., 2002), and Nurse–Family Partnership (Eckenrode et al., 2010) also found reductions in criminal behavior of 30 to 40 percent, which also match those from CPC. This latter effect is largely attributable to reductions in child maltreatment. Reductions in health compromising behavior and mental health problems have also been observed (Englund et al., 2014; O'Connell et al., 2009; Ou & Reynolds, 2010). Overall, these findings show that high-quality ECIs enhance participants' well-being across a range of contexts and over time. Some shorter-term studies (e.g., Early Head Start, Head Start) have found few gains (O'Connell et al., 2009), which may be a function of dosage, fidelity, attrition, and levels of family and school support (Reynolds et al., 2011a).

Summary of Processes of Influence

We summarize the contributions of the three processes of CPC and related programs for four youth and adult outcomes using the percentage contribution of each process to the total indirect (mediated) effect (Reynolds & Ou, 2011). The findings are summarized in Figure 10.2 and based on structural equation modeling of longitudinal associations in which measurement error, multiple indicators of each process, and alternative specifications are taken into account. After adjusting for gender, family risk, and the influence of other processes, CA-initiated pathways involving early achievement and need for remedial education accounted for 19 to 40% of the indirect effect. These are sizable contributions, both direct and indirect, in good-fitting models. FS-initiated pathways, which included parent involvement in school and avoidance of child maltreatment, independently accounted for 18 to 26% of the indirect effects. SS paths, measured by school quality and frequent mobility, accounted for 27 to 50% of the indirect effect of preschool (Reynolds & Ou, 2011; Reynolds, Ou & Topitzes, 2004). Domain crossover was evident as FS and SS accounted for sizable shares of impacts on arrests. Impacts on felony arrest were mediated by the number of school moves alone ($bs =$ -0.13 [program to moves] and 0.09 [moves to arrest]) and by paths involving parent involvement, school mobility, and high school completion (Reynolds & Ou, 2011). CA and SS accounted for substantial shares of impacts to adult depressive symptoms.

With regard to depressive symptoms, the majority of the indirect effect of CPC was attributable to paths initiated and contributed by CA, FS, and SS. CA showed the largest contribution. Similar to the other outcomes, one process was that the early CA advantage ($b = 0.36$) carried over to promote greater parent involvement ($b = 0.19$) and attendance in higher-quality schools ($b = 0.24$), which lowered rates of delinquency ($b = -0.12$) and improved the likelihood of school completion ($b = 0.18$) leading to lower rates of depressive symptoms (Reynolds & Ou, 2011). SS was the largest contributor to juvenile arrest, while the three processes made equal contributions to high school completion and felony arrest.

A similar pattern of findings has been found for school achievement and occupational attainment. Studies have also used structural equation modeling to strengthen validity. Re-analyses of the Perry, Abecedarian, and CPC programs (Englund et al., 2014; Reynolds et al., 2010b), which

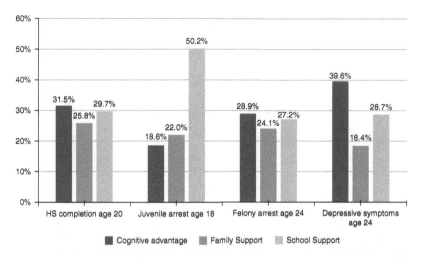

Figure 10.2 Percentage contributions of three processes to total indirect effects of CPC preschool participation. The chart summarizes the major contributing pathways to the long-term effects of CPC preschool as a proportion of the total standardized indirect effect. Estimates are from LISREL and take account of measurement errors and correlated errors across equations. The total indirect effect is the sum of all paths of influence from preschool leading to outcomes. The indirect effects are categorized by mediator, with the primary emphasis on the mediators that initiated the indirect effect

included matched measures and sequences of each process, revealed that the processes accounted for a majority of the observed impacts on educational attainment and health behaviors at age 21. Findings for each of these studies are summarized in Figure 10.3 (Reynolds et al., 2010). The studies also showed that classroom social adjustment helped transmit the effects of CA. CA contributed more to long-term effects for Perry and Abecedarian, whereas FS and SS influences were larger for CPC. In both Perry and CPC, the number of school moves was predicted by program participation ($bs = -0.11$ and -0.17) and directly linked to juvenile arrest ($bs = 0.20$ and 0.12, respectively). Many studies also show that the sustainability of effects in ECI and prevention programs is strengthened by SS (Jennings & Greenberg, 2009; Mashburn, 2015; Redden et al., 2001).

Feasibility and Cost-Effectiveness at a Larger Scale

Our review of the three processes shows their positive direct and indirect contributions to many indicators of well-being. These provide a strong

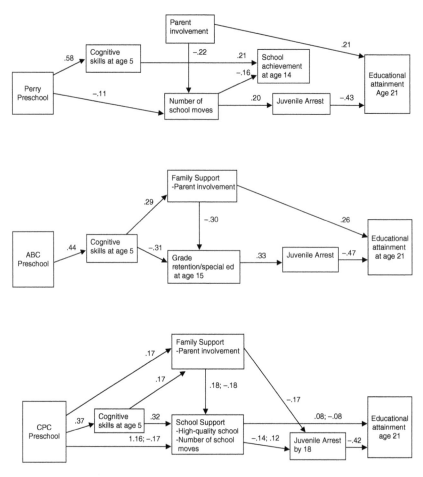

Figure 10.3 Summary paths of effects from preschool to years of education at age 21 in three studies. Selected coefficients are standardized and statistically significant, account for measurement errors, and are estimated from a larger model that included indicators of 5HM (Reynolds, 2012). A path not shown for Perry is from grade retention/special education to educational attainment ($b = -0.67$). For CPC, two coefficients on the same path are school quality and mobility, respectively. ABC = Abecedarian Project. CPC = Child–Parent Centers.

foundation for expanding effective ECIs that target these processes. For example, because FS is an established influence on children's outcomes, a variety of interventions (e.g., center-based, family-based) are being expanded as two-generational approaches (Avaller & Supplee, 2013). The No Child Left Behind Act also mandates that schools develop parent involvement and engagement plans. Parallel efforts to improve school quality through curricular reforms, increased alignment of instruction, and small classes also are feasible and scalable. Expanding access to effective programs can provide cumulative advantages which lead to enhanced well-being in multiple domains.

ECIs that operate by promoting CA, FS, and SS also show high economic returns (O'Connell et al., 2009). Table 10.2 shows the results of cost–benefit analyses for three programs: Abecedarian, Perry, and CPC. Although studies vary dramatically in cost per child and in age of measurement, each program demonstrates a positive economic return in regards to cost savings in remediation and increases in economic well-being due to higher levels of education. Abecedarian showed a return of roughly 3 dollars per dollar invested; CPC 7 to 11 dollars; and Perry 9 to 16 dollars (Barnett & Masse, 2007; Reynolds et al. 2011b; Reynolds & Temple, 2008; Schweinhart et al., 2005). The benefits were also spread among many outcome domains.

A meta-analysis of 49 state and school districts programs (WSIPP, 2014), primarily for children from economically disadvantaged contexts, shows a projected return of roughly four dollars per dollar invested, in large part because of early enrichments in cognitive and scholastic development, parent involvement, and socio-emotional learning. This indicates that implementation at larger scales can provide sizable economic benefits provided that program quality is relatively high. As shown in Table 10.2, the cost per child to achieve positive returns is lower than that of model programs.

Generalizability across Child, Family, and Community Contexts

The CPC program has recently been expanded to serve children from diverse ethnic backgrounds (e.g., Latinos, Hmong refugees) and other understudied groups. With funding from the US Department of Education's Office of Innovation, the Midwest CPC Expansion preschool to third-grade intervention is presently located at more than 30 urban and metropolitan schools in Illinois and Minnesota. A cohort of over 2,500 program and 1,300 comparison-group students in four districts is being followed to third grade. The comparison group participated in the usual preschool programs for 3- and 4-year-olds and attended 25 schools that were matched to program schools on propensity scores of economic disadvantage. School achievement and parent involvement are

Table 10.2 *Benefit–cost findings of selected early childhood interventions (2012 dollars)*

Program	Program Scale	Age at follow-up	Program cost per child ($)	Total Benefits to Society per Child ($)	Benefit – Cost Ratio
Abecedarian Project	Model	21	53,495	172,988	3.23
Chicago CPC Preschool-1	Large	21	9,426	67,271	7.14
Chicago CPC Preschool-2		26	9,426	102,117	10.83
Perry Preschool-1	Model	27	20,221	176,740	8.74
Perry Preschool-2		40	20,221	326,407	16.14
WSIPP (2014) meta-analysis	Large	4–17	6,974	29,210	4.20

Note. Values were converted for the original studies were converted to 2012 dollars using the Consumer Price Index for Urban Workers (CPI-U). Studies were as follows: Abecedarian (Barnett & Masse, 2007), CPC (Reynolds et al., 2002, 2011b), and Perry (Schweinhart et al. 2005). Washington State Institute for Public Policy (WSIPP) meta-analysis included 49 studies of state and school district programs.

the primary outcomes of investigation. The program elements (e.g., effective learning experiences, menu-based parent involvement system, continuity and stability) are tailored to needs of each community.

Initial findings show that Chicago and Saint Paul implementation in 2012–13 have effects on school readiness and parent involvement in school that are similar to CPC implemented in the 1980s (Reynolds et al., 2014). This pattern was observed in the presence of a significantly enhanced program in which baseline performance was equivalent and comparison groups received existing school-based preschool (i.e., state preschool or Head Start). For example, full-day compared to part-day preschool in the same schools was linked to higher rates of meeting school readiness norms (81% vs. 59%) at the end of preschool and lower rates of chronic absences (21% vs. 38%; Reynolds et al., 2014). These effects indicate the continued feasibility and effectiveness of the program across contexts. Other high-quality state and local programs show similar patterns of effectiveness (e.g., Camilli et al., 2010; WSIPP, 2014).

It will be important to assess effects on ethnic and geographic sub-groups. The original CLS sample was nearly all African-American. While this sample was representative of urban poverty, it does not reflect other types of contexts. The CPC program generally exerts its strongest effects on boys and children affected by the highest levels of socio-demographic risk (Ou & Reynolds, 2010; Reynolds et al., 2011b). Girls benefit more from school-age intervention (Reynolds et al., 2011a, 2011b). Impacts of extended intervention are similar for most groups.

Limitations of Knowledge

Although the processes substantially explained impacts on well-being, three limitations should be noted. First, studies primarily examined educational outcomes. Only a few have examined mental health, crime, and health behaviors. Individual processes may play different roles depending on the outcome and age of measurement. Further research is warranted.

Second, few studies have examined several processes together within a comprehensive model. The contributions of each process may vary by individual indicators and across programs and social contexts. Social and motivational factors, for example, may play significant yet complex roles. More extensive longitudinal studies into adulthood are needed. Although distinct, the processes are correlated and should be interpreted within the full model specification and program theory. Findings from life-course studies show the relative strength of the three processes. Alternative processes across a wide range of studies also warrant greater attention.

Finally, the three processes reviewed in our article have not been fully assessed for particular child and family subgroups, such as family economic status, different racial and ethnic groups, and for different levels of risk. The magnitude of influence for each will depend on the level of variation observed, which will be affected by child and family risk factors. However, the accumulated research in human development and health sciences (Braveman & Gotlieb, 2014; O'Connell et al., 2009) is consistent with the findings of our review.

Conclusion

Strengthening programs and sustaining their effects are key contributions of processes. Given the importance of entering kindergarten and the early grades proficient in multiple domains, it is expected that improving the quality of programs and increasing their length and intensity will strengthen the paths to well-being. Program features such as well-trained teachers and small classes are key sources of impacts and economic benefits (Table 10.2). The provision of comprehensive services can broaden the paths of influence necessary for sustained effects. Our review supports the generalizability of the processes in promoting well-being. A range of programs and practices that impact these processes would be expected to positively contribute. These could be independent or complementary of ECI. For example, interventions that prevent child maltreatment may exert longer-term effects on health and well-being by impacting juvenile delinquency, school achievement, and need for remedial education. The processes reviewed can promote sustained effects of intervention. Their reproducibility in a variety of contexts will help ensure that the demonstrated benefits of early childhood programs can be effectively scaled.

References

Avellar, S. A. & Supplee, L. H. (2013). Effectiveness of home visiting in improving child health and reducing child maltreatment. *Pediatrics*, 132 Suppl. (2), S90–S97.

Barnett, W. S. & Masse, L. N. (2007). Comparative benefit–cost analysis of the Abecedarian program and its policy implications. *Economics of Education Review*, 26, 113–125.

Bogard, K. & Takanishi, R. (2005). PK–3: An aligned and coordinated approach to education for children 3 to 8 years old. *Social Policy Report*, XIX, No. III. Washington: SRCD.

Braveman, P. & Gottlieb, L. (2014). The social determinants of health: it's time to consider the causes of the causes. *Public Health Reports*, 129 Suppl.(2), 19–31.

Camilli, G., Vargas, S., Ryan, S. & Barnett, W. S. (2010). Meta-analysis of the effects of early education interventions on cognitive and social development. *Teachers College Record*, 112(3), 579–620.

Campbell, F., Ramey, C. T. et al. (2002). Early childhood education: young adult outcomes from the Abecedarian Project. *Applied Developmental Science*, 6(1), 42–57.

Chicago Longitudinal Study. (2005). *User's Guide* (ver. 7). Minneapolis, MI: University of Minnesota.

Consortium for Longitudinal Studies. (1983). *As the Twig Is Bent ... Lasting Effects of Preschool Programs*. Hillsdale, NJ: Lawrence Erlbaum Associates.

Currie, J. & Thomas, D. (2000). School quality and the longer-term effects of Head Start. *The Journal of Human Resources*, 35(4), 755–774.

Eckenrode, J., Campa, M. et al. (2010). Long-term effects of prenatal and infancy nurse home visitation on the life course of youths: 19-year follow-up of a randomized trial. *Archives of Pediatrics and Adolescent Medicine*, 164, 9–16.

Englund, M. M., White, B., Reynolds, A. J., Schweinhart, L. J. & Campbell, F. A. (2014). Health outcomes of early childhood interventions: A 3-study analysis, in Reynolds, A. J. et al. (Eds.), *Health and Education in Early Childhood*. New York, NY: Cambridge University Press.

Farrington, D. P. & Welsh, B. C. (2007). *Saving Children from a Life of Crime*. New York, NY: Oxford University Press.

Finn, J. D., Suriani, A. & Achilles, C. (2010). Small classes in the early grades: one policy, multiple outcomes, in Reynolds, A. J. et al. (Eds.), *Childhood Programs and Practices in the First Decade of Life*. New York, NY: Cambridge University Press.

Garces, E., Currie, J. & Thomas, D. (2002). Longer-term effects of Head Start. *American Economic Review*, 92, 999–1013.

Gruman, D. H., Harachi, T. W., Abbott, R. D., Catalano, R. F. & Fleming, C. B. (2008). Longitudinal effects of student mobility on three dimensions of elementary school engagement. *Child Development*, 79(6), 1833–1852.

Han, S. (2014). School mobility and students' academic and behavioral outcomes. *International Journal of Education Policy & Leadership*, 9(6). Retrieved from www.ijepl.org.

Hayakawa, M., Englund, M. M., Warner-Richter, M. N. & Reynolds, A. J. (2013). The longitudinal process of early parent involvement on student achievement: a path analysis. *National Head Start Association Dialog*, 16, 103–126.

Jennings, P. A. & Greenberg, M. T. (2009). The prosocial classroom: teacher social and emotional competence in relation to student and classroom outcomes. *Review of Educational Research*, 79, 491–525.

Jeynes, W. H. (2007). The relationship between parental involvement and urban secondary school student academic achievement. *Urban Education*, 41(1), 82–110.

Lee, V. E. & Loeb, S. (1995). Where do Head Start attendees end up? One reason why preschool effects fade out. *Educational Evaluation and Policy Analysis*, 17, 62–82.

Kyriakides, L. et al. (2013). What matters for student learning outcomes: a meta-analysis of studies exploring factors of effective teaching. *Teaching & Teacher Education*, 36, 143–152.

Mashburn, A. (2015). *Maintaining the Impact of Head Start on Children' Long-Term Development* Paper presented at the National Invitational Conference on Sustaining Early Childhood Gains. Minneapolis: Federal Reserve Bank of Minneapolis.

O'Connell, M. E., Boat, T. & Warner, K. E. (Eds.), (2009). *Preventing Mental, Emotional, and Behavioral Disorders among Young People: Progress and Possibilities*. Washington: NAP.

Ou, S. & Reynolds, A. J. (2010). Mechanisms of effects of an early intervention program on educational attainment: a gender subgroup analysis. *Children & Youth Services Review*, 32(8), 1064–1076.

Pianta, R. C. (2005). A new elementary school for American children. *SRCD Social Policy Report*, 19(3), 4–5.

Power, C., Kuh, D. & Morton, S. (2013). From developmental origins of adult disease to life course research on adult disease and aging: Insights from birth cohort studies. *Annual Review of Public Health*, 34, 7–28.

Redden, S. C., Forness, S. R., Ramey, S. L., Ramey, C. T. et al. (2001). Children at risk: effects of a four-year Head Start Transition Program on special education identification. *Journal of Child and Family Studies*, 10(2), 255–270.

Reynolds A. J. (2012). *Success in Early Intervention: The Chicago Child–Parent Centers Program and Youth through Age 15* (Rev. paperback edn.) Lincoln, NE: University of Nebraska Press.

Reynolds, A. J., Chen, C. & Herbers, J. (2009). *School Mobility and Educational Success: A Research Synthesis and Evidence on Prevention.* Washington, DC: National Research Council.

Reynolds, A. J., Englund, M., Ou, S. et al. (2010b). Paths of effects of preschool participation to educational attainment at age 21: A 3-study analysis, in Reynolds A. J. et al., (Eds.) *Childhood Programs & Practices in the First Decade of Life.* New York, NY: Cambridge.

Reynolds, A. J., Magnuson, K. & Ou, S. (2010a). PK–3 programs and practices: a review of research. *Children and Youth Services Review*, 32, 1121–1131.

Reynolds, A. J. & Ou, S. (2011). Paths of effects from preschool to adult well-being: a confirmatory analysis of the Child–Parent Center Program. *Child Development*, 82, 555–582.

Reynolds, A. J., Ou, S. & Topitzes, J. (2004). Paths of effects of early childhood intervention on educational attainment and juvenile arrest: a confirmatory analysis of the Chicago Child–Parent Centers. *Child Development*, 75(5), 1299–1328.

Reynolds A. J., et al. (2014). Association of a full-day versus part-day preschool intervention with school readiness, attendance, and parent involvement. *JAMA*, 312(20), 2126–2134.

Reynolds, A. J., Temple, J. A., Robertson, D. L. & Mann, E. A. (2002). Age 21 cost–benefit analysis of the Title 1 Chicago Child–Parent Centers. *Educational Evaluation and Policy Analysis*, 24, 267–303.

Reynolds, A. J. & Temple, J. A. (2008). Cost-effective early childhood development programs from preschool to third grade. *Annual Review of Clinical Psychology*, 4, 109–139.

Reynolds, A. J., Temple, J. A., Ou, S., Arteaga, I. A. & White, B. A. B. (2011a). School-based early childhood education and age 28 well-being: Effects by timing, dosage, and subgroups. *Science*, 333(6040), 360–364.

Reynolds, A. J., Temple, J. A., White, B. A., Ou, S. & Robertson, D. L. (2011b). Age-26 cost–benefit analysis of the Child–Parent Center program. *Child Development*, 82, 782–804.

Schweinhart, L. J., Montie, J., Xiang, Z., Barnett, W. S. et al. (2005). *Lifetime Effects: The High/Scope Perry Preschool Study through Age 40.* Ypsilanti, MI: High/Scope.

Sullivan, L. M. (1971). *Let Us Not Underestimate the Children.*, Glenview IL: Scott Foreman.

Sweet, M. A. & Appelbaum, M. I. (2004). Is home visiting an effective strategy: a meta-analytic review of home visiting programs for families with young children. *Child Development*, 75, 1435–1456.

Takanishi, R. & Kauerz, K. (2008). PK inclusion: getting serious about a P–16 education system. *Phi Delta Kappan*, 89(7), 480–487.

Washington State Institute for Public Policy (WSIPP). (2014). *Early Childhood Education for Low-Income Students: A Review of the Evidence and Benefit–Cost Analysis*. Olympia, WA.

Zigler, E., Pfannenstiel, J. C. & Seitz, V. (2008). The Parents as Teachers Program and school success: a replication and extension. *Journal of Primary Prevention*, 29(2), 103–120.

11   Lessons on Sustaining Early Gains from the Life-Course Study of Perry Preschool

Lawrence J. Schweinhart

Introduction

This chapter summarizes the design of the HighScope Perry Preschool Study, the program itself, and the evidence for the program's short- and long-term effects. It looks at whether fade-out is really a problem and draws a conclusion from this study and others like it. Schweinhart, Montie, Xiang, Barnett, Belfield & Nores (2005) made a thorough presentation of the study's methodology and results through age 40, and presented the source of most of the figures in this presentation. Summaries through age 40 and extensions have been presented by Belfield, Nores, Barnett & Schweinhart (2006); Muennig, Schweinhart, Montie & Neidell (2009); Nores, Belfield, Barnett & Schweinhart (2005); Reynolds, Englund, Ou, Schweinhart & Campbell (2010); and Schweinhart (2006, 2007, 2010, 2011, 2012, and 2013).

The Context

Schooling as we know it began in the last two centuries. As it became more organized, age 6 became the age of entry into primary schools or first grade. Early childhood education was left to the dreamers, such as Johann Heinrich Pestalozzi (1746–1827) and his student Friedrich Froebel (1782–1852). Pestalozzi challenged the schools by emphasizing child-centered education, self-learning, free investigation, and internal control. Froebel applied these principles as he invented the first kindergartens for 5-year-olds with a curriculum of songs, stories, games, gifts, and occupations – a prepared environment for children to grow to their full potential (Froebel, 1897). Maria Montessori (1870–1952) continued in this vein by developing an educational approach that respected children's natural development, independence, and freedom within limits, starting the Casa dei Bambini in Rome's slums and articulating the approach in various books (e.g., Montessori, 1912).

In the 1960s, Bloom (1964) saw the volatility of early intelligence as an opportunity to improve it, and Hunt (1961) introduced Piaget (1896–1980) to an American audience, laying the educational ground-work for a renaissance of interest in early childhood education. In 1962 Susan Gray (1913–1992) began the Early Training Project in Murfreesboro, Tennessee (Gray, Ramsey & Klaus, 1982); David Weikart (1931–2003) began the HighScope Perry Preschool Study in Ypsilanti, Michigan (Weikart, Deloria, Lawser & Wiegerink, 1970); and Martin Deutsch (1917–2002) and his wife Cynthia began a preschool enrichment study in New York City (Jordan, Grallo, Deutsch & Deutsch, 1985). Three decades later, prompted by the failure of the initial national Head Start Study to find program effects (Westinghouse Learning Corporation and Ohio University, 1969) and Bronfenbrenner's (1917–2005) idea that parent education alone was the solution to sustaining early childhood program effects (1974), Gray, Weikart, Deutsch and directors of similar studies came together under the leadership of Irving Lazar to form the Consortium for Longitudinal Studies (1983). Bringing multiple studies together, Lazar, Darlington, Murray, Royce & Snipper (1982) found robust evidence of preschool program effects on children's intelligence at school entry, reduced need for placements in special education and grade retentions, and the first evidence of improvements in the high school graduation rate.

In the years since the Consortium, the HighScope Perry Preschool Study (Schweinhart et al., 2005), the Abecedarian Project (Campbell, Pungello, Kainz et al., 2012), and the Chicago Child–Parent Center Study (Reynolds, Temple, Ou et al., 2011) have become the standard-bearers for advocates of high-quality preschool programs. The Perry and Abecedarian studies employed random assignment techniques; the Chicago study examined a program operating across the large city. Together they have found evidence of long-term effects on high school graduation, earnings and employment, reduced crime, and strong returns on investment. Several other studies have found that certain preschool programs have strong short-term effects as well as long-term effects (Barnett, Lamy & Jung, 2005; Gormley, Gayer, Phillips & Dawson, 2005; Schweinhart, Xiang, Daniel-Echols, Browning & Wakabayashi, 2012; Weiland & Yoshikawa, 2013).

Other studies, however, have not found such promising effects as did these studies. The Head Start Impact Study (Puma, Bell, Cook et al., 2012) employed random assignment of children to Head Start or to a no Head Start condition. They found evidence of only weak, short-term effects on children's literacy, mathematics, and social skills. Employing a similar design, the Tennessee prekindergarten study (Lipsey, Farran &

Hofer, 2015) found similar short-term effects and negative effects at third grade. (The term "pre-kindergarten" is used in this chapter to refer specifically to state preschool programs.) The conclusion in both sets of studies begins with the observation that all preschool programs are not the same and do not have the same results.

Methodology

The HighScope Perry Preschool Study looks at the lives of African-American children born in poverty and at risk of failing in school. It employed randomizing procedures to assign children to a program or to no program, departing from randomizing procedures to place younger siblings in the same groups and to accommodate maternal employment. Heckman and his colleagues (Heckman, Moon, Pinto et al., 2010a; Heckman, Moon, Pinto et al., 2010b) employed swapping techniques that confirmed that the departures from random assignment did not substantially affect the pattern of results. The study investigators at HighScope Educational Research Foundation collected educational data annually from ages 3 to 11, and educational, economic, crime, family, and health data at 15, 19, 27, and 40; only 5 percent of the data are missing. Age 50 data collection is in progress, repeating previous measures and adding new attitude and health questions, and bio measures. It is notable that this preschool program follow-up at age 50 is funded by the National Institute on Aging.

The HighScope Perry Preschool program served African-American children living in poverty. Poverty was assessed by the low educational level of parents, their low occupational status, and their high household density. The program took place in a school that served African-Americans, served by Michigan's first African-American principal, Eugene Beatty. Some argue that preschool programs should serve all children, for empirical and logical reasons, but the evidence of this particular study and studies like it apply only to children living in poverty.

Each year from 1962 through 1967, four certified teachers served about 25 program-group children. The children attended at ages 3 and 4; about half of these children were 3 years old and the other half were 4 years old. The class met five mornings a week for eight months of the year, and the child's teacher visited each child and parent in their home each week.

In the HighScope Perry Preschool Curriculum, the forerunner of today's widely used HighScope Curriculum, teachers and children shared control by balanced conversation, with teachers and children talking and listening to each other. Following the plan–do–review sequence, children planned their own learning activities during planning time, did their own activities during work time, and reviewed these activities with others during recall time. The classroom setting and daily routine were designed to support these child-initiated learning activities. The curriculum focused on all aspects of children's development – cognitive, socio-emotional, and physical.

In the HighScope Curriculum, both adults and children are active. It may be distinguished from babysitting, in which both adults and children are passive; traditional nursery school free play, in which adults are passive and children are active; and direct teaching or programmed learning, in which adults are active and children are passive. Other curricula fit into these quadrants. Although the HighScope Curriculum was clearly used in the Perry program, in general reporting that one uses a curriculum does not mean that one's teachers are trained to use the curriculum or that they actually use it.

These, then, are the components of the HighScope Perry Preschool Study and the definition of quality that flows from it:
- An interactive child development curriculum
- Teachers certified to teach early childhood development
- A very high ratio of teachers to children (4 to 25)
- Weekly home visits and daily classes for children
- A thorough evaluation
- A high cost per child

The results do not generalize to programs that do not have most of these components substantially.

Results

Figure 11.1 shows the effect sizes – the group difference as a fraction of the sample standard deviation – of the differences between the program group and the no-program group on educational tests over time, with intelligence tests on the light gray line and achievement tests on the dark gray line. The program group performed better than the no-program group on intelligence tests during the program and through first grade. It performed better on achievement tests throughout the elementary grades and especially at eighth grade. The intelligence effect disappeared – faded out, as some say – even as the achievement effect got stronger.

The following graphs compare the percentages of the program group, in dark gray bars, to the percentages of the no-program group, in light gray bars.

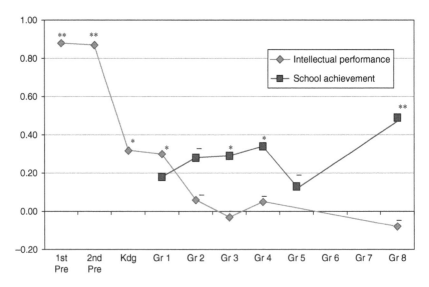

Figure 11.1 Preschool effect sizes on educational test scores
Note. **p < 0.01, *p < 0.05. Adapted from *Lifetime Effects: The HighScope Perry Preschool Study through Age 40,* by L. J. Schweinhart et al. (2005), Ypsilanti, MI: HighScope Press, pp. 61 and 62. Copyright © 2005 by HighScope Educational Research Foundation

As shown in Figure 11.2, 71 percent of the program group girls, but only 23 percent of the no-program girls, never required special education for mental impairment or retention in grade.

The preschool program appears to have prevented for girls a large portion of their need for special education for mental impairment or retention in grade. Similarly, 76 percent of the program girls, but only 38 percent of the no-program girls, graduated from regular high school. These differences were not found for boys, as most other effects were.

Figure 11.3 shows that the median earnings of the program group were higher than the median earnings of the no-program group at 27 and 40. Given the consistency of earnings differences – at 27 and 40, monthly (not shown) and annual – it's reasonable to conclude that the program group had higher career earnings than the no-program group.

Figure 11.4 shows that fewer in the program group than in the no-program group experienced five or more arrests – only 7 percent of them, compared to 29 percent of the no-program group by 27, and only 36 percent of them compared to 55 percent of the no-program group by 40 – i.e., significant reductions in an intractable lifetime problem.

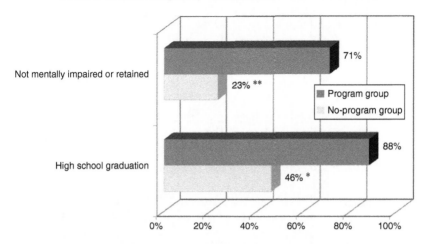

Figure 11.2 Placement and graduation of females
Note. **p < 0.01, *p < 0.05. Adapted from *Lifetime Effects: The HighScope Perry Preschool Study through Age 40,* by L. J. Schweinhart et al. (2005), Ypsilanti, MI: HighScope Press, pp. 52 and 56. Copyright © 2005 by HighScope Educational Research Foundation.

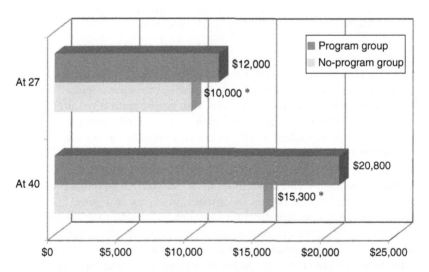

Figure 11.3 Adult median earnings
Note. *p < 0.05. Adapted from *Lifetime Effects: The HighScope Perry Preschool Study through Age 40,* by L. J. Schweinhart et al. (2005), Ypsilanti, MI: HighScope Press, p. 74. Copyright © 2005 by HighScope Educational Research Foundation

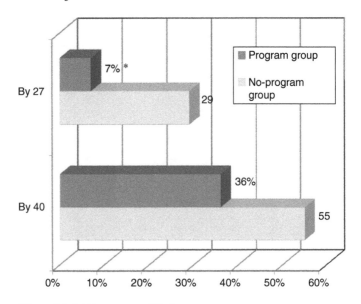

Figure 11.4 Five or more lifetime arrests
Note. *p < 0.05. Adapted from *Lifetime Effects: The HighScope Perry Preschool Study through Age 40,* by L. J. Schweinhart et al. (2005), Ypsilanti, MI: HighScope Press, p. 86. Copyright © 2005 by HighScope Educational Research Foundation.

Figure 11.5 presents a causal model of the study that fits the data well; that is, it represents the causal chains implicit in the effects looked for and found. Preschool experience combines with preprogram IQ to affect post-program IQ. Post-program IQ in turn affects achievement at 14 and commitment to schooling at 15. These two variables affect educational attainment by 40, which goes on to affect earnings at 40 and arrests by 40. Post-program IQ is the linchpin that holds this model together.

One of the most well-known findings of this study is that this preschool program had a large return on investment, as shown in Figure 11.6. Our estimate, using a 3 percent discount rate, which is similar to an interest rate over and above inflation, is that for each dollar invested, the program returned $16.14, four-fifths of it to the public and one-fifth to participants in the form of higher earnings. As the graph shows, the sources of the public return were savings in education due to less need for special education classes, higher taxes paid on greater earnings, and crime – both criminal justice system and victim costs. Savings in crime costs alone were over 11 times the cost of the program, but even without the crime savings, the

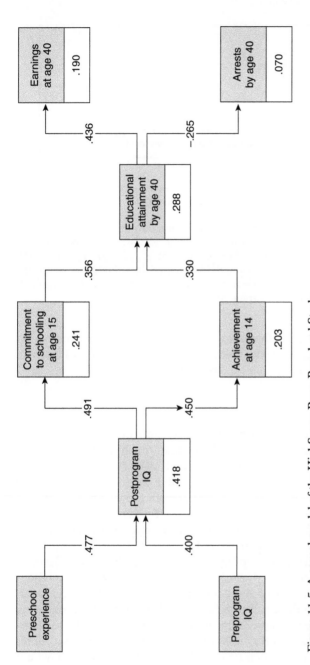

Figure 11.5 A causal model of the HighScope Perry Preschool Study

Note. Path coefficients are standardized regression weights, all statistically significant at p < 0.01; coefficients in each box are squared multiple correlations. Reproduced from *Lifetime Effects: The HighScope Perry Preschool Study through Age 40*, by L. J. Schweinhart et al. (2005), Ypsilanti, MI: HighScope Press, p. 164. Copyright © 2005 by HighScope Educational Research Foundation.

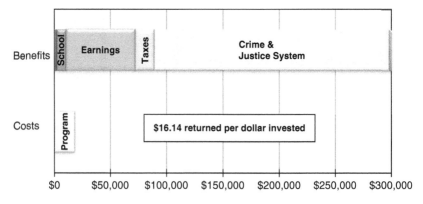

Figure 11.6 HighScope Perry Preschool return on investment
Note. Adapted from *Lifetime Effects: The HighScope Perry Preschool Study through Age 40*, by L. J. Schweinhart, et al., (2005), Ypsilanti, MI: HighScope Press, pp. xvii and 148. Copyright © 2005 by HighScope Educational Research Foundation. See also www.highscope.org/file/R esearch/PerryProject/Errata_3Final.pdf.

program paid for itself. Other analyses have arrived at other returns on investment, such as the sevenfold return on investment found by Heckman and others (2010b); in any case, the benefit far outweighs the cost.

Discussion

Some would say at $11,478 per year per child in 2014 dollars, the program is too expensive. It is about that much in the preschool programs operated in the Abbott school districts of New Jersey ($11,506; Sciarra, 2010), under court order to provide high-quality preschool programs; and only a bit higher than the cost per student in K–12 programs across the USA ($10,618; National Center for Education Statistics, Institute of Education Sciences, 2015). However, in general, states spend only about one third as much per child on pre-kindergarten programs ($4,125; Barnett, Carolan, Squires et al., 2015). On the other hand, our cost–benefit analyses show that the public cost of every poor child who does not receive this program is not zero dollars, but $329,000. Why do we keep choosing to spend this much money on big problems which we could substantially avoid by spending a tiny fraction of the amount to prevent them? In particular, why do we spend so much on prisons when we have not spent enough on preschool programs? Government deficits are real and large. One reason for them is our failure to make early childhood investments that significantly reduce our social problems before they get out of hand.

Is fade-out a problem? The title of this volume, *Sustaining Gains*, suggests that it is. I suggest that it is not, at least in the sense of a single outcome, such as intelligence, maintaining its gains over the years. Intelligence develops throughout childhood, as is obvious from the age-keyed items that comprise the intelligence test. The pattern of IQ effects suggests that the HighScope Perry Preschool program improved early childhood, but not later, intelligence. Even though the preschool effect on IQ diminished, it could still be the case that the early IQ gains were a central mediator of subsequent impacts on later attainments. That is the lasting value of the improvement in early childhood intelligence. Indeed, it is plausible that all of the Perry program's initial learning effects diminished, not just the preschool effect on IQ. IQ was passed over as the purpose of preschool not because it was not right for preschool programs, but because IQ tests fell into disfavor, as shown by the fact that Head Start never considered it as an intended or measured outcome. My suspicion is that early childhood intelligence may have been a proxy for what really mattered most: learning how to be a better student academically and behaviorally. This idea is buttressed by nonsignificant trends in teacher ratings of school motivation and in potential in kindergarten through third grade (not presented here). In other words, what drove the Perry program's long-term effects was its short-term effect on preparing children academically and behaviorally for school, the most obvious purpose of this endeavor. The conclusion from the HighScope Perry Preschool Study, and other studies reviewed in the introduction, is that some early childhood programs are highly effective – contributing to successful schooling, adult economic success, reduced crime, good health, and strong return on investment – while others are not. The implication is that we must substantially maintain the quality of early childhood programs as defined above and in other studies if we expect preschool programs to be found highly effective; and we need to continually evaluate their results to show which ones are highly effective. As a society, we need to invest in these programs and improve the less effective preschool programs that now exist.

Researchers have shown that they can run highly effective preschool programs. Some administrators and policymakers have shown that they can run efficient programs that cost substantially less per child. But with state pre-kindergarten programs and changes in Head Start, we are experimenting on a grand scale with how to run programs that are effective as well as efficient, and with no particular direction to the experimentation. Funds are allocated to programs annually on a cost per child basis, allowing effectiveness to vary freely. Why don't we allocate a small percentage of these funds to programs that demonstrate their effectiveness while allowing higher costs per child?

Efficient programs that are not effective are worthless, so why do we allow efficiency to dictate the design of our programs while ignoring their effectiveness, then ask why programs are ineffective when we have compromised their effectiveness from the start by insisting only on their efficiency? A good example is home visits. The HighScope Perry Preschool Program produced long-term effects and strong return on investment by a program that included weekly home visits as well as daily classes (although the research design does not allow us to distinguish between the relative contributions of the two components or their interactive effect). Yet, weekly home visits are not the policy in any state pre-kindergarten program nor in Head Start, where, instead, they may serve as a substitute for daily classes. In fact, many state pre-kindergarten programs render weekly home visits virtually impossible by requiring half-day programs to double up, leaving no time for weekly home visits.

Research has pointed the way to designing highly effective preschool programs. Unfortunately, we have followed this research only so far, preferring cheaper programs that leave the potential benefits of well-funded, well-designed preschool programs off the table.

References

Barnett, W. S., Carolan, M. E., Squires, J. H., Clarke Brown, K. & Horowitz, M. (2015). *The State of Preschool 2014: State Preschool Yearbook*. New Brunswick, NJ: National Institute for Early Education Research. Retrieved from http://nieer.org/yearbook.

Barnett, W. S., Lamy, C. & Jung, K., (2005). *The Effects of State Prekindergarten Programs on Young Children's School Readiness in Five States*. New Brunswick, NJ: Rutgers University, National Institute for Early Education Research. Retrieved from http://nieer.org/resources/research/multistate/fullreport.pdf.

Belfield, C. R., Nores, M., Barnett, W. S. & Schweinhart, L. J. (2006). The HighScope Perry Preschool Program: Cost–benefit analysis using data from the age-40 follow-up. *The Journal of Human Resources*, 41(1), 162–190.

Bloom, B. S. (1964). *Stability and Change in Human Characteristics*. New York, NY: Wiley.

Bronfenbrenner, U. (1974). Is early intervention effective? *Teachers College Record*, 76, 279–303.

Campbell, F. A., Pungello, E., Kainz, K. et al. (2012). Adult outcomes as a function of an early childhood educational program: an Abecedarian project follow-up. *Developmental Psychology*, 48, 1033–1043.

Consortium for Longitudinal Studies. (1983). *As the Twig Is Bent... Lasting Effects of Preschool Programs*. Hillsdale, NJ: Erlbaum.

Froebel, F. (1897). *Pedagogics of the Kindergarten*. Translated by J. Jarvis. London: Edward Arnold.

Gormley, W. T., Gayer, T., Phillips, D. & Dawson, B. (2005). The effects of universal pre-K on cognitive development. *Developmental Psychology*, 41(6), 872–884. Retrieved from http://dx.doi.org/10.1037/0012–1649.41.6.872.

Gray, S. W., Ramsey, B. K. & Klaus R. A. (1982). *From 3 to 20: The Early Training Project*. Baltimore, MD: University Park Press.

Heckman, J. J., Moon, S. H., Pinto, R., Savelyev, P. A. & Yavitz, A. Q. (2010a). Reanalysis of the Perry Preschool Program: multiple-hypothesis and permutation tests applied to a quasi-randomized experiment, *Quantitative Economics*, 1, 1–49. Retrieved from http://jenni.uchicago.edu/perry_reanalysis/general-090424–1808.pdf.

Heckman, J. J., Moon, S. H., Pinto, R., Savelyev, P. A. & Yavitz, A. (2010b). The rate of the return to the HighScope Perry Preschool Program, *Journal of Public Economics*, 94: 114–128. Retrieved from http://ftp.iza.org/dp4533.pdf.

Hunt, J. M. (1961). *Intelligence and Experience*. New York, NY: Ronald Press.

Jordan, T. J., Grallo, R., Deutsch, M. & Deutsch, C. P. (1985). Long-term effects of early enrichment. A 20-year perspective on persistence and change. *American Journal of Community Psychology*, 13, 393–415.

Lazar, I., Darlington, R., Murray, H., Royce, J., & Snipper, A. (1982). Lasting effects of early education: a report from the Consortium for Longitudinal Studies. *Monographs of the Society for Research in Child Development*, 47(2/3), 1–151.

Lipsey, M. W., Farran, D. C. & Hofer, K. G. (2015). *A randomized control trial of a statewide voluntary prekindergarten program on children's skills and behaviors through third grade*. Research Report. Peabody Research Institute, Vanderbilt Peabody College: Nashville, TN. Retrieved from http://peabody.vanderbilt.edu/research/pri/VPKthrough3rd_final_withcover.pdf.

Montessori, M. (1912). *The Montessori Method: Scientific Pedagogy as Applied to Child Education in the Children's Houses*. Translated by A. E. George. New York, NY: Frederick A. Stokes Company.

Muennig, P., Schweinhart, L., Montie, J. & Neidell, M. (2009). Effects of a prekindergarten education intervention on adult health: 37-year follow-up results of a randomized controlled trial. *American Journal of Public Health*, 99 (8), 1431–1437.

National Center for Education Statistics, Institute of Education Sciences (2015). *Fast Facts*. Washington, DC: Author. Retrieved from http://nces.ed.gov/fastfacts/display.asp?id=66.

Nores, M., Belfield, C. R., Barnett, W. S. & Schweinhart, L. J. (2005). Updating the economic impacts of the High/Scope Perry Preschool Program. *Educational Evaluation and Policy Analysis*, 27(3), 245–261.

Puma, M., Bell, S., Cook, R. et al. (2012). *Third Grade Follow-Up to the Head Start Impact Study Final Report*, OPRE Report # 2012–45, Washington, DC: Office of Planning, Research and Evaluation, Administration for Children and

Families, US Department of Health and Human Services. Retrieved from www
.acf.hhs.gov/sites/default/files/opre/head_start_report.pdf.

Reynolds, A. J., Englund, M. M., Ou, S., Schweinhart, L. & Campbell, F. (2010).
Paths of effects of preschool participation to educational attainment at age 21:
A three-year study analysis, in Reynolds, A. J., Rolnick, A. J., Englund, M. M.
& Temple, J. A. (Eds.), *Childhood Programs and Practices in the First Decade of
Life: A Human Capital Integration* (pp. 416–452). New York, NY: Cambridge
University Press.

Schweinhart, L. J. (2006). The HighScope approach: evidence that participatory
learning in early childhood contributes to human development, in Watt, N. F.,
Ayoub, C.C., Bradley, R. H., Puma, J. E. & Lebeouf, W.A. (Eds.), *The Crisis in
Youth Mental Health: Critical Issues and Effective Programs. Vol. 4: Early
Intervention Programs and Policies.* Westport: Praeger Press.

Schweinhart, L. J. (2007). Outcomes of the HighScope Perry Preschool Study and
Michigan School Readiness Program, in Young, M. E. & Richardson, L. M.
(Eds.), *Early Child Development: From Measurement to Action* (pp. 87–102).
Washington, DC: The International Bank for Reconstruction/The World Bank.

Schweinhart, L. J. (2010). The challenge of the HighScope Perry Preschool
Study, in Reynolds, A. J., Rolnick, A. J., Englund, M. M. & Temple, J. A.
(Eds.), *Childhood Programs and Practices in the First Decade of Life: A Human
Capital Integration* (pp. 157–167). New York, NY: Cambridge University
Press.

Schweinhart, L. J. (2011). How to make early childhood programs highly
effective, in Zigler, E., Gilliam, W. & Barnett, W. S. (Eds.), *The Pre-K Debates:
Current Controversies and Issues.* Baltimore, MD: Paul H. Brookes.

Schweinhart, L. J. (2012). Lifetime effects of participatory preschool education,
in Slaughter-Defoe, D. T. (Vol. Ed.) and Alston, J. (Series Ed.), *Messages for
Educational Leadership: The Constance E. Clayton Lectures 1998–2007: Black
Studies and Critical Thinking Series.* New York, NY: Peter Lang.

Schweinhart, L. J. (2013). Long-term follow-up of a preschool experiment.
Journal of Experimental Criminology, 9, 389–409. Retrieved from http://link
.springer.com/article/10.1007/s11292-013-9190-3.

Schweinhart, L. J., Montie, J., Xiang, Z., Barnett, W. S., Belfield, C. & Nores, M.
(2005). *Lifetime Effects: The HighScope Perry Preschool Study through Age 40.*
(Monographs of the HighScope Educational Research Foundation, 13).
Ypsilanti, MI: HighScope Press.

Schweinhart, L. J., Xiang, Z. Daniel-Echols, M., Browning, K. & Wakabayashi,
T. (2012). Michigan Great Start Readiness Program Evaluation 2012: High
School Graduation and Grade *Retention Findings*. Ypsilanti, MI: HighScope
Educational Research Foundation and Michigan Department of Education.
Retrieved from www.michigan.gov/documents/mde/GSRP_Evaluatio
n_397470_7.pdf

Sciarra, D. G. (2010). *New Jersey Abbott Preschool Program Profile*. Newark, NJ:
Education Law Center. Retrieved from http://blogs.tc.columbia.edu/transi
tions/files/2010/09/30.New-Jersey_Abbott-Preschool-Program_profile_.pdf

Weikart, D. P., Deloria, D., Lawser, S. & Wiegerink, R. (1970). *Longitudinal Results of the Ypsilanti Perry Preschool Project*. Ypsilanti, MI: High/Scope Press.

Weiland, C. & Yoshikawa, H. (2013). Impacts of a prekindergarten program on children's mathematics, language, literacy, executive function, and emotional skills. *Child Development*, 84, 2112–2130.

Westinghouse Learning Corporation and Ohio University. (1969). *The Impact of Head Start: An Evaluation of the Effects of Head Start on Children's Cognitive and Affective Development* (Vols. 1–2). Washington, DC: Clearinghouse for Federal, Scientific, and Technical Information.

12 Sustaining Gains from Early Childhood Intervention: The Abecedarian Program

Frances A. Campbell, Yi Pan, and Margaret Burchinal

This chapter describes the adult benefits associated with the Abecedarian Project, one of three scientific longitudinal studies of early intervention for high-risk children which had both low attrition and follow-up information extending 25 years or more past the end of early treatment. The other two studies are the Perry Preschool Project (Schweinhart, Montie, Xiang, Barnett, Belfield & Nores, 2005) and the Chicago Longitudinal Study (Reynolds, 2000; Reynolds, Temple & Ou, 2010). We describe important long-term gains seen to date for treated Abecedarian participants, then suggest factors that might have mediated these gains and test the extent to which they appear to have done so.

The Study

The Abecedarian Project was located in Chapel Hill, NC, a small college town whose population consisted primarily of students and families of university faculty and business-owners who supported the faculty and students. As such, the local residents tended to be highly educated and relatively affluent in the context of North Carolina. On the other hand, a stable group of low-income families, largely of African-American extraction, found employment within the university in low-paid service positions.

Between 1972 and 1977, the Abecedarian investigators admitted four cohorts of healthy infants (98 percent African-American) to the study, confining the enrollees to children deemed to be at high risk of developmental delay or academic failure, based on circumstances associated with poverty. A cohort consisted of 28 infants, 14 randomly assigned to the treatment group and 14 in a non-treated control group. From early infancy (1–4 months) until they entered public school, the treated children received educational child care. Treatment focused on overall child development (language, cognitive, social-emotional, and physical). The program developers provided, from infancy, an atmosphere that included warm, language-rich adult–child interactions, active participatory learning, and scaffolded, age-appropriate instructional activities offered in individualized or small-group settings (Ramey, Sparling & Ramey, 2012). On-site medical care was also provided, along with high-quality nutrition, and social support services as needed. A second randomized treatment phase offered a home–school support component, involving both children and parents for the first three years in public school (child aged 5–8 years).

Abecedarian Treatment

The Abecedarian study was unique among the three studies in that it began treatment in the first half of the first year of the children's lives, covering a wider developmental span than that provided by the other two programs. Its child care-based educational intervention operated for full days year-round, closing only for two weeks in the summer and 11 state mandated holidays per year. Eligibility for inclusion was based on a High-Risk Index whose categories measured socio-demographic circumstances associated with the risk for compromised cognitive development and academic failure (Ramey & Smith, 1977). Treated children were transported via the program's vans to and from the site each day.

Children randomly assigned to the control group were cared for during their preschool years in a variety of arrangements according to their family's needs and wishes. They might have been full-time at home with a parent, or in some kind of informal care in the home of a relative, or with a family day-care provider. Some attended other state-licensed group care programs, but, at the time, very few of those programs offered group care for infants. By the age of 4, approximately three-quarters of the control group children had attended some type of community child care center or preschool. All treated and control children were evaluated by psychologists not involved with developing or delivering the Abecedarian treatment, using a regular protocol of standardized measures. If the evaluators noted that a child from the control group appeared to be lagging in his or her development, the department of social services was alerted so the child might be referred for follow-up assessment and possible placement into a local resource such as Head Start. Thus, the treatment/control comparison in this study is conservative, contrasting children who had a stable, systematic infancy and preschool educational experience for the full five years with those who grew up in what has been called the "natural ecology" of their neighborhoods.

The original intent-to-treat sample consisted of 111 infants, 57 randomly assigned to the preschool treatment group and 54 in the control group. Maternal age averaged approximately 20 years when target infants were born, with a range from 13 to 46 years. Approximately one-third of the mothers were teenagers and three-quarters of them were single. Typically, children lived in multigenerational households headed by maternal grandparents, but their living circumstances ranged from intact two-parent households to a few cases where the mother was homeless and under protective surveillance by local social services.

The child care center was housed in a University-owned multipurpose building designed both for research and early childhood education. The child care center included an infant nursery suite with dedicated sleeping and play rooms and a feeding area. Older children had large, open classrooms where they played, napped, and were fed family style at low tables. Outside the classrooms were well-equipped play yards with customized climbing structures, swings, playhouses, sandboxes and a variety of outdoor toys. Weather permitting, morning and afternoon periods of active outdoor play were included in the daily schedule for all children; even infants spent time outside.

The infant care focused on providing emotional and linguistic support to the children. The youngest infants were held and cuddled while fed iron-fortified formula. An infant/toddler curriculum called *LearninGames* was jointly developed by Joe Sparling, an educational psychologist, and Isabel Lewis, a preschool teacher (Sparling and Lewis, 1978). These activities were individually assigned for each baby as the developers judged them appropriate. The earliest activities involved talking to and handling the infant; later activities involved playing reciprocal games, such as peek-a-boo, with them. A strong emphasis was placed on language development, responding to the infants' vocalizations, naming objects and describing actions for them. The environment was visually stimulating as well, with bright pictures or patterns on the wall, and toys and mobiles in the cribs and on the floor. Before they could sit unsupported, infants were sometimes placed prone on round pillows under their chests so they could reach and manipulate objects before them.

After infants graduated into toddler classrooms, their care continued to focus on warm, scaffolded interactions between themselves and the caregiver/teachers. The walls in toddler classrooms were lined with cubbies for individual belongings and with low shelves containing colorful toys from which children could self-select playthings. LearninGames continued to be used throughout the day with caregiver/teachers keeping notes on the activity assignments. See-saw rockers and stair pyramids encouraged gross motor play, and clay and finger paints offered fine motor activities. Teachers led musical games and dancing.

Breakfast and lunch were served in a special room whose tile floor was easy to clean; after lunch, rooms were darkened and soft music played while children napped.

For children aged 3 to 5 years, preschool classrooms were organized into areas dedicated to books, doll play, dress-up, large blocks for building, science centers, and quiet corners where children could spend time alone. Days were somewhat more structured, with teachers leading the children in planning daily activities. Preschool curricula were designed to guide children through a series of "graded presentations" involving sequential activities that the children planned and executed, leading to a "product" that they could then consume or play with. While fun and engaging for the children, these activities also taught words, numbers, and carrying out actions in an orderly manner (Harms, 1980). Older versions of the LearninGames were also utilized with the children (Sparling & Lewis, 1984). In addition, commercially available pre-literacy and pre-mathematics curricula were available for use. Again, language development was a focal point of the educational program. Teachers in the later years were trained in methods to "follow the child's lead" in conversations that both expanded vocabulary and encouraged children to ask questions (McGinness & Ramey, 1981).

Another unique feature of the multidisciplinary Abecedarian research program was its focus on the health of infants and young children in group care. Treated children received their primary pediatric care on site at the day care center. The on-site medical team included pediatricians, family nurse practitioners, and aides. Children were checked for wellness each day; regular data collection included nasal saline washes to detect the presence of viruses or bacteria. Except in the case of measles or chicken pox, children attended the center sick or well (Ramey, et al., 1976).

At the point of entry to public school the early childhood treatment and control groups were re-randomized such that half the children who had attended the Abecedarian preschool program and half the children in the preschool control group were provided a special school-age intervention. This program consisted of having a Home School Resource Teacher assigned to work with the child and family, encouraging parents to become involved in supporting the child's early learning, and providing a liaison between the child's classroom and home. Thus, the treatment model allowed a comparison between children who had either eight years of early childhood intervention (birth to 3 years in public school, EE), or five years of early intervention (preschool only, EC), or three years in the primary grades only (from kindergarten through the next two years, CE) to no systematic intervention at all (the untreated control group, CC).

The latter gives an estimate of the probable academic attainments of children from local high-risk backgrounds without access to the ABC treatment. Analyses of intellectual and academic skill data collected during and after the school-age phase of treatment (ages 5 to 8 years) provided little to no evidence of an independent impact of the school-age intervention, so we focus solely on the preschool intervention in this chapter.

Program Evaluation Data Collection

Children and parents in the treated and control groups were assessed regularly during the treatment years. Data were collected every six months until entry to kindergarten and thereafter in the fall and spring of the first three years of school. Follow-up assessments occurred when study participants were aged 12, 15, 21, 30, and 32–35 years. Standardized data on the children's intellectual development were collected across the infancy and preschool years, allowing their development to be measured using tests with nationally representative norms based on samples of same aged children. In all cases involving national norms the study's investigators required that African-Americans be included in the tested samples. Also during the preschool years, parental attitudes were assessed and annual visits to homes were made to score the degree of educational support the home appeared to provide.

After children entered public school, their intellectual development and academic skills were closely monitored during the primary grades, again using standardized scales with national norms based on same-aged children. Primary grade teachers also rated all children on adaptive behaviors in their classrooms. At the end of the first three years, second grade for children who had never been retained, first grade for those who had, a series of "endpoint" measures were taken that included a standardized intellectual test score, standardized age-referenced scores of reading and mathematics skills, teacher ratings of classroom adaptation and parent ratings of behaviors.

Follow-up measures of intellectual and academic skills were collected at age 12 when the students had completed seven years in school (the end of sixth grade and the last year in elementary school as the system was then configured). At age 15, the same measures of intellectual levels and academic skills were again collected when students had completed ten years in school. At that point, students should have completed ninth grade prior to transferring to Senior High. The protocol at age 15 included an extensive set of self-report measures of attitudes toward school and the family. Six years later, as near in time to the 21st birthday as possible, nationally normed standardized measures of intellectual development and academic skills were collected from the study participants along with self-reports of educational and vocational attainments and questionnaires that screened for mental health problems. However, a drawback of collecting data at age 21 was that those persons who had made continual educational progress past high school had not had time to graduate from college. For this reason, we considered a final round of data collection at age 30 to be a more telling indicator of actual adult benefits derived from the Abecedarian early childhood educational experience. To afford the most accurate possible comparison of adult attainments, tight control was maintained over assessment age for the 30-year follow-up. For purposes of the present analyses, the standardized cognitive measures from age 21 were combined with interview and self-report measures of social adjustment and educational and vocational attainments from age 30.

Adult Outcomes

Our indices of successful adult development and accomplishments included levels of intellectual and academic skills, educational and economic attainment, psychological adjustment, criminal activity, and biological risk factors for chronic health conditions (see Table 12.1). At the 21-year assessment, the Wechsler Adult Intelligence Scale – Revised (Wechsler, 1981) and the Woodcock–Johnson Academic Achievement Battery – Revised (Woodcock & Johnson, 1989) were administered by trained data collectors who were unaware of the examinee's early childhood status. The WAIS-R Full-scale IQ and Woodcock–Johnson age-referenced reading and mathematics standard scores are included in the analyses. Both IQ and achievement scores are standard scores with expected $M = 100$ and $SD = 15$ in the general population.

At the 30-year assessment, individuals were asked to indicate their final educational degree (coded as 12 = high school; 14 = some college; 16 = bachelor's degree; master's degree = 18; doctorate = 20) and to report the hours of employment for all jobs over the past two years and current income. The income was transformed into an income-to-needs ratio by dividing the reported household income by the income determined to define poverty for a given household size in federal government guidelines. Psychological adjustment was indexed by scores on two mental health screens completed by the individuals: the depressive symptom T score on the Brief Symptom Inventory (Derogatis, 1990) at age 21 and the externalizing T score from the Adult Self Report (Achenbach & Rescorla, 2003) at age 30. The T scores have an expected mean of 50 and

SD of 10 in the general population. At age 30, individuals were also asked to report all arrests and citations. Self-reported citations for lawbreaking up to age 30 were dichotomized as: none = 0, and any citation reported = 1. Finally, biomedical indicators of physical health in the form of measures of systolic and diastolic blood pressure were collected during a full physical examination, at approximately age 35, because high blood pressure is a strong risk factor for both cardiac and metabolic diseases.

As the first stage of the analyses designed to identify potential mechanisms, we examined these adult outcomes for treatment impacts (Table 12.1). The analyses tested for differences related to preschool treatment and gender because prior analyses had indicated long-term treatment impacts (Campbell et al., 2001, 2002, 2012) and gender differences in treatment impacts (Campbell et al., 2014). As reported previously, the treated children had significantly higher IQs ($F(1,100) = 5.71$, $p = 0.019$), reading scores ($F(1,100) = 3.91$, $p = 0.05$), math scores ($F(1,100) = 4.24$, $p = 0.042$), years of education ($F(1,96) = 8.62$, $p = 0.004$), systolic blood pressure ($F(1,64) = 4.88$, $p = 0.03$), and diastolic blood pressure ($F(1,64) = 4.36$, $p = 0.041$). While not reliably different from zero, sex appeared to moderate these treatment effects when we examined the treatment impacts by gender. There were large treatment impacts for females on IQ ($B = 7.26$, $SE = 2.58$, $p = 0.006$), reading ($B = 10.57$, $SE = 4.15$, $p = 0.012$), math ($B = 7.84$, $SE = 3.12$, $p = 0.014$), years of education ($B = 1.55$, $SE = 0.53$, $p = 0.004$), and depressive symptoms (BSI) ($B = -7.52$, $SE = 3.22$, $p = 0.02$), with small nonsignificant differences for males on all of these outcomes. In contrast, there were large treatment impacts for males on systolic blood pressure ($B = -17.54$, $SE = 8.37$, $p = 0.04$), and diastolic blood pressure ($B = -13.47$, $SE = 6.54$, $p = 0.04$), with smaller nonsignificant differences for females on these outcomes. In addition, a gender × treatment interaction ($F(1,97) = 3.25$, $p = 0.07$) suggested that treatment appeared to decrease externalizing problems at 30 years for females ($B = -3.37$, $SE = 2.67$, $p < 0.1$) and increase them for males ($B = 3.63$, $SE = 2.82$, $p < 0.1$) Based on these findings, we examined issues of mediation of treatment impacts on adult outcomes within gender.

Hypothesized Mediators

To identify possible mediators of early treatment on the sustainability of benefits, we selected plausible factors from among aspects of the child's life that might have been impacted by the early treatment. Our hypothesized mediators included treatment impacts on parenting, on the child's cognitive skills, executive functioning, behavioral regulation,

Table 12.1 *Adult outcomes for Abecedarian participants by preschool treatment and gender*

		Adult Outcomes										
		Females						Males				
		Control			Treatment			Control			Treatment	
	N	Mean	SD	N	Mean	SD	N	Mean	SD	N	Mean	SD
IQ and Academic Skills												
21y: Full-Scale WAIS-R IQ	28	84.18	8.90	25	91.44	11.22	23	86.52	8.24	28	88.07	8.88
21y WJ Reading Skills	28	86.11	13.60	25	96.68	16.37	23	89.13	12.71	28	90.29	16.95
21y WJ Math Skills	28	82.32	10.47	25	90.16	12.24	23	86.91	11.65	28	88.25	11.03
Educational and Economic Attainment												
30y *Final Educational Degree (y)*	28	12.07	1.76	24	13.63	2.24	21	12.62	1.60	27	13.30	1.88
30y Income/poverty Threshold	28	1.94	1.61	25	2.38	2.39	16	3.39	2.97	23	4.44	5.83
30y Hours/week Employed	20	44.10	15.72	20	38.50	10.34	12	45.00	16.81	21	48.71	12.37
Psychological Adjustment												
21y BSI Global Severity Index t	28	62.32	10.71	25	54.80	12.66	21	58.29	11.05	26	58.96	10.08
30y ARS Internalizing t	28	47.68	10.21	25	45.00	10.81	21	45.81	8.77	27	49.11	11.04
30y ARS Externalizing t	28	50.61	10.43	25	47.24	9.05	21	48.14	7.93	27	51.78	10.66
Criminal Activity												
30y Adult Criminal Citation/%	28	.18		25	.24		21	.62		26	.50	
Biological Risk Factors												
35y Systolic Blood Pressure	22	135.6	21.10	18	129.7	19.48	9	143.3	31.66	19	125.8	14.05
35y Diastolic Blood Pressure	22	89.23	16.68	18	85.33	16.72	9	92.00	22.45	19	78.53	10.76

and self-perceptions, and on kindergarten teacher's impressions of the children. We focused on potential mediators that were collected during or immediately following the treatment period, with the exception of the measures of student self-perceptions. These measures were from older ages because they were not (and perhaps could not be) collected earlier.

We selected these mediators because each has been advanced as a possible explanation for sustaining the gains of early childhood interventions. While changing parenting practices or attitudes was not a specific aim of the Abecedarian Project, it is possible that the treatment affected parenting, and that such impacts might carry through to adult outcomes. The primary goal of the Abecedarian treatment was to improve children's cognitive skills so, logically, enhancement of such skills is one of the most likely mediators of treatment impacts in this study. In recent years, however, children's behavior regulation and executive functioning have been widely viewed as more likely mediators (Cunha & Heckman, 2008; Yoshikawa et al., 2013). Working memory, mental flexibility, and self-control have been identified as key components of executive functioning, and are viewed as critical skills in early development (Fitzpatrick, McKinnon, Blair & Willoughby, 2014). These abilities represent approaches to learning and solving problems that are considered highly important for successfully negotiating the demands of school in childhood and of the working world later on, and they appear to account for the long-term impacts of the Perry Project on adult outcomes (Cunha & Heckman, 2008). Another behavioral style that treatment might have affected is task orientation, or the degree to which a child displays interest and persistence in learning. This characteristic in young children has been shown to predict later academic achievement (e.g., Hamre & Pianta, 2001). For years, researchers have shown that teachers' expectancies heavily influence students' gains in school (Rosenthal & Jacobson, 1963). Although teachers were not aware of the children's cognitive test scores, teachers have consciously or unconsciously expected more from children who appeared to be brighter. In turn, such children might have been encouraged to try harder, which could have mediated long-term treatment effects. Finally, the provision of on-site medical care and nutritious meals in the child care program might have translated into long-term treatment impacts on health.

Measures of Mediators

To describe parenting, we chose a measure of attitudes about childrearing and an assessment of the quality of the home environment (see Table

12.2). At 54 months, mothers were administered the Parent Attitude Research Instrument (Schaefer & Bell, 1958; Emmerich, 1969). One of its factors reflects "Authoritarian Attitudes," describing the extent to which parents endorse obedience rather than autonomy in their children. The quality of the cognitive stimulation and emotional support in the home environment was assessed using the Home Observation for Measurement of the Environment (HOME; Bradley & Caldwell, 1979) scored by a visitor to the child's home at 6, 18, 30, 42, and 54 months. The HOME takes note of the general physical condition of the dwelling, the kinds of toys and educational materials available to the child, the emotional tone of the mother–child interaction during the visit, and the mother's descriptions of the family's routines and the educational activities provided. The proportion of items passed at each age was computed and the mean of those total scores from 6 to 54 months was computed for each family to represent the overall quality of the preschool home environment.

The Bayley Scales of Infant Development (Bayley, 1969) were periodically administered to all children up to the age of 18 months. After each Bayley session, the testers completed the Infant Behavior Record (IBR), rating the infant's approach to the examiner and the testing materials and how interested he or she appeared to be in exploiting the materials. Most IBR items were nine-point scales ranging from positive to negative approaches to the construct in question. Four items formed a cluster we defined as Task Orientation: attention span, goal directedness, object orientation and interest in manipulation. These ratings represented direct assessment of persistence and task orientation based on the children's performance at 18 months. A later measure of task orientation among 5-year-olds was also collected based on teachers' ratings in the fall of the kindergarten year, as described below.

Measures of the child's cognitive and executive functioning skills were collected at age 5, which was about the same point as the end of the preschool treatment, using the Wechsler Preschool and Primary Scale of Intelligence (WPPSI; Wechsler, 1967). The WPPSI yields a Full-Scale IQ score, summing across all subtests, but also allows the child's level of competence to be described as reflective of Verbal and Performance (non-verbal) IQs. In addition, the WPPSI Block Design subtest can be construed as a measure of cognitive flexibility and working memory, two components of executive functioning (Table 12.2).

Kindergarten teachers rated the child's task orientation, ability to work independently, and behavior problems on the Classroom Behavior Inventory (CBI; Schaefer, Edgerton & Aaronson, 1978) in the fall of the kindergarten year. The CBI, with the exception of a scale measuring verbal intelligence, consists of bipolar scales measuring three dimensions of classroom adjustment: behavior problems, task orientation, and sociability. We created summary scores as follows: for behavior problems, consideration was reverse scored and combined with hostility; for task orientation, distractibility was reverse scored and added to task orientation and Independence, which were combined in our models due to their high correlation with one another ($r = .86$); the sociability measure consisted of extroversion minus introversion.

Children's self-esteem was measured at 8 years using the Purdue Self Concept scale (Cicirelli, 1972), and at 12 years using the Perceived Competence Scale for Children (Harter, 1982). The Purdue Self Concept scale consists of 40 bipolar pictorial items with accompanying words (e.g., "This child likes to read"; or "This child does not like to read."). The child indicates which best describes himself or herself. The Purdue score consists of the sum of positive choices. Harter's Perceived Competence Scale for Children consists of 36 bipolar items describing a student's self-perceptions of himself or herself in regard to scholastic competence, social acceptance, athletic competence, physical appearance, behavioral conduct, and global self-worth. Each domain is measured with six bipolar statements, such as, "Some kids are often unhappy with themselves but other kids are pretty pleased with themselves." The student indicates which pole best fits himself or herself and the extent to which the statements are "Really True for me" or "Sort of true for me." Scores can range from 1 to 4 with 4 being the most positive aspect. Thus, scores of 3 or higher indicate that the student views himself or herself more positively. Finally, the student's self-efficacy was measured at age 15 using the Self Evaluation Inventory (Schaefer, Edgerton & Hunter, n.d.). This measure of locus of control reflects the extent to which students believe their own efforts are responsible for their attainments rather than that forces beyond their control determine the major outcomes in their lives. We reasoned that this attitude toward responsibility for outcomes might mediate early treatment effects on adult accomplishments.

Measures of physical growth were collected annually during the preschool years. Psychological examiners routinely weighed and measured the children to monitor physical growth in both the treated and control groups. This allowed us to calculate the body mass index (BMI) for each child at age 5, giving a rough estimate of their health and nutritional status in the early years. We selected the BMI at 5 years to describe potential treatment impacts related to the on-site provision of medical care and nutritious meals.

To learn if early treatment had affected teacher perceptions, we compared public school kindergarten teacher's impressions of how bright the treated and control children appeared to be, based on their ratings of the child's verbal intelligence on the Classroom Behavior Inventory (Schaefer, Edgerton & Aaronson, 1978). Teachers had no prior knowledge of the children's actual test performance during the preschool years. Because teacher ratings of curiosity and verbal intelligence were highly correlated with one another (r > 0.80), we combined the ratings into a single impression reflecting how bright and how interested in learning the child appeared to be.

The descriptive statistics in Table 12.2 show treatment and gender effects on selected mediators. As the second stage of the analyses designed to identify potential mechanisms, we examined these hypothesized mediators for treatment impacts overall and within gender. The preschool treatment group had significantly lower scores than the control group on mother's 54-month Authoritarian Attitudes ($F(1,84) = 5.89, p = 0.017$), higher scores on children's 5-year WPPSI Verbal IQ ($F(1,89) = 11.97$, $p = 0.001$), on the 18-month IBR Task Orientation rating ($F(1,96) = 13.13, p = 0.0005$), and on kindergarten teacher ratings of verbal intelligence ($F(1,84) = 6.05, p = 0.016$). Unexpectedly, kindergarten teachers also rated treated children higher on the CBI measure of behavior problems ($F(1,84) = 18.44, p < .001$). Because our power to detect meaningful differences is compromised by limited power, we also report "marginal" differences found for treatment effects on kindergarten teacher ratings of CBI task orientation $F(1,84) = 3.33, p = 0.07$) and for the teens' ratings of self-efficacy or locus of control at age 15 ($F(1,99) = 3.12$, $p = 0.08$). A treatment by gender interactions was found for kindergarten teachers' ratings of task orientation: treated girls were rated by their kindergarten teacher as being more task oriented than control girls ($B = 0.19, SE = 0.15, p < 0.1$), treated boys were rated as less task oriented than control boys ($B = -0.19, SE = 0.15, p < 0.1$). We also found treatment × gender interactions for 5-year BMI ($F(1,85) = 3.35, p= 0.07$). Treated boys had lower BMIs than control boys ($B = -1.05$, $SE = 0.46, p = 0.02$), whereas there was little treatment effect on BMI for girls ($B = 0.14, SE = 0.46, p < 0.1$).

Mediation Analyses: Did Our Hypothesized Mediators Predict Sustainability?

The next set of analyses tested the extent to which the preschool treatment appears to have had long-term impacts on adult outcomes through the hypothesized mediators. Sobel tests of indirect effects were conducted that involved estimating the indirect path (ab) as the product of the path from treatment to the mediator (a) and the path from the mediator to the

Table 12.2 Hypothesized mediators for long-term Abecedarian treatment impacts

	Hypothesized Mediators											
	Female						Male					
	Control			Treatment			Control			Treatment		
	n	M	SD	n	M	SD	n	M	SD	n	M	SD
Parenting												
54m PARI Authoritarian	23	78.35	10.12	22	68.45	12.32	18	79.00	13.92	24	75.54	14.38
6-54m HOME Total	30	64.77	11.22	26	67.76	10.26	23	65.40	8.61	27	66.43	9.18
Child's Cognitive Skills												
5y WPPSI Verbal IQ	23	96.39	13.56	23	102.5	10.92	21	91.00	13.33	26	102.8	12.01
5y WPPSI Performance IQ	23	96.17	13.01	23	101.0	12.72	21	93.14	13.66	26	98.62	9.53
Child's Task Orientation												
18m IBR Task Orientation	28	21.39	4.13	24	24.33	2.81	21	19.95	4.28	27	22.63	3.96
Fall K: CB Task Orientation	23	2.96	0.44	22	3.16	0.58	20	3.23	0.44	23	3.04	0.50
Child's Executive Functioning												
5y WPPSI Block Design	23	9.91	1.93	23	10.57	2.37	21	9.33	3.17	26	10.35	2.13
Child's Social and Behavior Skills												
Fall K: CBI Sociability	23	3.22	0.49	22	2.96	0.68	20	2.88	0.68	23	2.92	0.71
Fall K: CBI Behavior Problems	23	1.96	0.66	22	2.57	0.91	20	1.84	0.70	23	3.04	0.50
8y Purdue Self-Concept	22	37.50	3.62	21	36.52	4.24	19	38.05	2.01	26	36.65	3.24
12y Harter Global Self-Esteem	24	2.71	0.68	25	2.02	0.75	23	2.32	0.94	27	2.07	0.89
15y Self-Evaluation Inventory	28	2.39	0.98	25	2.02	0.75	23	2.32	0.94	27	2.07	0.89
Child's Physical Development												
5y BMI	23	16.15	1.76	22	16.29	1.47	20	16.46	1.83	24	15.41	0.96
Teacher Perception												
Fall K: CBI Creativity and Verbal IQ	23	2.38	0.54	22	2.72	0.63	20	2.35	0.47	23	2.59	0.56

outcome (b). This is a correlational – not causal – analysis because we are not able fully to account for potential selection bias in the paths from the mediator to the outcome, even though the path from treatment to the mediator is from the randomized clinical trial. In these analyses, we focused on the adult outcomes in which we detected treatment main effects or treatment effects within male or females specifically.

Table 12.3 summarizes the results of these analyses. The most consistent findings implicated cognitive skills as a mediator at least for females. Indirect paths from treatment through 5-year verbal IQ to adult IQ, academic skills, and years of education were statistically significant for females; the same factor was marginally related to systolic blood pressure for males. In contrast, indirect paths involving 5-year performance IQ were only marginally significant for adult IQ and math for females.

Weak evidence indicated that "noncognitive" or executive functioning skills mediated treatment effects. Our early measure of executive functioning, the WPPSI Block Design score, was implicated in marginal indirect paths to adult IQ and academic achievement for females. Stronger effects were found for our measures of task orientation. For females, an indirect path from treatment through the 18-month toddler task orientation measure to adult IQ was statistically significant and it was marginally significant to the females' self-reports of externalizing behavior problems. For males, the indirect path from 18-month task orientation to adult income/needs ratio was marginally significant. Indirect paths through kindergarten teacher ratings of task orientation to female adult academic skills were statistically significant and to female years of education were marginally significant.

The kindergarten teacher's perception of children's verbal intelligence appeared to operate as a mediator in the same manner as did the child's WPPSI verbal IQ score. For females, indirect paths from treatment through the kindergarten teacher's rated impression of children's intelligence were statistically significant for adult intellectual levels and reading and math skills, and were marginally significant for females' adult educational attainment. These patterns were not found for males.

The child's BMI at 5 years was not implicated as a mediator in any analysis. Neither were the children's ratings of their self-esteem in elementary school, nor locus of control as teenagers, nor teacher's ratings of sociability or behavior problems in kindergarten.

In brief, our study of mediators of long-term benefits for the Abecedarian sample indicates that cognitive advantage, as indicated by the age 5 WPPSI intelligence test scores mediated adult intellectual levels and academic skills at age 21 and educational attainment at age 30. Independently, early treatment predicted all these adult outcomes.

Table 12.3 *Mediational analyses showing statistically significant and marginal indirect paths from treatment through mediators to adult outcomes*

Mediators	WAIS IQ	WJ Reading	WJ Math	Education (years)	BSI Depressive Symptoms	ASR External Problems	Income/ Needs Ratio	Systolic Blood Pressure
	B(SE)	B(SE)	B(SE)	B(SE)	B(SE)	B(SE)	B(SE)	B(SE)
Parenting								
54m Parental attitudes	1.10(.70)+	1.50(1.04)+		0.27(0.15)*				
6-54m HOME								
Child Cognition								
5y WPPSI Verbal IQ	3.54(1.19)***	4.94(1.75)**	3.23(1.22)**	0.22(0.16)+				3.05(2.02)+
5y WPPSI Perf IQ	2.21(1.15)*	2.15(1.23)*	2.00(1.09)*	0.17(0.12)+				
Child Executive Function								
18m IBR Task Orientation	(F)2.32(1.37)*	(F)2.94 (2.06)+						
K CBI Task Orientation								
Child Social and Behavior								
K CBI Behavior Prob.								
K CBI Sociability								
8y Self-esteem								
12y Self-esteem								
15y Locus of control								
Child Physical Health								
5y BMI								
Teacher Impression								
K CBI Intelligence	1.52(0.79)*	3.09(1.48)*	1.69(.90)*	0.19(0.13)+				

Significant and marginal indirect effects are reported for both female and male, unless noted otherwise (F = female)
*** = $p < 0.001$; ** = $p < 0.01$; * = $p < 05$; + = $p < .10$

The mediation of these adult scores through early test performance and verbal skills was clear in the case of females, whose early childhood language measures mediated adult intellectual and academic skills. The pathway to adult standardized test performance through verbal development is not as clear for males, although treated males and females earned similar scores on tests of intellectual development across ages from 5 to 21 years. In terms of standardized intellectual test performance, females appeared to maintain early gains to a greater extent than males.

At age 30, treated individuals had attained significantly more years of education; the prediction of this outcome by early verbal skills was significant for females only. However, despite the lack of as clear a predictive path, the probability of college graduation was greater for males than for females in both the treated and control groups. Fifteen individuals of the 101 individuals assessed at age 30 had graduated from a four-year college or university by that age; of these, 12 had been treated in early childhood compared to three cases in the control group, a 4-to-1 advantage. Of the college graduates in the control group, two were male, one female. Among the treated individuals, seven males compared to five females had college degrees. However, of the three persons who had, or were working on, advanced degrees at age 30, all were treated females.

Insofar as executive functioning is concerned, a trend was seen for WPPSI Block Design to predict adult intellectual and academic outcomes for females. Similarly, for females, toddler task orientation significantly predicted adult intellectual test scores at age 21 and marginally predicted female mental health scores at age 30. Despite finding no analogous pathways from early executive function and toddler task orientation to adult cognitive and educational levels among males, the Abecedarian data show males to be working more hours and to have higher incomes than females at age 30. In addition, toddler task orientation was weakly associated with higher incomes for 30-year-old males.

There was evidence that the teacher's perceptions of children's intellectual potential and task oriented behavior mediated later test performance, scholastic skills, and educational attainment for girls but not for boys.

We saw virtually no evidence that parental authoritarian attitudes were related to adult intellectual or scholastic outcomes, with one weak exception for this measure to predict adult IQ for females. There is no evidence that early treatment affected the quality of the children's home environments. However, there is evidence of "moderated mediation" in the Abecedarian longitudinal data. In a study of the synergistic influences of early childhood risk, the early home environment and early treatment on educational attainment in young adulthood, the findings indicated that the early home environment mediated the effects of risk of educational failure for those in the preschool control group, but that preschool treatment moderated this mediation for those who had preschool treatment (Pungello et al., 2010).

What we did not find was that our measures of childhood and adolescent self-esteem, or adolescent self-efficacy, mediated treatment effects on adult intellectual or academic measures. Nor did we see that our measure of behavior problems in early childhood affected adult test performance, academic scores, or vocational accomplishments.

We conclude that our data strongly support the cognitive advantage hypothesis as mediating sustained effects of early treatment on adult outcomes. We cannot conclude that the non-cognitive aspects of development had a more powerful effect. We do conclude, however, given the better economic indicators in the Abecedarian treated males that test performance and academic skills are only one mediator of adult attainments, and that many other factors that we did not include here undoubtedly contributed to the findings. For example, the possibility that some females were working less may have been because they had spouses or partners who contributed to their support. Another factor we did not include here was the effect of early childbearing which might have had a greater impact on vocational attainments among females.

A caveat of the Abecedarian research must always note the small sample size that depresses our ability to demonstrate reliably the effects of several circumstances that undoubtedly play important roles in the attainments of the treated and control adults in this sample. That we can see the effects described over the extended time period involved increases confidence in the reliability of the findings described.

References

Achenbach, T. M. & Rescorla, L. A. (2003). *Manual for the ASEBA Adult Forms & Profiles*. Burlington, VT: University of Vermont, Research Center for Children, Youth, & Families.

Bayley, N. (1969). *Bayley Scales of Infant Development*. New York, NY: The Psychological Corporation.

Bradley, R. H. & Caldwell, B. M. (1979). Home observation for measurement of the environment: A revision of the preschool scale. *American Journal of Mental Deficiency*, 84, 235–244.

Campbell, F. A., Pungello, E. P., Miller-Johnson, S., Burchinal, M. & Ramey, C. T. (2001). The development of cognitive and academic abilities: growth curves from an early childhood educational experiment. *Developmental Psychology*, 37, 231–242.

Campbell, F. A., Ramey, C. T., Pungello, E. P., Sparling, J. & Miller-Johnson, S. (2002). Early childhood education: young adult outcomes from the Abecedarian Project. *Applied Developmental Science*, 6, 42–57.

Campbell, F., Conti, G., Heckman, J. J. et al. (2014, March 28). Early childhood investments substantially boost adult health. *Science*, 343(6178), 1478–85. DOI: 10.1126/1248429. PMID: 24675955.

Campbell, F. A., Pungello, E. P., Burchinal, M. et al. (2012) Adult outcomes as a function of early childhood educational intervention: an Abecedarian Project follow-up. *Developmental Psychology*, 48(4), 1033–1043. DOI: 10.1037/a0026644.

Cicirelli, V. (1972). *Construction of the Purdue Self-Concept Scale for Young Children (Report of Contract #CG-5072)*. Washington, DC: Office of Economic Opportunity.

Cunha, F. & Heckman, J. J. (2008) Formulating, identifying and estimating the technology of cognitive and noncognitive skill formation. *Journal of Human Resources*, 43(4), 738–782. PMC2885826.

Derogatis, L. R. (1990). *Brief Symptom Inventory (BSI)*. Minneapolis, MI: National Computer Systems Assessments.

Emmerich, W. (1969). The parental role: a functional cognitive approach. *Monographs of the Society for Research in Child Development*, 34(8).

Fitzpatrick, C., McKinnon, R. D., Blair, C. B. & Willoughby, M. T. (2014). Do preschool executive function skills explain the school readiness gap between advantaged and disadvantaged children? *Learning and Instruction*, 30, 25–31.

Hamre, B. K. & Pianta, R. C. (2001). Early teacher-child relationships and the trajectory of children's school outcomes through eighth grade. *Child Development*, 72(2), 625–638.

Harms, T. (1980) *Learning from Cooking Experiences*. Menlo Park, CA: Addison-Wesley Publishing Company.

Harter, S. (1982). The perceived competence scale for children. *Child Development*, 53, 87–97.

McGinness, G. M. & Ramey, C. T. (1981). Developing sociolinguistic competence in children. *Canadian Journal of Early Childhood Education* 1(2), 22–43.

Pungello, E. P., Kainz, K., Burchinal, M. et al. (2010). Early educational intervention, early cumulative risk, and the early home environment as predictors of young adult outcomes within a high-risk sample. *Child Development*, 81(1), 410–426.

Ramey, C. T., Collier, A. M., Sparling, J. J. et al. (1976). The Carolina Abecedarian Project: a longitudinal and multidisciplinary approach to the prevention of developmental retardation, in Tjossem, T. (Ed.), *Intervention Strategies for High-Risk Infants and Young Children*, Baltimore, MD: University Park Press, (pp. 629–665).

Ramey, C. T. & Smith, B. (1977). Assessing the intellectual consequences of early intervention with high-risk infants. *American Journal of Mental Deficiency*, 81, 318–324.

Ramey, C. T., Sparling, J. J. & Ramey. S. L., (2012). *Abecedarian: the ideas, the approach, and the findings.* Los Angeles, CA: Sociometrics Corporation.

Reynolds, A. J. (2000). *Success in early intervention: the Chicago Child–Parent Centers.* Lincoln, NE: University of Nebraska Press.

Reynolds, A. J., Temple, J. A. & Ou, S.-R., (2010). Impacts and implication of the Child–Parent Center Preschool Program, In Reynolds, A. J., Rolnick, A. J., Englund, M. M. & Temple, J. A. (Eds.), *Childhood programs and practices in the first decade of life: human capital integration* (pp. 168–187). New York, NY: Cambridge University Press.

Rosenthal, R. & Jacobson, L. (1963). Teacher expectancies: determinants of pupils' IQ gains. *Psychological Reports*, 19, 115–118.

Schaefer, E. S. & Bell, R. (1958). Development of a parental attitude research instrument. *Child Development*, 29, 339–361.

Schaefer, E., Edgerton, M. & Aaronson, M. (1978). *Classroom Behavior Inventory.* (Unpublished. Available from the Frank Porter Graham Child Development Institute, University of North Carolina at Chapel Hill, Chapel Hill, NC, 27599.)

Schaefer, E. S., Edgerton, M. & Hunter, W. (n.d.). *Self-Evaluation Inventory.* Unpublished rating scale measuring locus of control and positive and negative self-concepts. Developed at the Frank Porter Graham Child Development Institute, University of North Carolina at Chapel Hill.

Schweinhart, L. J., Montie, J., Xiang, Z., Barnett, W. S., Belfield, C. R. & Nores, M. (2005) *Lifetime Effects: The High/Scope Perry Preschool Study through Age 40. Monographs of the High/Scope Educational Research Foundation, Number Fourteen.* Ypsilanti, MI: The High/Scope Press.

Sparling, J. J. & Lewis, I. (1978). *LearninGames for the first three years: a guide to parent–child play.* New York, NY: Walker.

Sparling, J. J. & Lewis, I. (1984). *LearninGames for threes and fours: A guide to adult and child play.* New York, NY: Walker.

Wechsler, D. (1967). *Wechsler Preschool and Primary Scale of Intelligence.* New York, NY: The Psychological Corporation.

Wechsler, D. (1981). *Wechsler Adult Intelligence Test – Revised.* Allen, TX: The Psychological Corporation.

Woodcock, R. W. & Johnson, M. B. (1989). *Woodcock–Johnson Psycho-Educational Battery – Revised.* Allen, TX: DLM.

Yoshikawa, H., Weiland, C., Brooks-Gunn, J. et al. (2013). *Investing in our future: the evidence base on preschool education.* Ann Arbor, MI: Society for Research in Child Development.

13 Differential Effects of High-Quality Early Care: Lessons from the Infant Health and Development Program

Juan C. Chaparro, Aaron J. Sojourner, and Nathan Huey[1]

The Infant Health and Development Program (IHDP) extended prior Abecedarian studies to a sample of low birth weight and premature infants (Infant Health and Development Program, 1990; Gross, Spiker & Haynes, 1997; Bradley et al., 1994). While the two predecessor studies, the Abecedarian Project and Project CARE, were both limited to one site and around 100 participating children, the IHDP was a multi-site study with nearly a thousand participating infants (Ramey, Sparling & Ramey, 2012). Since the intervention ended, papers have been written focusing on treatment effects such as child cognitive skill and behavior (Brooks-Gunn, Klebanov, Liaw & Spiker, 1993), quality of the home environment (Bradley et al., 1994), maternal employment (Brooks-Gunn, McCormick, Shapiro, Benasich & Black, 1994), the use of paid child care (Gross, Spiker & Haynes, 1997), and heterogeneity along demographic lines (Berlin, Brooks-Gunn, McCarton & McCormick, 1998). Because the IHDP program was effective, randomly assigned, and rich in data on both parents and children, it can be a valuable tool for understanding differences in how parents respond to an offer of free high-quality care and how this response relates to different developmental outcomes.

Design of the IHDP

The IHDP was a random-controlled trial conducted in eight cities with teaching hospitals throughout the United States of America. In order to be selected into the study, an infant must have been born in one of these hospitals at a weight of less than 2,500 grams and gestational age of 37 or fewer weeks. Two-thirds of the children who participated in the study

---

[1] This is a condensed, more accessible version of Chaparro, J. & Sojourner, A. J. (2015). *Same Program, Different Outcomes: Understanding Differential Effects from Access to Free, High-Quality Early Care*. Institute for the Study of Labor (IZA). Discussion Paper No. 9552.

287

were very low birth weight (below 2,000 grams); the rest were between 2,000 and 2,500 grams. There were no eligibility requirements based on race, ethnicity, or income, and as a result the participants were demographically diverse, a rare feature among early childhood intervention experiments. Enrollment began in October 1984 and ended in August 1985.

One-third of all participants were randomly assigned into a treatment group that received the full intervention. While the larger, control group got only follow-up pediatric examinations, the full IHDP intervention consisted of the offer of weekly home visits in the first year (reduced to every other week in the final two years), parent support groups, and care at a study-administered child development center in each city. The offer of center-based care began when the child turned 12 months old and lasted until the final child at each site reached 36 months (adjusted for prematurity). Though in previous Abecedarian studies infants entered care centers in their first year, entry was delayed in the IHDP due to the special health concerns of low birth weight, premature children (Gross, Spiker & Haynes, 1997). The centers were open five days a week for nine hours a day; children were scheduled to attend at least four hours a day (Brooks-Gunn et al., 1994). Free transportation was provided to the centers to ensure access for all families in the intervention group. The average hours attended per day was five, and the average days attended during the two years of the program was 267. During the infants' first year in the program, before they were eligible to attend the childcare center, there were no noticeable treatment effects.

Both the control and the intervention groups were given a variety of assessments and evaluations, focusing particularly on the mother and the child. Beginning at 40 weeks after conception and regularly until 36 months of age, children had pediatric check-ups at clinics established for the program. During these check-ups, data were gathered about the child's health, growth, and development, as well as about the demographic and social characteristics of the child and the family. Cognitive measurements were taken at 12, 24, and 36 months of age; behavioral information was collected at 24 and 36 months; home visits were made at 12 and 36 months to determine the quality of the child's living environment. Upon conclusion of the program, staff at each site worked to find community education programs for children in both the intervention and the control groups.

Dimensions of Heterogeneous Treatment Effects in the IHDP

Previous research established three main dimensions of heterogeneous effects: strong effects on children with higher birth weight, lower maternal education level (Gross, Spiker & Haynes, 1997), and lower family income (Duncan & Sojourner, 2013). Each of these dimensions can be parsed into distinct influences informed by economic theory. A child's birth weight is a consequence of characteristics of the family and mother that are fixed prior to pregnancy, choices made by the mother during pregnancy, and other factors that cause variation even when other elements are the same. The prior literature has not explored which of these three elements best explain the variation in treatment effects by child birth weight. The treatment had a larger impact on children from lower-income rather than higher-income families. This effect was so great that, at the conclusion of the intervention, the income-based gap in cognitive skill had been closed. However, family income also reflects a combination of different elements, including parents' potential hourly wage (which depends on their characteristics and the labor market), parental choices about how many hours to work, and availability of non-labor income.

Sound policy design requires understanding the drivers of desired effects. To what extent were treatment effects driven by differences in the opportunity cost of the mother's time; on parents' tendencies to invest time, effort, and resources in the development of their child; and on biological differences at the birth of the child that may impact the effectiveness of postnatal development choices? This study digs deeper into the causes behind heterogeneous effects of the IHDP.

Measures of Maternal Potential Wage, Prenatal Investment, and Child Endowment

Mothers' time is limited. They must choose how much maternal care to provide, how much time to place their child in non-maternal care (freeing up their own time and energy), how much to work for wages, and how much time to spend doing other activities. How they value their time and make these choices affects the extent to which they will take up any offer of free childcare. Rather than income, which reflects both fixed characteristics of the mother and time-use choices she makes, we focus on potential wage, which indicates how much an hour of her time is worth in the labor market. For workers, potential wage equals actual wage. For those not employed, potential wage is the wage someone would be capable of commanding if they were employed (Heckman, 1974).

In this study, the relationship between maternal potential wage and maternal characteristics is estimated using a sample of mothers of young children from the nationally representative Current Population Survey (CPS) March supplements for 1986–89 (Flood, King, Ruggles &

Warren, 2015). Using the estimates from this model, IHDP mothers are then scored to create a measure of their potential wage. The average potential wage is $8.08 for working mothers in the IHDP, and $6.62 for all IHDP mothers. Holding everything else constant, a mother whose time is worth more in the labor market would have more of an incentive to make use of the IHDP offer of free childcare since the hour of her time that is freed up is worth more in potential earnings. However, there may also be an incentive to take up fewer hours of this free care: mothers with higher potential wages may be able to improve their children's outcomes more efficiently with their parenting time (Bernal & Keane, 2011). The potential benefit of an hour at the care center to the child's development may, therefore, be smaller as maternal potential wage grows due to correlated maternal productivity in the labor market and parenting.

Differences across parents in willingness to devote their time, energy, and resources toward the development of their child may also be a factor in their choice to make use of free childcare and in its effectiveness at improving developmental outcomes. Parents have competing priorities between spending their time and resources on their child's cognitive growth and on all other aspects of their lives, and they may rank and trade off these priorities in different ways. Additionally, the child's birth condition, controlling for maternal potential wage and for different levels of investment in child development, may influence the potential effects of care options and, therefore, impact on the utilization of free childcare and on the outcomes associated with it. Birth condition may influence the productivity of postnatal investment (Cunha & Heckman, 2007).

Parents' willingness to invest in their child's development postnatally can be difficult to distinguish from the condition of the child at birth. There are two immediately apparent sources of this confusion. First, prenatal decisions to invest more in the child's development may improve the child's condition at birth beyond what it would have been with an otherwise identical mother less likely to invest pre- and postnatally. A child's better condition at birth may be due not to biological factors, but rather to choices the mother made during pregnancy driven by her propensity to invest more. Therefore, the child's physical measurements at birth do not provide a clear picture of the child's inborn cognitive and health conditions; instead, they may embody stable differences in maternal information and preferences that also led to differences in postnatal influences. Therefore, the observed heterogeneous treatment effects by birth weight may really be heterogeneous effects by the mother's preferences or her disposition to make personal sacrifices to invest in child development. A second confounding factor is that random shocks affecting the child's birth condition could affect the choices of the parent postnatally. If the child is born at a low weight compared to another child whose parents had similar characteristics and investment, the postnatal investment of the parents of the lighter child may be higher because of the perceived weakness of their child (Almond & Mazumder, 2013).

A measure of investment in the prenatal period gives leverage to disentangle the mother's stable willingness to invest from idiosyncratic influences on birth condition. Prenatal decisions are made without knowledge about the child's condition as revealed at birth (Aizer & Cunha, 2012). These decisions offer a clearer picture of the mother's propensity to invest in her child's development by excluding the additional effect of the mother's perception of her child's birth condition. Our model distinguishes three elements that make up the child's physical condition at birth: prenatal investment choices, observed maternal fixed characteristics that might affect birth outcomes, and the child's idiosyncratic biological makeup independent of these two factors. Birth weight and gestational age are used as measures of the observed condition at birth. Stable maternal characteristics are maternal ethnicity; marital status; maternal education; maternal age; whether or not the child was a multiple birth; whether or not the child was female; and the number of previous childbirths. The proxy for prenatal investment choices is made up of the following variables: average number of cigarettes smoked per day and average number of alcoholic drinks consumed per week during pregnancy; whether the mother used drugs while pregnant; amount of weight gained during pregnancy; and the trimester, if any, of first prenatal care.

The IHDP collected direct measures for prenatal investment. Interpreting these through the lens of nationally representative data makes them more descriptive and guards against bias that might arise from only studying a low birth weight, premature sample. Prenatal investment is scored by using the nationally representative Early Childhood Longitudinal Study, Birth Cohort (ECLS-B) of children born in 2001 (Nord, Edwards, Andreassen, Green & Wallner-Allen, 2006). Each mother–child pair in the ECLS-B is scored on a prenatal investment index and an index that measures the deviation of the child's birth weight and gestational age from expected based on prenatal investment and maternal characteristics. Each mother–child pair in the IHDP is then scored using the estimates of this model.

Residual unobserved influences on birth weight and gestational age (those that are not covered by maternal characteristics or prenatal investment) are mapped in the same way[2] to come up with a measure of the

---

[2] The variance of the residual is measured in the ECLS-B, yielding a z-score, and then residuals in the IHDP are measured in these units.

idiosyncratic influences on the child's conditions at birth, which will be referred to as the *child endowment*. This measures how that child's birth condition differs from that of children whose families had observably similar characteristics and made observably similar prenatal investment choices. As expected, children in the IHDP had particularly negative child endowments when compared to those born into similar situations in the general population. Though mothers in the IHDP tended also to invest somewhat less prenatally, the main reason that the children were eligible for the program seems to have been their unusually bad endowment shock.

Cognitive Effects of IHDP Treatment

Important outcomes on which there is heterogeneity of program effects, include child cognitive skill, quantity of care by type, and quality of care. The primary child cognitive measures are IQ tests at ages 3, 5, 8, and 18 years old.[3] Hours per week the child spent in maternal care comes from interviews conducted with the mother at 18 and 30 months, and the time each child spent at the IHDP care facility is available through administrative records. Supposing the child sleeps on average for 11.5 hours each night (Inglowstein et al., 2003), the time the child spent in non-maternal care not provided by the IHDP is found by subtracting hours of maternal care and hours of care at the IHDP facility from total waking hours. The Learning and Literacy component of the Infant-Toddler HOME score (Linver, Martin & Brooks-Gunn, 2004; Fuligni, Han & Brooks-Gunn, 2004), gathered at 12 and 36 months, measures the quality of maternal care; the yes–no questions used to generate this score are displayed in Table 13.1. Quality of care provided neither by the mother nor the IHDP is measured using IHDP data on what types of care the mother used (partner, sibling, grandmother, another relative, babysitter, day care home, day care center, someone else, or child's father if he lives in another home) and the characteristics of the family and the child together with information from the National Institute of Child Health and Development's Study of Early Child Care and Youth Development (NICHD Early Child Care Research Network, 2000; Vandell, 2004).

The relationship between child endowment and predicted IQ levels was not found to be significant, nor did endowment have any relationship

---

[3] The long-term effects of the IHDP intervention were first reported by McCormick, Brooks-Gunn, Buka, Goldman, Yu et al., (2006). These authors studied the effects on cognitive and behavioral outcomes of participants at 18 years of age. They found evidence of a positive although diminished effect on cognitive development of participants whose birth weight was above 2.0 kilograms.

Table 13.1 *Learning and literacy components (IT-home score) available in the IHDP sample*

12-month Home Assessment	36-month Home Assessment
At least 10 books are present and visible	Child has toys which teach color, size, shape
Muscle activity toys or equipment	Child has three or more puzzles
Push or pull toys	Child has toys permitting free expression
Parent provides toys for child during visit	Child has toys or games requiring refined movements
Learning equipment appropriate to age: cuddly toys or role-playing toys	Child has at least 10 children's books
Learning facilitators: mobile, table and chairs, high chair, play pen	At least 10 books are visible in the apartment
Complex eye–hand coordination toys	Child is encouraged to learn the alphabet
Toys for literature and music	Interior of apartment not dark or perceptually monotonous
Parent reads stories to child at least three times Weekly	Parent converses with child at least twice during visit
Child has three or more books of her own	Child is encouraged to learn spatial relationships
	Child is encouraged to learn to read a few words
	Child has real or toy musical instrument

Based on Linver, Martin & Brooks-Gunn (2004) and Fuligni, Han & Brooks-Gunn (2004).

to treatment effects. This suggests that, rather than the course of a child's development being predetermined at birth, it can be changed by the decisions of parents and policymakers. Higher prenatal investment (above the 33rd percentile of the sample distribution) was correlated with an IQ advantage of more than three points, and this gap persisted through age 18. This increased IQ could be a consequence of higher prenatal investments as well as correlated postnatal investments. Prenatal investment and treatment effects, in contrast, were not correlated: the mother's prenatal investment in her child's development apparently had no significant impact on the intervention's effectiveness. IQ increased with maternal potential wage for both treatment and control groups through age 18. Children of high-wage mothers had IQs four to eight points higher than children of low-wage mothers. The effects of treatment showed a different correlation, however: it boosted IQ for children of low-wage mothers but did not do so for children whose mothers were high-wage (above the 33rd percentile of the sample distribution). Children of low-wage mothers added around six points in IQ from the treatment. Those in more difficult economic circumstances gained more from the treatment. This disparity in treatment effect faded with age, but was still three points at 8 years old, five years after the end of the treatment. Treatment effects on child cognition across child endowment, prenatal investment, and maternal potential wage can be seen in Figure 13.1.

Childcare Effects of IHDP Treatment

Though the high quality of childcare provided at IHDP centers might seem to be the most important factor in these results, access to it is only one of many consequences for families given this opportunity. Making use of this new childcare resource for an hour also means that the mother does not have to care for the child during this time and could, therefore, open up an hour for wage work or another activity. An hour in the IHDP care facility could also be one hour fewer for which the family must plan some other form of non-maternal care, which often requires money, transportation, and other resource expenditures. Therefore, we examine how access to this free high-quality option affects the set of other childcare choices the family makes.

Though families in the intervention group were offered 40 hours of free care per week, the average hours used was only 16 per week. Surprisingly, hours used did not vary significantly depending on prenatal investment. With few resource or accessibility constraints – the IHDP childcare centers were free and transportation was provided – it might seem likely

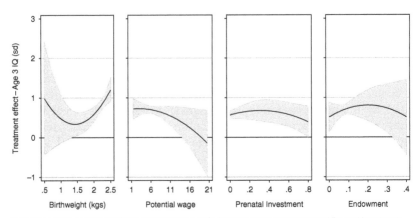

Estimate and 95% confidence interval. Potential wage: US$ of 2012 per hour. Endowment and Prenatal Investment: percentile in ECLS-B distribution. N = 858.

Figure 13.1 IHDP treatment effects on IQ at 36 months

that the main driving force in the take-up of the service would be how invested the mother is in child development, but this does not appear to be the case. Instead, wage and child endowment were the main variables across which heterogeneity was found. Mothers with the lowest potential wage used 15 hours of this service per week. Those with potential wages in the middle third used a similar amount. But those with the highest potential wages used only about seven hours of the free care per week on average.

How mothers with low and high potential wage would have allocated the time their child spent in IHDP care differed, as seen in Figure 13.2. The time children of higher-wage mothers spent at the IHDP childcare center mostly crowded out time they would have spent in other forms of non-maternal care rather than in maternal care. The opposite was true of lower-wage mothers: they reduced time directly caring for their children. One result of their newly free hours was an increase in maternal time spent in the labor market.[4]

The greatest cause of heterogeneity in take-up of the free care offer was child endowment. Parents of children with worse endowments took up significantly fewer care hours than those whose children were better off at birth. Mothers whose children were in the lowest 1 percent of child endowment relative to the national sample used an average of 15 hours per week of IHDP care, while those in the 40th percentile used more than 20 hours.

There were also changes in the quality of this reallocated care. One effect of IHDP enrollment was that the quality of non-maternal care settings other than IHDP centers decreased for those with higher potential wages (as shown in Figure 13.3). Children of high-wage mothers in the treatment group were in care settings of lower quality when they were not in either the mother's care or at the IHDP center than similar children in the control group. However, for low-wage mothers, non-maternal care outside of IHDP centers was unchanged in quality. This may be a result of higher wage mothers using IHDP centers as a substitute for high-quality care that, without access to the program, they would have bought on the market. With free care taking the place of these high-quality care hours, the remaining non-maternal hours were less expensive and lower in quality.

Figure 13.4 illustrates treatment effects on the quality of maternal care. This unpacks the differential effect by family income previously

---

[4] The long-term maternal employment effects of the IHDP intervention were reported by Martin, Brooks-Gunn, Klebanov, Buka & McCormick (2008). These authors also found important differential effects of the intervention, depending on children's birth weight.

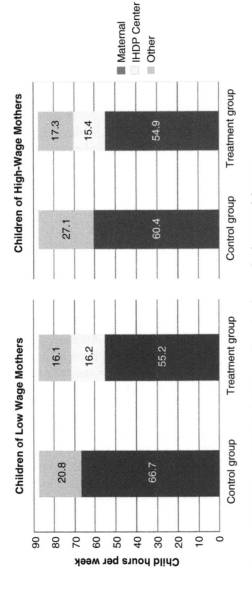

Figure 13.2 Effects of IHDP child-time allocation by mother's potential wage

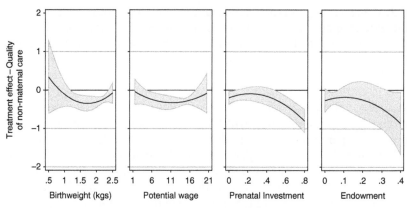

Estimate and 95% confidence interval. Potential wage: US$ of 2012 per hour.
Endowment and Prenatal Investment: percentile in ECLS-B distribution. N = 820.

Figure 13.3 IHDP treatment effects on quality of non-maternal care

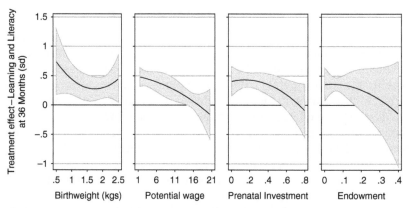

Estimate and 95% confidence interval. Potential wage: US$ of 2012 per hour.
Endowment and Prenatal Investment: percentile in ECLS-B distribution. N = 768.

Figure 13.4 IHDP treatment effects on quality of maternal care

reported (Duncan & Sojourner, 2013). Treatment effects on maternal
care quality are smaller when prenatal investment and child endowment are larger. This pattern was also observed with potential wage.
The treatment substantially increased the quality of maternal care of
low-wage mothers.

A decrease in maternal-care quantity therefore goes along with an increase in maternal-care quality for low-wage mothers, whereas treatment has no effect on quantity or quality for high-wage mothers. Conceptually, one intriguing interpretation of this pattern of results is that less time parenting may allow for greater effort to be applied over the decreased time that remains, raising average parenting quality. Parenting as an input of cognitive development may depend on effort exerted at any given time and the time over which this effort is exerted. If the amount of time spent parenting is decreased, a parent may be able to expend more effort when their child is in parental care. With access to the IHDP care centers, low-wage mothers could devote more time to activities other than parenting while still being assured that their children were being given high-quality care. As a result, not only were these children able to spend time in higher quality non-maternal care, but the time they spent being cared for by their mother also became more conducive to their cognitive development.

Policy Implications and Future Research

Young children's time is limited and experiences during this period have lifelong consequences. Therefore, childhood time can be fruitfully considered as a scarce resource that can be budgeted in different ways. How parents allocate their child's time with various caregivers is an important aspect of that child's development. However, the number of hours of free childcare service offered by a program will not on its own determine how families distribute child time. A family takes many factors into account when deciding how many hours to take up; a leading factor is the value of the parents' time. Moreover, the quality of the free care is an important consideration. Parents may be willing to make use of an offer of lower-quality free care over superior-quality care either from the market or that they would provide themselves (Peltzman, 1973) because of the cost saving. This could increase family income while being detrimental to a child's development. Childcare subsidies make all parents better off, but they do not necessarily improve developmental outcomes for all children.

How we structure our investments in child development influences their developmental outcomes. Achievement gaps are a result of the choices families make given an economic and policy environment. The experience of the families in the IHDP suggests that an offer of free high-quality care is effective in narrowing the income gap in cognitive development because it decreases some of the pressures on low-wage families. It seems that access to high-quality care frees up parents to parent better. The trade-off between parenting time and parenting quality must be accounted for in the design of future child care policy. Furthermore, the creation of an early intervention program does not guarantee its effectiveness. Those designing experiments and policies must take into account and respect how parents will respond – and respond in different ways – to the program. It seems useful to consider policy as an offer of quality, quantity, and price per hour of care. How parental take-up influences the effectiveness of already extant childcare subsidies can be studied using this economic framework.

Current policy makes the least public investment in children when children are youngest, although this is also the period when families have the least private resources to invest (Council of Economic Advisers, 2016). Total public investment averages less than $9,000 per child-year in children's first three years, $10,000 during the next two years, and over $16,000 per year in early elementary school. Public funding covers only 9 percent of child time during standard business hours in their first three years of life but increases dramatically during ages 3 and 4 due to Head Start and preschool programs, and exceeds 50 percent after age 5. However, parents have the least access to private resources – in the form of past income, current earning power, or credit against future income – precisely when children are younger and public investments are low.

There are three main objections to investing in childcare for infants and toddlers: low benefit, high cost, and concern about interfering in the child–parent relationship. This evidence should help dispel the first concern and balance against the other two. There is strong evidence of large benefits from access to high-quality care in terms of children's long-run skill development, especially for children whose parents have low earning power. Extra investments in the first three years of life alone can have long-term benefits for children from low-income families, though they may be larger, as well as more expensive, if followed up with additional enrichments later (Duncan & Magnuson, 2013). This echoes results from the original Abecedarian study, summarized in F. Campbell's chapter in this volume (Chapter 12). While the age 0–5 intervention had positive effects long-term – effects that parallel the IHDP's closely – the early elementary enrichment on top of the 0–5 intervention showed little additional effect. This evidence is in tension with a simple view that effects of early investment dissipate absent especially high levels of later investment.

In terms of cost, high-quality care for infants and toddlers is more expensive per child-hour than for preschoolers or elementary-school students. Younger children need more intensive care and attention, necessitating lower child-to-adult ratios. However, such care must be provided by someone in any case, whether or not it is provided by a parent. The opportunity cost of parents' time should be acknowledged as a cost of parental care. Though not on the public balance sheet, time in parenting is a real contribution and a real cost.

This leads to the final concern: that childcare subsidies for infants and toddlers will undermine the family by shifting incentives in favor of non-parental care. For those who want to help parents with young children manage the budget and time crunch but are deeply concerned about this issue, the alternative of cash transfers to parents when they have young children would accomplish this goal without affecting the incentives to use non-parental care. It would make it easier for parents to keep a roof over their family's head while also providing care themselves. Such transfers could be accomplished by a much higher Child Tax Credit – preferably one that is fully refundable in advance – or by a child allowance. Still, it is important to remember that the IHDP in fact raised maternal-care quality among those who used it the most. By reducing the burden of caring so much, it seems to have created psychological space for parents to parent better, and better parenting could conceivably be the foundation for a stronger family.

References

Aizer, A. & Cunha, F. (2012). *The Production of Human Capital: Endowments, Investments and Fertility* (No. w18429). Cambridge, MA: National Bureau of Economic Research.

Almond, D. & Mazumder, B. (2013). Fetal origins and parental responses. *Annual Review of Economics*, 5(1), 37–56.

Berlin, L. J., Brooks-Gunn, J., McCarton, C. & McCormick, M. C. (1998). The effectiveness of early intervention: examining risk factors and pathways to enhanced development. *Preventive Medicine*, 27(2), 238–245.

Bernal, R. & Keane, M. P. (2011). Child care choices and children's cognitive achievement: the case of single mothers. *Journal of Labor Economics*, 29(3), 459–512.

Bradley, R. H., Whiteside, L., Mundfrom, D. J., Casey, P. H., Caldwell, B. M. & Barrett, K. (1994). Impact of the Infant Health and Development Program (IHDP) on the home environments of infants born prematurely and with low birthweight. *Journal of Educational Psychology*, 86(4), 531.

Brooks-Gunn, J., Klebanov, P. K., Liaw, F. & Spiker, D. (1993). Enhancing the development of low-birthweight, premature infants: changes in cognition and behavior over the first three years. *Child Development*, 64(3), 736–753.

Brooks-Gunn, J., McCormick, M. C., Shapiro, S., Benasich, A. & Black, G. W. (1994). The effects of early education intervention on maternal employment, public assistance, and health insurance: the infant health and development program. *American Journal of Public Health*, 84(6), 924–931.

Council of Economic Advisers. (2016) The Disconnect Between Resources and Needs When Investing in Children.

Cunha, F. & Heckman, J. (2007). The technology of skill formation. *American Economic Review*, 97(2), 31–47.

Duncan, G. J. & Magnuson, K. (2013). Investing in preschool programs. *Journal of Economic Perspective*, 27(2), 109–132.

Duncan, G. J. & Sojourner, A. J. (2013). Can intensive early childhood intervention programs eliminate income-based cognitive and achievement gaps? *Journal of Human Resources*, 48(4), 945–968.

Flood, S., King, M. Ruggles, S. & Warren, J. R. (2015*). Integrated public use microdata series, Current Population Survey: Version 4.0.* [Machine-readable database]. *Minneapolis. MI: University of Minnesota.*

Fuligni, A. S., Han, W.-J. & Brooks-Gunn, J. (2004). The infant-toddler HOME in the 2nd and 3rd years of life. *Parenting*, 4(2–3), 139–159.

Gross, R. T., Spiker, D. & Haynes, C. W. (Eds.), (1997). *Helping low birth weight, premature babies: the infant health and development program.* Stanford, Calif: Stanford University Press.

Heckman, J. (1974). Shadow Prices, Market Wages, and Labor Supply. *Econometrica*, 42(4), 679–694.

Infant Health and Development Program. (1990). Enhancing the outcomes of low-birth-weight, premature infants. *Journal of the American Medical Association*, 263(22), 3035–3042.

Iglowstein, I., Jenni, O., Molinari, L. & Largo, R. (2003). Sleep duration from infancy to adolescence: reference values and generational trends. *Pediatrics*, 111 (2), 302–7.

Linver, M. R., Martin, A. & Brooks-Gunn, J. (2004). Measuring infants' home environment: the IT-HOME for infants between birth and 12 months in four national data sets. *Parenting*, 4(2–3), 115–137.

Martin, A., Brooks-Gunn, J., Klebanov, P., Buka, S. & McCormick, M. (2008). Long-term maternal effects of early childhood intervention: findings from the Infant Health and Development Program (IHDP). *Journal of Applied Developmental Psychology*, 29(2), 101–117.

McCormick, M., Brooks-Gunn, J., Buka, S. et al. (2006). Early intervention in low birth weight premature infants: results at 18 years of age for the Infant Health and Development Program. *Pediatrics*, 117(3), 771–780.

NICHD Early Child Care Research Network. (2000). Characteristics and quality of child care for toddlers and preschoolers. *Applied Developmental Science*, 4(3), 116–135.

Nord, C., Edwards, B., Andreassen, C., Green, J. L. & Wallner-Allen, K. (2006). *User's Manual for the ECLS-B Longitudinal 9-Month–2-Year Data File and Electronic Codebook (NCES 24006–046). Washington, DC: National Center for Educational Statistics.*

302   *Juan C. Chaparro, Aaron J. Sojourner, and Nathan Huey*

Peltzman, S. (1973). The effect of government subsidies-in-kind on private expenditures: the case of higher education. *The Journal of Political Economy*, 1–27.

Ramey, C. T., Sparling, J. & Ramey, S. L. (2012). *Abecedarian: the ideas, the approach, and the findings.* Los Altos, CA: Sociometrics Corp.

Vandell, D. (2004). Early child care: the known and the unknown. *Merrill-Palmer Quarterly*, 50(3), 387–414.

Part IV

Synthesis and Guiding Principles

14   Enhancing Children's Outcomes since "Eager to Learn"

Barbara T. Bowman

In 2000, the National Research Council (NRC) published a summary of research on early childhood education with an eye toward developing programs that would maximize learning for children (National Research Council, 2000). This chapter discusses some of the issues that were highlighted in the *Eager to Learn* report and reflects on what has happened since it was published.

The NRC report presented overwhelming evidence demonstrating the benefits of high-quality early education. It also summarized the then-current research on child development, on academic curriculum, and on social/emotional support. The report paid particular attention to children at risk of school failure and identified three reasons for this. First, some children, notably low-income black and brown children, were (and still are) failing in school. Assessments show that their vulnerability begins at an early age and that high school failure is predictable by the time students are in third grade. The underachievement of low-income children was (as it still is) viewed by many as a national crisis, with effects that include high rates of crime and incarceration, unemployment and underemployment, premature parenting, and other social ills.

A second reason for concern about early education was prompted by an explosion of research on young children. Over the past half-century, we had collected increasing evidence about how the first six years of life lay the foundation for later development and learning. Neuroscience research has led to greater understanding of how children's genes, both human and family ones, are translated into behavior through experience. Research also explained why some early deprivations are so difficult to remediate later in life.

The third reason for the attention to early childhood is a series of educational studies that verified the long-term effects of early experience. Three of these studies (HighScope, Chicago Child Parent Centers, and Abecedarian) all showed that the trajectory of the lives of poor children could be altered by the quality of their preschool experiences. Follow-up studies showed differences lasting at least 40 years in the lives of children who participated and did not participate in the three preschool programs.

While the Eager to Learn report addressed education for all children, it did consider social class as a factor that influences what and how children learn. The report said, "Young children who are living in circumstances that place them at greater risk of school failure – including poverty . . . are much more likely to succeed in school if they attend well-planned, high quality, early childhood programs." The report points out that there is "a significant association between children's performance on cognitive tasks and parent income and years of education." Although one of the report's firmest recommendations was that at-risk children have access to high-quality early childhood programs, it also made clear that early education is not a panacea for all social problems, even though there is evidence that it has a powerful role to play.

Since the publication of the report, new studies have confirmed the pernicious effects of poverty on student achievement. The younger the child and the deeper the poverty, the lower the child's educational achievement. And poverty is unevenly distributed across the population. For example, black families are both the poorest group and the group with the lowest-achieving children in terms of school performance. In 2014, 24 percent of children under age 5 were poor, and 37.1 percent of those were African American. Only 5.4 percent were non-Hispanic white children (CLASP). Black children also scored lower on achievement tests beginning at age 3. *The New York Times*, on August 19, 2014, commented, "Five decades past the era of legal segregation, [a] chasm remains between black and white Americans – and in some important respects it's as wide as ever."

The deeper the poverty, the less well children do in school. For a family of three, deep poverty, which refers to an income at or below 50% of the poverty threshold, equates to living with an annual income below $9,425 (DeNavas-Walt and Proctor, 2015). Certainly, the difficulties for these families are enormous and it is little wonder that the stresses of living compromise the opportunities for children. Unemployment and under-employment, segregated housing and schools, uneven distribution of educational resources, combine to make a devastating educational environment for many children. Despite the promise of early education, the increase in the number of black and brown children living in poverty makes school achievement an even more difficult task than we envisioned in 2000.

Current research is exploring why income disparity and the educational disparity go hand in hand. One theory is that families at the top of the wage scale are willing and able to devote more of their wealth to the development and learning of their children. This has led to new expectations for what parents do for their children. This theory is backed up to some extent by an annual survey of popular parent media. It found that, over the last 15 years, media messages have, increasingly, related to "stranger danger," unclean food, untrustworthy public officials, and accidents waiting to happen. Responsible parents are advised to safeguard their children against every conceivable danger, even at the expense of others. Aside from protecting children from real and imaginary dangers, the media recommended that parents buy educational toys, talk to their children, read to their children daily, and, most importantly, register them in high-quality preschool or child care centers. Since higher-earning families are also better educated, the educational environment for their children is likely to be rich in opportunities to learn school-related skills and knowledge.

Certainly, most low-income families do not have the luxury of devoting large amounts of time and money to the education of their young children. As the income gap widens, the challenge for programs will be to provide similar experiences to poor kids that more advantaged children enjoy. This makes one of the most contentious recommendations in Eager to Learn more important than it was at the time the report was produced. It was that teachers of young children should have the same level of education as teachers of older children: that is, a BA degree. Some people believed that the field could not financially support bachelor-level teachers because of the high ratio of adults to children in early childhood programs. Others do not believe that teaching young children requires much education – little kids don't know much, so their teachers don't have to either. Further, in many Head Start programs parents of the enrolled children, i.e. poor parents, were given priority for jobs, few of whom had higher education degrees.

The reasoning behind the teacher education recommendation in Eager to Learn is that the skills and knowledge necessary to teach young children are just as extensive and complex as those needed to teach older children. In addition, teachers with more education do more of the things that lead to higher achievement than teachers who are less educated. And, of course, there is a high correlation between mother's education and child achievement, and there is little reason to believe that more education does not have a similar value for teachers.

Since the report was published, there have been baby steps toward the implementation of this recommendation, primarily in public schools and high-tuition child care centers. However, not to the extent we wished. It was hoped, when Eager to Learn was published, that it would provide guidance as states increased their support for high-quality preschool programs. The early part of the twenty-first century saw a rapid increase in the number of states providing or increasing funding for early education programs. Unfortunately, this early enthusiasm was soon tempered by the recession in 2008, and progress stalled. In 2011–12, half a billion dollars were cut from state budgets and 4,000 seats were lost. Some recovery took place in 2013–14 as pre-K funding increased by $116 million, but early education is still making up for the losses during the recession rather than charting new territory. The good news is that, in some states, early education budgets are going up. A few states are renewing their call for universal preschool (New York being a notable example) and one State, Mississippi, was added to the 35 providing some state funding for preschool education. The bad news is that the ongoing fiscal crises in some states (Illinois being one) continue to constrain expansion of funding (NIEER: The State of Preschool, 2012–14).

The picture is a little more reassuring in the struggle for quality. The report stressed that it is the experience children have that determines whether a program is a benefit or hazard to development and learning. Despite the recession, many states are working on quality. Most, if not all, states' early childhood Advisory committees have developed early education standards (but, unfortunately, not ones aligned with common core kindergarten standards), and raised child care licensing standards. Nevertheless, NIEER reports, "Only 15 states could be verified as providing enough per-child funding to meet all 10 benchmarks for quality standards. As only 13 percent of the children enrolled in state-funded programs attend high quality programs, the vast majority of children served in state-funded pre-K are in programs where funding per child may be inadequate to provide a quality education" (NIEER: The State of Preschool, 2012–14).

Over the last few years, the federal government has become a more active supporter of early education. Since 2000, Head Start has had modest increases in funding and some standards were changed to better support quality. Head Start also began the process of requiring its teachers to have BA degrees. Another change at HEW is the focus though early Head Start, and other early intervention programs, on home visiting for infants and toddlers at risk of developmental difficulties. These programs are designed to prevent developmental failures caused when parents do not have access to needed childrearing information. Home visiting has a long history, with visiting nurses giving health information to low income parents; however, the effects of most parent education programs using non-nurses have best modest at best. The new home visiting programs will provide new information about the challenges of serving this age group and its benefits to children and families. The Department of

Education has also been active in the early childhood arena. Secretary Arne Duncan was a strong advocate and, under his leadership, the Department implemented the Race to the Top, a competitive grant program designed to encourage innovation in education.

The NRC report devoted considerable attention to the role of social/ emotional factors in development and learning. New concepts, like self-regulation and social competence, were discussed along with the traditional ones of play and interest areas. Eager to Learn focused on the skills and knowledge that lays the foundation for school, which included letters and numbers, well-developed oral language, literacy conventions, etc. as well as opportunities for play and social interaction. While the report tried to balance attention to both, it was read by some as overstressing academic achievement. Unfortunately, critics saw a dichotomy between a traditional social/emotional emphasis in curriculum and a skill-based one. This has continued to divide the professional community as well as parents. Play and activities based on young children's interests are often seen as compromised by more "school"-type learning (the alphabet) and instruction (listening to information).

The rationale for focusing on school-type skills, like alphabetic and number knowledge, was that prior knowledge facilitates later learning. Children who enter kindergarten with a beginning knowledge of literacy and mathematics are more successful in school. Greg Duncan and colleagues concluded from a meta-analysis of the research on school readiness, "the strongest predictors of later achievement are school-entry math, reading, and attention skills" (Duncan et al., 2007, p. 1428). Another reason to promote academic skills in preschool is that many low-income children are not likely to get this type of information at home, because parents are overwhelmed with other concerns, they don't understand the importance of beginning these skills early, or they don't have the skills themselves. It is interesting that most of the criticism of academic content has come from middle-class teachers and parents whose children already know and use these academic skills regularly. They know the alphabet, count to at least 20, and have a much more extensive vocabulary than poor children. Even before entering kindergarten, the average cognitive scores of children in families with the highest socioeconomic status (SES) are 60 percent above those of children from families with the lowest SES (Economic Policy Institute). Because economically advantaged children tend to learn these skills informally, in small bits over several years spent with educated parents, does not mean that this is the only way to acquire them.

Eager to Learn found there is no one curriculum or teaching style that's right for all children. It endorsed diversity in content and methods and favored a balance between teacher-directed and child-initiated activities. It also recommended that programs aim at providing a curriculum in which the academic content is specified and integrated across domains. Despite some reluctance, many early childhood educators have come around to the idea of adding academic content to preschool curriculum. Judging from the recommendations of early childhood professional organizations, there is an increased interest in intentional and evidence-based curriculum, instead of ones based solely on ideology. Nevertheless, many educators continue to demand a heavy diet of "free play" as an essential ingredient for preschool and gives short shrift to the achievement gap that awaits children from low-income families.

One of the major points made in Eager to Learn is that all experience affects subsequent ones. Children build on what they already know, adding to and refining, and occasionally misunderstanding as they grapple to integrate new ideas with old frameworks. When the framework is inadequate, too slim or too different for new learning to be meaningful, children lose focus and interest. This means, of course, that to maximize achievement new learning must be aligned and only a step above what children already know. While the report focused specifically on the years between 3 and 5, preschool was not seen as a standalone educational experience. Eager to Learn spoke to the importance of synchronizing preschool with infant toddler programs. It did not, however, specifically address the follow-up to preschool, which has had much more attention in recent years as pre-K–3 programming (Takanishi, 2016). This movement, which calls for aligning academic content and social demands between pre-kindergarten and third grade, has gained momentum. Although this grade range was intrinsic to the early Child Parent Centers that Arthur Reynolds described (and is currently being reassessed), pre-K–3 was dropped in the 1980s as more resources were put into preschool. The data showed that preschool paid off, so there was greater incentive to invest there.

Perhaps more importantly, few public schools or early childhood programs were seriously interested in joining pre-K to the primary grades. Early childhood programs were, and still are, in diverse settings with a variety of goals, organizational arrangements, and financing. Accustomed to a culture quite different from the public system, early childhood personnel feel little affinity towards K–12. Public schools were, and still are, faced with rising expectations and lowering budgets. They often have large numbers of low-income children who have not been enrolled in preschool, mobile school enrollment, and sporadic attendance. So, they must spend more time playing catch-up than building on the skills and knowledge of the children who attended preschool. There is little incentive in either system to form a coordinated whole.

Some advocates suggest we look to K–3 for the answer to fade-out. The argument is that preschool cannot be expected to compensate for the educational inadequacy of schools in low-income communities. If the kindergarten, first and second grade class rooms do not build on the foundation of preschool, it does not take long for a disconnect to show up. Stipek (Stipek, 2017) suggests that K–1 curricula designed to let non-preschool attendees catch up, are a boring repeat for children who had already learned these lessons in preschool. Further, peers offer little academic stimulation in the income- and racially-segregated schools that most poor children attend. Regression toward mean is inevitable.

There is a good deal of support for the notion that children learn best when there is an alignment between what they know and what we want them to know. This means that interventions that are sustained over time, building from one level to the next, are likely to result in better long-term achievement. For example, a number of alternative models have surfaced in various states to achieve greater alignment between pre-K and Head Start and child care. One that has some appeal is a half-day pre-K and Head Start in a K–3 public school, with wrap-around child care. The advantage of this model is that pre-K teachers would earn enough to amortize the cost of a four-year college education. In addition, being in close proximity to kindergarten teachers, they would be more likely to spend the necessary time to align and realign curricula and social expectations. The public school increasing appreciation of community and parent involvement in low income neighborhoods could also profit from the greater involvement of families in early childhood programs. There is yet little incentive in many states to join early childhood programs to public schools. One hopes Arthur Reynolds' reassessment of the Child–Parent Centers will energize more interest in pre-K–3.

Eager to Learn included in its report, a list of topics in need of additional research. Among the most important are:

1. **Child development:** We need to find new and better assessment strategies to find out what kids know and can do. Presently, we are limited to standardized tests, which are notoriously faulted particularly for young children, and teacher judgments, which tend to be biased by personal beliefs and inadequate data. We need multiple measures, some objective and some soft so that we can get a fairer picture of what individuals and groups of children are learning. More importantly, teachers need to be active participants in discussions about assessment. Beginning in pre-K, time and resources need to be directed to teacher teams who work with administration to assess

what children know and can do. External rules and expectations about teaching and learning cannot replace what is actually going on in the classroom. That, in the last analysis, depends on the teacher.

2. **Classrooms:** We do not need research to find the best curricula or teaching style; rather, we need to find out what kind of curricula and style works for which children and why. Diverse children living in diverse environments will not get ready for school with the same input. We also need better prepared teachers; teachers who can design appropriate curricula and select the appropriate styles for the children she teaches. We need teachers who are accountable, but who are well educated, have time to plan and consult with colleagues, and know how and what to teach young children.

3. **Parents:** We need to find new ways to engage parents. The PTA and Head Start models, which brought parents into the center or school to learn about and support the program, is no longer feasible as most parents are working or going to school. As with the children, we need to figure out what works for whom rather than expecting one model of parent involvement to work for all parents.

4. We need research to enable programs to "**go to scale**" with high quality. Local, small programs have demonstrated the potential of early childhood education. Just like public schools, however, early childhood programs are having trouble moving from a model school to a model system. What ingredients make a model work? and Can they be replicated? are important questions.

5. Finally, we need **economic analysis**. We need to answer such questions as: Does it make sense to spend less on child care so mothers can work, but then have to spend more on remediation? Should we fund pre-K for all, since all kids can profit from it, or give preference to low-income children who benefit more? Should we put more resources into interventions for infants and toddlers or does it make better sense to serve all eligible pre-K children first?

In summary, what has happened since Eager to Learn? There is good news and bad news. Among the discouraging aspects are the increased gaps in wealth and education without any serious effort to confront the elephant in the room: poverty. Further bad news: Early Childhood Education (ECE) programs that can help ameliorate some of the effects of poverty have not increased substantially in number and quality.

On the good news side, we have had small successes. There have been increases in the number of children participating in preschool from both advantaged and low-income families, and more efforts toward improving quality of the programs they attend have occurred. Programs are paying more attention to what and how they teach, and parents are paying more attention to the care and education of their children. There is also greater emphasis on alignment: on what comes before and after pre-K.

Resource Investments

Perhaps the best news is the number of people who understand the importance of the early childhood period of development and the need to support it. Having been in the field for a very long time, I remember quite well a time when most people would laugh at the idea that what you did with little children made much difference. This has changed. In 2013, the *First Five Years Fund* did a national survey of registered voters that indicated that early childhood education and services for children, from birth to age 8, was the second most important national priority – after the economy. Early childhood is now recognized by most Americans as both a critical period in human development **and** a critical national economic and social investment. That's progress.

References

DeNavas-Walt, C. & Proctor, B. D. (2015). *Income and Poverty in the United States: 2014.* Current Population Reports P60-252. US Census Bureau, Washington, DC: US Government Printing Office.

Duncan, G. J., Dowsett, C. J., Claessens, A., Magnuson, K., Huston, A. C. et al. (2007). School readiness and later achievement. *Developmental Psychology*, 43, 1428–1446.

National Research Council (2000). *Eager to Learn: Educating Our Preschoolers.* Washington, DC: The National Academies Press.

Stipek, D. (2017) The preschool fade-out effect is not inevitable: To sustain gains in preschool, look at what comes next, Education Week, March 17, 2017, Retrieved from www.edweek.org/ew/articles/2017/03/17/the-preschool-fade-out-effect-is-not-inevitable.html?qs=stipek.

Takanishi, R. (2016). *First Things First! Creating the New American Primary School.* New York, NY: Teachers College Press.

15   Reframing Policy and Practice Deliberations
Twelve Hallmarks of Strategies to Attain and Sustain Early Childhood Gains

Craig T. Ramey and Sharon Landesman Ramey

Early education experiments have produced varied outcomes. The "classic" long-term studies, as well as more recent studies, affirm many practical benefits that extend into elementary school – most consistently, reductions in grade repetition and special education placement – and result in healthier, more productive adult lives. Despite decades of thoughtful critique, the myth of a fade-out effect persists. We conclude that when early education yields large and enduring effects, this likely is the result of both (1) building a robust early learning foundation via high-quality and sufficient dosage supports in the first five years of life and (2) affording reasonably strong subsequent educational, family, and/or community experiences. This is because human competence and neuroplasticity benefit from cognitive, social, and health opportunities across the lifespan.

In this chapter, we reflect on our 40+ years of experience in this field – from directly designing and implementing randomized controlled trials of multiple types of center-based early care and education programs as well as home visiting programs to advising and often reviewing and evaluating large-scale community, state, national, and international programs. We propose a set of hallmarks that we think distinguish the majority of programs that produced large magnitude and multiple life-course (and intergenerational) benefits. We hope these hallmarks will contribute to a reframing of policy and practice deliberations, resulting in a far greater consensus about how our communities can realistically and promptly reduce the large and burdensome educational inequalities and health disparities that continue to plague our nation's lowest income and most marginalized children and families. The great divide within the USA, if not effectively curbed, will lessen the future for our democracy and will be a blight on all citizens and communities.

Background to Understanding Successful Life-Course Studies

The first set of pioneering early education experiments launched in the 1960s answered the question, "Can children born into poverty benefit from educational enrichment prior to entering school?" with a resounding "Yes" (Lazar et al., 1982; C. Ramey, 1982). These social experiments, fueled by humanitarian concerns about poverty and racism, also addressed the basic science question: "Can children's cognitive performance be improved by altering early experience?" Collectively, these studies challenged the widely accepted, but untested assumption undergirding the creation of standardized intelligence tests – namely, that intelligence was a fixed, innate trait. At the same time, these experiments incorporated new ideas derived from the fields of ethology and comparative psychology that yielded provocative findings about how profoundly learning (in birds, ducks, dogs, mice, rats, and monkeys) could be altered by manipulating early environments and early experiences.

The findings from the first set of 13 human experiments yielded both short- and longer-term data, rigorously and repeatedly analyzed and summarized through a peer-reviewed, consensus-building process. For scholars of early childhood development, the resulting 1982 monograph published by the Society for Research in Child Development served as a landmark publication. Remarkably, in the broader arena of early childhood education, the findings from more than three decades ago often are forgotten, misinterpreted, or discounted as being "back then" and "when our country was a lot different." There has been a vigorous and thoughtful second phase (in the 1970s and 1980s) and then a third phase (in the 1990s and the first decade of the 2000s) concerning scale-up, community-based, and even national projects. Yet we begin this chapter by reprinting the original full abstract (Box 15.1, next page) that summarizes what was concluded in the early 1980s. Of particular note, the effects applied widely to different subgroups of children and the benefits were *not* limited to a single or narrow cognitive outcome. Simply stated, and directly quoted, "Results showed that early education programs for children from low-income families had long-lasting effects in four areas: school competence, developed abilities, children's attitudes and values, and impact on family."

Box. 15.1

Abstract

This collaborative study assessed the long-term effects of early childhood education experience on children from low-income families. In 1976, 12 investigators, who had independently designed and implemented infant and preschool programs in the 1960s, pooled their original data and conducted a collaborative follow-up of the original subjects, who were aged 9–19 at the time. Coordination of data collection and joint analyses were supervised by two additional investigators. The multisample secondary analyses reported here addressed two general questions: Were there long-term effects of early childhood programs? Were programs more effective for some subgroups of the low-income population than for others?

Outcome measures included indicators of school competence (special education assignment and grade retention), developed abilities (standardized intelligence and achievement tests), children's attitudes and values, and impact on the family. Each early childhood project was considered separately for each hypothesis test and the results of the separate hypothesis tests were pooled using a pooled-z technique. This procedure tested the null hypothesis that there was no average effect of program participation across the different early education programs. Detailed attrition analyses indicated that attrition was essentially random, introducing no noticeable biases into the data analyses.

Results show that early education programs for children from low-income families had long-lasting effects in four areas: school competence, developed abilities, children's attitudes and values, and impact on the family. 1. Children who attended programs were significantly more likely to meet their school's basic requirements. Controlling for family background factors and initial ability, program graduates were significantly less likely to be assigned to special education classes and less likely to be retained in grade than were controls. The effect apparently operated for all the children regardless of sex, ethnic background, initial ability level, or early family background factors. 2. Children who attended early childhood programs surpassed their controls on the Stanford–Binet intelligence test for several years after the program had ended. There was no evidence that the programs differentially raised the IQ test scores of some subgroups of children (differing on sex, initial ability, and family background). There was some indication that program graduates performed better on achievement tests than did controls. 3. In 1976, children who had attended early education programs were significantly more likely than were controls to give achievement-related reasons, such as school or work accomplishments, for being proud of themselves. Older program graduates also rated their school performance significantly better than did controls. 4. Program participation also affected maternal attitudes toward school performance and vocational aspirations relative to those of the child. The school competence results are placed in a larger developmental context through exploration of two empirically derived paths from program participation to increased school competence. The educational, social, and economic significance of the results are discussed and implications for social policy are detailed.

(Lazar et al., 1982)

The socially valued and economically impactful outcome of making satisfactory school progress – including on-time grade promotion and not being placed in special education – appeared across almost all of the projects. The finding of enduring effects was repeatedly affirmed through rigorous experiments that were launched later (including the Abecedarian Project, Project CARE, and the Infant Health and Development Program [cf. Ramey, 2018]) and the large-scale community-based Chicago Parent–Child Centers (e.g., Reynolds, 2000; Reynolds, Temple & Ou, 2010). Similarly, substantial investments in conducting far more sophisticated and nuanced reviews and data analyses of even longer-term outcomes (concentrated primarily on the Perry Preschool Project, e.g., Schweinhart & Weikart, 1983; Heckman et al., 2010; the Abecedarian Project and its replication, Project CARE; and The Chicago Child–Parent Centers) endorse their value (e.g., Camilli et al., 2010; Dodge, 2017; Kay & Pennucci, 2014).

Yet surprisingly, what is all too often remembered from the first and second wave of early educational studies is that there was a "fade-out effect." The source of this misrepresentation of findings from both the early and subsequent studies, concerns primarily IQ scores. Specifically, the largest group differences on IQ scores between children who did and did not receive the experimental high-quality early education tended to be largest when the learning experiences were the most different between the experimental and control children. When control children in some studies received either high-quality community center-based care or when they entered high-quality public schools, their IQ scores increased, thus lowering the magnitude of significant group differences.

In contrast to the IQ outcome data, however, the practical academic benefits detected in terms of children's later reading and math achievement, lower grade repetition, and lowered special education placement rates remained strong (C. Ramey et al., 2000; Schweinhart et al., 2005). (For excellent reviews of "the myth of fade-out" and plausible reasons for declining group differences over time, see Barnett, 2004, 2014.) Even more impressively, a number of important adulthood benefits later emerged, including a variety of post-secondary educational and employment or income outcomes, and positive health indicators (e.g., C. Ramey et al., 2000; Campbell et al., 2002; Campbell et al., 2014). Further, high-quality public education *does* improve academic outcomes for children who enter kindergarten well below national average, so children in comparison groups often show significant early gains that contribute to smaller effect sizes than occurred during the younger years (e.g., S. Ramey et al., 2001). Even well-documented critiques of the fade-out effect (e.g., Barnett, 2014) have failed to dispel this belief.

In this chapter, we suggest that continuing to debate about the variations in long-term benefits and economic yield measured as "return-on-investments" (or cost savings to society by preventing negative outcomes) will be less productive and relevant for policy and practice than developing a new broadened paradigm that confronts the immediate consequences of permitting huge disparities to grow in the first decade of children's lives. We present a two-stage hypothesis, informed by our firsthand experiences of developing programs, conducting research, and reflecting on the findings from longitudinal studies of children born into entrenched poverty and extremely challenging life conditions.

The *first part of the hypothesis* is that **early life supports – both within and outside the family – must reach a threshold of high-quality and dosage to build a solid developmental foundation for later success in school, good health, and productivity in adulthood**. Accordingly, careful attention to the *multiple features* of those interventions that have produced both large short-term and later multiple long-term benefits is warranted. These features can inform efforts to design, improve, and coordinate current programs and community supports across a broad array of funding and administrative mechanisms; and may facilitate designing and implementing practically useful data collection, analysis, and reporting plans to maximize the likelihood that all children realize a strong early educational and health foundation.

The *second part of the hypothesis* is that **lifelong benefits of a strong early foundation in learning and health depend on what happens next** (C. Ramey & Ramey, 1998). That is, children need to have continuities in positive environments as they progress into next-stage educational, social, recreational, and creative endeavors. The conclusion that effective early education alone is not sufficient to guarantee success in life and health does *not* lessen the centrality or urgency of providing these early opportunities for all children, particularly those most vulnerable due to life circumstances when they were born. Rather, this recognizes basic principles of human learning and well-being, such that children (and their families, schools, and communities) continue to need strong supports to maintain good rates of learning and positive health and engagement in healthy activities. Fortunately, there is substantial evidence that high-intensity, theory-driven, carefully measured and monitored interventions – early and across the lifespan – can produce "gains" that do not fade, but rather well prepare children to realize the benefits of our major societal institutions and public programs.

Policy deliberations need to move beyond the limited and competitive debate about "early" education being the *only*, the *best*, or the *better time* to invest in children. This is not because the preponderance of evidence does not support this (e.g., Dodge, 2017). Rather, it is time to recognize the limits of the available data and analytic approaches and to confront the reality that children's well-being necessitates a 24/7, year-round, multi-year understanding of human development. We anticipate that a truly adequate inventory of the similarities and differences among children's daily realities – from this broadened perspective – will be critical to inform how we can best propel academic and social competence, health, and hope among our nation's most vulnerable children, starting early and then extending through adulthood in ways that build upon existing resources and scientific knowledge.

To the extent that we can create new broadened alliances that seek to conjoin improvements in education (pre-K through 12 plus higher education and vocational preparation) and parenting supports that extend far beyond the preschool years are likely to be productive, efficient, and endorsed by the general public. When education and positive environments for young children are "sold" to legislators and the business community primarily based on an economic model, this may have an unintended effect of reducing poor children and their families to commodities that are viewed as potential societal burdens, rather than accepting all children as integral to our larger communities and the future of our democracy. If investors do not "make money" on their bets in favor of these children being placed in evidence-based programs, then should we cease to provide early high-quality caring, educationally enriched, and socially integrated opportunities for these children? At the same time, we cannot ignore the fact that the economic return-on-investment, coupled with evidence that poor quality ("toxic") environments harm children's brain development, has captivated and stimulated many to take constructive actions within their communities.

The paradigm we advance is one that expands to consider group-level and societal human capital benefits (that is, beyond just measuring gains for the at-risk children) associated with providing early learning and health supports for all children. Similarly, we endorse the view that early supports and programs for all children (not just those at risk) should meet high standards that link to research evidence and that can be readily understood, valued, and measured (evaluated) by families and providers as well as scientists, administrators, and funding agencies.

Our reflections on the history and findings of a large body of research and program evaluation have led us to identify "hallmarks" of the most impactful projects. These hallmarks, somewhat surprisingly, do not necessarily drive up the cost of providing effective supports early in life, but they do require high levels of transparency, engagement of diverse sectors within our communities, and a bold willingness to take timely actions when children or families are in harm's way or when services and programs are below a quality and intensity threshold needed to support healthy growth and development. We present this list of hallmarks here to stimulate discussion so they can be further refined and incorporated into implementable policies and practices. These hallmarks may help provide a template to maximize the current and planned future investments in early childhood care and education initiatives – that is, these focus on the first part of our hypothesis: that high-quality early care and education are vital, but not necessarily sufficient, for later long-term success.

Part One: Hallmarks of Successful Programs that Improved the Lives of Vulnerable Children

The programs that produced enduring benefits have served as beacons and inspiration for launching many other efforts. They also have provided the data that economists use to estimate costs (often adjusted for operating in today's world) and their savings to society, measured in economic and human capital terms. Many of these proven programs served as the basis for designing newer studies that incorporate cutting-edge neuroscience methods to discover whether children's biology and particularly their brains are changed, and if so, in what ways and how much, as a result of participating in these types of programs. These programs are rightly celebrated for the exciting news and hope they bring to society.

Yet the good news is not met with uniform enthusiasm. To the contrary, the attacks on these "proven programs" have been vigorous and sustained; and skepticism abounds about whether these programs can be trusted to illuminate the pathways to improve the ways we choose to nurture and to educate our children, individually and collectively. The insider story of how these programs operated is often skipped over when sharing the good news. In this reflective chapter, we try to go behind the scenes and include ideas from those who led some of these programs.

The "Hothouse" versus the "Real World" Controversy: What This is All About

What are the attacks on these successful programs? Why so much pessimism? The most frequent attack on the well-known successful research programs is: *The positive results were obtained **only** under "hothouse" conditions.* The "hothouse experiments" accusation refers to the appearance that these projects operated under "ideal circumstances," in a rarified and protected environment, like a hothouse where the gardener can control all of the crucial conditions for growing plants. This controlled environment frees the gardener from dealing with the many uncertain whims of Mother Nature. Thus, by analogy, the gardener who succeeds in a hothouse may *not* achieve the same success in "the real world" of ordinary gardens. These references to hothouse conditions are usually accompanied with warnings to policymakers, politicians, administrators, practitioners, parents, and the general public: "Be careful. Do not think you can achieve the same results in your own communities (gardens)!"

A twist on the hothouse attack is the not-infrequent claim that the successful early childhood programs were "boutique programs." For those of us who designed and operated programs that served children with very challenging life conditions, we can assure the public that boutique is not an adjective that would readily come to mind for anyone who worked in or visited our early childhood programs. The term boutique makes it seem that what we did with and for these children and families was so elite and so out-of-reach that ordinary programs could never achieve the same conditions and thus could never yield equal benefits. Boutique also implies very expensive, and many of today's community-based, publicly funded programs cost as much, or even more, than the proven programs did, even adjusting for inflation

The expression "the real world" is shorthand for the morass of conditions providers and policymakers face as they decide what to do with and for children. "Real world" equates with complicated, out-of-control, overwhelming, unpredictable, resistant to change, vulnerable to fads, and often demoralizing. The "real world" often is used to explain, and offered as an excuse for, the abysmal state of services and supports for children and families in many places.

Many of our colleagues who led the successful early childhood programs would vigorously reject the claim that they worked in an ideal environment. They faced many serious operational problems, as well as threats that could have derailed their programs. Yet we think it is fair to acknowledge that the landmark studies were relatively small in scale, had reasonable levels of funding, and were mostly under the direct control of those who designed them. Without doubt, we consider these to be fortunate and desirable conditions; ones that probably helped to spare these programs from many of the daunting problems others often face when they operate within complex and large health, education, and social service delivery systems. So, taking the hothouse criticism to heart, we decided to ask, "What did these highly successful programs have working in their favor?"

The Search for Common Features of the Proven Programs: How to Detect These and How to Estimate the Magnitude of Their Importance?

To generate our preliminary list of hallmarks of successful programs, we first considered the same list of 20 programs reviewed by the RAND Corporation, focusing on the 15 that produced substantial evidence of lasting benefits. We have known many of the leaders of these programs, we have reviewed their scientific articles, read their program descriptions, and in various ways served as advisers and colleagues working together and frequently sharing what we have been learning. Some of the features we identify here include ones that were seldom written about in the scientific peer-reviewed publications about the programs. Thus, we cannot assert with absolute confidence that these hallmarks are decidedly the *only* factors that mattered, nor do we think that *every* successful program had *all* of these features. What we have reflected on is the plausibility that this combination of positive features contributed in a major way to the high quality, the consistency, and the measured success of the program. In the final analysis, we have difficulty imagining how the programs could have been launched and fully implemented so well if these features had not been present; these "hallmarks" appear to us to have operated in a synergistic fashion from the earliest stages of the program through all phases of operation and evaluation. We present this list in the spirit of capturing our best insights from our decades of experience – a list that captures what we consider instrumentally invaluable in launching and sustaining high quality, effective programs to benefit children. The programs have spanned the arenas of health, education, and social services, children of different ages and with widely varying needs, often children of single teen mothers, children of color, and children whose families had very limited resources and whose parents had inadequate educational experiences and opportunities.

The Nominated Hallmarks of Programs that Improved Children's Lives

We propose in Table 15.1 a set of "hallmarks" as distinctive characteristics that likely contributed to the success of many of the childhood intervention research programs that produced significant gains. Of particular salience is that these hallmarks seem to work as a set – in ways that provide natural feedback mechanisms and help to make the whole – the program being implemented – more than just the sum of its parts. Accordingly, we suggest that communities, policymakers, leaders,

Table 15.1 *Hallmarks of early childhood education programs that produced large benefits*

1. Leadership at the highest level was stable, highly engaged, and deeply knowledgeable about the content of the program. Program leaders had a strong professional stake in the conduct of the project.
2. The content of the programs was based on existing scientific findings and scientific theory about children's development, rather than ideology or philosophy alone.
3. The programs were relatively intensive – often engaging program children and/or family members over a fairly long period of time. Although program dosage is extremely difficult to equate across different types of programs for different types of children and families, in general higher intensity programs tend to yield greater benefits.
4. Multiple features and components were specified in the program to achieve maximum desired experiences for children, along with flexibility for intended individualization of the standardized protocol. That is, children's intertwined development and needs were recognized; this usually necessitated engagement of experts from diverse disciplines and specialty areas.
5. Before the program was implemented, it was supported by both external peer review (content experts) and by respected members or opinion leaders in the local community (local endorsement).
6. Program staff received strong training and professional development related to the intervention, and this included provision of active, ongoing supports and systematic supervision with feedback.
7. Implementation of the program was actively monitored by leaders, which helped to detect and resolve problems early as well as to reward staff. Performance expectations were clear to staff, as well as the immediate goals for improving children's education and health outcomes.
8. High levels of participation among all children and families were strongly supported from the very beginning and at all stages, including strategic plans to overcome the most likely potential barriers to full participation (e.g., transportation, illness policies, hours of operation, program schedule).
9. Children's progress was frequently assessed by objective and unbiased methods, and valued as vital to understanding whether the program was able to achieve its intended benefits on children's lives. Evaluation was viewed as something that was "externally imposed," or something that was intrusive or competed with program resources for children.
10. The information gathered about the program and about children's progress was analyzed and reported to both the program leadership team and to external groups, as appropriate, including presentation at leading professional organizations.
11. Program developers recognized that replication of the program would be an important next step if the results affirmed benefits to children and families. Thus, the program's content and procedures were documented sufficiently to allow replication.
12. The leadership had sufficient levels of resources and direct control over expenditures so that the key components of the planned program would be delivered, while knowing that they could rapidly make adjustments if and when problems occurred. The scale of these programs was small to moderate, and there was a good perceived match between resources available and the expectations for implementation.

direct providers, and parents consider how to maximize these hallmarks in their own efforts to increase children's school readiness and set the stage for enduring benefits.

These distinctive features also worked in a synergistic fashion. That is, each of these hallmarks received ongoing support from the presence of one or more of the other hallmarks. We elaborate in greater detail below.

1. **Leaders had a strong professional stake in the conduct of the project**. The leadership was present from the earliest stages of the program, a necessity since the people who led these projects were the originators of the ideas for the program and usually the ones who had to find the funds to conduct it. Sometimes external forces and opportunities encouraged the development of the program, but the compelling force behind and throughout these programs was the leadership. The individuals who led these programs were immersed in the content areas about human development addressed in their programs. They led the conceptualization and design of the program. In the world of science, they are designated Principal Investigators or Project Directors. Some had a history of working directly with children earlier in their careers, as teachers or clinicians or program administrators; others had firsthand experience observing and testing children in laboratory and community settings. Not all were experienced in leading large or complex projects when they began; neither were they all charismatic, singularly focused, or well-connected to influential people in the world of child and family policy. We can find little in common with their leadership style per se across these programs; rather, what surfaced was *their depth of commitment and knowledge about the theme or content of the intervention.*

In obvious ways, people who think of a new strategy to improve children's lives are highly invested in testing their ideas. They tend to be optimists, to the extent that they believe that meaningful change can occur, even in the lives of children and families facing serious life challenges. These programs – because they were in some ways original and not yet proven when they were launched – had to operate within the boundaries of science and its concomitant standards of proof. This meant that the leaders were constantly under scrutiny with multiple checks and balances used to yield what others would consider to be a fair or unbiased test of the program's impact on children's lives.

At the same time, these projects were exciting in their own right. The teams who worked together almost always included a mix of senior colleagues, graduate students and post-doctoral fellows, and experienced practitioners, as well as the new staff hired for the programs. There is little doubt these program leaders were active advocates for their programs.

Although they were hopeful, they did not claim success or promise benefits *before* the evidence came in. Indeed, excessive early claims can be the death of a scientific career.

2. **The successful programs were guided by both existing scientific findings and scientific theory about children's development, rather than ideology or philosophy alone**. The successful programs focused on changing specified aspects of a child's experiences that were highly likely to be important, based on findings from careful observational studies, from laboratory research with children, or from smaller (preliminary) studies that included at least some of the components of the final program that was implemented. These programs had a conceptual framework in which the rationale for the content of the program was described and defended. Sometimes the program added particular types of experiences to a child's life; sometimes it shielded the child from exposure to harmful experiences; sometimes the program changed the child's physical environment and health care to promote positive encounters and provide opportunities that otherwise were not as likely to occur, as well as to reduce or eliminate known environmental risks. The ideas guiding the program design – the package of services and activities that comprised the intervention, the treatment, or the prevention program – were formulated as scientific hypotheses about the ways that the components of the program would alter the process of human development. The hypothesized alterations in a child and family's life were then predicted to result in measurable changes in the short term, sometimes during the period that program was being provided, always at the end of the program, and often in the years after the child and family completed participation. This use of scientific findings and a guiding theory about children's developmental pathways was not just an academic exercise. To the contrary, this theoretical framework helped to shape the program itself. In all cases, these successful programs had a target group of children and families in mind when they were planned. Most of the programs concentrated primarily on directly changing the child's experiences – that is, the program actually provided specified learning experiences, types of interactional supports, and environmental opportunities to the children. Other programs, however, focused on changing the child's family first (such as home visiting and parenting programs) with the hypothesis that this would lead to changed opportunities and learning experiences to the children. Many programs had a theory that children would benefit from direct provision of certain experiences and these benefits would be better maintained if the child's family became better informed and more skillful in promoting their children's academic, social, and emotional development.

This conclusion that a scientific theory is an integral and important feature of the successful programs is one that many review panels have identified as well. In the landmark National Academies of Science report, *From Neurons to Neighborhoods* (Shonkoff & Phillips, 2000), the committee concluded that *every successful intervention was guided by a theoretical model with specification of the relationships between the stated goals of the intervention and the strategic approaches implemented to achieve these goals.* This strong consensus that theory matters brings currency to the words of Kurt Lewin, a highly innovative thinker in psychology and the founder of modern social psychology and what became known as "action research": Lewin (1951) promoted the idea that "There is nothing so practical as a good theory." He also admonished: "If you want to truly understand something, try to change it."

Most parents, teachers, and practitioners do not think in terms of formal theories about human development and life-course developmental trajectories in any detailed way when it comes to their everyday care, nurturance, and instruction of children. Many of these important people in children's lives do, however, have their own personal philosophies and their strong belief systems about children's "true nature" and how best to help a young child become a mature, healthy, responsible adult. Although strong differences of opinion exist about how much parents or anyone else can really influence a child (particularly when it comes to the topic of what area and when in the child's life the adult is trying to have an influence), there is almost universal agreement about some things that are harmful. But is there really an important difference between a philosophy and a scientific theory when it comes to children?

We argue strongly that there is a difference. A scientific theory is a formal set of ideas that are explicitly described and inter-connected, with linkages to objective data (evidence) about the phenomenon (the phenomenon here being the child's development). There is a rich and fascinating field known as the philosophy of science; most scientists view theories as representing a highly evolved and elevated form of scientific reasoning. Then there are smaller theories or detailed elaborations of portions of major theories. Most human developmental scientists today are more modest in describing their ideas and prefer to use the expression "conceptual frameworks," rather than theory, to describe their layout of key ideas about the factors that contribute to and shape a child's life. Over time, these conceptual frameworks are refined, as more data become available and lend support to some ideas, but not others, and as unanticipated relationships emerge. These conceptual frameworks thus become increasingly specified about causality or something called multi-determinism that posits there are mutually interacting, dynamic sets of probabilities that exert influences upon a child's development. (Science-speak is seldom easily understood; we will not try to defend ourselves or our colleagues for this occupational habit, but we will acknowledge that for many life scientists, each word or phrase they use has evolved through years of thinking, research, and re-formulation). Because so many of the terms scientists use also have an everyday connotation, there often is confusion about whether something is being used in the highly technical sense or the everyday sense. Examples of such confusion include terms related to areas such as: parent–child attachment, play, direct instruction, memory, emotions and feelings, intelligence, and personality. Scientific theories about human development are considered strong when they are highly specified in terms of how the different elements work individually and in combined ways with other elements, over time, and across set-tings – with these elements often changing in dynamic ways based on the engagement levels and the responses of a child. Scientific theories are designed so that they can be tested through research; thus, a theory – usually specified parts of a theory – can be proven wrong. In contrast, most philosophies and ideologies about children are judged largely by whether they seem to be logical, to match one's own experiences, or to be compatible with one's values and other belief systems about the world. Many philosophies are not organized so they can be disproved with evidence, or refined and improved based on facts that are collected about it.

In general, a philosophy or ideology is more similar to a world view than it is to a formal scientific theory. There are, of course, people who consider the life sciences as having their origins in philosophy and identify implicit assumptions about human nature that seem ideological. Historically, the philosophies and ideologies about human nature, in its individual and collective form, have garnered far greater sway than have scientific theories when it comes to societal decisions about taking care of and educating our children. (In all fairness, scientific theories about children are much newer; fewer people have studied them in depth; and for many, science represents something cold, distant, abstract, and very complex mathematically). A philosophy usually starts with some sweep-ing basic assumptions about the inherent nature of "man" (who first appears as a child) and then progresses to describe the ways in which children learn and become transformed into more or less competent and caring individuals.

A brief skip through some influential Western philosophers reminds us how different these basic assumptions can be. Consider John Locke, Thomas Hobbs, and Jean Jacques Rousseau. John Locke believed that a child was born as a blank slate (tabula rasa) and that experience would fill that slate. Locke did not believe man was fundamentally good or bad. Thomas Hobbs was the world's pessimist about man's basic nature: he proclaimed that human nature – when left alone – would result in a life that was predominately "solitary, poor, nasty, brutish, and short." The only way to escape would be to enter into mutually beneficial social contracts. So he saw some hope through external conditions. Rousseau had an idealist's view of man at birth – fundamentally pure and without sin, and only later lowered into a more beastly existence by a corrupt society. (By the way, Rousseau did not stick with this one view throughout his whole life.) These famous philosophers reflect starkly different views, generated in an era when there was little science about human beings in the early years of life or about which life experiences led to various adult outcomes. The debate about what mankind's true nature is – *independent* of the social and political environments where all human beings live – seems a bit preposterous to us. (It has captivated many, though, through the centuries.) The fact is, children cannot survive alone – and just thinking about this in the abstract, without empirical evidence, is unlikely to resolve the old philosophical debates. Even the tragic cases of children abandoned or reared in extremely isolated situations can hardly be considered proof about "man (woman) in his (her) natural state." In other words, babies need a social world – their species-specific and species-typical environments – to both survive in the short term and then to learn over time those behaviors and ways of thinking and reasoning that will allow later survival and reproduction.

Educators and the practice of education also have long been guided by various philosophies. Among the popular educational philosophies that have influenced children's early education are those put forward by John Dewey, Maria Montessori, Rudolf Steiner, and parents in the villages around Reggio Emilia in Italy. These philosophies can be highly inspirational for teachers, and often are associated with certain practices that have appeared to create positive learning environments for young children. These philosophies tend to be accepted as a matter of belief and faith by the teachers who follow them. Rarely are these philosophical assumptions ever tested, but we think there would be great merit in more rigorous scientific study to understand how the philosophies are used to inform the practices of teachers and how these practices then contribute to children's courses of development. We note that scientific theory about child development could be related directly to educational philosophies and practices, but this happens only rarely. We do not consider that philosophies and theories are inherently at odds or in competition. In fact, we think it is interesting that we have identified the use of scientific theory as a hallmark of the successful programs for children – and that many parents and practitioners strongly endorse the use of a particular philosophy to guide an educational program for children!

The use of scientific theory helps to establish a clear and practical guide for a program. The theory results in the program being *highly intentional* – focused in a well-thought-out way – in terms of what it does. The theory also helps to foster good communication in planning, implementing, monitoring, and evaluating the program. There is a "'big picture" with a common language of defined terms that correspond to the key aspects of the program. *This big picture and shared vocabulary of a theory go hand-in-hand with detailed explanations (a strong rationale) as to why key aspects of the program are likely to make a difference in the lives of participating children.* It is not just a vague idea that loving children and playing with them and teaching them will guarantee they grow up to be caring and smart adults, although nothing is wrong at all with love, play, or teaching per se. To the contrary, these *are* good things in a child's life. A theory would translate big concepts like love, play, and teaching into very clear dimensions as to what are the likely good ways of expressing love, playing with children, and teaching them – at different times in their lives. These words would not be used in ways that left it up to each parent or teacher or therapist with his or her own ideas about how to love, play, and teach children. What if an infant-toddler teacher thought that "tough love" is a very good kind of love, and then decided to start showing love by never "giving in" and never responding to a 4-month-old baby when crying in distress or trying to get the teacher's attention by making sounds, smiling, or moving his or her arms and legs? What if a child care provider believed that playing with a 2-year-old meant simply letting the child do anything and everything with absolutely no adult interference, no guidance, and no comments at all? Or what if a preschool teacher thought that teaching a 3-year-old in ways to help prepare the child for academic achievement in elementary school involved demanding that the child remain still, quiet, and totally attentive before any instruction begins, and that an effective method for teaching a very young child to try new skills involved immediate, sharp punishment every time the child does not follow (obey) what the adults asks (teaches) or every time the child makes a mistake? When a theory-based program for children emphasizes activities like responsive care (or love), exploration and natural play, and instruction that is appropriate for a child's age and stage of development, it is not just a matter of opinion for everyone to imagine how to express these qualities. In fact, the examples of how some adults show love, play with children, and teach children that we mentioned above are not made up or extreme examples – these examples are real ways that many well-intentioned adults we have met and observed have shown love, play, and teaching. We think these represent misconceptions about children and how they develop – and that these adults would greatly benefit, themselves, from seeing and then trying out new ways to express love, play, and teaching.

Note: we do not believe the scientific evidence supports a one-size-fits-all approach or there is a single theory that prescribes one and only one "best" way to nurture and educate all children. When scientists develop a theory-based program and discover that it is effective, some people may incorrectly conclude that this means all children will have to participate in that particular program, if they are to benefit. In general, most theories of science would argue against this interpretation, because the program was perhaps just one way of many possibilities of getting the right types of experiences to particular children at certain times or sequences in their lives. There likely are multiple routes to achieve the same benefits.

Scientific theory for the highly successful programs has functioned in much the same way that an educational philosophy has for many educators and parents. Both the theory and the philosophy can be used to foster a common understanding and promote effective communication about practices supported by the theory or philosophy.

Another important aspect of scientific theory is that each of its elements is defined in ways that are operationalized. When a scientist uses a theory that hypothesizes that "responsive care" of the child and that "cognitive stimulation" to optimally challenge the child beyond his or her current level are among the vital dimensions to promote healthy social, emotional, and intellectual development, then the scientist must define these terms specifically in behavioral and observable terms, so that someone can be taught to care for and to teach a child in these ways and so that these program elements can be directly and objectively measured as having occurred.

3. Program dosage (the amount of the program or treatment) was well matched to the program goals and the needs of participating children. Often, the programs that produced the largest and most lasting benefits were among the highest in their dosage, as measured by particular experiences indexed by hours per day, days per week, weeks per year, and number of total years. In everyday terms, the programs provided children and families with a lot of good and specifiable supports and opportunities over an extended period of time. This idea that the amount or the intensity of a program matters is highly consistent with most theories about children's learning and development. Complex skills, deep knowledge,

and life competencies benefit from multiple and varied learning opportunities, lots of review and practice, trial-and-error experiences, and
useful feedback. Most highly successful programs focused their efforts
on improving high-risk children's outcomes in multiple domains –
usually including social-emotional competence, cognitive and academic skills, and health promotion and risk avoidance – all areas that
have many controlling facets and thus benefit from programs that are
intensive or high in their dosage. So the conclusion that it takes more
than a short summer program, a few days per week of hourly tutoring,
or a monthly mentoring programs to produce large and lasting benefits
for very high-risk children is hardly surprising. At the same time, the
dosage principle always needs to be adjusted relative to a program's
specific goals and the children enrolled. For example, there are programs that are highly focused on teaching a particular skill set or
changing a child's motivation in a key but very limited area of development; for these programs, the dosage might be far lower than for
programs seeking to prepare at-risk children for successful transitions
to typical elementary schools or for programs that hope to change the
life course of students who are highly likely to drop out of high school
and not enter college because of limited knowledge, skills, and
motivation.

There are several ways of measuring a program's dosage, though
none is adequately precise or entirely satisfactory (cf. S. Ramey et al.,
2011). Many effective early childhood programs provided services to
high-risk children and families for multiple years. The Abecedarian
Project and Project Care, for example, provided each child with
a specified high quality educational program in a child development
center for a full day (ranging from 6 to 10 hours), 5 days per week, 50
weeks per year, for 5 years (until the child was old enough to enter public
school kindergarten. These were among the most intensive (high dosage)
programs ever studied. In contrast, the Perry Preschool Program enrolled
children at 3 or 4 years of age, after the children already showed considerable *delays* in their development (placing them substantially below the
normal range), and provided a half day, 5 days a week program for the
academic year for one or two years. This program also produced impressive long-term benefits for these children. The Chicago Parent–Child
Centers was a large-scale program that offered services over many years;
some of the children participated for only one or two years, while others
participated for three or four years. For some of the child outcomes, there
were benefits from the higher dosage, but not always.

Historically, the topic of intensity or dosage has been one that is
treated with great centrality in the health professions, but much less so in

behavioral and educational circles. At the same time, providing too little of something – even when it is of high quality – might not be better than nothing at all. This issue is a frontier issue in the science of education. We frame this issue as: How Much, When, For Whom, Why, and at What Cost? To What End? These are the kind of refined issues that belong to the next generation of program innovators and research scientists. To us this is an exciting point of embarkation and shows an advance from the question of "Can early intervention make a positive difference in children's current lives and school readiness?

4. Multiple features and pathways were included in the program to achieve maximum desired experiences for children, permitting individualization and flexibility that were inherent in the program models of education. Most programs for children that are in the educational and behavioral domains are seeking to instill a broad set of skills and good habits in children. This is also true of the new wave of programs seeking to curtail the epidemic of childhood obesity and associated increased health risks for diabetes, high cholesterol, and hypertension in young children – something unprecedented in earlier generations. These programs often are built directly upon developmental theory which advances the idea that the competencies, the receptivity, and the habits formed in certain domains of development (health, language, social interactions, emotional self-regulation) at one stage of development then serve to prepare the child for transition into more advanced stages of development. Most of what children learn and do requires lots of exposure, practice, and variation in the situations when these new skills and ideas are used. Accordingly, the programs themselves seek to help promote these aspects of a child's development through multiple activities. Sometimes these are encouraged through formal instruction combined with the child's opportunities for natural observation, exploratory guided play, and daily self-care and social activities. By building in many different ways to help a child learn about something and then practice and extend these new skills and knowledge, the outcomes are likely to be stronger, more flexible, and more useful to the child. This is why so many programs try to engage parents, as children's first and foremost teachers during the early years of life, and then alternate as important role models and monitors of their child's behavior and safety. The program flexibility that we know about is difficult to document or quantify; but the programs granted teachers and caregivers opportunities to propose changes, make adjustments in the pace of the curriculum, and identify concerns that warranted individual solutions. We think that had the programs been totally rigid in their protocol, they may have been less successful.

5. Before the program was implemented, it was supported by both external peer or expert review and members of the local community. The highly successful programs that have been so inspirational were funded through competitive peer review or through selection by foundations or governmental agencies that established criteria for selecting grantees. Many of these programs were reviewed frequently over their operational period and these competitive reviews undoubtedly motivated the program teams to plan carefully and to establish strong justification and evidence that their programs could be well implemented. In addition, the successful programs often engaged members of their local communities and practitioners/educators in helping to plan for and to launch the program. The external review and support for these programs truly was essential – but these factors also may have promoted greater openness and multiple layers of accountability. These programs did not operate in a closed system unto themselves. Further, the endorsements obtained from the community and outside professionals and scientists served to broaden the interest in the program and probably helped to increase the successful recruitment of children and families, as well as encourage the children and families to participate at high and sustained levels – thus receiving the intended "dosage" of the program.

6. Program staff were highly skilled and well prepared to fulfill their roles in the program – because they received strong initial training followed by active, ongoing professional development supports and systematic supervision. Many of the programs were highly original or innovative when they were launched. Thus, the programs had to develop training for the staff members who were responsible for working directly with families and children. These were not programs that simply relied on existing professionals who already knew exactly what to do – that is, the nurses, teachers, child care workers, or social workers were not just using their own individual professional opinions and judgments. Rather, the staff recognized that they were being asked to help pioneer and test new forms of interventions to benefit children. Accordingly, the initial training often was intensive, and because the programs were new, the training did not stop when the program was launched. Rather, almost all of these programs held frequent staff meetings and actively supervised and supported staff in frontline positions, providing additional on-the-job training in the form of supports, advice, information, and problem-solving. The professional development was an integral part of the program, and the staff understood the importance of having everyone being highly capable and consistent in their work. (Note: the amount of formal education required by staff varied widely across and sometimes even within programs. Regardless of job title, staff were considered team players vital to the program's success.)

7. Implementation of the program was actively monitored by the program leaders; this helped to detect and resolve problems early and served as a natural means of recognizing staff for excellence in their work. Performance expectations were clear to staff, as well as the immediate goals for improving children's outcomes. Programs that are scientifically studied necessitate careful documentation about what occurs. This open monitoring of a program serves to make clear to everyone exactly what is expected. These expectations or standards for the program ideally are linked to documentation procedures that the program was implemented on time and consistent with its proposed plans. The methods, however, varied across the successful programs, but often included written documentation by staff in a systematic manner, frequent and unannounced observations by program leaders and supervisors, outside site visits by funding entities, and independent observations by trained data collectors about the program delivery. A high level of monitoring also helped with early detection of problems – and was linked to efforts to correct these problems and avoid them in the future. This active monitoring of the programs came from the leadership and the entire team, who saw these procedures as necessary and positive – rather than as externally imposed, intrusive, arbitrary, or punitive.

8. There was a clear commitment to encouraging high levels of participation among all children and families, including planned strategies to overcome potential barriers to full participation. When a program is new and being tested, it is crucial to have high levels of participation from all children assigned to receive the new program or treatment. In a randomized controlled trial, one of the scientific standards is that all children and families assigned to the treatment or the control group will be studied and their outcomes will be measured, *regardless of whether they fully participate or not.* The insider phrase is, "Once randomized, always analyzed." Accordingly, a scientist testing a theory-guided program would predict the program will work if and only if the intended participants receive it. This means that if a program plans to have parent meetings, then all parents need to be encouraged to attend all meetings to fully test that aspect of the model. Understandably, some children and families have reasons that keep them from participating fully in all aspects of the program. This can, to some degree, be taken into account in later data analyses via statistical adjustments, but major problems with the level of participation of children or families (that is, receiving much less than the intended dosage level) would serve to reduce the program's potential efficacy. In some ways, this feature served as a motivator to staff at all levels to be sure that children and families had maximal opportunities to benefit from their program.

9. **Unbiased multiple assessments of children's progress were collected from the start and were explicitly valued as essential to understanding program effects.** The children in many of the successful programs came from life circumstances recognized as extremely challenging and far from ideal; thus the children had a high likelihood of not doing well. In some programs that included a mix of children from both high- and low-risk backgrounds, the children were still expected to benefit from what the program offered to them. (Even programs for highly academically gifted children may view the participants as potentially at risk if the children do not receive educational programs that truly meets their cognitive and social-emotional needs.) All of these programs for high-risk families measured the children at regular intervals using procedures that were considered valid and reliable as a way of measuring child development over time. These measures, similar to those about the program implementation and program quality, were highly valued by the program leaders, and were internally supported rather than externally imposed on the program. The programs did not feel threatened by these measures; to the contrary, they valued them as indicators of the extent to which the program was achieving its intended goals.

10. **The information gathered about the program and about children's progress was analyzed and reported to both the program team and to external groups.** When data are collected as part of scientific research funded by public dollars (as was true for the majority of the successful programs), the data are expected to be reported in a timely and open manner. (Note: currently, most federal research grants require that the datasets collected eventually enter the public domain, although this policy was not in effect when many of the landmark studies were conducted.) The information collected often was analyzed as soon as possible – because it was the basis for making new discoveries and for advancing the understanding about what promotes children's positive development. Team members and leaders were actively involved in developing plans for how the data would be analyzed. High levels of interest and excitement often accompanied the data analysis and interpretation phase of the successful projects. In many cases, the findings at one stage of children's development helped with decisions about the program and its future – and propelled the commitment to following the children longitudinally as they grew up.

11. Program developers recognized that replication of the program would be an important next step if the results affirmed benefits to children and families. Thus, the program's content and procedures were documented sufficiently to allow replication. The scientific framework demands that an experiment be replicable. Results from a project tested once and only once are not considered as strong as programs that have proven their benefits repeatedly. From the beginning, the successful programs were planned in ways that permitted replication if the results supported doing so. The detailed description of these programs, however, did not mean that they were readily exportable to all settings or that others who were not deeply knowledgeable about certain aspects of children's health or development could easily implement them on their own. Another factor is that replication often involves testing the same general program with a somewhat different group of children and families in a somewhat different social, cultural, geographic, and political context. This distinctive feature of many successful programs is a great strength, because this forms a solid foundation for future scale-up programs and adaptation of the successful treatments and interventions so that large numbers of children may benefit in the future.

12. The leadership had sufficient resources and control over expenditures so that the key components would be delivered, yet changes could be made quickly if problems arose. The scale of these programs ranged considerably, although many were small to moderate at first. More importantly, the programs perceived there was a good match between resources available and the expectations for implementation. Highly successful programs need to have resources sufficient to implement the program, including not just basic operations but the initial and ongoing training and professional development of staff, reaching out to and engaging parents and children in participating, measuring the program and its impact on children, and analyzing the data collected. These successful programs did not have to choose between providing services or evaluating their effects on children; rather, the resources were intended to be used for both purposes and this was viewed positively, for resources between funding the direct services and supports to children and funding the professional development, active monitoring, and data collection. The programs considered all of these features as essential.

How practically useful are these hallmarks for informing the planning, implementation, and assessment of scale-up and future quality improvement initiatives in real-world settings?
We have pondered whether some of these hallmarks are much more important than others. *At a minimum*, we cannot imagine how these

programs could have been as successful as they were without having strong and deeply knowledgeable leadership, a clear theory that guided their implementation of the program and was directly linked to potential benefits for the children, strong professional development and training for their frontline staff, and an active accountability system that measured both the program and the children.

A legitimate and longstanding concern remains about the transportability of these "hothouse experiments" to real world settings. Most were not designed initially in a way that tried to take into account the evolving complex regulations that today influence how public schools, Head Start programs, subsidized child care, pediatric health care, and other social supports service delivery systems currently operate. Indeed, there is no one standard template for how these real-world systems operate today, as we have learned in the more recent multi-site research we have conducted, where the scientific studies have included implementing highly comparable interventions in different cities, towns, and rural areas across different states and Indian nations. For us, the challenge is this: can these hallmarks of the highly successful programs provide a practically useful guide for what needs to be considered, and what might need to change, in the real world systems that serve children?

At first, the best of the research that sought to improve children's lives was focused on finding out *if* children could truly benefit from participating in these theory-guided and evidence-based programs. To the extent that the answers affirm the value of these programs, then the political and practical next steps need to build upon what is known. These hallmarks of highly successful programs are revealing. Together they force us to question as to what extent these hallmarks can become part of the existing systems of care and education.

Interestingly, these hallmarks of successful programs that benefited children also closely parallel the research process. Specifically,

- Both begin with rigorous planning and careful implementation. They continue by measuring the results and having the results reviewed by peers.
- The most successful interventions were *not* just inspirational or ideological, led by charismatic individuals. Nor were they externally imposed on project managers or frontline staff. Instead, they were solidly grounded in scientific evidence, and they were consistent with developmental (and often neurobiological) theory about children.
- The measures to assess individual children were not arbitrary or unrelated to the program's goals. Instead they were chosen by the program developers as germane to the program's goals.

- The enthusiasm of those involved in implementation often was high, and these projects had considerable degrees of freedom and control in how they operated.
- Reaching all children or families assigned to receive the intervention or treatment was considered a high priority – how else could the program impact a child except through active participation?

Science in the past 40 years has become increasingly competitive, strongly peer-reviewed, and closely monitored at all stages. Project participants are told in advance about the program, what its intended benefits are, what the risks might be, and they are counseled to understand their right to seek more information about a program and how they (parents and children) are progressing. Even when scientific research projects are conducted in schools and "real world" service settings, they require the same level of openness and peer review. This includes informing parents and children clearly and in advance about what the researchers intend to do, why they are doing it, who will be held responsible, how the child's safety and well-being will be monitored, and the ways in which the service or school system will use the information collected to modify and improve future services. In the real-world, many "experiments" occur all the time – often described as reforms, improvements, creative solutions, and new strategies – but seldom are the standards of science used at all levels to plan, monitor, and ultimately judge the effectiveness of these naturally occurring experiments.

The Ground Rules of Science. In looking for the hallmarks of the successful programs, we must realize that these were conceptualized as scientific experiments to test an idea. There are ground rules in our world of science – complex and unrelenting in their own right – regarding how to test the merit of a new (and thus unproven) treatment or program. We must first test our new program in a very careful and systematic manner, considered absolutely necessary to determine whether our strategy (supported by scientific hypotheses and building on what is known at that time) can generate at least some evidence of being right (correct, meritorious to pursue further, consistent with other evidence about how children develop and change over time). So as scientists we set up human experiments (clinical trials) that are vetted *in advance* by our peers as being worthy of pursuit, being ethical to conduct with minimal risks to participants and having a favorable ratio of possible adverse effects to potential benefits), and having the potential to generate robust knowledge that will be useful to scientists and practitioners in the future, *even if our program does not produce the hoped for benefits.* Accordingly, we are required by our professional standards to launch these studies in ways that allow us to have sufficient control over the factors (the study variables) that we hypothesize (think) will be important in changing the lives of children. So when scientists engage in testing a program, we must have confidence that the plans we generate for treatment will be implemented fully and that the individuals we invite and then enroll in our studies will actually receive the intended program. We are required to closely monitor the participants and their responses to the program. We build in many checks and balances on this process of documentation (data collection), and the information collected is analyzed in ways that are publicly verifiable, thus minimizing distortion of findings. *So, is it possible that some of the features of sound science were instrumental (causal) in producing effective programs?*

We think there now is ample evidence that many of the original successful projects have been replicated – with some variations – in other places, by other people, or with new groups of children. We also acknowledge that too few of these successful programs have been tested adequately when they are adapted for places where the children or the natural support systems differ considerably from the conditions in the landmark experiments. Similarly, we agree that many pioneering programs had advantages, including strong, passionate, and capable leadership with dedicated, caring staff who worked energetically and effectively, continuously learning on the job and being watched (monitored) by others. These projects had measurement systems in place, from the beginning and through to the end; these were measurement systems they selected and the findings about children and program quality were central to their existence – not viewed as burdensome and potentially punitive. If the measurement systems showed that things were not going as expected, then the programs themselves wanted to know this – so they could change, improve, and do whatever they needed to do to deliver on the promise of helping children truly thrive. Freedom to modify the program, to increase the training and supports for teachers or home visitors, and to ask staff to do something extra or new was definitely a feature of these pioneering studies as well. Above all, what we can tell others – after 40+ years' worth of frontline experiences and immersion in detailed statistical analyses about these pioneering studies is that what changed the children and gave them brighter futures were *the adults* who on an everyday basis nurtured them, taught them, challenged them, protected them, promoted their health and curiosity, and showed respect for and helped to support and educate the children's parents as well.

Part Two: The Significance of What Happens *After* Children Receive a Strong Early "School Readiness" foundation

We acknowledge how challenging and inadequate retrospective consideration is concerning precisely what was important for children who participated in the successful programs when they moved into public school settings that varied in quality. The data are sparse and thus opinions, including our own, abound. A landmark analysis by Currie and Thomas (1995) using large public databases about school quality supported the conclusion that when Head Start children enter reasonably adequate schools, the advantages from early learning continue, but when they enter very low-quality schools, there is an erosion of the benefits. Tragically, the economic and racial disparities in the matter of who attends high- versus low-quality schools are immense. We nominate that the same ideas that have guided the early care and education programs – summed succinctly in the statement "It is the cumulative relevant learning and life experiences – inside and outside the home – that produce more or less competent, caring, and creative children" – should extend more vigorously into our consideration of what it will take to ensure that children continue to progress well after they receive a strong foundation and enter school well prepared.

School occupies many hours of the children's weekly waking hours, and produces large amounts of learning. At the same time, children are profoundly influenced by what happens before and after school during the weekdays, what occurs on the weekend, and their summer learning experiences. Ample scientific evidence from both observational and interventional studies affirms the totality of experiences statement assumption above. Ironically, when we try to simplify measure of the quality and impact of school by a simplistic set of measures – such as relying on average group performance on standardized tests once a year – we defy much of the scientific evidence about human growth and development. We know that children's school progress and overall well-being are far more than what their standardized test scores capture (not to discount these entirely, however). One inherent problem is that standardized test scores are not necessarily attributable primarily to what occurred in the classroom – although a year in an excellent classroom can make a big difference. As we shift the study paradigm from a "maintain the gains from investments prior to kindergarten" to a more integrated life course perspective, we advocate strongly that measuring children's learning opportunities more comprehensively could set the stage for parents, communities, schools, and health care providers to work more efficiently and collaboratively. We do not favor continuing the model of designing special demonstration projects that operate under auspices largely outside the existing natural institutions and local support systems or that depend primarily on infusion of new dollars that are not likely to be sustainable under current policies and funding mechanisms. In fact, we suspect that decades of this approach has created a strong natural backlash and a set of attitudes that decrease receptivity to change – a "here today, gone tomorrow" or a "didn't we try that a while back and whatever happened to that report?" mindset toward educational and community reforms. We do harken back to the proposed set of hallmarks of successful early childhood programs and ask the question of how applicable these features might be to facilitate the following: creating stronger and more effective schools, to implementing parent engagement programs that produce measurable benefits for children and families (unfortunately, some appear to have been iatrogenic), providing high quality and multi-year sports and artistic-pursuit programs for children from all walks of life, offering summer programs filled with experiences that are mentally, physically, and socially rewarding, and ensuring that children who work hard in their childhood tasks of learning, inside and outside of school, will be confident that they have a certain chance to keep on working hard as they grow older and transition into young adulthood. We often have envisioned issuing a Birth to Adulthood "report card" that measures for each child the quality, amount, and types of environmental supports and experiences they have to learn, play, socialize, create, and be healthy; and checks whether systems are in place to limit their exposure to adverse life events and toxic environments. If such a contextualized and lifespan card existed, perhaps embedded within health care records and school records, and shared with families directly, then we would be able to monitor our population in new and highly innovative ways.

We have been immensely fortunate in getting to know and work with so many dedicated individuals, groups, foundations, and public agencies and institutions that have supported the knowledge growth about early childhood interventions. We do not think we have all the answers, yet we hope that deep reflection and constructive debate can move into new arenas and engage a wider group of stakeholders, including the parents and children directly affected by this body of research.

In this presentation, we introduce – albeit late and only briefly – a broad systems framework we developed to capture multiple levels of influence that contribute to the provision of high-quality early child care and education. Figure 15.1 illustrates some, but not all, of the variables operative in the systems framework. The Four Diamond Model resulted from three years of intensive statewide collaboration in Alabama with

Four Diamond Model for Improving the Quality and Benefits of Early Care and Education

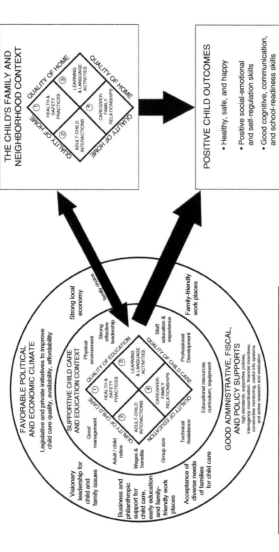

Figure 15.1 Four Diamond model for improving the quality and benefits of early care and education

hundreds of stakeholders. The framework allowed highly diverse individuals and entities to think about what matters most for producing positive outcomes for children. Of highest saliency is that this model does *not* assume that all potentially supportive factors must be present for children to experience the critical proximal experiences deemed valuable (through scientific research and direct observations of many parents and providers). That is, this model explicitly showed that there could be multiple pathways to support positive outcomes for children, thus avoiding the longstanding conflicts that seem to pit programs against one another, or takes sides about whether out-of-home programs are better or worse than a family-based approach. This multiple pathways idea also implies that the contextual and more distal factors – such as well-educated staff who receive excellent salaries and benefits, low child-to-adult ratios, high quality physical settings with lots of materials and supplies, high standards for licensing certain providers, or a strongly supportive citywide or statewide initiative with high levels of funding – can serve as a proxy to indicate that children are receiving high-quality care and education. All too often, formal systems of rating have relied on the distal supportive factors, rather than directly observed what is happening when children are in non-parental care and when they are in their own family. We then continued to adapt and use this, not for a theoretical framework about children's development per se, but as a perspective on what can facilitate versus impede successful real-world implementation. The model includes a multi-pronged set of child outcomes, recognizes the distinctive and useful roles of multiple individuals and groups, yet places as *the central most important factor on a child's life the amount and quality of experiences under the fours domains (diamonds) of Health and Safety Practices, Learning and Language Activities, Adult–Child Interactions (sometimes labeled warm and responsive caregiving), and Caregiver–Family Relationships.* Accompanying this model we developed, in collaboration with others, and through systematic review of many other environmental and assessment tools, a brief checklist of what we consider to be absolute basic essentials that should be present in every single child's life for the first five years. This is but one of many frameworks, but we leave these as examples of how partnerships can generate shared understandings and move forward to agree on how to invest wisely and strategically in improving the future for children and nation.

Conclusion

A remarkably rich set of scientific publications and program evaluations affirm that some early childhood initiatives and programs can produce outcomes that have strong, practical value for individuals, families, and communities. Further, under some conditions, increasing the positive outcomes for young children has proven to be crucial in setting the stage for continued positive progress as children transition into public school and later into adulthood. We conclude that the existing databases on these topics, although certainly amenable to more and more data analyses, create a strong, instructive set of working principles to consider in today's highly diverse settings with major shifts in demographics and support systems. That is, the findings from successful programs repeatedly affirm human potential (neuroplasticity) and the universal needs of young children in terms of the inter-related domains of cognition, language, social-emotional development, and physical health. At the same time, the programs that failed to produce large and enduring effects mostly ignored the working principles and failed to meet the universal needs of young children.

In this presentation, we have reflected on features of some of the most successful programs that altered the lives of highly vulnerable young children, and nominated a set of 12 features we label "hallmarks." The success of these programs depended on many levels of support, adequate training, resources, and ongoing and objective measures of both the programs and the children's progress. These programs understood children's development and had guiding theories of how children learn. When the early benefits appear to lead to later positive outcomes, this often reflects the fact that children entered schools that continued to support their development, had supportive families, and/or lived in communities with multiple ways to assist children and families at the next stages of development. This is consonant with an abundance of biobehavioral data that both prior and concurrent opportunities exert significant influences on performance and health. Additionally, the perception that there are future good prospects may comprise an operationalized portrayal for children, families, teachers, and clinicians to have hope (i.e., to value rather than discount the future) (Bickel et al., 2014) and to be motivated to do their best and stay active and healthy.

Finally, we recognize that our notion that it would be a good thing to run the real world like a scientific experiment may appear to be quite science-centric. Yet at the heart of science is an unrelenting set of standards for discovering truth and then using what we know now (the best iteration of truth) to take actions that have applied value. Continuing the process of gathering useful data, analyzing the information, sharing it widely, promoting vigorous and constructive debates, and trying to do things even better, more efficiently, at lower cost, or with exciting novel additions is an amazing story of what has happened since the 1960s and 1970s – showing that under the right conditions, most children can overcome the dire predictions based on the circumstances of their birth, becoming productive citizens in a vibrant democracy and complex world.

Inventing and Delivering a Better Future for Young Children

If we in the United States of America are to achieve a more supportive and equitable landscape for children from birth on, there are several strong recommendations that we advocate.

First, we must acknowledge that early childhood programs can support adequate school readiness and subsequent school progress spanning academic achievement and social-emotional adjustment. Quality matters! Poorly implemented programs of low dosage are ineffective investments and need to be rapidly improved or eliminated. As Phillips et al. (2017) recently affirmed, not all pre-K programs are equal.

Second, investments in early childhood programs must be monitored and consequential. We think that unannounced and behaviorally focused "quality monitoring" visits should become the expected norm in all publicly funded programs. These visits should be directly coupled with specific and timely professional development activities and technical assistance. Parents, too, should have a formal voice in ongoing evaluations of early childhood programs.

Third, credentialing standards and compensation for pre-K teachers and assistant teachers should be made equivalent to comparable K–12 personnel.

Fourth, all early childhood programs should be required to develop plans for coordinating health and mental health supports, before and after childcare, and family social services. This recognizes that children's success in school and, later, into adulthood depends on recognizing and meeting their multiple needs at each stage of development. Schools cannot do this alone; families and communities need to be active partners in supporting children's holistic growth and development.

Fifth, there needs to be an unwavering commitment to measuring and publicly reporting each child's development, not only for mandatory reporting but for use to inform adjustments to a child's education plan.

Sixth, partnerships are an effective way of sharing expertise to mutual

√ = Pass
√– = Partial
Blank = not passed

THE Q-STAR CHECKLIST (2013)
The Foundational Cornerstones for High-Quality Care and Education: Birth to age 5
Sharon L. Ramey, Libbie Sonnier-Netto, & Craig T. Ramey

Place:	Date:	Time Observed:
Observer:	# of adults :	# of children:
Age group:	Infant/Toddler:	Preschool:

Adult IDs	A₁	A₂	A₃	
				WARM AND RESPONSE CARE
				1. Children's names used often with real warmth.
				2. Adults show joy, liking, and concern for every child.
				3. Adults & children have back-and-forth play and conversations.
				4. Children encouraged to explore and try new things.
				5. Children's needs and questions responded to positively and promptly.
				6. Adults care and teach about children's feelings and good ways to handle them.
				7. Adults encourage and teach children to play and cooperate with others.
				8. Adults observe individual children and adjust activities as needed.
				9. Children are not teased or bullied. If so, adults act quickly to help.
				10. For a child with special/extra needs, adults actively address their social and emotional needs.
Total √s				
				LANGUAGE AND LEARNING
				1. Adults use children's interests and activities to teach new skills and ideas.
				2. Adults use daily routines and "in between" times to teach many things.
				3. Adults actively teach children many words and communication skills.
				4. Adults praise children for specific new things they are learning.
				5. Toys, books, and materials organized so children can find and use them often.
				6. Adults read a lot with children, in ways that teach early literacy skills.
				7. Adults teach children a lot about math and science.
				8. Children get to practice new skills and improve through play.
				9. Adults help children learn to plan, pay attention, ask questions, and problem solve.
				10. For a child with special/extra needs, adults actively address language and learning needs.
Total √s				
				HEALTH AND SAFETY
				1. Good hygiene practices evident.
				2. Indoor and outdoor areas safe and secure.
				3. Children physically active throughout the day.
				4. Children not made to be still or quiet, except briefly.
				5. Nap and quiet time offered, but not forced.
				6. Safe practices for sleeping/napping, feeding, and going places.
				7. TV, video, and screen time limited and positive.
				8. Almost all food and drinks are healthy.
				9. Adults can administer First Aid and handle emergencies.
				10. All adults look for and immediately report possible child neglect and abuse.
Total √s				
				FAMILY CONNECTIONS WITH OTHERS WHO CARE FOR & TEACH THEIR CHILDREN
				1. Parents encouraged to visit and share ideas with providers/teachers; and parents do this.
				2. Providers/teachers & parents know one another by name and their role in the child's life.
				3. Providers/teachers & parents share with one another what a child is learning and ways to practice.
				4. Providers/teachers keep up-to-date about each child's family and home life.
				5. Providers/teachers & parents meet often to talk about the child's progress, strengths, and needs.
				6. Providers/teachers & parents work together to solve any problems that arise.
				7. Providers/teachers & parents work together to prepare a child for major transitions.
				8. Providers/teachers & parents show mutual caring and respect.
				9. Providers/teachers & parents understand the rules and values in their settings.
				10. Providers/teachers & parents together make sure children are not at risk for neglect, abuse, or harsh treatment
Total √s				

Figure 15.2 The Q-STAR checklist (2013)

advantage and to realize cost-effectiveness and efficiency. University/ community partnerships can exist in all states as well as in most communities. State and land-grant universities with an explicit mandate to service their local and regional populations are particularly attractive potential partners. These partnerships can help bridge the gaps between scientific knowledge, human development, relevant educational and healthcare practices, and public policy.

We think these six recommendations are accomplishable with the knowledge base that currently exists and with a rearrangement of many of the resources already in place. We cannot think of any acceptable excuses for failing to provide high-quality opportunities for learning and development to all children who live in our country. We know the serious personal, family, and community toll – economically, socially, and psychologically – of allowing young children to grow up without the essentials to succeed in school and life. The future of our democracy is inextricably linked to the future of children. If high-quality early childhood programs become the norm, our country as a whole, as well as particular children and their communities, will benefit.

References

Barnett, W. S. (2004). Does Head Start have lasting cognitive effects? The myth of fade out, in Zigler, E. & Styfco S. J. (Eds.), *Head Start Debates* (pp. 221–249). Baltimore, MD: Paul H. Brookes.

Barnett, W. S. & Carolan, M. E. (2014). *Facts about* Fadeout: *The Research Base on Long-Term Impacts of High Quality Pre-K (CEELO FastFact)*. New Brunswick, NJ: Center on Enhancing Early Learning Outcomes.

Bickel, W. K., Moody, L., Quisenberry, A. J., Ramey, C. T. & Sheffer, C. E. (2014). A competing neurobehavioral decision systems model of SES-related health and behavioral disparities. *Preventive Medicine*, 68, 37–43. PMID: 25008219.

Camilli, G., Vargas, S., Ryan, S. & Barnett, W. S. (2010). Meta-analysis of the effects of early education interventions on cognitive and social development. *Teachers College Record*, 112(3), 579–620. Available at: http://rci.rutgers.edu/~camilli/Papers/38_15440.pdf.

Campbell, F. A., Conti, G., Heckman, J. J. et al. (2014). Early childhood investments substantially boost adult health. *Science*, 343, 1478–1485.

Campbell, F. A., Ramey, C. T., Pungello, E., Sparling, J. & Miller-Johnson, S. (2002). Early childhood education: young adult outcomes from the Abecedarian Project. *Applied Developmental Science*, 6, 42–57.

Currie, J. & Thomas, D. (1995). Does Head Start make a difference?, *American Economic Review*, 83, 241–364.

Dodge, K. A. (Ed.) (2017). *The Current State of Scientific Knowledge on Pre-Kindergarten Effects*. Durham, NC: Duke University.

Heckman, J. J., Moon, S. H., Pinto, R., Savelyev, P. A. & Yavitz, A. (2010). The rate of return to the HighScope Perry Preschool Program. *Journal of Public Health*, 94, 114–128.

Kay, N. & Pennucci, A. (2014). *Early Childhood Education for Low-Income Students: A Review of the Evidence and Benefit–Cost Analysis* (Doc. No. 14–01-2201). Olympia, WA: Washington State Institute for Public Policy. Retrieved from: www.wsipp.wa.gov/ReportFile/1547/Wsipp_Early-Childhood-Education-for-

348   *Craig T. Ramey and Sharon Landesman Ramey*

Low-Income-Students-A-Review-of-the-Evidence-and-Benefit-Cost-Analysis_ Full-Report.pdf.

Lazar, I. & Darlington, R. (Eds.). (1982). *Lasting effects of early education: A report from the consortium for longitudinal studies.* Monographs of the Society for Research in Child Development.

Lewin, K., (1951). *Field Theory in Social Science: Selected Theoretical Papers.* Oxford: Harpers.

Phillips, D. A., Lipsey, M. W., Dodge, K. A. et al. (2017). Puzzling it out: the current state of scientific knowledge on pre-kindergarten effects: a consensus statement, in Dodge, K. A. (Ed.), *The Current State of Scientific Knowledge on Pre-Kindergarten Effects* (pp. 19–30). Durham, NC: Duke University.

Ramey, C. T. (1982). Commentary, in Lazar, I. & Darlington, R. (Eds.), *Lasting Effects of Early Education: A Report from the Consortium for Longitudinal Studies. Monographs of the Society for Research in Child Development*, 195, 142–151.

Ramey, C. T. (2018). The Abecedarian approach to social, educational, and health disparities. *Clinical Child and Family Psychology Review.* PMID:29637322

Ramey, C. T., Campbell, F. A., Burchinal, M. et al. (2000). Persistent effects of early childhood education on high-risk children and their mothers. *Applied Developmental Science*, 4, 2–14.

Ramey, C. T. & Ramey, S. L. (1998). Early intervention and early experience. *American Psychologist*, 53, 109–120.

Ramey, C.T., Sparling, J. J. & Ramey, S. L. (2012). *Abecedarian: The Ideas, The Approach, and The Findings.* Los Altos, CA: Sociometrics Corporation.

Ramey, S. L., Crowell, N. A., Ramey, C. T., Grace, C., Timraz, N. & Davis, L. E. (2011). The dosage of professional development for early childhood professionals: how the amount and density of professional development may influence its effectiveness. *Advances in Early Education and Day Care*, 15, 11–32.

Ramey S. L. & Ramey C. T. (2005). How to create and sustain a high quality workforce in child care, early intervention, and school readiness programs, in Zaslow, M. & Martinez-Beck, I. (Eds.), *Critical Issues in Early Childhood Professional Development* (pp. 355–368). Baltimore, MD: Paul H. Brookes.

Ramey S. L. & Ramey C. T. (2007). Establishing a science of professional development for early education programs: the Knowledge Application Information Systems (KAIS) theory of professional development, in Justice, L. M. & Vukelich, C. (Eds.), *Achieving Excellence in Preschool Language and Literacy Instruction.* (pp. 41–63) New York, NY: Guilford Press.

Ramey, S. L., Ramey, C. T., Phillips, M. M. et al. (2001). *Head Start Children's Entry into Public Schools: A Report on the National Head Start/Public School Early Childhood Transition Demonstration Study* (Contract No. 105-95-1935). Washington, DC: US Department of Health and Human Services, Administration on Children, Youth, and Families.

Reynolds, A. J. (2000). *Success in Early Intervention: The Chicago Child–Parent Centers.* Lincoln, NE: University of Nebraska Press.

Reynolds, A. J., Temple, J. A. & Ou, S. (2010). Impacts and implications of the child–parent center preschool program, in Reynolds, A. J., Rolnick, A. J., Englund, M. M. & Temple, J. (Eds.), *Childhood Programs and Practices in the First Decade of Life: A Human Capital Integration.* New York, NY: Cambridge University Press.

Schweinhart, L. J. & Weikart, D. P. (1983). The effects of the Perry Preschool Program on youths through age 15, in Consortium for Longitudinal Studies (Ed.), *As the Twig Is Bent: Lasting Effects of Preschool Programs* (pp. 71–101). Hillsdale, NJ: Erlbaum.

Schweinhart, L. J., Montie, J., Xiang, Z. et al. (2005). *Lifetime Effects: The High/Scope Perry Preschool Study through Age 40.* Ypsilanti, MI: High/Scope Press.

Shonkoff, J. P. & Phillips, D. A. (2000). *From Neurons to Neighborhoods: The Science of Early Childhood Development.* Washington, DC: National Academy Press.

Subject Index

Name Index